CHASE THE
RABBIT

F. A. GRIEGER

WestBow®
PRESS
A DIVISION OF THOMAS NELSON
& ZONDERVAN

WestBow Press books may be ordered through booksellers or by contacting:

WestBow Press
A Division of Thomas Nelson & Zondervan
1663 Liberty Drive
Bloomington, IN 47403
www.westbowpress.com
1 (866) 928-1240

ISBN: 978-1-4908-6288-0 (sc)
ISBN: 978-1-4908-6290-3 (hc)
ISBN: 978-1-4908-6289-7 (e)

Library of Congress Control Number: 2014922069

Print information available on the last page.

WestBow Press rev. date: 05/19/2015

For my Bloopie

... and for the rest of the children of the United States.

I prefer peace, but if trouble must come, let it come in my time, so that my children can live in peace.

—Thomas Paine

CONTENTS

ACKNOWLEDGMENTS

This book would not have been possible but for the encouragement, mentoring, kindness, and direct assistance offered freely by many people.

Since some of the content is critical of some very powerful institutions, I am obligated to protect the identities of those who contributed their time and assistance to ensure that they will not become targets of reprisal by those institutions. Therefore, I will mention them here only by their first names. You all know who you are, and you know that you have my deepest respect and gratitude.

To *Mutti*, the most inspiring person I've ever known, my loving mother Dorothea, who gave me my life, my values and my love of music. I am who I am because of you and you will forever be my light and my guide. There is not a single person that you have touched during your lifetime who wasn't the better for it. You truly are a *Gift from God*. I Love You.

To my father, Paul, who showed me the world, who taught me about self-reliance, perseverance, character, taking care of your own, and to always question authority. Thank You Vati, we miss you.

To Ana G. for your outstanding work on the cover art, and to Eric V. K. for contributing to the cover design.

To Eva K., who contributed content, editorial expertise, and invaluable advice and encouragement. To Donna B., Sheilah M., and Carla K., who advised me on both the content and readability; and to Vera for always being there for the ones you love. You're truly an angel.

To Virginia "Kiki," who taught me about forgiveness and unconditional love, even after she was gone. We miss you terribly, and you're always in our hearts.

Special thanks to two truly brilliant men: Mike K—mentor, guide, and the embodiment of leading by example, thank you for your friendship; and to Jack

S., for your courage, constructive criticism, contributions to the content, research material, and invaluable advice.

To my brothers-in-arms and dear friends: Pete, Armin, Jeff H, Ray F., Rick M., Robert M. T., Thierry S., and Mathieu N.

To Bob P. for your insights into Thomas Jefferson, The Declaration of Independence, and property rights, to Larry F. for unknowingly inspiring me, and to Rashad T. for your keen insights into the Civil War, slavery, and Thomas Jefferson.

To Kevin O., whose inspiring words were the catalyst that encouraged me to finally start writing.

And ... to my dear friend Franklin B., who is missed and always remembered.

PART 1

Who Stole My House?
Who Stole My Life?

INTRODUCTION

People all over the world used to call America "The Land of Opportunity." Practically no one says that anymore. More than ever before Americans are actually emigrating, leaving the country permanently. In 2013, the number of American taxpayers who renounced their US citizenship reached an all-time high—a 233 percent increase over the year before. In 2014, the number of Americans who have renounced their US citizenship again reached a record high, so the pace is accelerating.

Why?

America has been in decline for some time. Those who doubt this are in denial. This decline is apparent within our economy, our culture, our entertainment media, our education system, and most disturbingly our current system of governance. There are many issues people point to that they believe are the cause of this decline, but most of these are only symptoms, not causes. It is like a systemic disease that has festered for decades but whose symptoms are only now becoming intolerable. Yet in addressing only the symptoms of this disease, its root cause continues to elude us. It strengthens while our nation's immune system is made weaker. As a consequence, we the people have become powerless to fight it. Unable to identify the root cause, we resort to fighting one another.

That disease—the root cause of our ills—is the eradication of our property rights.

The consequences affect every one of us, independent of our politics, our races, our genders, or our religions. Herein, we will examine these effects in that context—how each of our lives as individuals is impacted.

Herein we will look at how our model of public school funding and property taxes function to eradicate real home ownership. We will explore how this funding model deliberately erodes educational standards in order to dumb down our children. We will look at how income taxes and our inherently inflationary monetary system function to rob us of the fruits of our labor through forced confiscation of our earnings and the continual devaluation of our savings. We will also identify the forces behind these policies, why they are being imposed upon us, and how our system of governance has been corrupted in order to achieve those ends.

This book is an effort to connect the dots in terms of what appears to most people to be an assortment of seemingly unrelated, yet highly destructive social problems. In fact, these problems are parts of a broader mechanism, acting together to deliberately destroy our individual property rights, our liberty, and our national sovereignty. *We the people* must gain a comprehensive understanding of these issues so that we can each act to make the necessary course correction to the destructive path that our country, and in fact the world, is currently set upon.

More importantly the most viable solutions to these issues will be presented. The self-serving career politicians who have entrenched themselves in our local, state, and federal governments will resist these solutions with every fiber of their being. Implementing them will by necessity reduce or remove the political class's power and put an end to their incessant and irresponsible largess. There are no easy solutions, and some of them cannot be implemented without some near-term sacrifice. However, to restore prosperity for individual citizens today and for our children of tomorrow, we have no other choice.

That Was Then ... This Is Now

America's founders had a deep understanding of economics and property, an understanding that had never before in the history of civilization been laid down as a national policy. America was the first country in history to establish within its constitution a bill of individual unalienable rights to life, liberty, and property. There were numerous bitter disputes between the founders about specific policies, but the key issue in which there was total consensus was property rights. In fact, the American Revolution was fought largely to secure real property rights for individual citizens. In particular, there were three key policies over which the founders all agreed—the legal right to acquire and own private property in land and other goods; the right to sell, exchange, or give property to others on terms of one's own choosing; and the most fundamental policy of all, government's guarantee of a system of sound money.

Not one of these policies remains in effect today. Many would dispute this assertion; however, this book will prove its veracity. It is evident in almost every aspect of our lives and across almost all economic classes that our property rights are gone. Furthermore, almost everything our federal government does today is unconstitutional and is intended to eradicate the few rights that remain.

As a consequence, there is a rising tide of anger and frustration developing among the hardworking middle class. Most of our elected government employees ignore it rather than examine what their actions have been to foster this anger. They instead are surreptitiously working to establish a police state in order to quell any dissent that might arise from the citizenry regardless of the legitimacy of our grievances. However, our nation's history was founded on the premise of questioning authority. We must resurrect this basic American principle—to question authority and to force government to address our grievances as our servant and not as our oppressor.

Are you a parent who feels powerless and frustrated with the substandard education and immoral values with which your child is being indoctrinated in their public school—a school that is accountable solely to government bureaucrats because it's funded with property taxes extorted from you under the threat of seizing your home? Are you a small business owner drowning in the quicksand of increasing taxes, crippling regulation, and the imposition of more costly government programs like Obamacare? Is your small business finding it difficult or impossible to borrow needed capital from banks who instead of lending to you, acquire or invest in large corporations that compete against you? Perhaps you are elderly, burdened with constant worry about surviving on a fixed income from social security—while property taxes and basic monthly expenses skyrocket out of control. Instead of being able to retire and enjoy your golden years, you find yourself competing against teenagers for a minimum-wage job at a fast-food joint. If you're lucky, you might earn enough to keep from being thrown out of the home whose mortgage you spent thirty years paying off. Maybe you're a college student or recent graduate crippled with student loan debt, struggling or even unable to find a decent paying job. Do you wonder if you'll ever manage to get out from under your enormous debt burden? Or are you simply fed up with government lies and propaganda touting false hope and change for greater economic prosperity, financial security, and opportunity—all of which remain perpetually out of reach?

If you count yourself or anyone you love among the aforementioned categories, this book is for you.

Our country is disintegrating, and the middle class is disappearing. The number of American citizens living below the poverty line has increased by more than 33 percent in just five years.[1] Virtually all of those citizens used to live above the poverty line. You and your children could be next. The media reports that the country is in a period of economic recovery, yet poverty continues to expand, the middle class continues to contract, and the only jobs being created are part-time minimum-wage jobs previously filled by teenagers. All the while the real cost of living is soaring while household incomes are declining. And what goes largely unreported is that hundreds of thousands of families across America lose their homes every year not only to foreclosure but to seizure for nonpayment of property taxes. Tens of thousands of these homes are being snapped up by private equity funds and other banking institutions. They use their money-creation power to finance these acquisitions as corporate-owned residential rentals.[2] These firms are profiting from the financial crisis and housing bubble, which they helped to create. This little-known process is transforming home ownership into pervasive rent slavery all across the country. Real home ownership has been systematically wiped out in America.

Americans have accepted a form of freedom that is actually the opposite. They no longer recognize the difference between a free-enterprise system that respects individual property rights and a collectivist system that confiscates your property and conscripts your labor. This confusion over what is and is not freedom has morphed into a continual conflict between the left and right. Our socioeconomic model has been infected with a social pathogen, and like some sort of autoimmune response, *we the people* have been engaged in a relentless attack against one another, fighting over a false left-right paradigm. All the while every one of us is being fleeced of our earnings, our savings, our homes, and our property.

The United States was founded in the cause of individual liberty, whose cornerstone is a respect for individual property rights. Establishment Republicans have perverted that cause to justify the construction of a global empire through a persistent policy of foreign interventionism disguised as "spreading Democracy around the globe." Establishment Democrats have abandoned the cause of liberty altogether in favor of democratic socialism, dependency, and expanding the welfare state. Both political parties are primarily interested in expanding and then abusing their power over the citizenry. They accomplish this by colluding to surreptitiously confiscate your property and earnings, and turning you into a total dependent.

Our current political process consists in Republicans fighting against statist-socialism espoused by the Democrats and Democrats fighting against corporate-socialism espoused by the Republicans. Both falsely claim to be devoted to the free market and the US Constitution while in truth they act to distort the spirit and intent of our

---

[1] Associated Press, "4 in 5 Americans live in danger of falling into poverty, joblessness," July 28, 2013

[2] Whelan, Robbie, "Big Money Gets Into Landlord Game," Wall St. Journal, Aug 4, 2011

founding principles as they vie for dominance between two variants of collectivism. Neither upholds the fundamental tenets of the constitution—respect for individual liberty, property rights, and personal responsibility. Both parties willfully ignore the fact that the constitution mandated a socioeconomic model that is the antithesis of any form of collectivism. On the few occasions that the constitution is raised during public discourse, they resort to arguing the myth of a *living constitution*. However, this idea could only be based upon a premise that ethical principles and fundamental moral values should change with the times. By that way of thinking one must ask, "Do moral truths become immoral and immoral behaviors become moral just because we live in a different century?" The unalienable rights of individuals are based on ethics, fundamental morals and natural laws that are enduring and unchanging. The framers derived these principles from natural law, which is why they are the basis for our constitution and Bill of Rights.

Nevertheless, both political parties along with all branches of our government collude to neuter The Constitution in order to further the agenda of the political class. This collusion has subverted the separation of powers doctrine, which was central to our founding principles of governance. Through numerous unconstitutional acts passed by Congress, including the Patriot Act, the National Defense Authorization Act, and the misnamed Patient Protection and Affordable Care Act, We, the American people, both liberal and conservative, are being subjected to illegal federal government spying and intrusion into our private lives to an extent that is unprecedented. America's *shining beacon of freedom* has been replaced—by an antenna, intercepting your phone calls and emails for surveillance by the NSA and the IRS. Our property and the fruits of our labor are systematically confiscated while the obscenely wealthy global banking establishment continues to be enriched at our expense—not coincidentally but as a direct consequence. Government pretends to be concerned with helping the poor as a means to justify fleecing the middle class. They then transfer the fruits of our individual labor and control of most real property to the obscenely rich ruling class. As government takes more and more control over our lives, the middle class evaporates, poverty expands, and the obscenely rich continue to get obscenely richer. How is this happening right under the noses of such a vast, relatively well-educated population?

Divide and Conquer

The mainstream media, complicit in the *mis-education* of the American people, broadcasts entertainment news about issues that are selected as emotional hot—buttons for specifically targeted groups. A series of stories are put out that are intended to instill a sense of disenfranchisement, and then fan the flames of anger among a subgroup of the population. This action is followed by a different series of stories targeted at a different group. It is a process of manufacturing opposition. We are relentlessly bombarded with news stories about Latinos and illegal immigration, single mothers, deadbeat dads, African-American issues, school shootings, race-baiting, the war on drugs, so-called conservative issues versus so-called liberal issues.

We continually hear about gay rights, black rights, Hispanic rights, women's rights, animal rights, but never a single word is uttered about individual property rights, which apply to everyone equally. The American people are so distracted, confused, and polarized against one another by the barrage of conflicting and often irrelevant information that very few have even noticed that the only rights that truly matter to all of us, our constitutional rights and in particular our property rights, have been systematically eradicated.

The mechanism being employed is as old as it is simple—*divide and conquer.* Subgroups of American society are pitted against one another over manufactured controversies so that everyone is kept confused, busy, and distracted by our culture of envy and celebrity worship. In public, the political class continually argues over things that are completely outside the scope of the proper role of government and should otherwise be private matters for every individual or family. In private, they collude to destroy our individual rights to life, liberty, and property. All the while every American's bank account is being raided, while their homes and properties are confiscated with little or no objection.

This has been enabled largely because the true meaning of property ownership has been distorted for so many generations that today the vast majority of Americans have little or no understanding about what property rights really are. People have been conditioned to believe that home ownership consists in taking on an enormous debt that will likely never be paid off in order to purchase a home whose price has been inflated far beyond its true value through fraudulent lending practices and loose monetary policy. To service that debt, you make monthly payments more or less for your entire adult life, the lion's share of which is interest expense. At the same time and further for all eternity, you are subject to a perpetually increasing rate of property tax (assessed in direct proportion to the artificially inflated value of your home). If you were to simply stop paying the tax on your "private property," you are deemed a criminal tax evader. Your home is forcibly seized and is then auctioned off to the highest bidder, with the state and the bank sharing the proceeds. If you're lucky, you will be spared a prison sentence.

Most Americans call this "home ownership."

Coincident to this process, every person's savings and retirement is constantly devalued due to the Federal Reserve's incessant debasement of the dollar through money printing (quantitative easing).

Inflation—The Hidden Tax

Most people in the modern industrialized world have been conditioned to believe that inflation (demonstrated as rising prices) is a naturally occurring and unavoidable phenomenon. This is absolutely false.

Before the housing bubble burst in late 2007, most home owners were deceived by propaganda claiming that the inflation in home prices indicated a strong and growing economy. Most were actually delighted at seeing the value of their homes increase, believing that this was an indication of their becoming wealthier. Unfortunately, they had little or no understanding that this was due to a deliberately engineered, market-specific inflation, rather than the natural forces of supply and demand. These false economic signals encouraged people and many businesses to mal-invest and subsequently lose their hard-earned money. More problematic, they willfully ignored the consequent escalating property tax right along with and in proportion to the rising home prices. Many borrowed against the artificially inflated value of their homes and then used those funds to acquire more junk they didn't need. Few questioned the logic or integrity of banks that offered home equity loans amounting to 125 percent of their already inflated market value. The absurdity of this notwithstanding, many people took the bait and then mortgaged their family's future in order to fund a new SUV, a big-screen TV, a vacation cruise, or worse—a second overvalued home also financed with a mortgage—while knowingly putting their homes underwater in debt. This played directly into the hands of the ruling class's corporatocracy and their political cronies who used this concept to disguise unsustainable overconsumption as *economic growth*. In spite of the experience from the housing collapse that started in 2007, banks again are practicing these same destructive lending practices. As recently as June, 2014, new advertisements have begun to emerge for home equity loan offers of up to 110% of the home's market value. Indeed, a secondary housing bubble has been forming since mid—2011.

Follow the Money Printers

The public, too distracted and confused by the entertainment media's mass-distraction campaigns, finds it almost impossible to discern the root causes of our economic ills. In fact, it boils down to one of the most common expressions we've all heard before, "Follow the money." By this, I mean follow the money to its source. A small group of very powerful, international, financial elites have implemented a mechanism to centralize—under their control—our means of production (land, labor, and natural resources). That mechanism is found within our monetary system and central banking.

The corporatocracy uses the media to distract the citizenry from the alarming fact that they have gained control of our lives, property, and future through an economic model based on a corrupt and unconstitutional monetary system. The Federal Reserve system is an exclusive monopoly on money printing that benefits an elite group of global bankers to whom the government has become beholden, all at the expense of every individual who must work for a living. The former government of the people, by the people, and for the people was usurped by central bankers long before anyone of the current generation was born.

Very few Americans even realize that our current monetary model—the Federal Reserve system—was not only described by Karl Marx in *The Communist Manifesto* as a cornerstone of Communism[3] but is prohibited by the US Constitution. This is not a conspiracy theory. It is a conspiracy fact. Our Federal Reserve system is unconstitutional, and the monetary system we have been living under is designed to deliberately transfer the wealth earned by individual labor to an unelected ruling class that remains practically anonymous. The ruling elite control the puppet strings of our government, which enforces that wealth transfer under the guise of wealth redistribution for the so-called "common good." At the same time the mainstream media perpetuates our envy-driven culture of overconsumption through a sophisticated form of propaganda called advertising and public relations.

You Can't Own Your House

A country's monetary system determines the nature of that country's property rights. A nation whose currency is based upon debt cannot at the same time enjoy a system that respects the right to property ownership. When all money is created out of debt, all property is by default actually controlled by the lender. That property includes your house, your savings, and your labor (and therefore your life itself).

If the American people ever allow private banks to control the issue of their currency, first by inflation, then by deflation, the banks and corporations that will grow up around them will deprive the people of all property until their children wake up homeless on the continent their Fathers conquered. I believe that banking institutions are more dangerous to our liberties than standing armies ... The issuing power should be taken from the banks and restored to the people, to whom it properly belongs.

—Thomas Jefferson

In spite of these facts, this monetary model has been implemented in every industrialized country. Whether we are talking about the US dollar, the euro, the yen, or the British pound, there is no currency that is immune from the artificial

---

3   Marx, Karl; Engels, Friedrich. 1848. *The Communist Manifesto, The Ten Planks of Communism.*

manipulations of inflation and that is not controlled by a central bank run by a select and powerful group of individuals.

This was not always the case. From the time of the ratification of the US Constitution in 1789 until 1913, a period of 124 years, the US economy had essentially zero inflation—except during the US Civil War and two short periods when chartered central banks were established.[4] The charters for those first central banks, however, had expiration dates, so their destructive monetary manipulation was short-lived. Even after the establishment of the Federal Reserve in 1913, the United States still had a vestige of a sound currency. Until 1933, the United States remained on the gold standard.

In the very first official act of his presidency, Franklin Delano Roosevelt put an end to the requirement that paper US dollars be redeemable in gold domestically while he retained a gold standard only for foreign exchange transactions (this was called the gold *exchange* standard, as distinct from the gold standard). With the stroke of a pen, FDR declared individual gold ownership illegal—a direct violation of the US Constitution. The final nail in the coffin came in 1971 when President Richard Nixon defaulted on America's promise to exchange gold for paper dollars presented for conversion by foreign central banks. In rescinding America's adoption of the Bretton Woods Agreement, Nixon disconnected the US dollar from the gold *exchange* standard altogether. On that date, the price of Gold was $35 per ounce. What followed next was a succession of international currency wars.[5] We are currently engaged in the most destructive currency war in history, yet this is largely unknown to most Americans and is not reported in the mainstream news media.

The US dollar has lost more than 98 percent of its value since the creation of the Federal Reserve system. In a system such as ours, continuous money printing relentlessly devalues your savings, your retirement, and the purchasing power of your earnings. It is intended to do so.

Our Monetary System Creates and Guarantees Sustained Poverty

Throughout the 1800s and into the early 1900s, those who were poor but diligent, hardworking, and frugal were able to save and accumulate wealth over a period of time in order to escape poverty. Our current monetary model, however, precludes the poor from saving their way to prosperity, for savings will become worthless after any extended period of time. It is designed to ensure that the poor remain in poverty and the middle class remain under a constant threat of being reduced to poverty. This is one of the means by which the middle class is ruled by fear. This monetary system has been adopted by every industrialized nation on earth. As such, there is now nowhere in the world that a

---

4   Mullins, Eustace. *The Secrets of The Federal Reserve*, Bridger House Publishers, June 22, 2009

5   Rickards, James, *Currency Wars* (Portfolio Trade, 2012)

moral, self-reliant individual can simply live within his or her means and be able to save enough to retire or leave something of value to his or her children. No matter how frugal you are, it is now virtually impossible to save enough money over time in order to purchase a home without using mortgage debt. Forcing every poor and middle-class worker into a life of perpetual, inescapable, debt servitude has been one of the main goals of the statists. We have allowed them to succeed.

The people of the Western world have been conditioned to believe that a form of currency that can be wished into existence, created out of thin air, and expanded to a theoretically infinite supply of money is a sound medium of exchange. In adopting this system, we can create a theoretically infinite demand for goods and services. Those goods, however, are limited in physical supply by the laws of nature. Infinite demand for a limited supply is incompatible with the laws of nature and is the basis for forming artificial economic bubbles. The overconsumption encouraged by this model ultimately pollutes our environment, wipes out our natural resources, and impoverishes the working middle class, all while it enriches a small entitled group that is obsessed with power—the power to create money from nothing. While inflation creates a continuously rising cost of living, the central bankers sit back to enjoy their unremitting windfall, laughing all the way to their bank.

All the while we the people spin our wheels, incessantly running in circles, choking on the increasing pollution of our air and water, working ourselves to death in a noble but futile effort to try to earn sustainable financial security for ourselves and our families. Most of us are painfully unaware that real economic freedom for the individual has become an unattainable goal. The principal beneficiaries of our relentless productive efforts are the political class and the international bankers whom they have authorized to create money out of nothing (legalized counterfeiting). They profit not only from the productive wealth generated by the entire working class but also from the relentless infighting amongst the fragmented citizenry of this once-great country. Indeed, divide and conquer has again been demonstrated as one of the most effective tactics to establish tyranny.

It's time that we let go of our personal biases, our prejudices, our race-baiting, and our counterproductive political correctness and see through this fraud. It's time that *we the people* stop fighting against one another, driven by the culture of envy and distracted by our adolescent celebrity worship, both of which have been instilled through the corporate media, our government, and our public education system. We the people must all come to recognize this autoimmune disease for what it is and attack it instead of one another.

Our country and our children's future are in serious trouble. Although the situation is daunting and some kind of worst-case scenario appears to be almost inevitable, there still remains the means by which to turn the tide back in favor of the American citizen. Doing so will first require that more people gain the knowledge and understanding about what has happened to our property rights and why. And secondly it will require the citizenry to act, each of us for our own interest and for the good of our own families.

Finally it is vital for the reader to understand that no president, senator, congressman, supreme court justice, or any combination thereof will restore your individual rights to property and liberty. Only you can act to restore your rights and your liberty—or they will not be restored.

It's time that we take back what we have earned—our property, the fruits of our labor, and most important of all, our families and our children. We the people must act now. Our children's lives and futures are at stake.

CHAPTER 1

The Rabbit

They call it the American dream ... because you have to be asleep
to believe it.

—George Carlin, 2005

Greyhound dog racing is a fascinating business model. It's also a fitting metaphor
for American life as we know it.

Greyhounds are naturally gentle, intelligent, and unaggressive dogs. They are born
and bred to race because of their exceptional speed. It is in the prime of their lives
when they are young, healthy, fit, and eager to taste life that they are enslaved and
trained to race against one another solely for the profit of the track owner. During
their tenure as racing dogs they are kept rather hungry. They are fed well enough to
maintain their health, strength, and speed but not so well that they are ever fully
satisfied. During race season some may be kept on the verge of starvation during
the approach to post time. This is done so that just as they are about to sprint from
the starting gate, they will be highly motivated to beat the other dogs to the prize,
which they believe will satiate their hunger. At this point the prize, a fake rabbit, is
presented just in front of them on the track. As their starting gates fly open, they are
overcome with a tremendous urge to pursue a singular goal—to beat the other dogs
and be first to catch the rabbit. They are perpetually hungry and believe the rabbit to
be their salvation. They become aggressive, relentless, and almost mindless in their
pursuit of this deceptive goal.

During their off-time they are trained to dislike, resent, and fear the other dogs. This
is done so that they will feel a strong desire to battle against and try to dominate one
another. This reinforces each of their beliefs that the other dogs are trying to deny
them their rabbit. Thus they try to outcompete one another in order to catch the

rabbit on which they believe their lives depend. What the dogs never realize is that it is all a fraud. None of them can catch the rabbit no matter how hard they try, no matter how fast they run, no matter how well they outcompete or outsmart the other dogs. The rabbit is controlled by the track owner, who either speeds it up or slows it down as required, always keeping it just out of reach. This goes on and on race after race literally for the dogs' entire lives so that they are never able to catch up to their goal, and they never quite realize why.

Throughout the course of their lives the dogs remain somewhat loyal to the owner because they're dependent upon him for the scraps of food he gives them. He conditions them to see these scraps as their reward for a race well run. The owners are sometimes kind and friendly to the dogs, and at other times they are cruel, occasionally depriving them of their scraps. This inspires dependency, fear, uncertainty, and confusion all at the same time. Like people, dogs that are kept hungry, fearful, and confused are easy to control and manipulate. But their greatest fear by far is the fear of rejection by their handler because they're trained to believe that if they are rejected they will starve. This ensures they will remain obedient and will not try to escape. The owners treat the dogs in such a way as to garner both strong loyalty and dependence while at the same time convincing them that the other dogs are their enemies, competitors who are trying to deprive them of their *fair share* of rabbits.

Normally these dogs are kind, gentle, and unaggressive, but by using sophisticated training techniques developed over decades, their owners are able to polarize them against one another, while simultaneously instilling in them a fear of deprivation. They therefore work and compete harder and harder throughout their lives in a relentless effort to defeat one another and gain the love of their masters while they maximize his revenues in the process. In effect, the dogs become addicted to their own servitude. All the while they never realize that they are nothing more than tools of profit, all being equally exploited. The owners and managers who run the track continue this process until the dogs are too old and worn out to race. No longer useful as a resource, they're euthanized, discarded, and replaced.[6]

What must go through the greyhound's mind at the moment the owner delivers the lethal injection? Does he realize that he's been duped? Has the fraud been so sophisticated that the dog goes to his grave actually feeling love and loyalty to the ones who have exploited and then eventually done him in? Does the dog look up at his owner while the needle is casually stabbed into his thigh and wonder, *Why did you lie to me? Why did you destroy my life just to make yourself rich?*

It's likely that at the end the dogs still have no understanding that their whole existence of running around the track to the best of their ability was for nothing. They probably have no idea that the real beneficiary of their life of hard work and

---

[6]   Klas, Mary Ellen. "Greyhound deaths, and Florida's racing industry." *Miami Herald,* Feb. 16, 2014

sacrifice was their owner, whose only interest was to coerce them into striving to achieve an illusory goal that has been deliberately rendered unattainable. Even if they could catch the rabbit, it wouldn't matter because the rabbit is a fake—they can't eat it anyway—but they will never know that. They go to their deaths actually feeling love and loyalty to their oppressor, painfully unaware that they have been had.

Like these greyhound dogs, Americans are being lied to. We are lied to by our government, misled by the entertainment media, indoctrinated by our educational institutions, defrauded by our banking institutions, and subjugated by our employers. Nevertheless, we willingly grant these institutions power over every aspect of our lives, and we even admire and assist those who are exploiting us. What is the purpose of the lies?

To con each and every one of us out of our property rights and to coerce us into consenting to our own fleecing—while venerating and revering the thieves.

This is true no matter if one is truly poor or one is a member of the upper-middle class. It doesn't matter if you are black, white, Latino, Asian, straight, gay, lesbian, Democrat, Republican, employee, manager, small-business owner, or greyhound dog. No matter how you earn your living, all those in the middle class have one thing in common. Like the greyhounds, we have all been duped into pursuing an illusion, a goal that has been held in front us as *the American dream*, the dream of individual freedom that comes from attaining economic security for ourselves and our children—the dream of becoming a self-reliant home owner. Like the rabbit on the dog track, the so-called American dream is today an illusory and unattainable goal.

This is because the act itself of chasing the rabbit is what enriches those few who benefit from our daily economic activity. Making the rabbit uncatchable ensures that we can never stop running after it. We pursue hard work and productive effort as a means to survive, intending to achieve sustainable self-reliance. However, the game has been rigged so that real long-term economic security for individuals and their families is unattainable. We spend the best and healthiest part of our lives working like dogs for forty, fifty, or more years while paying most of our earnings to tax collectors and mortgage lenders mainly in an effort to become home owners. However, in reality, home ownership does not truly exist in America. Real property rights were eradicated a long time ago.

The Inversion: Lies Become Truth, Immoral Becomes Moral

Most Americans don't realize this situation for what it is, and once confronted with this reality, they initially object to the notion that we have no real freedom and no real property rights. There are several reasons for this:

- It is too emotionally painful to consider that we are actually nothing more than work mules. People would feel degraded and humiliated to realize that they are nothing more than an economic resource for a ruling class to exploit. Most people would rather live a comfortable lie than face the painful and unvarnished truth. But it is a fact. To the ruling class we are not human beings. We are *human resources.*

- Research psychologists have discovered that it actually requires more cognitive effort to reject false information than it does to simply accept it as being true. Therefore, misinformation is especially likely to stick when it conforms to our preexisting political, religious, or social point of view. Because of this, misguided ideology and personal worldviews can be especially difficult barriers to overcome. One study notes that efforts to retract misinformation often backfire and actually lead to the strengthening of an erroneous belief.[7]

> This persistence of misinformation has fairly alarming implications in a democracy because people may base decisions on information that, at some level, they know to be false.
> —Dr. Stephan Lewandowsky,
> University of Western Australia

Over time, most people develop a vested emotional interest in supporting their own errors. It would bruise a person's ego to admit that he or she had been conned, duped, or coerced into believing a falsehood. This principle is even more powerful when those falsehoods are foisted upon an entire society, for then peer pressure comes into play. This is the force behind today's propensity to label those seeking truth as "conspiracy theorists." If you swim against the tide and reject commonly held beliefs— no matter how absurd those beliefs may be—you are an outcast. In truth, there may be conspiracy theories, but there are also conspiracy facts. It takes courage, character, integrity, and humility to admit when one's own beliefs are in error, even when it's the result of deliberate misinformation. Nevertheless, at the risk of using a cliché, "the truth shall set you free." This book will deal only in facts and conclusions that can be supported with facts.

> To argue with a person who has renounced the use of reason, is like administering medicine to the dead.
>
> —Thomas Paine

---

[7]   Wood, Janice. "Why Do We Believe Lies Even After They Have Been Proven Wrong?" *Psych Central*, Sep. 22, 2012

We are constantly lied to. Joseph Goebbels (Adolf Hitler's minister of propaganda), has been quoted as having said that lies are seen to be true if they are repeated often enough. Truth, however, since it is generally self-evident, is rarely repeated over and over again. Truth tellers don't feel the need to repeat what is self-evident, but liars, on the other hand, are relentless and persistent in their efforts to convince others of falsehoods.

If you tell a lie big enough and keep repeating it, people will eventually come to believe it. The lie can be maintained only for such time as the State can shield the people from the political, economic and/or military consequences of the lie. It thus becomes vitally important for the State to use all of its powers to repress dissent, for the truth is the mortal enemy of the lie, and thus by extension, the truth is the greatest enemy of the State.

—Joseph Goebbels, minister of propaganda
in the German Third Reich

- Most Americans have neither the time nor the resources to research, study, learn, and then critically analyze the many spheres of knowledge required to fully understand what is going on in American socioeconomics and politics. It requires both depth and breadth of understanding in economics, mathematics, finance, banking, global geopolitics, sociology, and American history to fully grasp the economic consequences of our government's actions. People are too busy running on the hamster wheel, just trying to keep roofs over their heads and their children fed. They have precious little time or energy needed to gather the knowledge and experience necessary to be able to connect the dots and figure out what is being done to them and for what purpose. Most have little choice but to accept their information from the mainstream media and public education system at face value. Few are able to challenge the information they are given. This is part of the design.

A *Newsweek* poll conducted in 2011 found that of a thousand Americans, 70 percent could not identify the US Constitution as the law of the land. More than 75 percent of high school seniors could not name a single power granted to Congress by the constitution.[8] A random poll conducted recently of 1,500 American voters found that less than 19 percent had actually read the US Constitution in its entirety at least once

---

8 Hentoff, Nat, "Our Constitution: How many of us know it?" The Cato Institute, May 19, 2011.

in their lifetime, and less than 1.1 percent had ever read *The Communist Manifesto*. In spite of these facts, 36 percent of Americans (and 45 percent of Democrats)[9] view socialism favorably. [10] Yet clearly since most have never read either *The Communist Manifesto* or the US Constitution, they cannot possibly know what socialism actually is and how it differs from America's founding principles and the free enterprise system.

It seems that most Americans choose to follow a political ideology based upon a distorted understanding of what these different systems stand for. Many simply choose to identify with one or the other political party much in the same way they would follow their favorite NFL team—based on what is most popular among their closest friends and family members. We are trained from childhood by our schools and by the entertainment media to pick and then root for our favorite team. Most adults view the political process in the same way. Deprived of truthful and objective information with which to educate themselves, people are open to the underhanded influence of those seeking power over them. Most Americans who favor socialism believe it to be an effective means to fairly distribute wealth in order to take care of the poor. They are very well intentioned, but grossly misinformed about what the fundamental and moral differences between socialism and the free enterprise system really are. This book is intended to remedy that.

- Most people suffer from normalcy bias. This is a condition that is well known to psychologists. It refers to a state of denial. Like an infant with a security blanket, we cling to our habitual and repetitive way of life and consider it normal regardless of its dysfunctions. Normalcy bias tends to make people ignore looming danger or even catastrophe. Many casually dismiss obvious signs of impending disaster. Most people are generally hopeful, so they project a falsely optimistic outcome that further deepens their state of denial. When entire societies fall prey to normalcy bias, we end up with events like World War II. During the rise of the Nazis, millions of Germans ignored the warning signs. Over time, the regime implemented gun control and censorship of the press. Jews and other disenfranchised groups were required to wear identifying symbols and to carry numbered identification. Many who could have left the country stayed and were exterminated. Think of this when the subject of a US national ID card or RFID implantation for Americans is brought up in public discourse.

The current and most relevant example of normalcy bias is our model of home ownership. This has persisted for several generations, so it has

---

9   Gardiner, Nile, "45% of US Democrats favor Socialism," *The Telegraph* Nov. 30, 2012.
10   Newport, Frank, "Socialism viewed positively by 36% of Americans," *Gallup Politics*, Feb 4, 2010.

become accepted as the normal definition of ownership and of property rights in general. It consists in borrowing money from a bank for a period of thirty or forty years—money that the bank is authorized to create from nothing—so that by the time the mortgage is paid off, you will have paid three times or more than what the house is actually worth (assuming one actually ever pays off his or her home, which is a rarity today). At least two thirds or more of the total payments will have been interest on the debt. All the while you are subject to a continually increasing property tax that is levied against your home for all eternity. Nonpayment of the tax results in the seizure of your home by the local authorities—at the point of a gun if necessary—even if you have paid off the mortgage in full. If you sell the home for a capital gain (resulting from the artificial inflation created by our bubble economy), you are taxed on that gain, benefitting the government and not you—the property *owner*. When you mortgage your home, you are required to purchase a full coverage insurance policy against fire, flood, damage, or any potential disaster that could destroy the home. The beneficiary however is not you who pay the premium, but the bank that holds the mortgage.

Furthermore, our homes are subject to zoning regulations that restrict us from certain uses of our property, such as operating a small business within the home. If you want to change the structure, build an addition, or erect a separate garage, you must first ask permission from the local authorities and even pay them a fee to obtain that permission. If the local authorities decide that some public use of your property takes precedence, they will *condemn* and then seize your home through eminent domain.

Therefore, we have a model of ownership without control. Americans have been persuaded to believe that this model is normal. However, ownership without control is a contradiction in terms. America's model of *property ownership* is anything but normal.

- Many people suffer from confirmation bias. This is where we have a persistent bias toward sources of information that confirm the beliefs we already have. We then consciously reject information that disagrees with our preconceived ideas. People would rather feel good about what they hear than learn absolute truth. That makes us easily trainable, and in the same way as the greyhounds, we are conditioned to become loyal to and dependent on our leaders even when they lie to us repeatedly. We rarely if ever question their motives or intentions. We want to believe that they have our best interests at heart, so we rarely question what we're told by those in authority.[11]

---

[11] Pohl, Rüdiger F. Cognitive Illusions—A Handbook on Fallacies and Biases in Thinking, Judgment, and Memory.

If Anderson Cooper, Sean Hannity, or President Obama said it on TV, it must be true. We like to believe they wouldn't lie to us because they are charming, likeable celebrities who tell us what we want to hear. Liberals watch CNN or MSNBC and feel good about what they're told. Conservatives watch Fox News or read *Newsmax*, and they feel good about hearing the exact opposite information. Neither considers the others' news sources as having any credibility, so they refuse to listen to each other. In actual fact, neither source is completely truthful, so neither side is hearing the absolute truth. Upon debating with each other, while one party states its case, the other plugs their ears with their fingers and sings, "La, la, la, la, la, la, la, la." If a third voice of reason comes along to try to talk some sense into them, they both plug their ears and sing.

Most people are more interested in proving that their particular team is right instead of being devoted to finding objective truth. This isn't entirely their fault, as it is to some extent a feature of everyone's biology. When asked to accept a principle that conflicts with an established belief system, almost everyone experiences *cognitive dissonance*. This can be physically painful to some people. Note how listening to some politicians literally makes your skin crawl. According to "the father of advertising and public relations," Edward Bernays, this feature of our biology makes mass indoctrination possible.

> The conscious and intelligent manipulation of the organized habits and opinions of the masses is an important element in democratic society. Those who manipulate this unseen mechanism of society constitute an invisible government which is the true ruling power of our country. ... We are governed, our minds are molded, our tastes formed, our ideas suggested, largely by men we have never heard of. This is a logical result of the way in which our democratic society is organized. Vast numbers of human beings must cooperate in this manner if they are to live together as a smoothly functioning society. ... In almost every act of our daily lives, whether in the sphere of politics or business, in our social conduct or our ethical thinking, we are dominated by the relatively small number of persons ... who understand the mental processes and social patterns of the masses. It is they who pull the wires which control the public mind.
>
> —Edward Bernays

Being devoted to absolute truth requires that one have the humility to accept the possibility of being proven wrong, even if the truth hurts. Career politicians have stated repeatedly that their goal in any argument is to win. To a career politician, the truth is not only irrelevant but should be perverted or obfuscated whenever necessary to prove his or her case. Career politicians consider truth as an obstacle to be overcome. Winning an argument, regardless of truth, is one of the cornerstones of legal training and is why most successful career politicians are trained as lawyers. This reveals that most politicians are motivated by power, not by the opportunity to serve the best interest of their constituents. Only truth will serve the people's best interests. When people are less devoted to absolute truth than they are to a feel-good exercise of validating what they have been taught to believe, they can be deceived into believing any falsehood. They might even believe that occupying a residence under the control of a mortgage lender for thirty years and a property tax collector for eternity constitutes ownership.

> When you want to help people, you tell them the truth. When you want to help yourself, you tell them what they want to hear.
>
> —Dr. Thomas Sowell – Sr. Fellow, The Hoover Institute – Stanford University

Government Lies—"Read My Lips"

The following are just a small sample of the lies our government tells to the American People:

Lie: Social security is a trust fund.

Truth: If it were truly a trust fund, they would be reimbursing us with the same money our employers withheld from our earnings while we were employed. Why then is it financially structured as a welfare benefit? The fact is that social security is a tax (payroll tax), and those funds are spent by Congress even before they are collected (on whatever Congress wants to spend them). There is no fund, no money on deposit in an account for any retiree. Current taxpayers fund the retirement costs of former taxpayers whose withholdings had already been spent long before they retired. The financial analogy is an investment scheme where new investors are lured in so that earlier investors can be paid off with that new money. When critics refer to the social security system as a Ponzi scheme, they are being completely accurate. Social security operates on the same financial model for which Bernie Madoff was sent to federal prison. More problematic is that the massive baby-boom population is now entering the line to collect their social security from a trust fund that doesn't exist. Their benefits will have to be paid by future taxpayers who will be fewer in number, paying fewer dollars into the system. Furthermore, they will be doing so with money that has been devalued through our inflationary monetary policy.

> Congress says they're looking into the Bernie Madoff scandal. So the guy who made $50 billion disappear, is being investigated by the people who made $750 billion disappear.
>
> —Jay Leno

To say that the social security system will be broke is a gross understatement. This constitutes only one part of our projected national debt that is often referred to as an *unfunded liability*. It is completely unaccounted for in terms of our current 18 trillion dollar national debt. When unfunded liabilities like social security, Medicare, and Medicaid are taken into account, our national debt comes out to an estimate of more than $145 trillion dollars. That amounts to more than $1.2 million dollars per US taxpayer. This figure continues to grow mainly through the federal government's deficit spending of a staggering $4.6 billion per day.[12]

Lie: The Federal Reserve controls inflation.

Truth: The Federal Reserve deliberately creates inflation. Every US dollar in existence is a debt (an IOU) called a Federal Reserve note. This currency is the very instrument of inflation. Since the Federal Reserve Act was passed in 1913, the Fed has destroyed more than 98 percent of the dollar's purchasing power—deliberately. During the 124 years prior to the founding of the Federal Reserve, the US dollar was a gold-backed currency that retained its value during long periods of time. In other words, there was essentially zero inflation. Under those conditions, even those poor who were frugal, thrifty, and hardworking could accumulate wealth and save their way to prosperity. Our inherently inflationary system has made that impossible. Our Federal Reserve debt-based monetary system is designed to guarantee sustained poverty.

Lie: The recession ended, and we are having an economic recovery.

Truth: The United States has been in a nearly perpetual state of recession for at least the last fifty years. The few short periods of growth were illusory, artificially stimulated by unsustainable consumption rather than by real investment. Today there is no measure by which the economy is showing a rebound. While the official

---

[12] www.usdebtclock.org, Oct 31, 2013.

unemployment rate (reported as U-3 by the Bureau of Labor Statistics) dropped to below 8 percent—conveniently just weeks before the 2012 presidential election—the rate of full unemployment (called the U-6) climbed from 14.5 percent to 14.9 percent at that same time. Some economists point to other uncalculated factors such as the labor participation rate, which suggests that real unemployment is more than 20 percent. Average household income has actually declined since the beginning of the Obama administration. The largest decline has been among African-American heads of households with an 11.5 percent decline in median income between June 2009 and June 2013. This is more than twice the 5.5 percent overall decline in median household income nationally.[13] In 2003 the inflation-adjusted *net worth* for the typical American household was $87,992. By December 2013, it was only $56,335—a 36 percent decline.[14] Net worth has to do with assets—property rights. This is a clear measure of how much our property rights have been destroyed over the past 10 years alone.

President Obama can lay claim to having achieved the lowest labor participation rate (63.2 percent) since the Carter administration in 1978. The main reason the rate was lower than this in previous decades was because there were far fewer women in the workforce before the mid-1970s, predating the women's liberation movement.

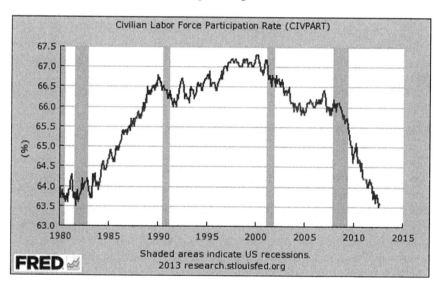

Understanding labor force participation is crucial in assessing the state of the economy and in putting the current level of unemployment in its proper perspective. Millions of people who would like to be employed have literally given up on finding work.

13   Reiland, Ralph R. "The Poor: Reagan vs Obama"—*The Pittsburgh Tribune-Review, Sept 17, 2013.*

14   Pfeffer, Fabian T., Danziger, Sheldon, and Schoeni, Robert F. Wealth Levels, Wealth Inequality, and The Great Recession. *Russel Sage Foundation Report.* June, 2014

Many of these are former higher level professionals and highly educated white-collar workers who cannot find anything more than a part-time minimum-wage job, so they simply stay out of the game. Once they have exhausted their unemployment benefits, they are no longer counted as unemployed. As a consequence, although the rate of unemployment has the appearance of having declined since the end of 2012, the actual ratio of employed people to the entire population has declined, so the real rate of unemployment is going up, not down.

The Highest Welfare Population in the Industrialized World

Americans are no longer capable of feeding themselves. More than forty-six million people are on food stamps, and the number is climbing rapidly.[15] In fact, the full-time private sector workforce is now smaller than the number of people receiving some form of federal food assistance. The US Department of Agriculture estimates that a total of 101 million Americans currently participate in at least one of the fifteen food assistance programs offered by the government at a cost of $114 billion in 2012.

Since the population of the United States currently stands at approximately 316 million people, this means that nearly one third of the entire US population receives food aid from the government. This bestows upon the United States the honor of having the highest welfare population in the industrialized world.[16] The rate at which this condition is deteriorating is alarming. The number of people living at or below the poverty line has increased by an astounding 33 percent from 2009 through 2013.

These facts are a glaring indictment of the notion that our economy is improving.

Lie: Your congressman is working on your behalf.

Truth: The elites in Congress and the appointed bureaucrats who do their work are career politicians, permanent employees of the government. Their purpose is to expand the government, increase their political power, confiscate the productive wealth created by the middle class—and finally—to serve the interests of the private Federal Reserve system and their other corporatist masters in the military industrial complex. They view the American people as nothing more than a means to an end—labor resources. They view The Constitution (or anything having to do with individual property rights) as an obstacle to achieving their goal of absolute power and control over property, labor, and natural resources.

---

[15] Plumer, Brad. "Median household incomes have collapsed since the recession." *The Washington Post*: March, 29, 2013.

[16] Hayward, John, "Food stamp nation is now larger than full-time private-sector workforce" *Human Events Journal, July 9, 2011.*

Lie: We have a two-party system, and there is a difference between the Republican party and the Democratic party.

Truth: There is only one party—the political class. Each new presidential election demonstrates the same pattern. The incumbent party's policies are denounced by the faux-opposition party. Whenever the opposition party wins and takes office, they proceed to continue those same basic policies they had earlier denounced. The two political parties exist solely to provide a false left-right paradigm to keep Americans divided. Only in public do they differ on superficial issues that are not even within the proper role of the federal government. Behind closed doors they collude to rob us of our property, savings, and earnings. Whatever legislation the government enacts is certain to reduce your liberty and steal something from you. They pretend to be a bunch of hapless bystanders to world events that are happening beyond their control. In fact, they are complicit in provoking global tension in order to appear heroic when they offer the solutions to those conflicts they themselves have instigated. Those "solutions" always consist in taking more of your money, more of your property, and restricting more of your freedom. Their sole aim is to accumulate power, undermine the separation of powers doctrine by consolidating power in the executive branch, and ensure that their selected benefactors will be handsomely rewarded from the Federal Treasury.

Lie: Income taxes fund the government.

Truth: The purpose of the federal and state income tax system is threefold. First it is a mechanism to confiscate at least half of your earnings in order to ensure that you can never pay off your debts or accumulate enough savings to become self-reliant. Second it enables the government to collect personal financial data and to maintain dossiers on individual citizens in order to facilitate the transfer of their wealth and property to the ruling class. Third it also provides a means to have all citizens willingly yet unknowingly waive their fifth-amendment right to avoid self-incrimination (when you *voluntarily* file your income tax returns you are implicitly waiving your fifth-amendment rights). And finally one must ask, "If the government can and does print all the money it needs, why would it need taxes from you?"

Lie: There is a war on terror.

Truth: The war on terror is in reality a war against the American people. Al–Qaeda is continually portrayed as our enemy, yet in 2012, we provided that organization financing, aid, weapons, and even US military assets in Libya. In 2013, we provided them aid in Syria. The original underwear bomber had no passport yet was able to board his plane. It was later proven that he was actually a CIA informant and several eyewitnesses observed him being assisted onto the plane by what has been suggested was a CIA asset.[17] It is noteworthy to observe that every major terrorist

---

[17]   Miller, John, "Would-Be Underwear Bomber A Double Agent" CBS News, May 8, 2012.

act perpetrated against civilians over the past decade, has ultimately been foiled by other civilians—not our militarized law enforcement. The underwear and shoe-bomber were both stopped by other passengers. The Boston Marathon bomber was discovered and caught by a private citizen. In spite of this we are continually indoctrinated with the notion that our ever-expanding police state is necessary to protect us from terrorists. The so-called war on terror is simply the current straw man used to replace the former Cold War justification for wasting trillions of taxpayer dollars on manufactured conflicts in the process of enriching those who run the military-industrial complex. In 2011, the total number of American citizens killed worldwide as the result of terrorism was seventeen. In comparison, according to data published by the US Department of State, an American citizen is more than twenty-two thousand times more likely to be killed accidently by a trained medical doctor while he or she is undergoing treatment in a US hospital or 17,600 times more likely to die of heart disease than to be killed deliberately in a terrorist attack.[18]

Lie: America is a democracy.

Truth: The United States was founded as a constitutional republic under the rule of law and not as a democracy under the rule of a majority of potentially corrupt, self-serving men and women. The fact that democratic processes are used, such as the selection of representatives through a majority vote, does not obviate the fact that in a republic every individual as well as the government itself is obligated to abide by the law of the land—the US Constitution. Today our federal, state, and local governments routinely violate the constitution. The population has been surreptitiously deceived through propaganda and incrementalism into believing that America is a democracy. The former Soviet Union, former East Germany, and dozens of other socialist countries around the world have also been democracies (rule by a majority). Democracy is a euphemism for fascism and was characterized by Benjamin Franklin in his famous quote as "three wolves and a lamb voting on what to have for lunch; liberty is a well-armed lamb contesting the vote." American democracy has the appearance of representative government but has actually devolved over the past hundred years into corporate socialist fascism. The Central Bank (Federal Reserve) and their corporate interests control the president and Congress and thereby the workings of government. We the people have been reduced to little more than labor resources for the ruling class to exploit and manipulate with our consent—work dogs fighting over scraps.

Lie: Abraham Lincoln freed the slaves.

Truth: Abraham Lincoln is considered by many historians to have been the nation's most tyrannical president as compared to all of his predecessors. Most Americans have been taught to believe that Lincoln waged the Civil War against the South

---

18   US Department of State, Terrorism, Deaths, Injuries, Kidnappings, of Private US Citizens, July 31, 2011. http://www.state.gov/j/ct/rls/crt/2011/195556.htm

solely in order to end slavery. However, much of the historical documentation, including Lincoln's own letters reveals that it was an effort to stop the Southern states from secession mainly for economic reasons. In fact, Lincoln misused the law and violated the US Constitution in order to justify waging a bloody war on his own countrymen. The Civil War led to the slaughter of more than 750,000 Americans, a third of which were civilian noncombatants, and more than a hundred thousand of those were women and children. More soldiers died during the American Civil War than in World War I, World War II, the Korean War, and Viet Nam combined. More children were killed during the Civil War than the total number of American combat soldiers lost in Viet Nam. Lincoln's emancipation proclamation not only did *not* end slavery, but in fact, in an act of political bribery, it protected slavery in the border-states, allowing it to continue in the five slave states that had elected not to join the Confederacy. Lincoln actually suggested that freed slaves should either be deported back to Africa or to Central and South America in a colonization program for which he called for a constitutional amendment.

Lincoln justified the Civil War by twisting the law under the claim that the secession of the Confederate states constituted a breach of contract (the US Constitution). Under common law, a party can only rescind a contract by mutual consent of all parties to it, and the Union states did not consent to the Southern states' secession. The US Constitution, however, is not nor has it ever been a legal contract but is instead a treaty among the sovereign US states, and there is no constitutional prohibition on secession. The Constitution can be rescinded by any party to it without the consent of any other party as per international law on treaties. Nevertheless, that did not stop Lincoln from perverting the law in order to justify an invasion of the Confederate states. The North objected to the Southern secession primarily for economic reasons while they disguised the purpose of the war as a benevolent and principled effort to end slavery, revisionist history notwithstanding.

Government lies are so pervasive and far-reaching in number that an entire book would be inadequate to cover all of them. Nevertheless, an outstanding summary of government's most egregious lies has been published by the honorable Judge Andrew P. Napolitano in his acclaimed nonfiction work *Lies the Government Told You*, published on March 2, 2010. I very highly recommend this book.

There is but one straight course, and that is to seek truth and pursue it steadily.

—George Washington

The Arrogance of the Political Class

Government's consistent pattern of lies stems from another cognitive bias from which practically all career politicians suffer. It is called attribution bias. This is a bias from which politicians assume only good and noble attributes for themselves while they assign bad and ignoble attributes to others. This plays directly to their egos, and an all-too-common behavior that results is a persistent desire to *be right* as opposed to finding absolute truth in any issue. It is the reason that politicians always try incessantly to prove their point, even long after irrefutable facts have proven them wrong. There is nothing more dangerous to a person, a family, a corporation, or an entire country than leaders who are certain about and confident in their ability to convince others of absolute falsehoods. This is even more important when it comes to politics and governance, for we all know that politicians lie not only to us but to one another, which makes their actions particularly damaging to the country they govern.[19]

Why Americans Can't Get Ahead

Most middle-class Americans are coming to realize that they just can't get ahead no matter how hard they work, no matter how much they invest in savings, education, training, or the development of new skills, or no matter how diligently they serve their employers. Most know that something is systemically wrong, but they just can't put their finger on what it is.

The fundamental reason is because property rights in the United States have been eradicated through three basic mechanisms—property taxes, income taxes, and our monetary system's inherently inflationary structure. Every election cycle politicians incessantly debate the topic of job creation. However, **the most important economic issue facing Americans is not jobs. It is property rights**. If you doubt this assertion, consider that the former Soviet Union had 100 percent employment—with no economic prosperity for individuals. This is because under Soviet-style socialism, there is no property ownership.

A fully employed worker who cannot own property has been called many names throughout history—serf, indentured servant, and most appropriately slave.

> None are more hopelessly enslaved, than those who falsely believe they are free.
>
> —Johann Wolfgang Von Goethe

---

[19]   Hafner, Ferdinand. Phase IV Policy and Plans for Iraq. *Cognitive Biases and Structural Failures in United States Foreign Policy: Explaining Decision-Making Dissonance.*

Home Ownership

The ambition to own your home and be truly self-reliant is a universal desire, whether Democrat or Republican, conservative or liberal. Decent and respectable people all want basically the same thing—to be able to achieve sustainable economic security and prosperity for themselves and their families through their own hard work and achievement. That requires the right to private property ownership. However, home ownership in the United States under our current model is an illusion.

Property Taxes

Libertarians and fiscal conservatives who are devoted to The Constitution are often accused of being against taxation. "You just don't want to pay your fair share," is the accusation most often proffered. In fact, it is not taxation in general that constitutional conservatives object to. It is the form of taxation wherein lies the inherent fairness or unfairness of the tax. It is also the form of tax that reveals the true intentions and long-term agenda of those with the power to levy tax.

Economists often say, "If you want to discourage an activity, tax it." This statement is based on the fundamental economic principle that taxing any activity distorts the demand of that activity. Increasing the cost of something through taxes reduces its demand. Thus, if you want to discourage smoking, tax cigarettes. If you want to discourage drinking alcohol, tax alcohol. It follows then that if you are interested in establishing and maintaining a tyrannical government with the power to enslave its people, you must first diminish individual freedom and self-reliance while expanding dependency. To do this, you must therefore discourage (or eliminate) property ownership and wealth accumulation. Therefore, you must tax property and income. Property and income taxes work together to subvert self-reliance and individual freedom. Such taxes are anti-free market, antifamily, and to coin a phrase, un-American. They are two of the principal tools used to establish tyranny. It is because of this basic principle that Karl Marx cited these as two of the cornerstones of Socialism. The effort to counter this trend toward Marxism is the reason that the movement to promote the Fair Tax came into being in 2006.[20]

Take the actual case of an elderly ninety-nine-year-old woman still living in her modest Pennsylvania home. Her home was paid off in full more than forty years ago, and she has never had a mortgage on it. She paid cash for it with money she painstakingly saved during the prior forty years of hard work. She has not had a child in the public school system for more than thirty-five years. In spite of this she is subject to an annual property tax that consumes more than a third of her income from social security (money that she supposedly already earned but which had been confiscated by her employer for the fraudulent social security *trust fund*). If she cannot pay this onerous property tax, her home will be taken from her by the local authorities at the

---

[20]   Boortz, Neil. The Fair Tax. William Morrow Paperbacks. May 2, 2006

point of a gun if necessary. Her home would be auctioned off, and she would receive nothing. In spite of her ninety-nine years of age, she would be made homeless, labeled a criminal tax evader, and would be accused of defrauding the government. That does not constitute home ownership but rather extortion perpetrated by the government. The largest segment of the US population that owns their home debt-free is the elderly and retired. Our system of property taxation discriminates against the elderly and is an affront to a culture that should respect its elders.

Taxing your home ensures that you will always live in fear of losing it and will never have absolute control of your property. This condition ensures that even if you have paid it off, you can never truly retire in peace since you will forever be subject to a perpetually increasing tax on your home until the day you die. If you bequeath it to your children, their inheritance will consist of a tax liability and total cost of ownership that continuously increase—forever. Government's proper role under The Constitution is to protect your property rights—your wealth. Instead, government consistently acts to destroy your wealth and confiscate your property.

Income Tax

As stated earlier, most people mistakenly believe that the purpose of federal income tax is so that the US government can raise revenue to fund public services. The Grace Commission under the Reagan administration, however, proved otherwise.[21] Virtually all of the income tax revenue collected by the IRS is used to pay only the interest on the national debt with almost nothing going toward public services. This has been the case since at least the 1970s. The fact that virtually 100 percent of your income tax revenue is paid to the private Federal Reserve Central Bank as interest on the money our government has borrowed demonstrates precisely how the fruits of our labor are transferred to those who control the monetary system. Furthermore, the government doesn't need your money. They can print all they wish, and they have been doing so with reckless abandon for decades. The primary purpose in taxing individual income is to ensure that you cannot save enough money within a reasonable amount of time in order to become economically secure on your own. The system is engineered to ensure that you never quite get ahead enough in order to become sustainably self-reliant (through real property ownership). At the same time you are forced to feed the very beast that is robbing you of your earnings. This is the essence of *chasing the rabbit*.

The Untold Truth

Governments can raise revenue in many ways other than threatening to seize your home or forcing your employer to confiscate half of your earnings on behalf of federal and state tax authorities. For example, sales, or consumption taxes are more compatible with free

---

21   Congressional Budget Office, "Analysis of the Grace Commission's Proposal for Cost Control," Feb, 1984.

market principles and do not impede real economic growth through investment and savings. Sales taxes are fair because individuals choose what they buy, how much they buy, and how frugal or wasteful they intend to be. If you want to discourage an activity, tax it. Taxing consumption therefore encourages frugality and discourages wastefulness. What could be better for our environment than reducing waste and overconsumption? Government employees are not interested in reducing overconsumption to help protect the environment. In fact, it is quite the opposite. Instead, they must satisfy their corporate donors by continuing to *stimulate* the consumption-based economy so that the citizenry will continue to buy crap they don't really need from US companies that have outsourced the manufacturing of those things to their financial partners in China.

Most politicians, both Democrat and Republican, claim to be pro-environment. However, protecting the environment is completely at odds with what they consider to be a healthy, growing economy, which they define as perpetual and infinite growth in consumption. Our world is finite with finite resources and a finite environment able to absorb the waste and pollution generated. Infinite growth in consumption is a physical, mathematical, and scientific impossibility. The best way to strike a healthy balance between economic growth, respect for our environment, and protection of our natural resources is to focus on the kind of growth that comes from savings and investment, not from perpetually increasing consumption of disposable junk through artificially stimulated demand.

The Hidden Tax—What Is Inflation?

It is important to understand that rising prices is not the cause but instead the consequence of inflation. Most people intuitively understand how supply and demand affects prices, but what escapes them is how inflation enters into the supply and demand dynamic. The word *inflation* refers to an expansion of the supply of money. The increased amount of money in circulation causes each unit of money to be devalued in terms of its purchasing power, so more dollars are required to buy the same goods, giving the appearance of higher prices. This will be explained in much greater detail in chapter 4, but for now suffice it to say that rising prices are an effect, not a cause of inflation and that inflation itself is an artificially created phenomenon under the direct control of those with the power to print money.

A Debtor Nation

Until the 1930s, most people in America purchased their homes by saving their money over a few years' time and then paying cash or by making term payments to the seller upon privately agreed terms (owner financing). Until the Great Depression, fewer than 30 percent of Americans actually borrowed from a bank in order to purchase a home, and the mortgages at that time were only for terms of up to five years with a balloon payment at the end of the term.[22]

---

[22]   Green, Richard K. The American Mortgage in Historical and International Context, "University of Pennsylvania Penn IUR Publications," Sept. 21, 2005.

The now ubiquitous thirty-year mortgage is a relatively recent phenomenon, first coming into practice after World War II. Mortgages were extended out to thirty years as part of the GI Bill, a government program established to reward returning servicemen with easy lending and to stimulate the new home construction industry. As mortgage lending became more pervasive, the artificially stimulated demand for homes caused their prices to rise, forcing more and more individuals to use the new long-term debt in order to purchase a home. This eventually led to the system of inescapable mortgage borrowing in place of real home ownership that we have today.

Nowadays most responsible Americans find it impossible to live frugally enough in order to diligently save their money over time to be able to pay cash for their home (the way our great-grandparents bought their homes). The rate at which you could accumulate the money required would never keep up with the rate at which its purchasing power is destroyed through inflation. You never quite get there. You can never catch the rabbit. The current system forces most people into having no choice but to use long-term debt financing to purchase a home that they will likely never be able to pay off before they drop dead from exhaustion.

We have seen the negative effects of this system in practice through the formation of the housing bubble. In the following graph, the median sales price of existing homes sold in the United States is compared with the median income for an individual between 1950 and the present day.

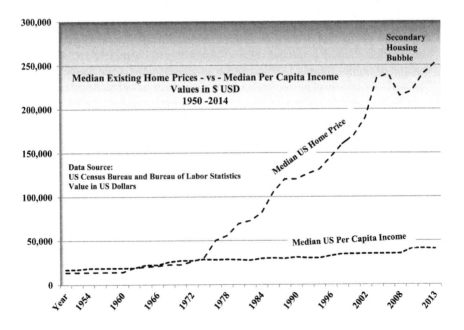

The unmistakable pattern shows that since the mid-1970s the rate at which the income for middle-class Americans increased is substantially outstripped by the disproportionately high rate of inflation targeted at the housing market. This is a consequence of the relentless expansion of credit directed specifically toward home mortgages.[23] This is called a market-specific inflation. It is created deliberately by those with the power to print money.

Government's Policy to Eradicate Real Home Ownership

Note that since before 1952 through 1977, the median home price and the median national per-capita income were roughly equal. For example, in 1970 the median individual income was about $21,000 while the median price of an existing single family home was $21,500.[24] In fact, from the end of World War II until approximately 1963, the average annual per-capita income in America was slightly greater than the price of a new home. By August 2013, home prices had climbed to more than six times the median per-capita income. (The price of an existing home sold in the United States was $260,000, while the median per-capita income was $41,000.)[25]

The divergence of the two curves in the graph above began in 1977. This was the year that President Jimmy Carter signed into law the first version of the Housing and Community Development Act. This later evolved into the Community Reinvestment Act.[26] Along the way, legislative changes were made to the original act in 1989, 1992, 1994, and 1999. When one analyzes the data closely, each time those legislative changes were made, the rate of divergence increases, further widening the gap between income and home prices. This was a systematic process designed to diminish real home affordability for the average middle class worker. This clear long-term trend was a direct consequence of the legislative actions taken by our Congress and presidential administrations (both Republican and Democrat). Its purpose was to slowly and deliberately inflate the prices of homes far beyond the earnings and consequent savings rates of most middle-class Americans. The housing bubble, was simply a market-specific inflation, engineered by the government and Federal Reserve, to deliberately drive every hard working American, into inescapable and perpetual mortgage debt servitude.

---

[23]   Prices versus Wages. *Forbes Magazine.* June 26, 2007.

[24]   US Census Bureau, Data from tables F-5, H-5, and P-4 from historical income tables, 2011.

[25]   US Census Bureau, "Median and Average Sales Prices of New Home Sales in the United States," Sept., 2013. http://www.census.gov/construction/nrs/pdf/uspricemon. pdf, and National Association of Realtors Data http://www.nahb.org/fileUpload_details. aspx?contentID=55764

[26]   Bernanke, Ben. Prepared Speech, *The Community Reinvestment Act, Its Evolution and New Challenges.* March 30, 2007. http://www.federalreserve.gov/newsevents/speech/ Bernanke20070330a.htm

Fiduciary Irresponsibility

The Federal Reserve's official mandate is to promote maximum employment, stable prices, and moderate long-term interest rates. This presupposes that the Fed's actions have a predictable impact on employment (and therefore individual income). The Federal Reserve (the Fed) also controls interest rates and lending standards, so they directly control the credit available to home purchasers. Therefore, the Fed directly controls the conditions that affect both of the parameters represented by the previous graph. Since wages are a direct consequence of the level of employment, one can then conclude that the Federal Reserve in collusion with the federal government have enacted policies designed to deliberately increase the gap between the median per-capita income and the median home price. In other words, government regulators and the Federal Reserve work together to systematically make real home ownership unaffordable for the average American. They deliberately force every citizen into perpetual debt servitude. It is clear that they have been doing so as a matter of policy for the past half century.

The principal beneficiaries of this trend have been the banking and mortgage lending industry as well as those government agencies with the power to levy property taxes. It also benefits a government intent on eliminating real property ownership in order to expand dependency and therefore its own power. This trend has been taking place over such an extended period of time and with such a clear, deliberate, and predictable outcome that it could not possibly have occurred by mistake. Our government, under the direction of the Federal Reserve, has been acting to deliberately legislate the citizenry out of the possibility of real home ownership and turn us all permanently into renters and debt slaves. They achieve this through their power to create money from nothing.

This assertion is supported by a recent phenomenon taking place in the private equity business. Since the collapse of the housing bubble hit its zenith, some of the world's largest private equity funds have been buying up swaths of foreclosed homes. These companies have become the country's newest slumlords, setting up divisions to own literally tens of thousands of single-family homes as rental properties. Some of the institutional investors in these funds are actually investing capital they received as part of the Troubled Asset Relief Program (TARP) bailouts. By using their enormous financial resources (most of it courtesy of the American taxpayer) to acquire huge swaths of foreclosed homes, they are able to take those homes out of the existing supply, thereby perverting the supply side of the economic equation. This again acts to artificially inflate housing prices above what their actual market value should be, ensuring that the affordability gap is maximized and sustained. Indeed, looking again at the previous graph shows a secondary housing bubble forming since 2011 and trending upward into 2014. As this trend continues, banks and their political conspirators become America's landlords, and the poor and middle class become permanent rent-paying tenants precluded from any possibility of real home ownership.

It is clear that our system is engineered at the government level to force every middle-class American into debt for their entire natural lives, whether they want to take on debt or not. Confiscating half or more of your income through taxes further ensures that you will remain perpetually in debt, will never have any hope to catch up, and will therefore always be a submissive and compliant rent-paying employee, always on the verge of homelessness until you're too old to enjoy your life. Income taxes is one of the basic means by which to control the labor market and to keep American citizens in fear of losing their jobs, their homes, or even their freedom by making innocent mistakes on their tax returns, landing them in prison. A controlled labor market is anti-free market and anti-capitalism.

By our current economic model, trying to save for a future investment on the scale of a home purchase or to start a small business without using debt is impossible. In the past even the hardworking poor had the possibility to save their way to prosperity. That, too, has become impossible because the purchasing power of savings degrades at a rate faster than one can accumulate that savings. Our monetary system works together with our tax policy to keep the poor in poverty and to keep the middle class under the constant threat of sinking into poverty.

We are all chasing a rabbit that has deliberately been made uncatchable.

Phony Economic Growth for Political Gain

When our elected government employees talk about growing the economy, they are really talking about increasing consumption. That is what stimulus is all about. Stimulating the economy (money printing) is centered mainly in expanding consumerism—coercing average people to buy and consume far more than they really need or even want while discouraging them to save for the future. This leads directly to environmental degradation. When people overconsume, they also overpollute.

There are two kinds of economic growth—growth in value (increasing assets, savings, and investment) or growth in consumption (increasing sales and economic turnover by getting people to buy more stuff). Only the former type of growth makes a nation sustainably wealthier. This is also true for any individual. A person's wealth or net worth is not measured in terms of how much one can consume in a given period of time. It is measured by assets, savings, and property ownership. From real wealth comes self-reliance.

Growing assets can be done sustainably and with a respect for the environment (e.g., green building practices, investment in manufacturing capacity, development of intellectual property, etc.). This requires savings and investment over time. Growth in pure consumption, on the other hand, can be realized in the near term by stimulating economic activity, discouraging savings, and coercing people to spend their money as soon as they earn it, before inflation destroys its purchasing power. This is achieved by keeping interest rates artificially low while creating inflation through credit expansion (money printing) and loose lending practices. This type of economic growth isn't really growth at all because it is unsustainable. You cannot have your cake and eat it too. Once value has been consumed, it is gone. To show continued growth by this model, you must consume more and more and more. Or you can make it look like more by raising the price of everything through inflation, giving the appearance of growth.

Because it shows up in GDP (gross domestic product), politicians can point to overconsumption and falsely claim that they are shepherding a healthy, growing economy. However, consumption has natural limits. When unrestrained, it always leads to more pollution, waste, and rapid exhaustion of natural resources. Politicians favor this kind of growth because it can be realized in the short time frame of a political term. This kind of growth is disguised as a healthy and expanding economy for which politicians can take credit but which in reality is an unsustainable short-term indulgence that contributes to the long-term destruction of our environment.

Infinite Money

Our current system allows the government to repeatedly raise the debt ceiling in order to create what amounts to an infinite supply of money. This in turn enables those who centrally plan our economy to create a theoretically infinite demand for consumable goods and services (also known as stimulus). This leads to unrestrained overconsumption. True fiscal conservatives, constitutionalists, or Libertarians if you prefer, who are calling for an end to the Federal Reserve system and a restoration of a sound monetary system, are the true environmental conservationists. They seek to restrain this kind of overconsumption disguised as economic growth for political purposes. They are among the few voices who are calling for real fiscal restraint and discipline and who are calling for government and all of society to live within their means. Living within our means is the best way to immediately reduce our environmental impact. A system of sound money is also the only means by which to create a true value-based economy under which price and value will mean the same thing—where the natural forces of supply and demand and not artificial inflation will determine the price of things. Most importantly sound money is the only mechanism by which savings can retain its purchasing power over time so that even the poor have the possibility to escape poverty by accumulating a savings—a savings that will have real value in the future.

The rabbit that Americans have been chasing since the founding of this country is the promise of individual liberty and sustainable self-reliance. In the 124 years that followed this country's founding, earning one's economic freedom was actually achievable. For today's middle class and poor, it is not.

Property Rights—The Fundamental Precondition for Individual Liberty

Unless one can truly own his or her home, the land on which it sits, and the fruits of his or her own labor, that individual cannot become self-reliant and free. Our current socioeconomic model has been designed to enslave the best among us for the benefit of the worst. The thieves who have taken control of this nation's government and monetary system have skewed the rules in their favor. We are no longer functioning on a level playing field, as is required for a true free-market, capitalist system. Not a single American citizen, whether poor, middle class, or even upper-middle class, truly owns his or her home or has full control over the value of his or her labor.

Ownership without control consists of bearing all of the costs and risks of ownership while the bureaucrats who control the disposition of your property reap the benefits. In return they offer nothing but grief. Americans have been subject to exactly this model of illusory property ownership for the past sixty years or more. Americans today must spend more than two thirds of their adult lives paying off mortgages, while during that entire period and forever thereafter, they are subject to an onerous property tax, nonpayment for which results in the seizure of their homes. Does that truly constitute ownership?

If you answered yes, I impress upon you to remember the plight of the greyhound. Question what you have been taught and reflect critically on what you truly believe. Remember that wanting to be right is not the same as finding truth. Feeling good about the falsehoods you believe in ultimately hurts you and your family in the long run. Therefore, seek truth, even if the truth hurts.

> No persons are more frequently wrong, than those who will not admit they are wrong.
>
> —François de La Rochefoucauld

We must all stop blindly following those we perceive to be in authority. We must all gain the courage and integrity to question our own closely held beliefs, to let go of our normalcy bias and our confirmation bias, and to seek truth as opposed to validation. We must question those in authority on their true intentions. Ask them, "Why have you lied to me?" If you're a Democrat, why is your political party in Washington and in your state acting to eradicate your property rights and thereby threatening to make your children homeless? If you are a Republican, you need to ask exactly the same question of the representatives belonging to your political party.

Humans were originally hunters and gatherers. We became farmers and inventors independently cultivating our lives by the sweat of our own brows. Today we are allowing ourselves to be born, bred, and educated to work as obedient employees, principally for the benefit of an unknown ruling class that hides in plain sight. We are all just chasing a rabbit that is actually uncatchable. This is not by accident or error. It is by design. It is certainly not what the founding fathers of this country intended for their countrymen to whom they bequeathed this great nation. It is certainly not the country that we should bequeath to our beloved children.

CHAPTER 2

The Rubicon

Government big enough to supply everything you need is big enough to take everything you have.

Has the United States reached or possibly even surpassed the point of no return?

America today resembles nothing that was intended for it by our founders. We have become a dependency society where entitlements are the new normal. We have become a police state where we must live in fear that any words stated in jest in an e-mail are monitored by a federal agency that labels it a threat and puts us on a watch list. We are now subject to the possibility of indefinite detention without charge, trial, or conviction of any crime. We have become an entertainment culture, where our celebrity worship turns talk-show hosts and golfers into multibillionaires, while our politicians claim that a neurosurgeon or small business owner earning a miniscule fraction of that is *rich* and has not been paying his or her *fair share*. We have transformed from a republic of rugged individualists aspiring to self-reliance and functioning under the rule of law into a bunch of whiney little girls complaining to our government about what they are going to do to take care of us. We have lost the basic understanding that liberty must be accompanied by self-restraint, personal responsibility, discipline, respect for individual property rights, and delayed gratification.

As a child of the 1960s and 1970s, I grew up on the idea that we live in a free country. But what is freedom? Some people have been led to believe that it is a state of being free of responsibility, free of care, free of stress, and free of pain or being able to get free stuff. But these are conditions of dependency, not American freedom. American freedom was founded on the idea of becoming self-reliant. It is the antithesis of dependence. It is independence.

Freedom is not defined by safety. Freedom is defined by the ability of the citizens to live without government interference. Government cannot create a world without risks, nor would we really wish to live in such a fictional place. Only a totalitarian society would even claim absolute safety as a worthy ideal, because it would require total state control over its citizens' lives.

—Congressman Dr. Ron Paul

The archenemy of a tyrannical government is a healthy, wealthy, and self-reliant citizenry for such people have no need of a big and powerful government. In fact, such people find government to be an impediment. Everything that our government does is based on expanding its power for its own sake. Thus, their aim is to expand and maximize our dependency. Therefore, they act to make the achievement of self-reliance unattainable, ensure that our wealth cannot be passed on to our children, and work to make our dependency irreversible. By keeping the poor and middle class impoverished, the corporatocracy will have an endless supply of employees who are desperate, underpaid, overambitious, over-consuming, homeless, dependent debt slaves for generation after generation. Thus, we have witnessed the incremental elimination of our property rights, and the systematic dismantling of The US Constitution. Our current government is deliberately and irreversibly extinguishing the concept of American freedom, and *we the people* are allowing them to do it.

Our founding fathers pledged their fortunes, their lives, and their sacred honor to achieve our freedom and independence not just for themselves but for every American living today. Now more than two centuries later, after so many gave their lives and the lives of their sons to win that independence, what are we doing to honor their legacy?

We are living beyond our means and have become a nation of entitled, overfed, over-consuming hoarders of stuff. This is not consistent with values centered on freedom and self-reliance. Self-reliance demands self-discipline.

In his epic work on psychoanalysis *The Road Less Traveled*, Dr. M. Scott Peck discusses self-discipline at great length.[27] One of the cornerstones of self-discipline is delayed gratification. Becoming a self-reliant individual depends upon living within one's means. Doing so requires discipline and delaying gratification so that one can save for the future (however our inherently inflationary monetary system is designed to discourage saving).

Most Americans today are living on a basis diametrically opposed to this principle. We buy now and pay later. Or we don't pay at all. We simply take on an unserviceable debt burden and then pass it onto someone else's children or to faceless taxpayers who

---

[27] Peck, Dr. M. Scott. 1988, Sept. 15. *The Road Less Traveled*, Touchstone Publishing.

are forced into funding bailouts for bad loans made by corrupt banks. "Let somebody else worry about it. I want what I want ... right now." This model of living beyond one's means is being practiced today by most individuals, most corporations, most institutions, and every component of our federal, state, and local governments.

What are the consequences of this?

The standard of living for the entire middle class is declining rapidly. Over the next three to five years we will see an even more precipitous decline as hyperinflation kicks in. This is not hyperbole or speculation. As a consequence of years of artificial stimulus and quantitative easing conducted by our Federal Reserve central bank, it is mathematically inevitable. The obscenely rich bankers who control the nation's money supply, will continue to get even richer. They will also expand their control of most real assets, including the best land, preferred shares of the largest corporations, natural resources, and most of the physical gold and silver. Through their monetary manipulation, they indirectly control the rate of unemployment and therefore the labor market and the value of our time. Furthermore, they control the media, and therefore they carefully control and manipulate the information we receive. Upon that information we base all of our decisions in terms of what we purchase, our career choices, and who we vote for.

The Bubble Economy

The housing bubble clearly demonstrated what happens when value and price become mutually exclusive. Our economic model is constructed in such a way as to create many kinds of bubbles. The '90s saw the dot-com bubble, and the early 2000s saw the telecom industry bubble. We've had repeated stock-market bubbles for many decades, and today we are facing a bond bubble, a currency bubble, a debt bubble, and a derivatives bubble. But it was the recent housing bubble more than anything before, which clearly revealed the blatant and deliberate fleecing of the middle class's property and wealth through the bubble economy.

In 1995, the Clinton administration together with HUD (Department of Housing and Urban Development), revised the National Affordable Housing Act in order to make credit more easily available to formerly credit-unworthy borrowers.[28] The operative word there is unworthy. If unqualified borrowers couldn't afford to service a debt before that act was passed, what made any of our government employees believe those same people could service a debt after it was passed?

The ultimate consequence was to artificially spike demand in the housing market. This caused the rise in housing prices to accelerate which continued unabated until

---

[28] Financial Services Modernization Act, Community Reinvestment Act Amendments in the Gramm-Leach Act, United States Senate Committee on Banking, Housing, and Urban Affairs, 1999.

the bubble burst in late 2007. The Federal Reserve kept interest rates artificially low for most of that time. With the flood of loose credit granted on diminished lending standards, the effect was to expand the money supply (in the form of debt) available exclusively to home buyers. The definition of inflation is an expansion of the supply of money and credit. Skyrocketing housing prices and the resultant housing bubble were due to a market-specific inflation deliberately engineered by government and the Federal Reserve's monetary policy. It had very little to do with the natural forces of supply and demand as many people mistakenly believe.

These events clearly came as a surprise to the general public. But they could not possibly have been surprising to the central planners at the Federal Reserve who engineered these events. The principle of inflation through monetary expansion is an elementary aspect of economics. The events of 2007–2008 could not possibly have been a shock to the doctorate-level economists at the Federal Reserve, unless they had been absent from their university courses in economics. Therefore, there are only two possibilities. They are either totally incompetent about basic economics, or they engineered this housing inflation and resultant catastrophe intentionally. These men are among the most highly educated and intellectually gifted people this country has produced. It is unlikely that it was a consequence of incompetence. To conclude that it was engineered reveals a criminal act of biblical proportions, and in that case they should be ushered into federal prison posthaste. US prisons house tens of thousands of highly educated, extremely gifted, and intelligent con men who have defrauded victims out of billions of dollars. Education and intelligence are not necessarily synonymous with integrity and good intentions. Given the facts, the most likely conclusion is that the housing bubble did not happen by accident. It was planned, engineered, and executed for a specific purpose. Its ultimate effect has been to further eliminate individual property rights in the United States and transfer those rights to the banks and to the government.

What few people then or today would acknowledge was the increase in property taxes that took place right along with and in proportion to the artificial inflation in home prices. The average annual property tax rate in Western New Jersey for my own 1600-square-foot, single-family home was about $1,700 in 1994. Today the annual property tax on that same home is just over $11,000. That's more than a sixfold increase over 20 years (or an average of 10% annually).

It's painfully ironic that the Housing Affordability Act, which was touted as making home ownership affordable for low-income people, has instead rendered housing unaffordable for most, including upper-income people. The ideal of real home ownership is becoming unachievable for the entire middle class. This assertion is supported by the fact that the rate of home renting is rising substantially faster today than at any other time in US history.

All of these issues beg this question: How and why has this occurred? Most people believe it is by some error, mistake, or unforeseen consequence that was beyond the control of any government official. Those officials do nothing to dispel that notion.

Others believe that what we are witnessing is part of some naturally recurring business cycle. Still others believe that all it will take to correct is a few manipulations by our Nobel Prize-winning community organizer and his group of czars and then everything will somehow miraculously turn around for the better. Nothing could be farther from the truth.

Alan Shrugged

On October 23, 2008, CSPAN broadcast a congressional hearing in which Dr. Alan Greenspan testified before Congress in relation to the financial crisis. In his testimony he defended the concept of using derivatives as a means to spread the risk of subprime lending practices and then went on to state, "I still don't understand fully why it happened [the financial collapse in 2008], and obviously to the extent where it happened and why ... I will change my views." However, it doesn't require a Ph.D. in economics to understand that loaning hundreds of billions of dollars to people who have no means with which to repay it and then hiding the financial risks in the form of derivative investment products, is going to end badly. Furthermore, the individuals running The Federal Reserve system and their cohorts in government are not just hapless innocent bystanders. If the political class and leaders of the Federal Reserve are truly so incompetent that our economic ills are a consequence of their innocent mistakes, then every now and then by the law of averages, they would make a mistake from which the citizenry would benefit. But that never happens.

An error? The business cycle? Have our economic ills occurred on their own by happenstance? Not a chance. And nothing can turn around an $18 trillion national debt on top of another $145 trillion in unfunded liabilities yet to be felt. Furthermore, the truth is far more sinister.

More than thirty years ago a journalist named Charley Reese of the *Orlando Sentinel* newspaper wrote the following rather thought-provoking article titled "Looking for Someone to Blame? Congress is a Good Place to Start"

Used with permission of the **Orlando Sentinel, copyright 1984**

If both the Democrats and the Republicans are against deficits, why do we have deficits?

If all the politicians are against inflation and high taxes, Why do we have inflation and high taxes?

You and I don't propose a federal budget. The president does.

You and I don't have the Constitutional authority to vote on appropriations. The House of Representatives does.

You and I don't write the tax code, Congress does.

You and I don't set fiscal policy, Congress does.

You and I don't control monetary policy, the Federal Reserve Bank does.

One hundred senators, 435 congressmen, one president, and nine Supreme Court justices equates to 545 human beings out of the more than 300 million, who are directly, legally, morally, and individually responsible for the domestic problems that plague this country.

Excluded are the members of the Federal Reserve Board because that problem was created by the Congress. < In 1913, Congress delegated its Constitutional duty to provide a sound currency to a private, central bank, which now has a monopoly on the creation of an "elastic" or un-sound fiat currency.>

Excluded are all the special interests and lobbyists for a sound reason. They have no legal authority. They have no ability to coerce a senator, a congressman, or a president to do one cotton-picking thing. It doesn't matter if they offer a politician $1 million dollars in cash. The politician has the power to accept or reject it. No matter what the lobbyist promises, it is the legislator's responsibility to determine how he votes.

Those 545 human beings spend much of their energy convincing you that what they did is not their fault. Both parties cooperate in this common fraud.

The Constitution, which is the supreme law of the land, gives sole responsibility to the House of Representatives for originating and approving appropriations and taxes. The Speaker of the House is leader of the majority party. That individual and fellow House members and not the president, can approve any budget they want. If the president vetoes it, they can pass it over his veto if they agree to.

It seems inconceivable that a nation of 300+ million cannot replace 545 people who stand convicted -- by present facts -- of incompetence and irresponsibility. I can't think of a single domestic problem that is not traceable directly to those 545 people. When you fully grasp the plain truth that 545 people exercise the power of the federal government, then it must follow that what exists is what they want to exist.

If the tax code is unfair, it's because they want it to be unfair.

If the budget is in the red, it's because they want it to be in the red.

If they do not receive social security but are on an elite retirement plan not available to the people, it's because they want it that way.

There are no insoluble government problems.

Do not let these 545 people shift blame to bureaucrats, whom they hire and whose jobs they can abolish; to lobbyists, whose gifts and advice they can reject; to regulators, to whom they give the power to regulate and from whom they can take this power. Above all, do not let them con you into the belief that there exists disembodied mystical forces like "the economy," "inflation," or "politics" that prevent them from doing what they take an oath to do.

Those 545 people and they alone, are responsible.

This piece is as true today, as it was in 1984. It demonstrates that when it comes to the dysfunction of our federal government and of our overall economy, nothing is going to change anytime soon. Why should it? Nothing has changed in the thirty years and five different presidential administrations (two Democrat and three Republican) since this article was first published.

Most people in the United States know that something is amiss, so they speculate on a vast number of possible reasons. From the abject poor on welfare to upper-middle-class professionals, the vast majority of people have the sense that something is deeply wrong in this country. They can't quite put their finger on exactly what the root cause is, and so they believe there is nothing they can do about it. This sense of hopelessness leads to apathy, further enabling the ruling class and their enforcers in the political class to impose a top-down approach to governance. As a result, we continue with the status quo. In spite of all the political hyperbole on hope and change, most of us have no choice but to deal with the fact that nothing substantive ever changes, and we can't get ahead no matter how hard we work or how diligently we try to save. All the hope in the world will change nothing.

So why are *we the people* not asserting our unalienable rights? Why are we not standing up to act on our own behalf? Why are we not advocating for our children's future?

Ruling a People by Fear and Coercion
Is the Essence of Tyranny

The middle class is ruled by fear—fear of losing their jobs, their credit rating, their health, and their homes. Americans feel powerless because we are all caught in a vise that is slowly and incrementally squeezing the life out of each and every one of us. One jaw of the vise is the federal government, which extracts the wealth out of hardworking citizens through income taxes, payroll (social security) taxes, Medicare taxes, and Medicaid taxes. They squeeze us further through their corrupt partnership with the Federal Reserve system by debasing our fiat money in order to devalue any savings we might manage to scrape together.

The other jaw of the vise is the state and local government that holds de facto title on every home in America through our system of property tax extortion. More and more as time goes on, the citizenry is realizing that their homes aren't really their own but are instead balls and chains with perpetually increasing tax liabilities that will be levied for all eternity.

There is a way out. Implementing the solution will require that you accept a devotion to truth as your principal value, and that you respect property rights as the cornerstone of a free and just society—not just your own property rights but that of your neighbors and countrymen. You must reject the unjustified use of force against others as your moral imperative. These are some of the basic elements of a free-market system, one that is no longer practiced in the United States. Most importantly we all must let go of our personal biases and see things as they are, not as we wish them to be.

Monopoly Money

In the preceding paragraphs I mentioned fiat money. Nowadays we sometimes hear the term fiat currency or fiat money without any explanation as to what that actually means. In fact, few people understand what money itself truly is. I have yet to meet a single individual whose public school, college, or even graduate school curriculum taught the origins, definition, or true purpose of money.

Money is often referred to by economists and in textbooks as a medium of exchange. However, this is only one of its three main functions. It is better defined as a tool of communication. Its purpose is to represent a standard of value that all those within a society who use it have agreed upon. When someone purchases a gallon of milk, both the seller and the buyer agree as to the amount of money that represents what a gallon of milk is worth to both of them. In fact, to the buyer, the milk is worth more than the money being traded, or he wouldn't make the trade. And likewise for the seller, the money is worth more to him than the milk he is offering, or he as well wouldn't make the trade. Therefore, in the free market the transaction is a win-win. If the milk-seller wishes to purchase a new tractor, he isn't required to carry thousands of gallons of milk to the tractor-seller to trade as he would under a pure barter system. Money provides important properties that barter cannot, such as divisibility and transferability.

Another important and often overlooked characteristic of money could be referred to as shelf life. It provides a means by which to store value over time. Milk is a perishable commodity. If the tractor seller were to accept one thousand gallons of milk in exchange for a tractor, much of that milk would likely spoil before he would have a chance to use it or trade it for other things that he might need such as steel, rubber tires, or manufacturing machinery. It follows then that the shelf life or the ability to reliably store value over time is one of the most important properties of money. It must be able to not only honestly communicate but also preserve value. In this regard, money has been said to be the keystone of civilization.

Therefore, the three main functions of money are to act as a medium of exchange, a unit of account, and a store of value. Some socioeconomic models, however, overemphasize money's use primarily as a medium of exchange while they trivialize or even ignore its purpose as a store of value. Therefore, there are different kinds of money. Which kind is used by a given society is a reflection of that society's moral values. If the purchasing power that a unit of money represents can change unpredictably over time, then it can neither honestly communicate the value of any given transaction nor reliably store value over time. Like the milk used for barter, unstable money can also *spoil*, in terms of its purchasing power. For money to function with integrity, it must fulfill all three functions. It must have *shelf-life*. This is called honest money.

There are only two different kinds of money. The first is money with inherent value, and the second is money that has an arbitrarily assigned value. The former has value that is inherent because it is based on a defined amount of a physical commodity that itself is valuable and for which there is an actual demand (like gold or silver). The latter type of money has a value that is determined mainly by those granted with the power to create it and then assign its value. Those who have this power can further manipulate its value (purchasing power) by controlling the quantity of money that exists in circulation (inflation or deflation) and the cost imposed to borrow it (interest rates).

Economists refer to money with inherent value as *sound money* or *honest money*. Its purchasing power is a consequence solely of the natural forces of supply and demand. On the other hand, money that has been created by a government-authorized body that then assigned an arbitrary value is referred to as *fiat* money. Its purchasing power is a consequence primarily of the volume of currency in circulation—the money supply—which can vary widely from one period to another. From an economic perspective a country whose monetary system is based on sound money will see the prices of goods and services remain stable over very long periods of time. On the other hand, a country whose monetary system is based on fiat money will see the prices of goods and services fluctuate unpredictably in accordance with the volume of currency in existence, which is largely determined by the central bank that issues it. This is often referred to as an *elastic* currency. In effect, under a fiat monetary model, the laws of supply and demand can more easily be manipulated and even deliberately distorted, while under a sound monetary system they cannot.

Money Printing

The US Constitution guaranteed that our economy would function under a sound monetary system. The Federal Reserve Act, which was passed in 1913, undermined this constitutional mandate and set the stage to convert the US dollar into the pure fiat currency we now know as Federal Reserve notes.

Today our money is issued not only as fiat but as debt. Our treasury prints Federal Reserve notes (also called bills of credit) on behalf of the Federal Reserve Central Bank and then declares those notes as legal tender. The Federal Reserve then loans that money to the government or to member banks at interest. A note is a debt or an IOU owed to the bank that issued it. The purchasing power of any single US dollar is a function of both the volume of money that exists and the interest rate charged by the central bank that issued it as debt. Therefore, the US dollar is an inherently unstable store of value. Since the Federal Reserve has the authority to regulate the volume of the money supply as well as the interest rate applied to its debt, it then has the ability to directly control and manipulate its purchasing power.

Since all of our money is created as debt, the Federal Reserve then also has the ability to deliberately create market-specific inflations (bubbles). The housing bubble for example was created by providing more credit at lower interest rates while also applying lower lending standards to mortgages than to any other form of lending. This disproportionately expanded the money supply (in the form of credit) available solely for home purchases and therefore artificially inflated home prices.

Prior to the founding of the Federal Reserve in 1913, the US Treasury also issued currency, but it did so in the form of US dollars (not Federal Reserve notes), and it was able to do so at zero interest without creating debt. Those US dollars were legal tender only because the law required that type of paper money to be redeemable for a fixed quantity of gold or silver. This ensured that even that type of paper money was a sound currency. This is what is meant by money that is "backed by gold."

If you remove a paper US bill from your wallet right now and read the text across the top front of the bill, it will not state US dollar but instead, "Federal Reserve Note," and under that, a small bit of text which states, "This Note is Legal Tender For All Debts, Public and Private." This means that every dollar in existence today is a note or a debt instrument. We are obligated by law to accept this IOU as payment for all goods and services (including our own labor). Its purchasing power is completely unrelated to any asset value. Every Federal Reserve note that has been created and issued by the Federal Reserve is owed back to the Fed with interest. This is where part of our national debt comes from.

The Deficit and the National Debt

Many people confuse national debt with budget deficit. These are two completely different things, although they are related. The budget deficit is the amount of money that the government spends in excess of the amount of taxes it is able to collect in any given year. That overspending is compensated for by government borrowing, which is what increases the total national debt over time. Every hour of every day without interruption our government spends $200 million it does not have. (That's almost $4.8 billion per day). This is adding more than $1.75 trillion to our national debt each year, and there is no end in sight. In the six-year period from 2007 through 2013 the national debt doubled. This represented a debt increase greater than that of the previous ninety years combined. The interest on that debt must be repaid by the future labor provided by the working poor and middle class.

Our government's ability to engage in deficit spending without immediate consequences is made possible by the fact that we have a fiat rather than a sound monetary system. It allows the government to surreptitiously conscript the future labor of the citizenry to cover its debts. If we had a sound currency, the government would have no choice but to live within its means.

What Is Fiscal Stimulus?

There is a school of thought known as Keynesian economics. It is named for John Maynard Keynes, who developed the idea that an economy's output is strongly influenced by *aggregate demand* or total spending in the economy. Part of that spending includes government spending. Keynesian economists generally argue that private-sector decisions "sometimes lead to inefficient macroeconomic outcomes which require active policy responses by the public sector." "Active policy responses," is code for printing money. In particular, they espouse monetary policy actions (printing money) by the central bank and fiscal policy actions (deficit spending and tax increases) by the government with the intent to stabilize output over the business cycle.[29] In other words, Keynesian economics advocates a mixed economy instead of a pure free-market system.

The most influential economic book of the 20th and current centuries, in terms of theory and economic policy, has been Keynes's *General Theory of Employment, Interest, and Money*. G.D. H. Cole, the socialist economist called Keynes's General Theory,

> The most important theoretical economic writing since Marx's 'Capital,' … what he has done, triumphantly and conclusively, is

---

[29] Sullivan, Arthur; Steven M. Sheffrin. *Economics: Principles in Action*. Prentice Hall, 2003.

to demonstrate the falsity, even from a capitalist standpoint, of the most cherished practical 'morals,' of the orthodox economists and to construct an alternative theory of the working of capitalist enterprise so clearly nearer to the facts that it will be impossible for it to be ignored or set aside.

Notwithstanding the socialists' political agenda, there are numerous weaknesses in Keynes's economic theories and assertions. First he never actually proved that private sector decisions sometimes lead to *inefficient* macroeconomic outcomes. Friedrich Hayek actually proved quantitatively the exact opposite in several of his subsequent works, including *The Pure Theory of Capital* and *The Fatal Conceit*. Acute market imbalances can occur because of the natural forces of supply and demand. Such events do not necessarily constitute *inefficiency* but are sometimes due to unavoidable facts of nature. Furthermore, the fallacy in the notion of aggregate demand is that it lumps together demand for goods and services that are consumption-based (such as food, gasoline, etc.) along with durable goods that are acquired for the long term (such as automobiles, televisions, furniture, home improvements, investment in education, etc.). The respective demand cycles for such items is clearly disparate and cannot be aggregated in reality. People have no choice but to purchase items like food, gasoline, water, and energy for their day-to-day survival regardless of what they desire to spend on luxuries. An entire population choosing between needs and wants yields vastly different demand cycles.

Therefore, it is misleading to aggregate demand for life's absolute necessities along with luxuries and conveniences since the relative demand for these different categories of products is highly variable. In addition, all individuals must decide between alternatives when they are making any buying or investment decisions. Spending money on a convenience or a luxury instead of on one of life's necessities always carries an opportunity cost for the spender. When the relative price and value of all items in an economy are distorted through this aggregation, it is impossible for anyone to assess the real opportunity cost for choosing one alternative over another.

When the money supply is expanded through government deficit spending in order to artificially stimulate economic activity in specific targeted markets, people may be encouraged to spend more on nonessentials and durable goods that they might not otherwise need for their day-to-day survival. The mathematics associated with aggregate demand obscures this behavior in terms of different classes of goods purchased, and therefore, it perverts real supply and demand across all categories of goods.

This is explained in great detail in economist Henry Hazlitt's *The Failure of the "New Economics," An Analysis of the Keynesian Fallacies*. Hazlitt states, "I have found in Keynes's General Theory an incredible number of fallacies, inconsistencies, vagueness, shifting definitions and usages of words, and plain errors of fact." Hazlitt logically and through calculation refutes most of Keynes's theories. He then correctly assesses Keynes's aversion and bias against individual thrift, prudence, and delayed gratification, in other words living within one's means. It was this mentality that led Keynes to make the fallacious claim that individual saving is ultimately damaging to economic growth. For this reason, Keynes was a proponent of fiat monetary models and the use of inflationary devaluation as a means to discourage individual savings.

From Keynes's General Theory:

> Though an individual whose transactions are small in relation to the market can safely neglect the fact that demand is not a one-sided transaction, it makes nonsense to neglect it when we come to aggregate demand. This is the vital difference between the economic theory of the aggregate and the theory of the behavior of the individual unit, in which we assume that changes in the individual's own demand do not affect his income.

If this passage seems unintelligible, vague, and difficult to make sense of, you are not alone. Most of Keynes's writings follow this pattern of what I call *plausible deniability of meaning*. The most logical interpretation is that Keynes refers to savings merely as the act of not purchasing something that would be consumed, while he refers to investment as purchasing something that is a capital good. This would contradict much of what Keynes had written earlier in which he claimed that savings and investment were "necessarily equal." It also completely contradicts his notion of aggregate demand. This is because consumption destroys value. Investment preserves and even enables the creation of more value. There are numerous other fallacies in Keynes's thinking. For one thing, one of the main reasons for saving is in order to enable a capital good purchase at a later time so the first act is not only necessary for the second; they are part of the same transaction.

Furthermore, what might fall into the category of a capital good for an individual (such as a television, refrigerator, or automobile) is different in terms of its utility than a capital good purchased by a profit-making industrial company. Companies make capital expenditures on plant and equipment solely for the purpose of generating more income. Clearly, the respective demand cycles for a capital good purchased by individuals cannot be aggregated with the demand for capital goods purchased by industrial companies, as they serve a completely different purpose. True purpose, is part of what creates demand.

With respect to opportunity costs Hazlitt writes:

A man's tastes change and he switches from chicken to lamb. We don't scold him at one moment for hurting the poultry raisers and praise him the next for aiding the sheep raisers. We recognize that his purchasing power has gone in one direction rather than another and that if he had not given up the chicken, he would not have had the money to buy the lamb. Unless a man refrains from spending all of his money on consumption goods (i.e. unless he saves), he will not have the funds to buy investment good, or to lend to others to buy investment goods … there cannot be a given amount of real net investment in a community without an equal amount of real net saving.

Page 64 of Keynes's *General Theory* reveals the true basis for his thinking: "The decisions to consume and the decisions to invest between them determine income." So according to Keynes, it is not the fruits of labor and productive work that determine income but consumption and investment? This of course is an absurd perversion of cause and effect.[30] It is reminiscent of the equally absurd Marxist doctrine "from those according to their ability, to those according to their need." The need of an individual to consume is not what determines their income. It is solely a matter of what fruits one's labor can produce that does. Keynes's own illogical theories and writings reveal his Marxist leanings.

Keynes's theories further ignore the unintended consequences when individuals in government are charged with the power to borrow and spend rather than to solely tax and spend. The consequences to politicians for taxing and spending are almost immediate. Raising taxes is the best way to lose your government post. But the consequences of borrowing and spending (deficit spending) is felt by the electorate long after the perpetrators in government have come and gone, so such a system is fraught with corruption, incompetence, and irresponsibility leading to mal-investment.

Nevertheless, Keynesians continue to ascribe to the notion that any spending by government will stimulate the overall economy and lead to growth. To Keynesians, whether or not that spending results in real value creation is irrelevant. These are the *economists* who espouse the notion of paying one group of people to dig a bunch of holes in the ground and a different group of people to fill them in again as a means to create jobs and economic activity. However, you cannot have your cake and eat it too. Activity is not growth. And what is worse, when this spending is not made from savings but from more borrowing—deficit spending—you get negative growth. Deficit spending on projects that provide no sustainable economic value is destructive. The economic equivalent in a private business is called *negative return*

---

30   Hazlitt, Henry. The Failure of "The New Economics" An Analysis of the Keynesian Fallacies. Princeton, NJ: D. Van Nostrand Company. 1959.

on capital employed. When the cost of borrowing the money is greater than the economic value created by its employment, you destroy rather than create enterprise value overall. This is why borrowing money to fund government stimulus is not just counterproductive but destroys economic value in the long-run. The Keynesian model of government stimulus spending results in waste, the misuse of limited resources, irreversible environmental destruction, and incalculable opportunity costs.

Keynesian stimulus spending is therefore environmentally destructive. You can't protect the environment by punishing productivity. But you can certainly help the environment ceasing to reward counterproductivity.

Fiscal stimulus is not only expensive. It causes long-term harm to the overall economy by distorting real incentives and by consuming limited resources for purposes that add little or no value to society. When the government pumps hundreds of billions into the economy, it generally goes to corporate cronies chosen specifically by politicians seeking to gain political capital in return. More often than not, they support inefficient and poorly performing but politically connected businesses at the expense of more efficient ones. Companies like Solyndra, Sun Power, Enron, GM, or Global Crossing come to mind.

Keynesian economists attempt to justify this wasteful spending by claiming that "fiscal stimulus cures recessions." In fact, fiscal stimulus ultimately achieves the opposite. Stimulus exacerbates recessions. It does not cure them, and we have the negative consequences of a hundred years of deficit spending to prove it.

Keynesian economics also falls down analytically. Hayek explained that under centrally planned government stimulus spending, the resultant market-specific inflations (bubbles) distort supply and demand so that an accurate economic calculation cannot be made. In other words, there is no way to make a rational decision in terms of assessing the real value of any alternative. Buying and investment decisions in such an environment are therefore irrational.

Every purchase or investment is a consequence of deciding between several alternatives. The alternatives that are erroneously forsaken because of this miscalculation have an opportunity cost. The overall opportunity cost to society cannot be assessed quantitatively since it results from the hundreds of millions of independent decisions made daily across America by individual people—people being misled to choose erroneously on what to spend or invest in. The incalculable opportunity cost for these erroneous choices creates an enormous invisible drag on society as a whole. Therein lays the economic inefficiency inherent in the Keynesian economic model.

In a true free-market system recessions are natural self-corrections to acute market imbalances. Prior to the Federal Reserve and Keynes's ideas about government spending, the United States functioned under our constitutionally mandated free-enterprise system with a sound currency based on gold and silver coin. When a recession occurred, the policy was hands off, allowing the market to self-correct. (When your body is tired, you allow it to sleep.) There was no borrowing and spending your way out of a recession. In the pre-Federal Reserve days the United States averaged one recession approximately every four years. These recessions were minor, and each only lasted a few months before market forces corrected the supply-demand disparities.

The Federal Reserve System Has Exacerbated the Problems It Was Purported to Be Able to Resolve

The creation of the Federal Reserve in 1913 was originally sold to the voters as a means to smooth out the business cycle and avert those naturally occurring recessions. After the 1920s government stimulus became the drug of choice to treat economic downturns. Every successive president ranging from Roosevelt to Kennedy to Obama has used fiscal stimulus to try to counter every recession. The result is that recessions have been longer, deeper, more protracted, and more damaging than anything encountered in the years before government intervention. The Great Depression was the first of many of these. The 2009 crash is several times worse and has lasted several times longer than the worst recession on record before 1913. According to official criteria that define recessionary conditions, the United States has had recession approximately every 5.7 years since the creation of the Fed.[31] So although they are a little less frequent, they are far more economically damaging and last substantially longer. Contrary to the government's distorted economic reporting, we have been in an almost perpetual state of recession for the past fifty years with a few exceptions during artificially engineered economic bubbles.

Nowadays fiscal stimulus is promoted as the best means by which to cure recessions. However, the original propaganda used to sell the public on the creation of the Federal Reserve system was that recessions could be averted altogether. The past hundred years of continual recessions have proved otherwise. In fact, what were formerly normal, acute imbalances in supply and demand that would simply self-adjust have been transformed into chronic economically destructive ailments to our society. Keynesians claim that fiscal stimulus is so important that it justifies going perpetually deeper into debt because they consider it a cure-all for our economic woes. However, it has been demonstrated by numerous Austrian-school economists that fiscal stimulus makes worse the very problems it aims to solve. Any grade-school child with rudimentary math skills can understand that problems created by debt cannot be solved by going even deeper into debt.

---

[31]   Adorney, Julien, "Keynesians Sleepy? The case against economic stimulus," Sept. 30, 2013. http://www.fee.org/the_freeman/detail/keynesians-sleepy-down-a-red-bull#axzz2hTRWD3Gi

Keynesian Stimulus Depends on a Fiat Currency System

Government stimulus is accomplished through deficit spending and money printing, which in turn is paid for with the future labor of every American citizen. Therefore, fiscal stimulus comes at a heavy price. It's not paid for by the politicians who enact it but by the citizenry it is purported to help. Therefore, it makes recessions more protracted and more costly than if the market were simply allowed to self-correct. Furthermore, the deficit spending used to create that stimulus will push onto future generations a more onerous debt burden, exacerbating that generation's ability to deal with its own recessions. In other words, stimulus ensures that instead of allowing a recession to correct itself so that society can simply move on, it pushes the residual effects onto every following recession, exacerbating each successive one.

FDR's New Deal was the original Keynesian stimulus package. It cost $542 billion (inflation-adjusted) at that time. But the liabilities accumulated between 1935 and 2013 from that program alone amount to well over $27 trillion (and more than $100 trillion in addition for Lyndon Johnson's Great Society entitlements such as Medicare/Medicaid). The stimulus passed by presidents Bush and Obama to cope with the 2009 recession totaled more than $1.1 trillion. Just the aforementioned programs alone would require all American taxpayers more than thirty-one years of full-time labor to pay for them—that is, if everyone paid 100 percent of their income in taxes. The enactment of these few programs alone have conscripted every hour of labor from every hardworking American taxpayer for the next thirty-one years. This is the essence of debt slavery.

The hidden cost of fiscal stimulus is that it distorts economic incentives. All stimulus bills include bloated contracts to build unnecessary infrastructure or to fund unproven startup companies like Solyndra or, as Keynes famously suggested, "to dig and fill holes in the ground." Whether it's digging and refilling useless holes or building weapons with which to adventure into foreign countries to wage war, destroy their infrastructure, and kill their people, the true purpose is to generate economic activity that benefits a few banks, oil companies, and military contractors. It is government bureaucrats who pick and choose which industries and which companies eventually receive these contracts—companies who are the eventual donors to the campaign coffers of said bureaucrats. In other words, government rewards firms that are well-connected politically. They give contracts to companies that spend money on lobbyists instead of making a better or more useful product. In the long run, this mal-investment does permanent damage to the overall economy—not just in the United States, but all over the world.

Employing fiscal stimulus has become an addiction just like a chemical dependency whose grip on your life tightens with each new fix. Its repeated use has created a vicious cycle, yielding an economy that to continue functioning, is now dependent upon repeated applications of stimulus spending on pure consumption fueled by perpetually increasing debt. Eventually the government can only dig so many useless holes to be filled in again before they run out of shovels and laborers willing to dig for nothing. When more resources are spent on digging holes than are spent on building valuable assets for society, eventually the entire system can only self-destruct.

Fiat Is a Tool of Government Control

Fiat money derives its value from government regulation or law. The term comes from the Latin *fiat*, meaning "let it be done" or "it shall be." Its value is declared by its issuer rather than being a consequence of the natural demand for it. Fiat money is also often referred to as an elastic or soft currency. An elastic currency indicates a currency whose value is expected to fluctuate erratically or to depreciate against other currencies.

Fiat money has certain unique characteristics.[32]

Any money that is arbitrarily assigned a value and then declared by a government to be legal tender is fiat.

- Fiat is neither convertible by law to any other thing nor fixed in value in terms of any objective standard.

- Fiat is money without any intrinsic value, and its assigned value is unrelated to the value of any physical quantity of a valuable commodity.

Fiat cannot function as a reliable store of value. Therefore, neither can assets whose values are denominated in fiat. This includes your second most important asset— your home (your most important asset is your life). Since fiat's value can be arbitrarily assigned by the issuer, its value can be reassigned by the issuer at any time. Since fiat money is not convertible by law into any other commodity or thing, the issuer can cancel its legal-tender status any time it so chooses and thus render it completely worthless. In fact, this has been the fate of every single paper currency that has ever existed since the beginning of human civilization.

In contrast, sound money has an exact definition of its value in terms of weights and measures of a physical commodity. It entails the legal requirement that the bank of issue redeem it in fixed weights of gold or silver on demand. Even a coin containing valuable metal may be considered fiat currency if its face value is different from its market value as metal. The cost to produce a single penny is approximately 2.4 cents (and contains only 2.5 percent copper). Such a distortion of value is only possible under a fiat currency model.

Consider the purchase of a home in which you intend to live out your life. If you don't expand the home or change it in any appreciable manner, the physical asset

---

[32]   Keynes, John Maynard, *A Treatise on Money*, (MacMillan & Co., LTD, 1965) p 7.

itself doesn't change over the course of many decades. The value of its utility to you as a place to live also doesn't change over that time. In fact, the material of the home itself degrades, ages, and depreciates, and many components require replacement. So why then should we expect that its price should double or triple in the space of a decade or two? This is exactly what we have observed in America, but this has been the result of inflation caused by our fiat money and not the result of the supply and demand for homes. Since your home is valued in terms of our fiat money system, it, too, becomes an unreliable store of value.

When the housing bubble was becoming more obvious, many people mistakenly believed this inflation to their home's value represented an increase in their personal wealth. This is a fallacy. You must live somewhere, and all other homes are inflating in price right along with yours. If you sell yours at a higher value because of this market-specific inflation, not only will you be taxed on the capital gain, but you'll then have to purchase or rent another home that has also become inflated in value, so you wind up losing in the long run no matter what you do.

It is important to note that when people can have no confidence in the future value of their savings, there is little incentive to save. By coercing people to spend what they have now so they can avoid the unpredictable devaluation of their savings in the future, governments can artificially stimulate consumption and disguise that activity as economic growth. Through stimulus spending fueled by money printing (quantitative easing), the government pumps more money into the system, leading to increasing prices because of inflation. As people realize that saving their fiat money for a future purchase will be counterproductive over the long term, they spend it more quickly before it loses its purchasing power. As a consequence, the GDP (gross domestic product) will continually rise even if production remains stable or declines, giving the illusion of a healthy and growing economy. In fact, such growth is attributable primarily to inflation-induced overconsumption. When this happens, the false signs of prosperity encourage corporations to mal-invest their limited capital and to misallocate their resources. Individuals are encouraged to take on mortgages for homes they can't afford and then max out their credit cards to furnish them. The consequences of fiscal stimulus ultimately lead to corporate and individual bankruptcies. These are fundamentally Keynesian principles.

Keynes went so far as to claim that individuals who save their money actually hurt the overall economy by reducing aggregate demand. He called this "the paradox of thrift." Keynesianism holds that by encouraging people to go out and spend everything they earn, everyone is better off. Not only is this absurd, but this collectivist philosophy is fundamentally at odds with the free-enterprise system. Being thrifty, the traditional value of "a penny saved is a penny earned" is paradoxical only to one who holds the perverse notion that unrestrained and unsustainable consumption constitutes growth. Those who claim that a mixed economy based upon Keynesian principles is healthy and viable ignore the unintended consequences of mixing a little bit of socialism with free-market principles. The two models are fundamentally incompatible and cannot possibly coexist—particularly because each depends on a completely different type of monetary system.

The Keynesian viewpoint completely inverts the logic behind real economic growth. It confuses economic growth with economic activity. Economic activity consists in driving back and forth and burning up the gas in your car whether you need to go somewhere or not simply for the sake of consuming it. Real economic growth consists in filling up your gas tank and prudently consuming it only for a future productive use that will generate more value than the gas you consumed. Robust and sustainable economic growth does not come from consumption. It comes from savings, value creation, disciplined and judicious use of natural resources, and delayed gratification.

None of this is meant to imply that consumption spending is a bad thing. In fact, it is quite necessary. It merely is to say that spending on consumption does not make us wealthier either as individuals or as a society. To claim that consumption or consumerism is *the engine of economic growth* is absurd. It is putting the cart before the horse. Yet this is the exact mantra that has been stated by numerous mainstream *economists*.

"It's the Economy, Stupid"—Imaginary Wealth v. Real Wealth

President William J. Clinton (right) speaks with Federal Reserve board chairman Dr. Alan Greenspan after signing the Financial Services Modernization Act of 1999. The sweeping measure deregulated banks, securities firms, and insurance companies, allowing them to merge and sell one another's products. This launched the era of credit default swaps, derivatives, and the housing bubble, which eventually led to the 2008 financial meltdown.

When a central bank has a monopoly on the creation of fiat money and the power to regulate the amount of that currency in existence, it then has the ability to manipulate the value of everything denominated in that currency. Those things include not only goods and services but also property, assets, and labor. Under a fiat monetary system, the value of your home, your land, your work, your time, and your very life are all determined by those who are given the authority to create our money out of thin air.

Gold Is the Only Real Money

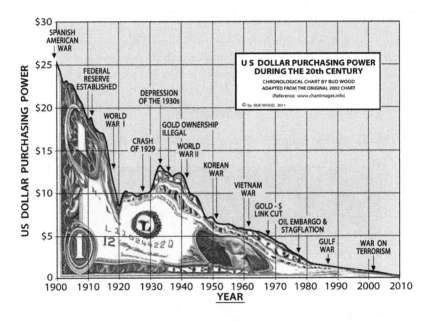

Every paper currency that has ever been put into circulation since the beginning of civilization has eventually become worthless.

In fact, the median age for the existence of every paper currency in history is only thirty-eight years. Not a single paper currency that has existed has ever remained in use in its original issued form for more than seventy-eight years.[33] Since the founding of the Federal Reserve system the US dollar's definition has changed several times. Most notably in 1933, when FDR removed it from the domestic gold standard and again in 1971 when Richard Nixon removed it from the international gold exchange

---

[33] Cate, Vincent. "Frequently Asked Questions on Hyperinflation," Silver Summit, 2012. http://www.financialsense.com/contributors/vincent-cate/frequently-asked-questions-hyperinflation

standard. Gold itself, on the other hand, has retained its intrinsic value and its purchasing power for more than five thousand years.

In 1985, Dr. Ron Paul and other congressmen challenged our country's currency system, which had been and continues to be monopolized by Federal Reserve notes. The congressmen successfully pursued the Gold Bullion Coin Act. Signed into law by President Ronald Reagan, it requires the US government to mint and place gold coins in denominations of $50, $25, $10, and $5 into circulation based upon demand. The coins are made of 91.67 percent pure gold. It was the first time since 1933 (when FDR outlawed gold coins as legal tender) [34] that gold coins were again minted and placed in circulation as legal tender in the United States.

The interesting point is that since then, the dollar has had two conflicting definitions. One is really not a definition as much as it is obfuscation. A Federal Reserve note's value is defined as "whatever a Federal Reserve note will buy." The other is a concrete definition based on a specified weight of gold. It is exactly such concrete definitions that central banks and legal tender acts are intended to erase. The fact is that since these coins carry a face value denominated in dollars, they are not mere bullion but legal tender. Technically since Ron Paul's Gold Bullion Coin Act was passed in 1985, we have had two competing currencies in the United States—Federal Reserve notes and gold bullion. This, however, does not mean that we again have a gold standard. Federal Reserve notes are not redeemable for a defined amount of gold. Instead, we have an unsound currency in Fed notes that are in competition with a sound currency in the form of gold bullion. [35]

The Gold Bullion Coin Act provides that a fifty-dollar gold coin is 32.7 millimeters in diameter, weighs 33.931 grams, and contains one troy ounce of fine gold. Therefore, under this definition it follows that a dollar is equivalent to one fiftieth of an ounce of fine gold. If you were paid fifty dollars per week in US gold coin, your annual income in terms of its face value would be $2,600, while the equivalent value in terms of Federal Reserve notes at current gold prices (about $1,300 per ounce) would be around $68,000. In that case, you would then legally be obligated to pay taxes on an income of $2,600, the face value of your income in gold coin since these, too, are legal tender.

In the 2006 court case *Robert Kahre v. the IRS*, it describes an employer who did exactly that. He paid his workers in gold coins in terms of their face value. As a consequence, their total earnings in terms of the coin's face value fell below the minimum income required to be reported to the IRS for income tax purposes. The IRS brought multiple criminal charges against Mr. Kahre and his workers for tax

---

34   Roosevelt, Franklin D., Executive Order 6102, April 5, 1933.

35   The Gold Bullion Coin Act of 1985, Pub L, 99-185, 99 Statute 1177 Dec. 17, 1985 Codified at 31 USC at 31 U.S.C. § 5112(a)(7) through (a)(10), 31 U.S.C. § 5112(i), 31 U.S.C. § 5116(a)(3), and amending 31 U.S.C. § 5118(d) and 31 U.S.C. § 5132(a)(1).

evasion in spite of the fact that there was no law or statute of any kind prohibiting him from paying his employees in terms of the face value of gold coins.

In May of 2003, federal agents raided several establishments belonging to the Southern Nevada businessman. Armed IRS officials held more than twenty of his employees in handcuffs and at gunpoint in the blistering sun on a 106-degree day, refusing them water as agents collected records and other materials.[36]

Neither Kahre nor any of his employees had committed a single crime or broken any IRS regulation. All he did to offend the Internal Revenue Service was to pay his workers based on the face value of gold coins versus their market value in terms of Federal Reserve notes (the value of the coin-metal in Fed-issued paper dollars). Both are legal tender in the eyes of the law. Even though the coins were in circulation, displayed a face value, were regulated by Congress, and authorized by the constitution, the IRS's confusing and nearly eighty-thousand-page tax code did not determine how to handle these gold coins if used for payroll. The IRS tax code only references dollars. It does not distinguish between coined money and paper money (sound or fiat).

In fact, two prior Supreme Court cases—*Ling Su Fan v. the United States* US302 (1910) and *Thompson v. Butler* US694 (1877)—both held the following:

1. "Public law gives to such coinage a value which does not attach as a mere consequence of intrinsic value. Their quality as a legal tender is an attribute of law aside from their bullion value. They bear, therefore, the impress of sovereign power which fixes value [as their face value] and authorizes their use in exchange."

2. "A coin dollar is worth no more for the purposes of tender in payment of an ordinary debt than a note dollar. The law has not made the note a standard of value any more than coin. It is true that in the market, as an article of merchandise, one is of greater value than the other; but as money, that is to say, as a medium of exchange, the law knows no difference between them."

"The Law knows no difference between them." Kahre didn't choose the precious metal bullion system as a means to transact with his employees without first doing his homework. He consulted monetary experts and lawyers, engaged in extensive research, and even met with congressmen. Kahre's conclusion was simple. While the bullion currency in the precious metal system was greater in value than the Federal Reserve currency (both legal tender), the law does not distinguish between the face values of either currency. So he paid his workers in terms of the face value of the bullion coins. There was no law or statute against it, and in fact, the

---

[36] *Robert Kahre v. the IRS and the DOJ*, (http://www.rapidtrends.com/robert-kahre-vs-the-irs-and-doj).

aforementioned Supreme Court decisions stated explicitly that what he did was legal and constitutional.

The IRS disagreed, expecting Kahre to report his workers' earnings based on the coins' market value if converted into notes issued by the Federal Reserve system. Instead, he didn't report or pay anything at all because the face value of the coins fell below the reporting threshold. The IRS alleged that Kahre and the other defendants paid at least $114 million (based on the Federal Reserve system) to workers. The use of these coins in trade was perfectly legal but represented a direct challenge to the fiat money system.

"Bobby Kahre is the only person in the world I know of with the courage to do that," said Joel Hansen, a Las Vegas attorney who represented one of the nine defendants in the case.

This story is a good example of what happens when a sound money system is able to compete with a fiat money system in the same jurisdiction. The inherent value provided by sound money is always preferable to the arbitrary and unstable purchasing power provided by fiat money. But outside of the courtroom the case draws attention to another significant issue—the ever-decreasing value of the Federal Reserve note. America's other monetary system, gold and silver coins, does not decrease in value. In fact, over the long term it appreciates in value in terms of Federal Reserve notes.

On September 17, 2007, after four months of trial and days of deliberation during the *Kahre v. IRS* case, the Las Vegas federal jury returned with not a single guilty verdict. Three defendants, who were all workers, were acquitted as well as Kahre's mother, who also worked for her son's businesses.

"I'm telling you that I have never seen such a dejected group of people leave a courtroom in my life," defense attorney Joel Hansen said of Department of Justice and Internal Revenue Service officials. "They were shocked."

Unfortunately this is not the end of the story. The heavy hand of tyranny is patient and relentless. The IRS continued to pursue Mr. Kahre by appealing as well as filing numerous follow-up prosecutions until finally they gained a successful conviction. On August 14, 2009, Mr. Kahre was convicted of tax evasion and conspiracy to defraud the IRS along with several other felony charges. According to the official court document, he was convicted of "intentionally and knowingly conspiring to defraud the federal government by deceit, craft, trickery and dishonest means for the purpose of impeding the IRS in its collection of income and employment taxes."[37]

---

[37] US Attorney's Office, District of Nevada Press Release, "Jury convicts Las Vegas business owner Robert Kahre and three others of tax fraud," Aug 14, 2009.

By this standard—one could conclude that our government's continual violation of the US Constitution during the past hundred years is an effort to *intentionally and knowingly conspire to defraud* every hardworking American citizen of their labor and property through inflation—deliberately created through an unconstitutional and fraudulent monetary system—thus perpetrated *by deceit, craft, trickery, and dishonest means* for the purpose of impeding every American citizen from trying to earn an honest living.

The Conscripts—Employers as the Government's Tax Collection Agents

We live under a system that confiscates the fruits of our labor before we even have a chance to touch it. This confiscation is carried out by the very institution on which we depend for our living—our employer. Every business in the United States has been conscripted by the US government to be its tax-collection agent as a condition of being in business. Furthermore, every one of us must agree to have our wage or salary garnished by our employer on behalf of the government as a condition of employment. Every business is required to spend enormous resources in time and manpower just to process withholdings from their employees' wages on behalf of the IRS, Medicare, Medicaid, social security, and state and local tax authorities. None of these government agencies compensates US companies for spending their own resources on acting as their tax enforcement agents. Companies are forced to garnish your wages and administer the collections at their own expense solely for the government's benefit.

Those companies have no choice but to account for their cost of compliance as part of their overhead. They must then pass those costs on to their customers in the price of every product or service they sell. Therefore, with every purchase you make you are funding the government's costs incurred in confiscating your own hard-earned money. It is like being stopped by a mugger in the street and then handing him a loaded gun with which he will proceed to rob you ... with your consent. We are feeding the beast that is bent on destroying us (or enslaving us—which are synonymous).

It could be argued that Robert Kahre's actions to pay his workers in gold bullion was a moral and just effort to try to find a legal circumvention around what should be viewed as an illegal extortion scheme—one that forces employers at their own expense to collect taxes from their employees against their will on behalf of a corrupt government that is intent on enforcing an unconstitutional tax system. The fact that Mr. Kahre found a perfectly legal loophole in the IRS's own tax code clearly did not protect him from their wrath when they discovered that their pervasive extortion system was imperfect. Mr. Kahre, whose private enterprise created jobs for hundreds of American citizens and who did not break a single law, faced up to 296 years in prison and fines of up to fourteen million dollars. In the end he was sentenced to eighteen years in prison. In prosecuting Mr. Kahre for a *noncrime*, the IRS successfully eliminated more than four hundred full-time jobs, thereby preventing those citizens from achieving self-reliance. Mr. Kahre's prosecution and subsequent incarceration will have cost taxpayers more than fifteen million dollars in court and imprisonment costs by the time he is released.

This absurd model is not compatible with free-market capitalism. In spite of that America is continually referred to as "a capitalist system." Those saying this are either misinformed themselves, or they are deliberately trying to misinform the rest of us. US Prisons house thousands of innocent people who are incarcerated for the noncrime of tax evasion, while real criminals like the owners of the Federal Reserve and their puppets in the political class live a free, luxurious, and lavish lifestyle on the backs of their conscripted servants—the American people.

Robert Kahre advocated on behalf of his employees and their efforts to honestly earn a livelihood for themselves and their families. He did so at an enormous personal cost. Our government considers Robert Kahre a criminal. In fact he is a man of courage and integrity who advocated for his employees in total compliance with the US Constitution.

How to Destroy Capitalism through Fiat Money and Taxes

In *The Communist Manifesto*, Karl Marx states that the most effective way to obliterate capitalism and the existence of a wealthy, self-reliant middle class is through a system of progressive taxation coupled with inflation (created through a central bank-controlled fiat monetary system). He was correct, and America is in the process of proving his hypothesis.

The true free-market system has not been practiced in America since 1913, when both the Federal Reserve system and the graduated individual income tax were instituted. Free-market capitalism is fundamentally incompatible with America's current monetary and tax systems. Karl Marx knew this, which is why he described in his *Communist Manifesto* the type of monetary system (fiat) and the graduated income tax, both of which America practices today, as the cornerstones of socialism and Communism.

Free and self-reliant people do not willingly subjugate themselves. They must be tricked into it.

Most Americans have never read *The Communist Manifesto*, so unfortunately very few people in America understand this. Of those who do, most believe that there is nothing that can be done about it. Since the middle class is ruled by fear, most of us just go on with our day-to-day lives, running on the hamster wheel, hoping to avoid being fired from our thankless job and possibly losing our coveted credit rating or getting kicked out of the home that we supposedly own. Those few who have connected the dots and understand these facts are mostly afraid to speak out against it (and rightfully so or they may wind up sharing a prison cell with Mr. Kahre). Most people are first and foremost concerned with keeping roofs over their children's heads and can't afford to lose their jobs over speaking politically incorrect truths. The truly poor and destitute are completely out of the game altogether. They have no hope, have accepted their fate, and feel powerless to try to change anything. Many realize from experience that our continually devaluing currency will prohibit them from saving their way to prosperity even if they are diligent and frugal. Therefore, they believe they have nothing to gain and nothing to lose no matter what they do. Every election cycle they run to the polls and vote for whichever charlatan has promised them a bigger piece of a pie that someone else has baked.

Overworked and Underpaid America—Increased Productivity in the Workplace

Increasing productivity today is a euphemism for squeezing your employees. Every year those Americans who still remain gainfully employed are working harder and longer hours for the same or lower pay and with fewer benefits. Even those being provided the so-called cost-of-living increase to their salary are being swindled. Those paltry few percentages are calculated from the official rate of inflation, which is grossly underreported by the government. Those hurt the most by this scheme are people on a fixed income from social security or a pension, whose annual cost-of-living increase is pegged to the grossly understated official rate of inflation. When one includes the rising costs of food, gas, water, energy, and all of the things we depend on for our survival, the real rate of inflation is more than three times the reported rate. As a consequence, corporate profits have been up double-digit percentage points every year since the so-called financial crisis began in 2007, while employee wages have declined during the same period.

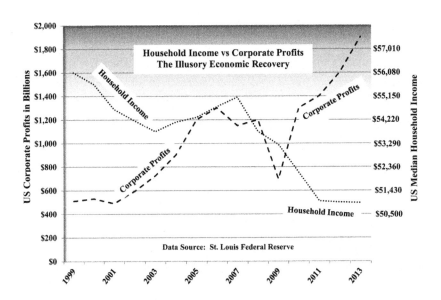

Having increasing productivity coincident with sustained high unemployment in reality means squeezing more work out of fewer employees in return for less pay and fewer benefits. Average worker productivity in terms of GDP has increased by between 2 and 6.6 percent per quarter since the financial crisis started in 2007. During that same time when figures are adjusted for inflation, average per-capita income has declined by as much as 16 percent, depending upon the industry. People are producing more while they are paid less. Since 70 percent of GDP growth comes from consumer spending, our economic stability is dependent upon an unsustainable source of growth. These employees are also consumers. Squeezing them will only exacerbate the situation. It is just a matter of time before we reach an economic tipping point again.

The Tipping Point?

During the 2012 presidential election it became clear that those who seek self-reliance and freedom through hard work and personal responsibility are vastly outnumbered. What happened in November of 2012 on election day was a demonstration that there are legitimately fewer Americans who desire to live in a free constitutional republic than those who want their government to give them free stuff at other people's expense. There are now fewer people who believe in the value of the free-enterprise system than those who actually think that Marxism is a legitimate way to end poverty and suffering (the demonstrable failure of every Communist country in history to have done so notwithstanding).

Furthermore, voting and elections are fraught with fraud. The presidential election is a process whereby candidates who have been preselected by the anonymous ruling class are elevated quickly to celebrity status by their corporate-owned media. Opinion polls are taken in order to determine what those politicians must say in order to ingratiate the voters. They then regurgitate the exact messages that the public have told them they want to hear. Both parties are controlled by the ruling class so it is irrelevant whether a Republican or Democrat gets into office. Either selected candidate will do the bidding of their handlers in the global international banking aristocracy. Elections may change the players, but they don't change the game. It is the game that is fundamentally flawed.

Media Bias—Shaping Public Perception

In the period leading up to the 2012 presidential election, the debates were carefully engineered to represent each candidate in a certain light. The purpose was to portray each candidate in such a way that voters would adopt their opinions of them based upon what the media intended, not on who they really were. Our knowledge and opinions about the candidates are whatever the media downloads to the viewers via sophisticated public relations and advertising techniques. Who the candidates really are in terms of their character is generally unknown to the public until long after we are able to witness the damage they inflict upon our nation with their self-serving and destructive actions.

During the Republican primaries an obvious pattern was demonstrated by the media in their repeated attempts to marginalize Dr. Ron Paul while at the same time inciting heated debate between Governor Mitt Romney and Senator Rick Santorum. It was clear from the beginning that former Governor Romney was the foregone nominee of the Republican National Committee and that the primaries were little more than a reality TV show. Furthermore, it was a virtual repeat of the media's anti-Paul agenda in 2008. This was orchestrated because Dr. Paul was one of the very few members of Congress that had consistently demonstrated an unwavering devotion to the constitution with a strict adherence to his oath of office. In other words, he is a man of character, integrity, and a champion of individual liberty—an enemy of the state.

The questions submitted to the candidates were carefully selected to elicit a predictable response and were clearly intended to shape the voters' opinions rather than to inform. More troubling is that the exact same questions were asked of Dr. Paul during the 2012 campaign as were asked during the prior 2008 campaign, and for the same purpose. One of the best examples of this was on January 10, 2008, when Fox News correspondent Carl Cameron asked Dr. Paul the question, "Congressman Paul, in another question about electability … do you have any, sir?" Cameron's disrespectful tone notwithstanding, Dr. Paul's reply was eloquent, profound, and thought-provoking. He received a rousing ovation for his response while his overall popularity with voters skyrocketed.

Nevertheless, four years later on December 15, 2011, during the Iowa debate, Fox's Megan Kelly asked him virtually the same question—whether he was electable as president. Only this time she preceded the question with a qualifying statement in which she falsely claimed, "Many people within this state (Iowa) doubt you could be elected." From where she drew that conclusion is unknown, as Dr. Paul had originally led the Iowa polling by a substantial margin in the months before that debate took place. Kelly's assertion that "many people within this state doubt you could be elected" was a blatant misrepresentation. Nevertheless, the obvious media bias

against Dr. Paul during both election primaries was palatable, much to the detriment of the American voting public and the cause of liberty. Just three weeks later Dr. Paul lost the Iowa primary by just 3 percent of the votes to Rick Santorum and Mitt Romney, who tied with 24 percent to Ron Paul's 21 percent. Whether or not the negative bias expressed by Megan Kelly against Dr. Paul contributed to his eventual loss is left to the reader to decide. However, it bears stating that the media's tactics in surreptitiously demeaning a candidate in the eyes of the public in order to shape their opinion and influence the vote is blatantly irresponsible and should constitute a criminal act of electoral fraud.

In trying to fully understand this pattern and the purpose behind it, I am reminded of another election that had taken place two decades before when a third-party candidate by the name of H. Ross Perot ran for president. Mr. Perot ran on a fiscally conservative platform in 1992 against Republican George H. W. Bush, and William J. Clinton. As part of Mr. Perot's campaign, he published a book titled *United We Stand*.[38] Mr. Perot quickly rose to enormous popularity, and his book was an immediate *New York Times* Best Seller. The first several chapters of that book centered on the issues of government largess and corruption, fiscal irresponsibility, and our runaway national debt, which then stood at nearly four trillion dollars (less than a quarter of what it is today). In his book he also discussed the dysfunctions of a congress made up of "corrupt, self-serving career politicians." Ironically many of those same self-serving career politicians he mentioned more than twenty years ago are still in Congress to this day.[39]

Perot financed his own campaign, rejecting any single donation of greater than $5.00. He relied on marketing and wide grassroots support.[40] Throughout the early part of the campaign all polls showed that Perot led the three-way race against Republican incumbent President George H. W. Bush and Democratic nominee Governor Bill Clinton of Arkansas.[41] A *Time Magazine* poll found that Perot had 37 percent support of all of the electorate, ahead of both Bush and Clinton, who tied for second at 24 percent. Perot quickly earned the trust and respect of Republican and Democrat voters alike.[42]

In spite of his comfortable lead, on July 16, 1992, Perot unexpectedly dropped out of the race amid massive controversy. Initially Perot announced on Larry King Live that he would not seek the presidency by explaining that he did not want the House of Representatives to decide the election if the result caused the electoral college to be split. Given his substantial lead in the polls, this explanation made absolutely no sense. Weeks afterward, however, there were numerous other stories of his having received credible threats against members of his family as well as himself, and some accredited his withdraw from the race to those events. Whatever the real reasons, it remains clear that dirty political tactics were employed behind the scenes to pressure

---

[38]   Perot, H. Ross. *United We Stand*. Hyperion Publishing. Aug. 24, 1992.

[39]   Dunham, Richard S. and Douglas Harbrecht. "Is Perot after the Presidency, or the President?" *Bloomberg Business Week*. April 6, 1992.

[40]   Griffith, Pat."Perot hearing the call of unhappy electorate," Pittsburgh Post-Gazette. March 30, 1992.

[41]   Poll finds solid support for Perot. *Los Angeles Times*. March 31, 1992.

[42]   "Perot The Front Runner," *Time*. June 15, 1992.

him to withdraw from the race since he was considered a Beltway outsider and was projected to win the 1992 presidential election. Perot eventually reentered the race in October and surpassed the 15 percent polling threshold in order to reach his goal of participating in all three presidential debates; however, his polling numbers never fully recovered.

What is most striking about Perot's 1992 book *United We Stand* is that the only thing that had changed between 1992 and the elections of 2012, a period of more than twenty years, is that the size of our national debt had quadrupled. Aside from that, Perot's *United We Stand* could have been written yesterday. During that twenty-year period with three different presidential administrations from both political parties, nothing substantial has changed for the better in this country. In this case, why should anyone be optimistic that things will improve in the next twenty years? It's clear that the actions of our political class over the past several decades have been to put this country on a path to cultural and economic disintegration. This has been accomplished by those in power irrespective of any party affiliation.

The only real qualifications to hold the office of the president of the United States are popularity, camera-friendliness, the ability to read a teleprompter, and a willingness to do whatever you're told regardless of the destructive consequences to the country or to your fellow citizens. If you are a sociopathic narcissist, you are particularly well qualified. The actual vote itself is more correctly a validation by the media-indoctrinated public of a preselected candidate.

It is about time that we admit that this is not where the battle for this country's redemption really lies. Our most important social institutions—education, the news media, the entertainment media, and others—have become nothing more than indoctrination camps and propaganda outlets whose job is to distort American history and the meaning of the constitution and to manufacture reliable Marxists. We have also allowed our government to undermine all of the institutions that we once depended upon to develop character and integrity among our youth—marriage, family, communities, schools, and churches.

We are reaping what we have sown. It has taken more than half a century to reach this point. To try to get back to an America that was the world's shining beacon on the hill, the standard of freedom and self-reliance for other countries to aspire to—to once again lead the world by example rather than by force—will probably not be accomplished by trying to restore sanity and integrity to our federal government. The pitifully few men and women in Congress that have the integrity to abide by their oaths of office, who uphold and defend the constitution, are too few in number to be able to turn it around by votes. Most true constitutionalists and statesmen don't seem to last long in Congress. However, the career politicians who remain indefinitely are living exactly what they espouse—to perpetually live off the government dole like parasites for their entire careers. Once in Congress they never leave unless they are forced to. The federal government has so vastly expanded its power that it now mainly attracts that same ilk—corrupt career politicians looking to get their piece of the public dole along with a lucrative lifelong pension. Government always attracts the type of men who desire power over others so that they can abuse it. There are numerous senators and representatives who have been in Congress continually for more years than the longest serving Supreme Court justice in history (thirty-six years), and Supreme Court judges are given lifetime appointments.

Since they won't leave on their own, it is up to the voters. Any current member who has served in Congress for more than twelve years should immediately be voted out of office. We must put an end to career politics.

Saving the Republic

Have we truly reached the Rubicon—the point of no return?

The American people have been stripped of their authority over their own lives, so we have all been trying to act from a position of weakness, hoping that a vote in a presidential election every four years means something. We must accept that it doesn't. If there is any possibility to turn this country back onto the right path, it will not be accomplished solely at the federal government level. In fact, it must be achieved by starting at the local community level, by taking back control of our homes, our property, our schools, and our families. Unless we reassert our individual sovereignty and restore our real property rights as home owners and thereby begin to loosen the vise in which we are all being squeezed, we will have little chance to assert any authority over the corrupt politicians who have entrenched themselves in our federal government. In order to be able to act from a position of strength we must make self-reliance achievable, restore our individual property rights, and rebuild the integrity of our educational institutions. We must do these things right now while we still can. The rest of this book explores why this is and how this could be done.

CHAPTER 3

Sesame Street—Property Rights for Dummies

Next to the right of liberty, the right of property is the most important individual right guaranteed by The Constitution and the one which, united with that of personal liberty, has contributed more to the growth of civilization than any other institution established by the human race.

—William Howard Taft, twenty-seventh president of the United States

The following is an article (reprinted with permission from David R. Henderson) by Janet Beales Kaidantzis:

Ever seen two children quarreling over a toy? Such squabbles had been commonplace in Katherine Hussman Klemp's household. But in the Sesame Street Parent's Guide she tells how she created peace in her family of eight children by assigning property rights to toys.

As a young mother, Klemp often brought home games and toys from garage sales. "I rarely matched a particular item with a particular child," she says. "Upon reflection, I could see how the fuzziness of ownership easily led to arguments. If everything belonged to everyone, then each child felt he had a right to use anything."

To solve the problem, Klemp introduced two simple rules: First, never bring anything into the house without assigning clear ownership to one child. The owner has ultimate authority over the use of the property. Second, the owner is not required to share. Before the rules were in place, Klemp recalls, "I suspected that much of the drama often centered less on who got the item in dispute and more on whom Mom would side with." Now, property rights, not parents, settle the arguments.

Instead of teaching selfishness, the introduction of property rights actually promoted sharing. The children were secure in their ownership and knew they could always get their toys back. Adds Klemp; "Sharing raised their self-esteem to see themselves as generous persons."

Not only do her children value their own property rights, but also they extend that respect to the property of others. "Rarely do our children use each other's things without asking first, and they respect a 'No' when they get one. Best of all, when someone who has every right to say 'No' to a request says 'Yes,' the borrower sees the gift for what it is and says 'Thanks' more often than not," says Klemp.[43]

Anyone who has been the parent of a young child has likely witnessed how children simply assume that any object within reach is their own. As they explore the world around them, they will grab any object they can get their hands on, and when you as the parent attempt to take it back, they throw a tantrum. "No, Daddy ... it's *my* Swiss Army knife!"

To say that intellectually most politicians are exactly like children would do a disservice to children. Politicians do, however, possess a similar notion of property rights. As they obtain political power over the world around them, they covet control over any desirable piece of property, resource, or asset that they can get their hands on—either so they can keep it for themselves or so they can redistribute it to others in return for votes and political favors. Since they know that you as the owner would object to your property being taken, they pass a law taxing it, or they confiscate it by misapplying other concepts like eminent domain. Politicians' (as well as the obscenely rich ruling class's) notion of property rights consists in a belief that what is theirs is theirs and what is yours is also theirs to dispose of as they see fit. They believe that they and their political supporters deserve your property more than you do even though you earned it.

---

[43]   Alchian, Armen. "Property Rights," *The Concise Encyclopedia of Economics,* The Library of Economics and Liberty. http://www.econlib.org/library/Enc/PropertyRights.html

The struggle for individuals' rights to property ownership goes back to the dawn of civilization. But true free-market capitalism is a relatively recent innovation. It is literally a construct of the US Constitution. Prior to the American Revolution all property on the European-settled parts of this continent was under the ownership of some European monarch. The use of all lands by colonists, even the wealthy ones, was only by the permission and good graces of the sovereign.

To a large extent, the American Revolution was about establishing the right to property ownership for individuals. This didn't mean that you were entitled to a piece of land. It meant that you were entitled to own it if you could earn it by the sweat of your own brow. Once individuals owned their land and home, it was theirs to do with as they pleased. Individual citizens were then free to cultivate their land, grow the food they needed to survive, and to produce wealth for themselves and their families. They then could trade freely and fairly amongst themselves by voluntary exchange for mutual benefit. For most hardworking people, that meant having the ability to accumulate a savings, to acquire a family home, and to eventually bequeath those assets as a legacy to their children.

Today the political class has set up a system of taxation and property confiscation designed to subvert this model of individual freedom and property rights. It works in combination with our fiat monetary system to ensure that most Americans by the time they reach the end of their lives will have few if any assets left to bequeath. What property or assets are handed down are taxed to such an extent that they are more of a liability to the heir than a valuable legacy.

An individual's right to private property ownership is the most fundamental requirement of a free-market (capitalist) economic system, yet it is one of the most misunderstood concepts. Many critics in the United States and throughout the Western world have complained that property rights often take precedence over human rights under the claim that people of lesser means are treated unequally and therefore have unequal opportunities. Once again this is an example of twisting the meaning of our founding principles. Equality of opportunity is not a guarantee of equal outcomes. In terms of the ability to create wealth, inequality exists within every society. But the alleged conflict between property rights and human rights is a fallacy. Property rights are human rights.[44]

This notion is also affirmed in the Bible. The first of God's laws for society are found in Exodus 22, and these were property rights laws. The commandment, "Thou shalt not steal," is the clearest declaration of the right to private property in the Old Testament. The concept also derives directly from our first founding document, the Declaration of Independence.

---

[44] Cato Institute Handbook for Policymakers, 7th Edition.

The US Declaration of Independence, which was primarily drafted by Thomas Jefferson, was adopted by the Second Continental Congress on July 4, 1776. The second section reads, "We hold these truths to be self-evident, that all men are created equal, that they are endowed by their creator with certain unalienable Rights; that among these are Life, Liberty, and the pursuit of Happiness"

Several possible inspirations for Jefferson's use of this phrase have been cited. Jefferson identified himself as an Epicurean. This is a philosophical principle that teaches the pursuit of happiness and proposes autarchism, which translates as individual self-reliance or individual liberty. For a larger society, this constitutes the notion of self-governance. Jefferson's inspiration for this idea may have originated with John Locke or possibly from his vast knowledge of ancient Greek philosophy. It's also likely that Jefferson's own life experience of losing his father when he was only fourteen led to his vehement devotion to the notion of self-reliance, a feature also of his unique character. Jefferson was known to have been an eminent scholar of ancient Greek history, and as a student, he had learned to read ancient Greek and Roman literature in their original Greek and Latin languages. Jefferson was a rare genius, a truly brilliant and gifted man. He was an accomplished building architect who designed his family estate, Monticello, and began construction on it by the time he was twenty-five. He was the chief philosophical architect of the Declaration of Independence at the young age of thirty-three. He was fully fluent in five languages, partly self-taught and partly learned during his studies at the College of William and Mary, where he also learned to play the violin.[45]

Although Jefferson's inspiration on the larger issue of self-governance and Republican principles emanated from his knowledge of ancient Greek writings, John Locke did indeed inspire Jefferson to a large extent on the issue of property rights. Locke argued in his *Two Treatises of Government* that political society existed for the sake of protecting property, which he defined as a person's "life, liberty, and estate." According to those scholars who saw the root of Jefferson's choice of words in Locke's doctrine, Jefferson replaced "estate" with "the pursuit of happiness."[46] The question has long been argued as to why Jefferson chose those words and didn't simply keep estate as an explicit protection of property rights in the founding documents.

Many scholars and historians have concluded that Jefferson wisely sought to implicitly rather than explicitly protect property rights. The reason was that at that time in history the concept of property included the ownership not only of one's home, land, and farm but also in the ownership of other humans. Physical slavery had existed for practically the entire history of human civilization, and although Jefferson himself was a slave owner by inheritance, he understood the concept of human servitude to be immoral. With the opportunity being presented for the first time in human history

---

[45]   The Thomas Jefferson Papers Timeline—1743 to 1827, Library of Congress.
[46]   Brown, Stuart Gerry, "The First Republicans—Political Philosophy and Public Policy in the Party of Jefferson and Madison," 1954.

to found a new country on the basis of the unalienable rights of the individual, many historians believe that Jefferson strove to set the stage for an eventual abolishment of slavery. However, he was wise enough to know that if he had included language in the new nation's founding documents to explicitly protect the right to all property ownership, it may have been misused to protect the right to own slaves and might thus have precluded their eventual emancipation. Therefore, he chose the language carefully in an effort to implicitly protect property rights such that the protected property was only in the context of home and land but not of other persons. This explains the use of the language "right to life, liberty, and pursuit of happiness."

Then—just as today—one's life and liberty depended upon private property ownership (that property being one's home). As far as pursuing happiness is concerned, it's doubtful that any slaves would have been happy about their condition. At that time in history most individual homes were also farms, which provided the citizens with their livelihoods as well as their residences. The citizens of that time depended on their homes and land for most or all of the food they cultivated and the livestock they raised. Their lives and personal security depended entirely upon their property.

Although the majority of Americans are no longer farmers, that condition is no different today. If you do not own your home, you are dependent upon the actual owner to allow you to use it (even if you are a renter). Such a dependency does not constitute freedom or liberty. To achieve life and liberty as well as the pursuit of happiness, one must have the right to not only use the land but to own it, to control its disposition, and to be a free man able to do both. This is what is meant by the unalienable right to life, liberty, and the pursuit of happiness, and it is as true today as it was in 1776. The right to one's own life, liberty, ownership of one's land, home, and the fruits of one's labor are the moral, unalienable rights of every man, woman, and child in America. These derive from natural law as endowed by our creator, who or whatever that may be.

In Defense of Jefferson

Jefferson's critics routinely accuse him of hypocrisy for having been a slave owner, but they fail to recognize the facts of his achievement. Jefferson had the foresight and intent to craft the founding documents in such a manner so as to establish the framework for an eventual abolishment of slavery once the newly formed country was on a stable enough economic footing to be able to do so. His implicit rather than explicit language protecting property rights is a testament to this.

Thomas Jefferson was not the only slave owner to have written voluminously about the paradox of continuing with the system that he admitted to be unjust and immoral. In the late eighteenth and nineteenth centuries, slavery was viewed by many of the founders as "an unfortunate inheritance, a problem of morality lacking a practical solution." As Jefferson put it, "There must doubtless be an unhappy influence on the manners of our people produced by the existence of slavery among us. The whole commerce between master and slave is a perpetual exercise of the most boisterous passions, the most unremitting despotism on one part, and degrading submissions on the other."

During this time, discussion surrounding an eventual abolition was fairly commonplace in the South. Slave owners discussed colonization, and some emancipated their own slaves. One of the more prominent slave owners who openly sought a way to abolish slavery without a consequent economic catastrophe was Henry Clay. His cousin, Cassius Clay once wrote,

> Slavery is an evil to the slave, by depriving nearly three millions of men of the best gift of God to man – Liberty. I stop here – this is enough of itself to give us a full anticipation of the long catalogue of human woe, and physical and intellectual and moral abasement which follows in the wake of Slavery. Slavery is an evil to the master. It is utterly subservient of the Christian religion. It violates the great law upon which that religion is based, and on account of which it vaunts its preeminence.

Why did most of the founders view slavery as a necessary evil that could not be simply done away with immediately?

Like the rest of the world at that time, the American colonies were an agrarian society. The global economy depended mainly upon agriculture and mining. Without the mechanized production provided by the industrial revolution (which would not be realized for another hundred years), it was conceivable that if slavery had been abolished immediately after America's founding, the economy of the new nation could have collapsed within a few weeks. The economy, which depended to a large extent on a model of slave labor in spite of its inherent inefficiencies (as did the economies of the rest of Europe and Africa at that time), was a legacy of more than a thousand years of global slave-based agriculture. Many of the framers believed that the newly established United States could not have endured an immediate eradication of slavery without a consequent economic catastrophe. Jefferson understood this as a possible threat to the new nation's ability to endure, but he also understood that the rights to individual liberty as well as private property ownership were the most important cornerstones to a free society. This presented a paradox or a no-win situation with respect to the issue of slavery. Never before in human history had the opportunity presented itself to establish a new nation founded on principles of individual liberty and property rights—with the consequent abolishment of physical slavery as the moral imperative. At that time in history it was economically and politically impossible to do both at the same time, or so many of the founders believed.

This is not meant to justify or condone the fact that such an immoral institution as slavery continued in America after its founding. Whether or not the founders were mistaken in their belief that there was a real risk of economic collapse without slavery was a matter only they could have assessed based on the best knowledge they had at the time. Nevertheless, the framers' idea to legally establish the right to private property ownership as an unalienable right for every citizen was new in the history of human civilization. It is what allowed the eventual abolishment of slavery to happen. It is a construct purely from the founding of the United States of America, and it is the foundation of the free enterprise system.

Therefore, it must be clarified that from the time of America's founding until the passage of the thirteenth amendment, which abolished slavery in 1865, America cannot truly be considered to have functioned under a pure free market, although it was the freest market in the world at that time. Free-market economics is fundamentally about a respect for individual property rights. The fruits of a man's labor are his property, so institutionalized bondage for purposes of conscripting one's labor is fundamentally incompatible with a free-enterprise system. The moral implications notwithstanding, slavery has also been shown to have been economically inefficient. Economist Ludwig Von Mises explains it as follows:

> The price paid for a slave, is determined by the net yield from his 'employment,' just as the price paid for a cow is determined by the expected net yield of its utilization. The owner of the slave does not pocket specific revenue. For him there is no specific exploitation boon derived from the fact that the slave's work is not remunerated. If one treats men like cattle, one cannot squeeze more out of them than 'cattle-like' performance. Then it becomes significant that man is physically weaker than oxen or horses, and feeding and guarding a slave is, in proportion to the performance to be reaped, more expensive than feeding and guarding cattle. If one asks from an unfree laborer human performance, one must provide him with specifically human inducements. If an employer aims at obtaining products which in quality and quantity excel those whose production can be extorted by the whip, he must interest the toiler in the yield of his contribution. Instead of punishing laziness and sloth, he must reward diligence, skill, and eagerness. It is this fact that has made all systems of compulsory labor disappear. (Mises, 2008)

Some people believe that pure capitalism can include the buying and selling of human beings and that only government intervention (such as in the American Civil War) could have ended this practice. However, slavery is inherently inefficient from an economic perspective. Furthermore, the practice of slavery was also ended by other major participants of the slave trade during that era without waging bloody wars. In fact, only government-imposed limitations on private property rights can allow slavery as a viable economic system. Indeed Lincoln's emancipation proclamation actually mandated that slavery be allowed to continue in the border-states.

Calling Out the Revisionists

At the time Lincoln wrote the Emancipation Proclamation, England and France had recognized the Confederacy and were considering assisting the South in the war effort. About his own proclamation Lincoln wrote, "I view the matter (the Emancipation Proclamation) as a practical war measure, to be decided upon according to the advantages or disadvantages it may offer to the suppression of the rebellion." He further wrote, "I will also concede that emancipation would help us in Europe, and convince them that we are incited by something more than ambition."

In other words, according to Lincoln, the principal benefits derived from emancipation were in suppressing the South's secession and in demonstrating to Europe a ruse of benevolent intentions. Lincoln was not truly interested in ending slavery, and his own writings demonstrated a complete lack of concern surrounding the issue. In an 1858 letter for example, Lincoln said, "I have declared a thousand times, and now repeat that in my opinion, neither the General Government, nor any other power outside of slave states, can constitutionally or rightfully interfere with slaves or slavery where it already exists." Given the facts, what was Lincoln really after? Why did he object to Southern secession so vehemently that he was willing to pervert constitutional law and falsely claim secession to be illegal as a justification to invade the South?

Ironically earlier in his political career Lincoln supported the notion of secession. In an 1848 speech to the House of Representatives, Lincoln supported Texas's secession from Mexico by stating:

> Any people anywhere, being inclined and having the power, have the right to rise up and shake off the existing government and form a new one that suits them better ... nor is this right confined to cases in which the whole people of an existing government may choose to exercise it. Any portion of such people that can may revolutionize and make their own of so much of the territory as they inhabit.
>
> —Abraham Lincoln

Why didn't Lincoln hold the same values regarding Southern secession? Once again just follow the money. From the time of the nation's founding until 1913, the only sources of tax revenue for the federal government that were allowed by the constitution were excise taxes and tariffs. During the 1850s, 90 percent of federal revenue came from tariffs, and 75 percent of that was generated by the seaports in the Southern states. Allowing the Southern states to secede would have deprived Lincoln's government of almost 70 percent of its total tax revenues. Going to war was not the best means to end slavery, but it was the only means to keep the Union intact for the sake of maximizing future tax revenues for the federal government.

Some have suggested that if the Lincoln government had truly been interested solely in ending slavery, it would have been far more cost effective and humane for the US government to simply purchase their freedom from the Southern plantation owners at a fair market price. Although this might have been possible, there are legitimate arguments against this idea. For one thing, it has been asserted that some slave masters actually enjoyed being slave masters. There is a great deal of truth to this, as our current model of debt slavery can attest to. Furthermore, simply purchasing the slaves in order to free them would have legitimized the concept that humans could be owned and sold as property. And finally slavery indeed was a social institution in addition to an economic one.

History has proven that economic reality always trumps social norms in the long run. As the previous commentary by Mises pointed out, physical slavery has been proven to be economically inefficient. Social institution or not, slavery was quickly fizzling out on its own all over the world. It's part of the reason that between 1800 and 1865, slavery was legally abolished in France, Norway, Haiti, the United Kingdom, Prussia, Spain, Mexico, Argentina, the Netherlands, Uruguay, Estonia, Venezuela, Livonia, Canada, Liberia, Greece, Chile, the Federal Republic of Central America, Sweden, Bolivia, Brazil, Serbia, Portugal, Denmark, New Grenada (Columbia), the Kingdom of Hawaii, Peru, and Russia, all without firing a single shot.

The best solution (and only constitutional one) would have been to simply allow the South to secede peacefully and then offer free status and sovereign citizenship to any slaves who crossed over to the North thereafter. Instead, Lincoln chose to invade the South and wage a bloody four-year war that took more than 750,000 American lives at an unfathomable economic cost. It wasn't long before the free-enterprise system in combination with the industrial revolution dramatically expanded economic prosperity. With this prosperity, the injustice and economic inefficiency of slavery became more starkly revealed. Slavery would have come to a rapid end with or without the American Civil War as a direct consequence of the free-enterprise system.

Labor Is Property

Slave labor is a theft of property. The concept of individual property rights is based in natural law, from which are derived all of our unalienable constitutional rights. The natural law theory rests on the insight that man has a specific nature, as does the world around him and his means of interacting with it. As noted economist

68

Murray Rothbard writes, "The activity of each entity, whether organic or inorganic is determined by its own nature and by the nature of other entities with which it comes into contact. The nature of man is such that each individual person must, in order to act, choose his own ends and employ his own means, in order to attain them."[47]

Each man must learn about himself and the world around him and then employ his own ability to think, to reason, to select values, to learn about cause and effect, and then to act of his own volition. Each man does so for his own purpose in order to maintain himself and advance his life. Each of these acts constitutes an attribute of an individual's thinking mind.

To think, feel, evaluate, and act are attributes only of the individual, so it is vital for each person's survival and prosperity to be free to learn, develop his intellect, choose, and act upon his knowledge and values without coercion. This is the basis of human nature. To interfere with this process by force goes profoundly against what is necessary by man's nature for his life, prosperity, and survival.[48]

Therefore, it is the use of force by one against another (except in the case of justifiable self-defense), which is inherently unethical and immoral.

> No man can put a chain about the ankle of his fellow man, without at last finding the other end fastened about his own neck.
>
> —Frederick Douglass

---

47 Rothbard, Murray, "For a New Liberty," (Ludwig Von Mises Institute, 1973) ISBN 978-1-61016-264-7.

48 Tannehill, Morris and Linda. The Market for Liberty. (Ludwig Von Mises Institute, 1970).

John Locke, widely known as *the father of classical liberalism*, addresses the issue of property rights in this way:[49]

> Every man has property in his own person. This, nobody has any right to but himself. The labour of his body, and the work of his hands, we may say are properly his. Whatsoever then, he removes out of the state that nature hath provided and left it in, he hath mixed his labour with it, and joined it, to something that is his own, and thereby makes it his property. It being removed from the common state nature placed it in, it hath by this labour something annexed to it that excludes the common right of other men. For this labour being the unquestionable property of the labourer, no man but he can give a right to what that is once joined to.

The relevancy of this in terms of Locke's influence on America's founding principles is that a man's first property right is in his own person. In other words, your body is your own, which is self-evident. Each person owns himself and has the right to his own life. Locke takes this further to say that the labor (and the fruits thereof), which are a product of one's own body, must therefore also be one's own property. This, too, is self-evident. But more importantly it implies that when a man creates value by mixing his labor with something inanimate (a natural resource for example), the product that is produced becomes his property. Considering this principal in the context of our current monetary system, it can therefore be said that fiat money (also an inanimate object—albeit one that is created out of thin air) has no real value until labor has been exchanged for it, making that money the private property of the laborer who earned it. Therefore, taxing earnings from labor compensation constitutes a theft of property.

The Moral Defense of the Right to Individual Liberty and Property Rights

Any act, whether thinking or laboring in the production of wealth, is an attribute of each individual's existence. Therefore, freedom of action is a critical aspect of every person's life. If a man is not free to use his mind, his body, and his time in the conduct of any action he wishes (so long as he doesn't violate the unalienable rights of another person), then he is to some degree a slave. The right to individual liberty, like the right to property, is a fundamental aspect of the right to one's own life. This philosophical concept is critical in terms of the moral implications of slavery. To be enslaved is to have the property of one's own body stolen by another. Having

---

[49]   Locke, John, *Two Treatises of Government.* Cambridge: Cambridge University Press. 1764, sec 87. p 123, 209.

the fruits of one's labor taken against one's will is the essence of physical slavery. It follows then that to be taxed on a portion of the fruits of one's labor is nothing less than an act of limited slavery.

Given the many variants of socialism (Communism, national socialism, fascism, corporatism, etc.), each one treats the issue of property rights somewhat differently. But what they all have in common is that they universally seek to eradicate the right of individual ownership and/or control of private property, most especially the disposition of one's home and one's labor. Under all forms of socialism, citizens are conscripted to work for the state (either wholly or partially through income taxation) rather than for themselves, and this constitutes a basic violation of property rights. All forms of socialism constitute slavery. They are only distinguished in terms of degree.

Fiat Money—The Tool of Debt-Slavery

The worker who earns sound money is paid with a real asset in exchange for real labor—value for equivalent value. In contrast, the worker who is forced by law to accept fiat money in exchange for his labor (as in the United States and the rest of the modern world), is accepting a debt instrument, nothing more than an IOU. Since it is the future labor of the citizenry that begets value to fiat money after it is issued, the purchasing power of that IOU is determined in part by the labor of his fellow citizens, which has also been exchanged for every Federal Reserve note that they, too, have been paid. In effect, every worker accepts payment in the form of some part of the fruits of the labors of his fellow citizens who are also forced to accept fiat-debt in exchange for their work. As a consequence, every hardworking citizen is forced to cannibalize the wealth created by every other hardworking citizen in order to survive, while the issuer of the fiat money skims off a portion of the labors of all workers collectively.

In return, the central bankers who create fiat currency offer nothing of value to society. The money they print only derives its value from the labor provided by the citizens they exploit. In effect, a fiat currency model is designed to enable the issuing authorities (and their partners in government) to conscript the labor of the citizenry in order to beget value to the counterfeit money they issue. They then transfer most of the fruits of that labor back to the issuer through taxation. It is the basic tool by which governments can take control of your labor and therefore your life. It is the basic tool used to impose debt slavery on the entire working class.

It should be noted that under a system of physical slavery the slave owner must at his expense provide his workers with shelter, food, clothing, and even health care. Conversely (or to be more correct—perversely), under our current system of debt slavery, the workers must provide those things for themselves at their own expense.

The Tax on Individual Income from Wages Is Unconstitutional

Congress's power to lay and collect taxes is given in Article 1 of the US Constitution. This power only allowed Congress to impose those taxes as long as they were subject to another provision that required direct taxes to be apportioned among the states according to the census. This prohibited any kind of tax on income (as income was then defined) or capitation (a tax per head).

The sixteenth amendment, which was passed in 1913 and was signed into law by President Woodrow Wilson (just a few months before signing the Federal Reserve Act), sought to overrule this by stating, "The Congress shall have power to lay and collect taxes on incomes, from whatever source derived, without apportionment among the several States, and without regard to any census or enumeration."

The graduated income tax as we now know it was instituted in America in the same year just prior to establishing the Federal Reserve system and its fiat currency model. These two institutions were implemented at the same time and for the same purpose. They work together to fleece the working population of the fruits of their labor in order to profit the cartel that owns of the Federal Reserve system.

Compensation Is Not Income

A little-known fact, however, is that the sixteenth amendment did not redefine income. The definition of what constitutes income has never changed. So how do we define income in terms of the spirit and intent of the US Constitution since that definition still holds?

As has been demonstrated, an individual's labor constitutes his or her private property. When you work for a wage or salary, you are exchanging your time and your physical and intellectual efforts in return for property in the form of money. Trading labor for money constitutes a property exchange (which is why employers call this compensation). From the time of America's founding, a wage or a salary was not defined as income but as *just compensation*. It was not thought to constitute a net gain for the individual. In other words, you have to give something up in exchange for something that both parties agree is of an equivalent value. According to the spirit and intent of the constitution as well as several subsequent Supreme Court decisions, money that an individual received was only considered income if it provided the individual with a net capital gain from non-labor related activity.

In fact, the word income is not defined anywhere in the Internal Revenue Code; however, the Supreme Court has defined it for us in numerous cases.

In Stratton's Independence v. Howbert 231 US 399 (1913), the Supreme Court's decision stated,[50]

> As to what should be deemed "income" within the meaning of Sec. 38, it of course need not be such an income as would have been taxable as such, for at that time income was not taxable as such by Congress without apportionment according to population, and this tax was not apportioned. Evidently Congress adopted the income as the measure of the tax to be imposed with the respect to the doing of business in corporate form because it desired that the excise should be imposed, approximately at least, with regard to the amount of benefit presumably derived by such corporations from the current operations of the government.

The Supreme Court defines income tax, as "an excise tax imposed with respect to the doing of business in corporate form." Being employed to work in return for equal compensation does not constitute being engaged in any corporate activity since it does not provide the worker with a net gain in value. The meaning of this is that for purposes of federal taxation, income was originally defined as earnings from corporate activity, not from labor compensation as in a salary or a wage. That legal definition per the Supreme Court's decision has never been changed. Therefore, per the constitution and the Supreme Court's decision on its intent, it is only income from interest and dividends that are legitimately taxable as income but not salary, wages, or tips.

It is interesting to note that this principle is inverted in terms of our current tax policy. Today individual labor compensation is taxed at the highest rates, while capital gains taxes are assessed at the lowest. This condition benefits those with the highest earnings capacity—those with enough wealth to be able to invest their cash savings in corporate activities. It punishes those who are lower earners and ensures they are unable to accumulate enough savings within a reasonable amount of time to be able to do anything more than just pay their weekly living expenses. It's the reason that the vast majority of the middle class lives paycheck to paycheck and continues to get poorer, while the rich get richer. Our system of unfair taxation is designed to achieve this result. The median net worth of all of the members of Congress is over one million dollars. As such, the bulk of their individual earnings are from investment dividends, and not from their salaries. Therefore, they directly benefit from this inversion of principles. This represents a conflict of interest for every member of Congress.

---

[50]   US Supreme Court, Stratton's *Independence Ltd., v. Howbert*, 231 US 399 (1913), Dec 1, 1913.

This is also the reason that the IRS has officially established that filing federal taxes is *voluntary* in spite of the fact that a prison sentence awaits if you fail to do so. The government falsely claims that filing is voluntary in order that the taxpayers will then have voluntarily (or unwittingly to be more accurate) paid the government a tax on their compensation—in spite of the fact that an enforced tax on compensation is prohibited by the constitution and subsequent Supreme Court decisions. In effect, filing a federal income tax return is the filer's implied voluntary waiver of the constitution's prohibitions against taxes on compensation.

When you earn money from interest on your savings, a dividend from a stock's earnings or a capital gain on the sale of a stock, it constitutes a windfall. It is not money you were paid in return for your time and effort or for which you traded a piece of your life. It is money you gained by speculating or by taking an investment risk and then sitting back to let others do the work. This is what is meant by a gain on corporate activity. Gambling and stock investing both fall into this category. Working hard to earn a living does not.

The framers considered an individual's property to be sovereign. Labor is property and they objected to any kind of tax on labor—wages, salaries, and tips. They never intended that an individual's private property of any kind (including labor compensation) should be taxed by the federal government.

The Fifth Amendment to the US Constitution, which is part of the Bill of Rights, protects against abuse of government authority in a legal procedure. Its guarantees stem from English common law, which traces back to the Magna Carte in 1215. The actual text of the Fifth Amendment states:

> No person shall be held to answer for a capital, or otherwise infamous crime, unless on a presentment or indictment of a Grand Jury, except in cases arising in the land or naval forces, or in the Militia, when in actual service in time of War or public danger; nor shall any person be subject for the same offense to be twice put in jeopardy of life or limb; nor shall be compelled in any criminal case to be a witness against himself, nor be deprived of life, liberty, or property, without due process of law; nor shall private property be taken for public use, without just compensation.

"No person shall be deprived of property, without due process of law; nor shall private property be taken for public use, without just compensation." Taxing income by means of confiscation by one's employer through payroll withholdings is *by definition* the taking of private property for public use without just compensation. In fact, it is taken without any compensation—neither for the worker who earned it nor for their employer who used its own resources to confiscate it on behalf of the government. Employer-enforced tax withholdings from workers is a direct violation of the US Constitution. But when you file your tax return "voluntarily," you are in effect waiving those provisions as well as your Fifth Amendment rights. Since the government will send you to prison for not *voluntarily* filing your tax return, this constitutes an act of extortion—forcing you to waive your Constitutional right under threat of physical force leading to the loss of your liberty.

Property Rights in Home, Land, and Resources

Many attempt to confuse the issue by referring to property ownership as being something different from property rights. They claim that one can still have property rights even if that property is owned by the government. This fallacy is part of the same fraud the Fascists used in the 1930s to convince the European people that fascism, which permitted limited property rights, was the better and only alternative to Communism, which permitted no property rights.

With respect to real property (land and resources), socialists seek to transfer property from private to government ownership. This empowers the government to selectively grant rights of use without the right of ownership. The purpose is to give the ruling class the ability to pick and choose who gets what property and what they can do with it as well as the authority to take it away any time they choose. More insidious is a system that allows private individuals to retain superficial ownership, while government retains the basic control authority over property. This leaves all financial risk, liabilities, costs, and burdens of property ownership with the citizen, who is then beholden to the government for permission to use that property. This latter description is exactly the system we have today in the United States.[51]

Such authority to grant rights of use without real ownership allows rulers to subordinate and rule the citizenry by fear—fear of losing access to your property. This allows the rulers to remain in power indefinitely as well as to expand that power continuously over time. These are the primary objectives of career politicians.

Tightening the Vise—Holding Your Home Hostage

When local authorities levy a tax on an individual's private property, they must at the same time have a provision to be able to seize that property in the event of nonpayment of the tax. However, the Fifth Amendment prohibits the seizure of private property without due process and further states that "private property shall not be taken for public use without just compensation." Since taxing private property requires that the state be able to seize it for nonpayment, this presents a paradox. Taxing individuals' property and in particular their residential homes is therefore not compatible with the spirit and intent of the fifth amendment to the US Constitution.

---

[51]   Coyle, Dennis J. Property Rights and The Constitution: Shaping Society Through Land. Albany, NY: SUNY Press. 1993.

In other words, when a state or local government arbitrarily imposes a tax on an individual's home and then deems that property owner a criminal for nonpayment of that tax—then seizes that property without providing just compensation to that property owner—it should be viewed not only as a violation of the US Constitution but as an act of criminal theft by extortion perpetrated by the local government against one of its own citizens.

Private property rights do not conflict with human rights. They *are* human rights. Private property rights are the rights of humans to acquire and use specified property and goods and to exchange them value for value. Any restraint on private property rights shifts the balance of power from individual citizens to politicians, subjecting people to more government authority.[52] Since more authority is what a tyrannical government is after, eradicating property rights is its principal goal.

Government Overreach

The separation of powers doctrine is intended to prevent the federal government from acquiring enough power to establish laws that would potentially deprive individual citizens of any of their unalienable rights to life, liberty, and property. It bears repeating that private property rights are the basic foundation of individual liberty. The continual subversion of our property rights and our other constitutional rights are a consequence of a government bent on deliberately destroying our liberty so that it can consolidate and expand its power over the citizenry. This is why limited government and the separation of powers doctrine must be restored if we are to save America from complete dissolution into a tyrannical police-state.

Establishing the right to private property ownership as the cornerstone of a free and just society was perhaps the single most important aspect of the history of this nation's founding because it laid the philosophical foundation for the end of human slavery. The issue of slavery in terms of property rights cannot be emphasized enough. When men, women, and children were forced to provide their labor in exchange for no payment, it was a theft of their private property, a theft of their very lives. To advocate for limited government is not to advocate for the ridiculous notion of limited slavery. Limited government is intended to protect individual property rights and not to violate them only to some limited extent. The taking of just a part of one's property in the form of a property tax or a part of one's labor in the form of a tax on wages or salaries is exactly that—an act of limited slavery.

Where Is Your Income Tax Going?

This last assertion is most glaring when one considers it in the context of the Grace Commission report. The Grace Commission was an investigation requested by

---

[52]   Alchian, Armen, "Property Rights," The Concise Encyclopedia of Economics, The Library of Economics and Liberty.

President Ronald Reagan in 1982.[53] The focus of it was to reveal waste and inefficiency in the federal government. Its head was businessman J. Peter Grace. When launched, Reagan specifically asked the members of that commission to "be bold and work like tireless bloodhounds. Don't leave any stone unturned in your search to root out inefficiency."[54] The most relevant findings in terms of the government's use of federal income tax revenues were the following:

> One-third of all income taxes are consumed by waste and inefficiency in the federal government. Another one-third escapes collection owing to the 'underground economy.' With two thirds of everyone's personal income taxes wasted or not collected, 100 percent of what is collected is absorbed solely by interest on the federal debt and by federal government contributions to transfer payments. In other words, all individual income tax revenues are gone before one nickel is spent on the services [that] taxpayers expect from their government.[55]

Before 1913, the individual income tax did not exist. Today every nickel of it is wasted on inefficiency and interest on the national debt. The original Constitution of the United States of America prohibited this kind of tax and is quite clear as to how we are to be subjected to a direct tax. The framers included not one but two limitations in the constitution. The limitations forbidding direct taxation of individuals are found first in article 1, section 2, clause 3, which states, "Representatives and direct Taxes shall be apportioned among the several States which may be included within this Union, according to their respective Numbers."

Furthermore, the US Constitution, article 1, section 9, clause 4 states, "No Capitation, or other direct, Tax shall be laid unless in Proportion to the Census or Enumeration here in before directed to be taken."

Nevertheless, the federal government has long demonstrated a willingness to impose unconstitutional tax policy under threat of property seizure or loss of liberty if one refuses to comply. The most recent demonstration of this has been Obamacare (the misnamed Patient Protection and Affordable Care Act). Justice Roberts' decision to declare the constitutionality of Obamacare on the basis that it is a tax reveals the

---

[53] Reagan, Ronald. Remarks at a White House Luncheon with the Chairman and Executive Committee of the Private Sector Survey on Cost Control. March 10, 1982. http://www.reagan.utexas.edu/archives/speeches/1982/31082d.htm

[54] Grace Commission, IP0281G "The Presidents Private Sector Survey on Cost Control" Library of Congress, Jan 31, 1985.

[55] Analysis of the Grace Commission's Proposals for Cost Control, United States Congressional Budget Office – United States Congress, Feb., 1984.

Supreme Court's willingness to pervert the US Constitution in order to violate its basic principles.

The sixteenth amendment to the US Constitution, which was passed in 1913, precisely states, "The Congress shall have power to lay and collect taxes on incomes, from whatever source derived, without apportionment among the several States, and without regard to any census or enumeration."

Once again it is important to understand that what constitutes income has never been redefined by the constitution. Nor has it been defined anywhere in the IRS tax code. As such, earlier Supreme Court decisions that defined income as gains from corporate activity and not as wages or equivalent property exchanges still hold. Nevertheless, the Obamacare tax in spite of its noncompliance with even the sixteenth amendment was deemed constitutional as a tax by Justice Roberts.

> I will not raise taxes for individuals earning less than $200,000 annually by one single dime.
>
> —Barack Hussein Obama, II

Obama campaigned heavily on the promise that he would not raise taxes on the middle class. In order to pretend compliance with this campaign promise, the Obama administration repeatedly asserted that the Obamacare provision was not a tax but was instead a penalty. Once this went before the Supreme Court for a decision on its constitutionality, it miraculously became a tax. Justice Roberts asserted that the financial penalty is a tax. However, it must be understood that it is not assessed on the basis of income, so it cannot be considered as any form of income tax. Therefore, it is not authorized by the sixteenth amendment. Furthermore, as a tax it also does not satisfy the three types of taxes listed as valid in the constitution—income, excise, or direct. In spite of Roberts' perversion of meaning in regards to what a tax on income actually is, he is referring to the penalty that is assessed for being uninsured. The fact that the penalty is accounted for and collected as part of the annual federal income tax filing process doesn't obviate that it is still just a penalty and not a true tax. Furthermore, the penalty is not assessed uniformly. It is triggered by economic inactivity, so it is not a valid excise tax, and finally Obamacare fails to apportion the tax among the states by population. The Constitution only allows for direct taxation of individuals by census or enumeration or by the sixteenth amendment as a proportion of income.

There is not a single feature of the Obamacare penalty that validates it as a direct tax according to the constitution's definition thereof or by any other part of the constitution, including the sixteenth amendment.

The Constitution does not grant Congress an independent power to use taxation as a means to regulate activity (or inactivity as in this case) unless that regulation is authorized by the constitution. Furthermore, the tenth amendment reserves powers not granted to the federal government—to the states and to the people. Nowhere in the constitution is Congress granted the power to force citizens to purchase a product (health insurance) as a condition of legal residency in the United States.

Most troubling is that Roberts' decision is another blatant demonstration of the consequences of the elimination of the separation of powers doctrine. The Supreme Court has devolved into nothing more than an extended tentacle of the executive branch of government. Its purpose today is to pervert the meaning and intent—rather than to uphold and defend—the constitution as a means to further the personal agenda of whatever tyrant sits in the White House. Another unintended consequence of this is that today there are thousands of American citizens incarcerated in our already overburdened prison system for the non-crime of tax evasion. Their incarceration costs taxpayers far more than the amount of taxes they allegedly evaded.

The Assault on Individual Property Rights

The basic sections of the constitution that provided protections to our right to property ownership have never been amended. The right to property ownership without threat of seizure provided by the Fifth Amendment should prohibit states from levying tax on individual homes that constitute private property. Furthermore, when the value of that property is subject to the Federal Reserve's manipulation of our inflationary money, deceiving citizens into paying a tax based on that deliberately inflated value constitutes fraud. Today the enforcement for the collection of property taxes is accomplished through extortion, intimidation, and fear—fear that people will lose their family homes to seizure for nonpayment of the tax, homes that those people may have worked entire lifetimes to own. Our property and income tax systems are nothing short of a vast criminal enterprise.

Toward the end of its 2004 term the US Supreme Court decided three property rights cases in which the owners had legitimate complaints. In all three cases the owners lost. One of the most noteworthy was *Kelo v. City of New London*.[56] In this case the city condemned Susette Kelo's property and seized it, intending to transfer it to another private party—Pfizer Corporation—that the city "believed could make better use of it." Normally one thinks of a condemned property as being a decrepit, vacant slum, but Mrs. Kelo had just invested a substantial sum into renovating her family home a year before the city condemned it. This was one example of a blatant theft of property perpetrated by the city of New London against Mrs. Kelo and more than a dozen other citizens in favor of another private entity—in this case a huge pharmaceutical corporation. In finding on behalf of the city, the Supreme Court simply ignored the

---

[56]   US Supreme Court, *Kelo v. City of New London* (04-108) 545 U.S. 469 (2005) 268 Conn. 1, 843 A. 2d 500—Retrieved from Cornell University School of Law Library.

"public use" restraint on the power of government to seize private property under eminent domain.[57]

It should be noted that between 2003 and 2013, Pfizer Corporation spent over $130 million on lobbyists, promoting their interests to various federal and state government agencies. Mrs. Kelo and the dozen home owners have no lobbyists and could not afford them. Only bankers and large bank-owned corporations can afford to buy politicians—using money they are able to create from nothing.

This case had centered on a plan by the city of New London, CT, to develop ninety-two acres of waterfront land into office buildings, a marina, and new upscale multifamily housing adjacent to a $300 million research center that was planned by Pfizer Corporation on the same land. Pfizer would be allowed to lease the land from the city for $1 per year. The owners of more than a dozen homes located on that property, however, refused to move. Suzette Kelo's home had been in her family for several generations, and she had just invested extensively in its remodeling. She enjoyed the view of the water and had no intention of giving up her unique location. One of her elderly neighbors named Wilhelmina Dery had been born in her house in 1918 and had lived there for her entire life. Well into her eighties, she had a deep sentimental attachment to her childhood home, and also had no intention of moving. Nevertheless, the city of New London misused several provisions of eminent domain and condemned the homes of dozens of citizens, including Ms. Kelo and Ms. Dery. The property owners were forcibly evicted, and their homes were then seized and demolished. Numerous court cases and appeals by the home owners went all the way to the Supreme Court but were unsuccessful. Imagine the sadness experienced by 85 year old Ms. Dery, at seeing her birthplace demolished, for the sake of a huge Pharmaceutical company that would be granted a $1 annual lease of the land under her former home—a home her parents worked a lifetime to own.

Not long after all of the residents were displaced and their homes leveled into an empty lot, Pfizer Corporation decided not to locate their research center to New London after all, and the entire project was scrapped. To this day, the neighborhood known as Fort Trumbull remains an abandoned, dust-strewn empty lot.

There were absolutely no consequences to this senseless theft of property for Pfizer or for the city, and the property owners whose family homes had been demolished were left with no recourse whatsoever. They were forced to accept compensation in an amount that the city itself determined to be *fair market value*.

Property Rights and FDRs New Deal

Clearly the eradication of our property rights has much more to do with the actions of the US Supreme Court than with the US Constitution itself. In the pre-New

---

[57]   Benedict, Jeff, *Little Pink House: A True Story of Defiance and Courage*, Jan 26, 2009.

Deal era before 1934, the US Constitution's protections on private property were respected because the court enforced those protections *to the letter of the law*. Those protections have remained unchanged to this day. However, for today's activist judges property rights means something very different. The progressive era spawned people like Oliver Wendell Holmes, Lewis Brandeis, and John Dewey, who regarded property as "a privilege that society granted to individuals for society's purposes." To them, property consisted not in an individual's right to his own life, to authority over himself, to the fruits of his labor, or his liberty; but of "a discretionary realm of freedom that the individual enjoyed thanks to the state's decision to protect that realm." Brandeis himself wrote in his dissenting opinion on Traux v. Corrigan, 257 US 312, 376 (1921), that "rights of property and the liberty of the individual must be remolded, from time to time, to meet the changing needs of society."

The reader should read that quote again. According to progressive Supreme Court justice Brandeis, your rights of property and your liberty, "must be remolded from time to time," to meet society's changing needs.

However, society is just a concept. It is what we call a group of individuals interacting with one another, each of their own accord. To claim that society has needs that supersede the rights of an individual is fallacious. A society cannot think, decide, or act, for these are attributes purely of an individual. No man, group of men, or society can lay claim to the right of any other individual man or his property. To do so is to espouse theft and slavery as being a moral imperative so long as it is perpetrated by those in a majority.

Brandeis, like Holmes, was frequently in dissent when writing such decisions. They were present through the transition of the Supreme Court to an activist body during FDR's 12-year reign. The result was this second conception of property rights which became law only a decade later. The New Deal era Supreme Court adopted this notion of property rights as a "privilege" granted by the federal government whose authority can expand or contract "in the service of the changing needs of society."[58] This is what has led to such clear violations of The Constitution as the Kelo decision. The framers would be mortified at this perversion of our founding principles.

FDR was the US president for more than 12 years. During that time, he was able to appoint 8 of the 9 sitting Supreme Court justices. He wasted no effort in packing the court with progressive activists who shared his contempt for The Constitution and his leftist ideology. It was Roosevelt's progressive Supreme Court that came to regard the US Constitution not as a doctrine based in natural law—acknowledging as unalienable, the rights of every American citizen—but as a living document open to their own whim of interpretation. As such, they came to regard property as a social privilege which can be manipulated to serve whatever ends lawmakers decide. This

---

[58]   White, G. Edward. The Constitution and The New Deal. Harvard University Press. 2002.

notion is the antithesis of our founding principles. However, it is perfectly aligned with the Marxist concept of no individual property rights.

Without Property Rights, There Is No Freedom

It is fundamental in common law and grounded in reason that property is what separates one individual from another. Individuals are independent or free only to the extent that they have sole or exclusive control over whatever property they own. Indeed, Americans go to work every day for most of their adult lives solely to acquire property for the purpose of becoming self-reliant and to achieve their independence. The ability to achieve that independence, however, has been totally undermined by our system of property taxation, income taxes, the consequences of our fiat monetary system and other examples of government abuse like the *Kelo v. the City of New London* case.

America's founders understood clearly that private property ownership is the foundation not only of individual prosperity but of freedom itself. Thus, through the common law, state law, and the US Constitution, they sought to protect property rights—the rights of people to freely acquire, control, use, and dispose of property as they saw fit without government interference. Today not a single American citizen retains true ownership and control over their home or their labor. Even the US Supreme Court has demonstrated in recent years that it will no longer respect the spirit and intent of the constitution in protecting the individual right to property ownership.

The founders would be disgusted to see what has happened to individual property rights during the course of the twentieth century. They waged a bloody and costly war over far less. Despotic governments have long understood that if you control property, you can then control the media, the schools, the labor market, religious institutions, and the political process itself. America reached that point more than three generations ago. When our Congress gave up their authority over our monetary system in 1913, they transferred control of every citizen's life and property to the owners of a private banking institution—the Federal Reserve—and to their political cronies. They did so by fraud and deceit and without the consent of the citizenry. This literally constituted the crime of the century.

On December 23, 1913, several months after the institution of the federal income tax (the sixteenth amendment), President Woodrow Wilson signed into law the Federal Reserve Act. He did this while more than half of Congress was away for the Christmas holiday, precluding their participation in the vote.[59] Not long afterward

---

[59]   Senate Documents Col. 3, No. 23, Page 100, National Economy and the Banking System—Woodrow Wilson, 1916.

the president then claimed that he had been duped by the banking aristocracy into enacting this unconstitutional law. So Wilson had this to say,[60]

I am a most unhappy man. I have unwittingly ruined my country. A great industrial nation is controlled by its system of credit. Our system of credit is concentrated. The growth of the nation, therefore, and all our activities are in the hands of a few men. We have come to be one of the worst ruled, one of the most completely controlled and dominated Governments in the civilized world, no longer a Government by free opinion, no longer a Government by conviction and the vote of the majority, but a Government by the opinion and duress of a small group of dominant men.

—President Woodrow Wilson

With this confession, Wilson admits that with the passing of the Federal Reserve Act of 1913, the US government fell under the control of the owners of the private Federal Reserve banking cartel.

Ruined his country indeed, and it has yet to recover.

Did Wilson make this statement because he suddenly realized the ramifications of what he had done or to feign his foregone knowledge of it and therefore claim innocence in the matter in an attempt to protect his legacy? Was Wilson truly unwitting in his participation in the ruin of his country as he claims? Prior to seeking the US presidency, Wilson had been the president of Princeton University and was the first doctorate-level academic elected as president of the United States. Could a man of such a prestigious education truly have been so naïve, so obtuse, so stupid?

Whenever we look back in history on those events where government elites have imposed some destructive policy designed to obliterate the intent of the constitution,

---

[60]   Wilson, Woodrow, *The New Freedom: A Call for the Emancipation of the Generous Energies of a People,* New York, (Doubleday, Page & Co. Publishers, 1913).

the pattern is the same. The officials responsible pretend to have been hapless innocent bystanders that were unknowingly duped along with the rest of their countrymen. Politicians hoping to escape blame for their ruinous actions almost always hide behind the notion that world events are driven by some inexplicable tide of history. This may be true for natural disasters but not for the social conflict that corrupt career politicians deliberately instigate. There is always a cause and effect, and the ruling class has had thousands of years to figure out how to cheat the peasants out of their hard-earned wealth and their hard-won freedom. When highly educated and well-connected government officials feign innocence by playing dumb, one should be exceedingly skeptical of their sincerity.

We have long been witnessing the economic consequences of this deliberate, surreptitious, and incremental eradication of our property rights. We see it in the heavy price we pay for the continually increasing economic uncertainty and inefficiencies of our current system. We see it as public entitlement benefits continue to grow at the expense of those from whom those resources are confiscated. We incrementally slide further and further to a point of total servitude by debt and taxes.

Our founders went to extraordinary lengths and bore enormous personal risk in order to secure our freedom. It is a painful irony they thus set the stage for us to eradicate the physical slavery that was imposed upon a small portion of the population only to have it replaced with debt slavery imposed upon the entire population.

We are paying a monstrous price to maintain these destructive models of taxation and our fiat monetary system. The highest price, however, has been to our system of law, justice, and governance, which have been corrupted in order to expand and perpetuate these institutions. We the people, who have a right to self-governance and who aspire to be self-reliant property owners, are asking simply that our government obey the law, the same law we must all abide—the common law and the law of the constitution. The essence of this request is to tell of our government simply this: "Stop stealing our property and just let us live our lives in peace."

> The right to life is the source of all rights—and the right to property is their only implementation. Without property rights, no other rights are possible. Since man has to sustain his life by his own effort, the man who has no right to the product of his effort has no means to sustain his life. The man who produces while others dispose of his product, is a slave.
>
> —Ayn Rand

CHAPTER 4

The Monetary System
and Socioeconomics

A penny saved, is a penny earned.

—Benjamin Franklin

This statement was true during Mr. Franklin's time, but if he were alive today, he would rephrase it as, "A penny saved is a penny eventually lost." This is due to the fact that under our current fiat monetary system, your savings continually loses purchasing power until it eventually reaches its intrinsic value of zero. It is part of the design.

Understanding money and its essential role in civilization is probably the most important issue about which our public schools refuse to teach us. Money is a civil society's most important tool of communication. Its purpose is to enable individuals to appraise and then communicate the economic value of any given alternative in order to conduct voluntary transactions on a basis of fairness and honesty. These transactions include not only trade and purchasing but also working for compensation and saving and investing for the future. For a transaction to be honest, the money representing the value of that transaction must be honest. That is why sound money is often referred to as honest money, and therefore, it is the basis of capitalism and the free-market system.

Free-market capitalism is defined as an economic system in which trade, industry, and the means of production are controlled by private owners with the goal of earning profits in a free-market economy. Capitalism's main characteristic is that it functions in competitive markets, where private parties to any transaction are free to agree on the prices at which assets, goods, and services are exchanged on a voluntary basis and on terms of each party's choosing. For such a system to function with efficiency and integrity, the money used for such transactions must accurately reflect equivalent value to both parties. Therefore, only sound money is compatible with the free-enterprise system, as its medium of exchange.

Time Is Money

Everything we do in life constitutes an economic transaction. Even if a particular activity does not involve a transfer of money, it is still an economic matter, for the time taken to do anything—or time spent doing nothing—has an opportunity cost. In other words, time spent doing something unproductive is time that could otherwise be spent on something that creates value. The value creation that is forsaken represents the opportunity cost of having instead done something unproductive or having done nothing at all. Therefore, it could be argued that everything we do (and even what we don't do) represents either the creation or exchange of value—value which is measured in terms of our accepted monetary unit. This is also what is meant by the mantras "time is money" and "everything has a price." From this also stems the concept of financial risk. Anytime you make an investment for the prospect of a future gain, you are risking the potential loss of that investment. This is true whether your investment is in the form of money or time.

Death and Taxes

Consider this concept from a more personal perspective. According to the Bureau of Labor Statistics, the median per-capita income in the United States in 2013 was about $14.00 per hour. That is $112.00 per eight-hour day. Now imagine that you are at the end of your life. You are lying on a cold slab looking up at your loved ones who have come to see you off to the afterlife, if there is such a thing. You know that these are your last moments on earth. Never again will you see your children, be able to play with your grandchildren, or share the love of your family. Never again will you enjoy the warmth of a beautiful sunset. You have at most a few hours left before the eternal sleep. Once you cross that threshold, you will never be able to come back. Before tomorrow your only mortal life, the most precious gift you will have ever received will be gone—forever.

How much would you pay to have one more day? What is one day of your finite life worth? And yet observe how many of us are willing to sell an entire day of our lives to our employer for $112.00—before tax.

Money is the prime motive of human labor. If you want food, clothing, and shelter, you must have money. Unless you are fortunate enough to be part of the tiny minority that has inherited more money than you could spend in your lifetime, you must work for, beg for, borrow, or steal it. Only one of the aforementioned provides for self-reliance. Stealing is unethical and a crime. Begging depends upon the charity of others. Borrowing makes you beholden to the lender. Laboring—*earning* your money—is the one and only means of obtaining wealth that allows you to become self-reliant and therefore free. Therefore, those who wish to control society must ensure that the people have no choice but to either beg for or borrow money, whether they want to or not. A fiat monetary system provides this feature since it is created as debt—from nothing. Since all fiat money is debt—when you are paid for your labor you are forced to accept money that is actually owed to someone else. It is through this system that rulers are able to make self-reliance unachievable. Their purpose is to expand social and economic dependency in order to ensure their status and permanence as rulers. Thus, the archenemy of any ruling class is a sound monetary system.

Since the value of every transaction and every asset is based upon the monetary system under which the economy functions, the one who controls the monetary system controls the value of everything. This includes the value of our time and therefore our labor.

Section 8, clause 5 of the US Constitution states, "The Congress shall have the power to coin Money, regulate the Value thereof, and of foreign Coin, and fix the Standard of Weights and Measures." This clause guaranteed the United States a system of sound money. This means that money must be created only as coin—a precious metal commodity—as opposed to fiat (paper notes), and that its unit of value should be fixed in terms of a standard of weight of that precious metal.

Gold and silver cannot be created out of thin air. Under a sound money system based on gold or silver, the overall supply of money remains stable, and therefore, prices are stable over time. Prices of all goods and services as well as the value of all real assets are then based solely on the market forces of supply and demand. These market forces result from the daily actions of the whole of the people. Under such a system there is no inflation. If prices rise, it is solely due to the demand for something increasing relative to its supply. When that occurs, suppliers increase production to meet the increasing demand, and prices then re-stabilize on that basis. Suppliers do so out of self-interest just as those who demand more of their products also act in their self-interest. It is an economy in symbiotic, albeit dynamic equilibrium. It is perfectly natural.

Fiat money is unnatural. Its value is not defined in terms of any weight or measure of anything. We have already seen how fiat money is used as the instrument of inflation and how central bankers are able to create market-specific inflations—market bubbles. We also demonstrated how they deliberately destabilize the economy by deciding into which markets to loan the most money (expanding credit) and at which interest rates—thus allowing them to distort supply and demand differentially across markets. The last and more important piece of this insidious puzzle, however, is that central bankers conduct their monetary manipulations in secret. Therefore, they are in a position to pick and choose which of their corporate and political cronies will benefit from having foregone knowledge of their actions, while the general public is kept in the dark.

This is why the cost of virtually everything that we in the middle class depend on for our daily lives is increasing at a disproportionately faster rate than our individual incomes. It is also one of the reasons that average middle-class citizens continually get poorer and poorer, while certain privileged individuals get richer and richer regardless of how the overall economy is doing. Like the plight of the greyhounds, the race has been rigged, coercing us to incessantly chase a fake, uncatchable rabbit solely for the profit of our owners.

Inflation Is Not a Naturally Occurring Phenomenon

The Oxford English Dictionary defines inflation as follows:

- An increase in the amount of currency in circulation, resulting in a relatively sharp and sudden fall in its value, with a consequent rise in prices due to the currency's reduced purchasing power. It is caused by an increase in the volume of paper [fiat] money issued.

- A persistent increase in the level of consumer prices resulting from a persistent decline in the purchasing power of money, caused by an increase in the amount of available currency and/or credit beyond the proportion of available goods and services.

These conditions indicate that inflation is not defined as the increase in prices but as the increase in the supply of money causing its reduced purchasing power. When your money has been devalued, you need more of it to purchase the same things as before giving the appearance of higher prices (in spite of the intrinsic value of those things remaining unchanged). Inflation is the cause while rising prices are the effect and not the other way around. When all money is issued as debt, this then also holds true for an increase in the amount of available credit (such as mortgages). Therefore, printing money is nothing more than a euphemism for expanding credit (debt). The many other euphemisms used by the Federal Reserve and banking industry to describe this include: quantitative easing (QE); active policy responses; accommodative monetary policy; adding liquidity; adding to bank reserves; asset swap; creating excess reserves; currency intervention; deficit accommodation; easing credit; debasing the currency; expansionary monetary policy; expanding The Fed's balance sheet; Fed purchasing debt; securities purchase program; funding the deficit; helicopter drop; liquidity enhancement; monetizing debt—all of these are bankers' code names for exactly the same thing—creating money from nothing.

The reader should note that the word credit is used by the banking industry in place of the word debt. This is because when you take on a debt, the bank has issued you credit. Bankers use the words credit and debt interchangeably because the choice of words *expanding credit* sounds much kinder than the words *expanding debt*, although they mean exactly the same thing.

In summary, the most important aspect of this to remember is that inflation or expansion of the money supply is the cause, while the rising prices are the effect, and not the other way around.

Money for Nothin'—Fractional Reserve Banking

I should point out that when I refer to money printing or paper money, I use these terms loosely. Paper money in this context means all fiat money. Given today's technology only about 7 percent of all US currency in existence is physical paper. The rest resides only as digital ones and zeroes on various financial computer databases around the world. In other words, whenever the Federal Reserve creates money, they simply type a number followed by a dozen zeroes into a computer and *voila!* We have another trillion of new *liquidity*, and the economy has once again been *stimulated*. Commercial banks also create money from thin air when they engage in fractional reserve lending. This is a principle whereby banks are only required to retain a fraction of their total depositors' funds on hand while they are permitted to loan out the rest at interest. In fact, the lion's share of the total money supply is created in this way.

How Fractional Reserve Lending Creates Money Out of Thin Air

Most of the total money supply (in US dollars) is created by commercial banks. Commercial banks are required to keep a certain amount of depositors' cash in their vaults at any given time. This is called the reserve requirement. In the United States the reserve requirement is 10 percent. This means that if the bank has one million dollars in deposits, it can loan out $900 thousand of that amount at interest, even though it belongs to the depositors. The new money creation process takes place from this point forward. When the eventual borrowers of that $900 thousand then deposit that money into their own bank, their receiving bank considers that as part of its reserve and can then re-loan all but 10 percent of that amount—another $810 thousand. The bank that in turn receives this $810 thousand then adds this money to its reserve and can again loan out 90 percent of that—another $729 thousand— and so on and so forth. The banking industry calls this the money-multiplier effect. This is a misnomer, however, since it is in truth a debt-multiplier. In effect, this same $729 thousand is owed to more than three different depositors. The last dollar of the original million is owed to 132 different depositors. Therefore, banks collectively earn interest on the same money loaned out to multiple borrowers. When all is said and done, this initial one-million-dollar deposit yields a total of nine million dollars in new virtual money, every penny of which is debt, and all of which is earning interest for the banks.

Banks are allowed to create virtual money in this way because every borrower who signs a loan application pledges their future labor and earnings as the means to pay it back (while also pledging assets as collateral to be seized in the event of nonpayment). In other words, your signature on a loan agreement authorizes the bank to create the money you are borrowing out of thin air. In effect, that newly created money is infused with new purchasing power by virtue of the future labor that the borrower has promised to exchange for it upon repayment of the debt.

We the People Are Complicit in Our Own Fleecing

Although it is commercial banks that create most of the money supply through fractional reserve lending (expanding credit), there are always two parties involved in a loan agreement—the lender and the borrower. Monetary expansion is created by the people themselves, people who either refuse to live within their means or have no choice but to use debt just to survive. Most of the government's monetary and tax policies are designed to impose this latter condition upon the people. The more debt you use to fund your lifestyle, the more you contribute to monetary expansion and the further you devalue every single US dollar in existence. Every time you use debt to finance a purchase, you increase the money supply, create inflation and devalue your own savings. With every dollar you borrow you further impoverish yourself, your neighbors, and your children. As the basic standard of living in this country becomes less and less affordable because of the resultant inflation, more people are driven more deeply into debt just to survive. The system has entered a death spiral toward self-destruction. This is one of the reasons that the rate at which the number of people who are descending from the middle class into the ranks of poverty is increasing.

During the run up to the housing collapse—banks offered home equity loans of up to 125% of the *value* of the home. This is a called a 125-LTV (loan-to-value) mortgage or a "no-equity home loan." These mortgage products continue to be offered in spite of what happened during the housing bubble, and they allow borrowers to deliberately put their homes underwater in debt. Once the housing bubble burst, many of the same borrowers who knowingly took on these absurd levels of debt were then complaining that they should be bailed out by the government.

Unless you pay cash for your house—in full—it is not your house. Furthermore, your neighbors and other taxpayers don't owe you a bailout if you have knowingly buried yourself under a mountain of debt you couldn't afford in the first place.

The Infinite Bubble

Credit card debt is also created through fractional reserve lending. Every time you swipe your credit card, whether it is to fill your gas tank, buy groceries, or take a vacation with your family, you have created new virtual money that did not exist before. The banking industry encourages people to use revolving credit to fuel their consumerism because the average interest rates they can charge for this is more than 20 percent annually. This does not even include the transaction fees levied against the merchant, which can be as much as 4 percent of the amount charged. While banks are paying on average about 0.5 percent interest on depositors' savings, those same banks are earning more than 20 percent annually on credit card debt. This represents a more than 4,000 percent rate of return for the bank by lending money that doesn't actually exist until you swipe the card.

With every credit card transaction, you expand the money supply, devaluing your real-money assets, your savings, and your retirement. Therefore, with every credit card swipe, you enrich the bank and impoverish yourself and your neighbors. This is one of the reasons that the banking industry is trying to drive the financial system away from using cash for most transactions. They instead want people to use credit cards for just about everything. When consumers use cash, the bank doesn't get *a piece of the action*. For this reason the banking industry and the government are intent on moving us toward a cashless society, based entirely on digital fiat money.

Finally the most important aspect of this is that all fractional reserve institutions are simply bankruptcies waiting to happen. It takes only a relatively small number of depositors all withdrawing their money at the same time to put any bank out of business. Such an event is what is known as a run on the banks.

The Puppet Masters

Recall the graph presented in chapter 1, which compared the inflation in median home prices to the median per-capita income. This demonstrated clearly that the ratio of the median price of a home relative to per-capita income has increased more than sixfold between 1977 and today. This condition has been deliberately created by the money manipulators in the Federal Reserve system by differentially targeting the housing market versus the labor market with different levels of liquidity and different interest rates on the debt offered in each market category. At the same time the federal government distorts individual income further through taxes.

It is the Fed's board of governors and open market committee who determine how much capital to deploy, the interbank interest rates, and what the reserve requirements for the member banks shall be. Therefore, the rate of monetary expansion and thus the rate of inflation is under the direct control of the Federal Reserve. While inflation decimates the purchasing power of your money, you are taxed on your earnings and property. This ensures that you are unable to earn enough to keep up with the rising cost of living without using increasing levels of debt. The system is intended to drive you further and further into debt and keep you there. This enriches both the banking aristocracy and the political class with the fruits of your labor. This is the essence of *chasing the rabbit*—a prize that has been deliberately made uncatchable.

In a free market economy based on sound money, the forces of supply and demand are a consequence of the actions of the whole of the people. In contrast, in a centrally controlled economy based on fiat money, the forces of inflation are a consequence of the actions of a few very powerful men and women—the people who run the Federal Reserve system. They use inflation to pervert the natural forces of supply and demand in order to achieve certain ends that are known only to them. In other words, they attempt to centrally plan our entire economy through the authority they have been granted to create and issue our money (all of which is debt) and to manipulate its purchasing power.

Central Planning's Fatal Flaw

In 1920, the economist Ludwig von Mises demonstrated that since a socialist economy destroys price information through government intervention, the innumerable participants in the economy are unable to make a rational calculation about value or about profit and loss.[61] Any economic activity that operates at a loss cannot be sustainable. Furthermore, Nobel Prize-winning economist Friedrich A. Hayek demonstrated that a national economy has such an immense number of dynamic economic relationships that no single committee or bureaucracy, no matter how intellectually gifted or well-staffed could ever know enough to direct prices or production levels. He referred to this as socialism's fatal flaw.[62]

---

[61] Mises, Ludwig Von. Economic Calculation in the Soviet Commonwealth. 1920.

[62] Hayek, F.A. The Fatal Conceit, The Errors of Socialism. University of Chicago Press. 1991.

No central planner can possibly possess enough knowledge about local changes in the economy and localized supply and demand as experienced by the entire US population going about their daily lives. It is the billions of daily choices made from moment to moment by the more than 320 million American citizens that should determine the real value and the price of everything. This is why a free market is the most efficient and honest system. Money and investment flows through transactions made by the whole of the people based upon each and every individual's unique knowledge about their particular part of the macroeconomic landscape. A small boardroom of central bankers sitting in Washington could never have the collective knowledge about market dynamics driven by 320 million or more people. However, central economic planning via a central bank has been the principal objective of those seeking to rule society for centuries. It is one of the foundations of Marxist-Socialist dogma.

Fiat Money—The Cornerstone of Socialism

Among those who are devoted to socialism many are well-intentioned idealists believing that it has the possibility to improve society as a whole and to provide for the poor. They believe this only because they have been misinformed by more than a century of relentless propaganda. They have been spoon-fed that propaganda by those who are devoted to socialism for a different reason. These are the people who recognize socialism's ability to centralize power in the hands of a few with the consent of the masses. Their goal is to be among those few who gain that power over other men so that they can abuse it. These people have long understood that having authority over the creation of a nation's fiat money system is the main catalyst to acquiring absolute power over society. It gives the issuer control over all property, natural resources, and especially labor. Consider the alarming consequences of this fact when the idea of a single global currency is raised during public discourse.

In 1919, Austrian Otto Bauer, a lawyer, social democrat, and "father of Euro-communism" wrote, "If all banks are amalgamated into a single central bank, then its administrative board becomes the supreme economic authority, the chief administrative organ of the whole economy."

He went on to say, "Only by nationalization [centralization] of the banks and monetary powers does *society* obtain the power to regulate its labor according to a plan, and to distribute its resources rationally among the various branches of production, so as to adapt them to the nation's needs."

In his book *Der Weg Zum Sozialismus* (The Way to Socialism), Bauer's premise, nationalization of the banks, is to centralize the fiat money-creation powers under the sole control of a central bank.

Central banking is the essence of central economic planning with the intent to control the means of production through financial manipulation. This idea's practical failure is the inability for central planners to possess the collective knowledge of

93

hundreds of millions of people who make market decisions every waking hour of every day. This is why central planning does not work for the benefit of the citizenry and never will.

It can, however, be employed to work for the benefit of a corrupt few who have been granted the control authority.

Now consider for a moment the following hypothetical: A corrupt, power-mongering sociopath bent on dominating society reads Otto Bauer's previous passage. Such a person would see the following:

"Only by centralizing the banks and the monetary powers under *my* control can *I* obtain the power to regulate labor, according to a plan, and then distribute society's resources to *myself, my family, my political supporters, and to my own corporate institutions*, so as to adapt them to *my own needs.*"

If one seriously considers the ramifications of this hypothetical statement, it sheds an ominous light on the following well-known quotation made by Mayer Amschel Bauer Rothschild,

"Give me the power to issue and control a nation's money, and I care not who makes its laws."

Rothschild understood that a fiat monetary system controlled by a few privileged men (preferably he and his family) would enable the issuer to "make the nation's laws." In other words, it would give him control of the government as well as the economy, effectively placing him above the law. Whoever controls the issuance of a nation's fiat money system controls the government, the economy, and therefore the people.

Karl Marx's idea was that the government would control the central bank. Rothschild's idea was that the central bank would control the government. The former yields a system of state socialism (Communism). The latter yields a model of corporate socialism (Fascism). MIT professor Noam Chomsky calls this 'state capitalism,' but it is actually fascism (the merger of state and corporate financial power). Both models are the antithesis of the concept of self-governance as espoused in the US Constitution. Both models depend upon a central bank-controlled fiat monetary system, a system that is explicitly prohibited by the US Constitution.

Therefore, the clear distinction between a sound currency and a fiat currency represents the difference between a nation of free individuals with the possibility of self-governance—and one that is ruled by a totalitarian oligarchy that absolutely prohibits self-governance and has few or no property rights. Which would you prefer to live under?

The United States was founded as the former. Since 1913, we have devolved into the latter.

From an economic perspective there is no difference between Socialism and Communism. Both terms denote central control of the means of production. Planning consists in the plans of the government being substituted for the plans of individual citizens. The result is that entrepreneurs and businessmen will be deprived of the discretion to employ their capital in accordance with their own vision. They must instead comply unconditionally with the central planners' goals, even though those goals are kept secret. In America it is by taxation and our debt-based fiat system of capital through which control of the means of production has been transferred from entrepreneurs and businessmen to the banking corporatocracy and their cronies in government.[63]

From the ethical perspective socialism is morally bankrupt. Its premise is that we can each live at the expense of others in spite of the fact that this violates both natural law and the biblical commandments that forbid coveting and theft. Indeed, socialism in practice depends upon the use of force applied by one group of people over others. It is the essence of human parasitism. The use of force by one man against another except in self-defense is unjust and immoral. Nevertheless, this reality has never stopped the statists from attempting to centralize their power over the economy.

As a side note, I should point out that the term capitalism is often misused to describe the opposite of the free-enterprise system. This creates a great deal of confusion for many people. For example, the term *state capitalism* is actually used to describe the opposite of free-market capitalism. *State* capitalism describes a system in which the state undertakes commercial economic activity and where the means of production are dominated by state-owned or controlled enterprises, or corporatized government agencies that are highly regulated. Therefore, state capitalism is actually fascism. It would be more accurate to refer to it as corporate socialism than as state capitalism. Those who control such a system are referred to throughout this book as corporatists, or the corporatocracy.

When I use the word capitalism throughout this text, I am referring to free-market capitalism and not its opposite—state capitalism. The distinctions are stark. Free-market capitalism is about individual liberty and respect for individual property rights. Its basis is a system of sound money. State capitalism, on the other hand, is corporate socialism. It is founded in having no or at most very limited property rights for individuals so that the means of production (particularly labor) can be centrally controlled by state or huge corporate interests. Its basis is a system of fiat money. The two are complete opposites. Their respective monetary systems are incompatible with one another.

---

[63] Mises, Ludwig Von. The Anti-Capitalistic Mentality, Ludwig Von Mises Institute.

A sound monetary system requires that money has a fixed and defined value based on a precious metal commodity such as gold or silver. For more gold or silver to come into existence, industrious men must mine and refine it, creating value through their labor and earning their living in the process. This is purely a consequence of supply and demand. Only nature can create that kind of money, and it will only come into existence in response to there being enough demand to justify the investment required to mine and process it. Therefore, only sound money is compatible with a nation founded in self-governance, functioning with the efficiency of a free market under the rule of natural law—where only supply and demand determine value.

Instead of the sound currency system that was guaranteed to us in the US Constitution, today we have a monetary system that is controlled by a cartel of private financial institutions who own the Federal Reserve. The US government has granted that cartel a monopoly on the creation and issuance of Federal Reserve notes—fiat money in the form of debt that is created from nothing.

How to Establish a Corrupt, Self-Serving, Totalitarian Oligarchy in One Easy Lesson

In order to convert a free and prosperous nation that is self-governed by the rule of natural law into a tyranny ruled by a few corrupt men, one must first replace its sound monetary system with a fiat monetary system. Once those men have been empowered with a monopoly on the creation of that nation's money, they can control the value of all labor and the disposition of all property. Otto Bauer said exactly that with his statement, "By nationalizing [centralizing] the banks and the monetary powers under my control, I can obtain the power to regulate labor."

Karl Marx understood this as well and described the central banking model on which our Federal Reserve system is based in his ten planks of Communism. It is the basic monetary system required for a nation to destroy capitalism and replace it with socialist central governance. The current American fiat monetary system is a fundamentally Marxist construct and is entirely incompatible with free-market capitalism. Its central purpose is to enable the surreptitious control of your labor and your property, through perpetual debt expansion.

The majority of the middle class is completely oblivious to these facts. Most Americans get up every morning and go to work to earn a paycheck solely so they can pay most of their earnings to mortgage lenders and tax collectors. Most are so indebted that they are willing to spend more than half of their waking hours for 40 or 50 years performing menial tasks in a fluorescent lit cubicle—even if they hate their jobs. They don't even object to their employer withholding (confiscating) between a third and half of their *compensation* on behalf of the government. Possibly the only employer in America who ever attempted to advocate for his employees by objecting to this corrupt system was Robert Kahre (see chapter 2). He is now serving 18 years in federal prison for his trouble.

The need for food, shelter, and clothing, as well as for social validation and even status within our society, is a very powerful motivator. The accumulation of money is therefore an accumulation of social and psychological power. As such, one who controls the creation of money controls the source of this power.

The Debt Ceiling—To Infinity and Beyond

Since our money is created from nothing and loaned out as debt, the Federal Reserve can theoretically create an infinite amount of money, and therefore nearly infinite demand for goods and services. The earth and all of her natural resources, however, are finite, so goods and services are limited in supply by the laws of nature. Infinite demand for limited supply will yield infinitely high prices (hyperinflation). This is not only theoretical. It has been demonstrated in practice. It is because of this principle that the German hyperinflation of the early 1920s produced postage stamps denominated in tens of billions of German marks. The most recent example of hyperinflation occurred in Zimbabwe from 2007 through 2010, which produced banknotes in denominations of one hundred trillion Zimbabwe dollars. At the height of their hyperinflation it required a hundred-billion-Zimbabwe-dollar banknote to purchase just three chicken eggs.

Fiat money printing has been especially capacious in the last hundred years. This has led to the total destruction of most currencies, including the US dollar. Money printing gives the people the illusion of economic growth and wealth creation since it permits people, institutions, and governments to live beyond their means. However, this constitutes nothing more than unsustainable overconsumption fueled by borrowing. People must come to understand that governments act to deliberately destroy the value of their currency. They must do this in order to minimize the effects of the debt obligations they incur from their irresponsible deficit spending.

There is one currency governments cannot print. Gold has been real money for almost five thousand years, and it is the only currency that has survived throughout history. Gold has a virtually infinite shelf life. It cannot be created from nothing, and no government controls it. Therefore, gold will over time always reveal governments' fraudulent actions in creating money out of thin air. This was one of the principal reasons that in 1933, Franklin D. Roosevelt used his executive order power to confiscate all gold and prohibit its use as money. Observe what we are experiencing currently. Gold is fluctuating, but it is not going down precipitously. Instead gold is doing what it has done for thousands of years—maintaining its purchasing power. Acute declines in the gold price can be traced to manipulation through short-selling of *paper gold*, gold-backed bonds, or gold mining stocks. But physical gold itself has remained the most stable store of intrinsic value for five millennia. Currently no country on earth uses a gold standard as the basis of its monetary system, although most hold substantial gold reserves in their treasuries.

The Global Currency War

Before the founding of the Federal Reserve in 1913, the US monetary system was based on gold and silver coin, and the issue of our sound money was controlled by Congress, and therefore, by *we the people*. Before 1910, most of the countries of Europe had also been on the gold standard for several generations. But just before the outbreak of World War I, Germany and most of the rest of Europe abandoned the gold standard and adopted a model that was based on paper fiat currency. It's important to understand that in 1913, although the United States had passed the Federal Reserve Act, the country remained on the gold standard for another twenty years.

In 1913, the exchange rate between the US dollar and the German mark was $1 USD (US dollar) to 4 DM (Deutsche Mark). Starting around 1920, Germany rapidly expanded their money supply in an effort to try to deal with the high cost of reparations of World War I. The terms of the Versailles Treaty had forced Germany to pay huge reparations for the cost incurred by the countries that were victorious. The treaty required that Germany repay this debt in gold bullion. This impoverished Germany and forced the country to fund its deficits internally by issuing bonds and expanding credit.

The only way for the German government to deal with its onerous debt was to make it irrelevant in proportion to the value of its currency. The subsequent unrestrained expansion of their money supply led to hyperinflation and a complete devaluation of German money. Economists call this "inflating their way out of debt."

Countries devalue their fiat currencies for two main reasons—to diminish their debt burden and to make their goods cheaper in terms of foreign currencies, thereby stimulating exports in order to bring foreign money into the country. Those foreign countries in turn must begin to devalue their own currencies (by printing more) in order to balance the resultant trade deficits. Therefore, fiat money generates competitive devaluations or "currency wars" between nations.

By 1923 at the height of the German hyperinflation, the exchange rate had gone from $1 USD for 4 DM three years earlier to $1 USD for 50,000 DM. Within less than three years of unrestrained *quantitative easing*, Germany had destroyed the value of its currency with a loss of 99.999 percent of the Deutsche Mark's purchasing power. In those days, before the advent of computers and digital electronics, all new money had to be printed as physical paper. The sheer volume of paper Deutsch Marks was staggering. Money was so worthless that it was more cost-effective to burn these notes for home heating than to use it to purchase firewood.

With the founding of the Federal Reserve in 1913, America began the incremental conversion of its monetary system from coin to fiat. Since then, we have taken a hundred years to accomplish what it took Germany only three years. Between 1913 and 2013, the dollar has lost more than 98 percent of its purchasing power.

A Word about Deflation

Since inflation results from of an expansion of the money supply, deflation then is the result of the opposite—a contraction of the money supply. Occasionally one hears about the Fed's fear of deflation, claiming that it would be far more disastrous to the US economy than simply continuing to inflate. In light of such assertions, the reader must understand that the government and the Federal Reserve benefit from inflation. They do not benefit from deflation.

The nation's *experts* on money and finance—generally central bankers and academics—almost universally condemn deflation as an evil specter that should be feared. They then seek to convince the public that the only means to avert a deflationary death-spiral which they claim will wipe out the entire economy—is to further stimulate the economy with more inflation—money printing. However, this is a distortion of the truth. And while most economists claim that inflation is beneficial if used to combat deflation, they fail to compare the long term consequences of either condition. Practically no one ever asks the basic question: "What is actually wrong with deflating the money supply in terms of economics?"

Economist Murray Rothbard conducted a critical analysis which demonstrated that deflation can benefit society by "accelerating the readjustment of the structure of production after a financial crisis." Other than this, and the pamphlet *Deflation and Liberty*, by Jörg Guido Hülsmann, few economists have produced any objective analysis of the impact deflation has on market processes or the resultant social and political consequences. This is because most noted economists work for the banking industry—the main beneficiary of our inflationary fiat model. Those who are not bankers are entrenched in academia and other politically funded think-tanks that are in the pocket of the ruling class. As such, they relentlessly incriminate deflation as a scapegoat in order to perpetuate the Federal Reserve's pro-inflation agenda.

This state of affairs raises the following two questions (the first a rhetorical one): If inflation is so good and deflation so evil, why have we repeatedly experienced deeply damaging financial crises for several generations while functioning under a purely inflationary monetary system? And the more obvious question: Can one actually improve or worsen the state of an economy by increasing (inflating) or decreasing (deflating) the quantity of money?

Since deflation consists in a contraction of the money supply, it is accompanied by an increase in money's purchasing power. Therefore, deflation makes savings and earnings more valuable. The result is a decline in prices in response to the increased purchasing power of your money. Your savings will purchase more goods and services than before, as its purchasing power goes up. Your salary, as long as it remains unchanged, will also purchase more than before. These conditions are actually good for the average citizen and especially for diligent savers who live within their means. It benefits those on a fixed income like retirees on social security, pensioners, students, and people with no debt. Deflation would be damaging however to the political class (the Federal Reserve and our government) and those who use debt to finance their purchases and acquisitions.

Furthermore, according to Adam Smith and Étienne de Condillac,[64] money is neither a consumers' good nor a producers' good. Therefore, its quantity is irrelevant for the overall wealth of a nation.[65] In other words, neither inflation nor deflation has any impact whatsoever on the real overall wealth of a nation.

The alleged short-term benefits of inflation regarding employment and economic growth are illusory. Inflationary stimulus mainly generates more consumption as opposed to more real investment. Furthermore, an increasing GDP that results from

---

[64] Étienne Bonnot de Condillac (French: [bɔno də kɔ̃dijak]; 30 September 1714[2] – 3 August 1780) was a French philosopher and epistemologist. Condillac is important both as a psychologist and as having established systematically in France the principles of John Locke.

[65] Hume, David. "On Money." Essays (Indianapolis: Liberty Fund, 1752, 1985), p 288. Smith, Adam. Wealth of Nations. New York, Random House. 1776.

rising prices is not a valid measure of increasing economic value. A dozen eggs which used to cost one dollar but doubles in price due to inflation is still just a dozen eggs. Its intrinsic value does not change. A pickup truck that once cost $20 thousand and now costs $40 thousand due to inflation does not provide twice the value to its owner in terms of utility. Whatever benefits that might result from inflationary expansion of the money supply, are temporary and are enjoyed only by certain members of society. Those benefits result from the redistribution of resources derived from the other members of society.

Imagine for a moment that it would become legally permissible for you and every other American with your same birthdate, to take every one dollar bill in your wallet, and simply use an ink pen to add two zeroes to the bill. This would transform each of your one dollar bills into a one hundred dollar bill and constitute an expansion of the overall money supply—inflation. With this instant access to "new money," you and all of those people who share your birthdate would be the first to spend that money into the economy. You would uniquely benefit because market prices would only adjust to that newly added money after it has entered circulation. As soon as it enters circulation, the purchasing power of the existing money supply is diluted and everyone who receives those new dollars will be able to purchase less with them than you did.

The last person to receive those dollars will not only have money with less purchasing power than the one who first created that new money, but their income and any existing savings they had before you added your zeroes will have been diluted in purchasing power as well. Your gain will become their loss. Now imagine that instead of spending the new money which you created, you loan it to another person, at interest, who then spends it into the economy. Your economic gain is even greater since you're earning interest on money you created from nothing, and you *spent* it into the economy first. The benefit to the borrower is diminished since he or she must now pay you interest on that newly created money. Every subsequent borrower of that money then has to pay more for less purchasing power.

Now imagine the government grants you the exclusive power to do this as much as you wish, but only under the condition that you will also create and loan the government as much as it wishes to borrow and spend—the interest for which will be paid to you by the citizenry through taxes confiscated from them under threat of seizure of their *private* property.

Congratulations, you are now the Federal Reserve Central Bank.

There is no valid reason why inflationary expansion of the money supply should create more instead of less real overall growth. While those institutions that create the new money are benefited (primarily banking institutions and lenders), all others down the financial food chain are harmed because their money is left with reduced purchasing power than it would otherwise have had. Similarly, there is no reason that inflation should decrease rather than increase unemployment.

In truth, any quantity of money in a society provides all of the services that a medium of exchange can provide both in the long-term as well as in the short-term. Deflation, like inflation, is just another monetary phenomenon and as such, it simply affects the distribution of wealth among the individuals and various classes of society. But neither inflation nor deflation has any effect on the aggregate wealth of society in terms of real assets.[66]

Although deflation is demonstrated in falling prices it does not necessarily have a negative impact on businesses' profits. Profit does not depend upon the price at which we sell something. It depends upon the difference between the price of what we sell, and our cost to produce or buy whatever we sell. In deflation, prices decline overall so profitable production continues just as before. Prices may go down, but so do costs of production—in direct proportion.

If Inflation is "A Hidden Tax," Deflation is "A Visible Dividend."

The only fundamental change that deflation brings about is that it modifies the structure of property ownership. Firms and individuals who have lived beyond their means—financed their expenditures with debt—go bankrupt because their falling level of income cannot support the debt they incurred before the deflation. Conversely, firms and individuals who have lived within their means and financed their expenditures only from savings and earnings can purchase and invest more favorably with money that has increased purchasing power. In effect, the ownership of companies, homes, and other assets will shift to a different group of people—those who espouse living within one's means, avoiding debt, and who spend no more than they earn. Those who borrow and spend recklessly (the buy now and pay later crowd) will lose their property (but in truth debtors never really *own* their property in the first place—the lender does). In principle, ownership of assets shifts from those with the power to create debt out of thin air to those who only acquire assets using money they have actually earned in the course of real productive effort.

The bottom line of deflation is that it reveals the redistribution of wealth that goes along with changes in the quantity of money. It is transparent, and results in visible misery for some (debtors) along with the visible benefit of others (savers). In contrast, inflation creates anonymous winners at the expense of anonymous losers.[67] Inflation and deflation are both zero-sum games. But inflation is a deceitful fraud. It is the vehicle through which a society's false elites can surreptitiously exploit an entire population. Deflation is not inherently bad for society as a whole but it is bad for

66 Hülsmann, Jörg Guido. *Deflation and Liberty*. 2008. Ludwig Von Mises Institute.
67 Hülsmann, Jörg Guido. Deflation and Liberty. 2008. Ludwig Von Mises Institute.

a ruling class that has financed its expansion of power and influence through debt creation and money printing.

Why the Government and the Federal Reserve Truly Fear Deflation

Deflation creates as many winners as it does losers. It punishes the government's corporate cronies who thrived on their intimate connections to those who control the creation of fiat money. It also deprives the political class of the ability to relentlessly deficit spend the country into bankruptcy in order to fund entitlements for themselves and for the misinformed voters who keep them in office.

Deflation destroys those companies and institutions that exist as parasites at the expense of the rest of the economy, and which owe their debt-fueled existence solely to our inflationary fiat system. The political and ruling classes will never admit this, because they are at the heart of those parasitic institutions. For this reason, the media continually tries to convince the American public that deflation would devastate the economy. In truth, it would mainly hurt the ruling and political class's ability to continue robbing the citizenry of their property and income, while providing a windfall for those with a savings and little or no debt.

Deflation, like inflation, is nothing more than a monetary policy with redistributive effects. Therefore, it is erroneous to claim that a period of deflation following a period of inflation is somehow harmful from an economic perspective. Neither policy benefits the nation as a whole but simply confers benefits to certain groups at the expense of other groups. Therefore, it is only logical that the political class, bankers, the corporatocracy, and their wholly owned subsidiaries in the entertainment media will promote the policy that uniquely benefits them—inflation. They then relentlessly deride the policy that would benefit the rest of us—deflation.

What a direct comparison of the two reveals is that inflation constitutes an unjustifiable redistribution of income in favor of those who create the new money, while disadvantaging all those who receive (borrow) it afterward. In practice, this means that the producers of fiat money—the central banks and their partners in the financial sector—are the principal beneficiaries. They are milking the system and we are its cows. Inflationary fiat money is the mechanism through which these people enrich themselves at the expense of the citizenry. It is a system that enables the wealthy and powerful to become far wealthier and far more powerful than if all of society had to depend exclusively on sound money, over which they would have no control and which they could not perpetually inflate at their own whim.

Sound money is neither inflationary nor deflationary. Its quantity is only increased or decreased in response to actual supply and demand generated by the market economy. This further demonstrates why sound money is the only type of money that is compatible with the free enterprise system. It is why sound money is the only monetary system allowed by the US Constitution. Economist Hans Sennholz praised deflation as a means to abolish fiat money and restore sound money in its place.

In his pamphlet *Deflation and Liberty*, Jörg Guido Hülsmann eloquently characterizes the situation as follows:

> It would not be uncharitable to characterize inflation as a large-scale rip-off, in favor of the politically well-connected few, and to the detriment of the politically destitute masses. It always goes in hand with the concentration of political power in the hands of those who are privileged to own a banking license and of those who control the production of the monopoly paper money. It promotes endless debts, puts society at the mercy of "monetary authorities" such as central banks, and to that extent entails **the moral corruption of society**.

Hülsmann went on to say:

> We come to the conclusion that deflation is not a mere redistribution game that benefits some individuals and groups at the expense of other individuals and groups. Rather, deflation appears as a great harbinger of liberty. It stops inflation and destroys the institutions that produce inflation. It abolishes the advantage that inflation-based debt finance enjoys over savings-based equity finance. It therefore decentralizes financial decision-making and makes banks, firms, and individuals more prudent and self-reliant than they would have been under inflation. Most importantly, deflation eradicates the re-channeling of incomes that result from the monopoly privileges of central banks. It thus destroys the economic basis for the false elites and obliges them to become true elites rather quickly, or abdicate and make way for new entrepreneurs and other social leaders.

Deflation impedes the consolidation and expansion of power of the federal government, and in particular in the executive branch. It also obviates the growth of the welfare state. When deflation causes the purchasing power of money to increase, it benefits those on a fixed income and welfare expansion becomes unnecessary.

Deflation destroys the economic basis of the social engineers, spin doctors, and the brain washers.[68]

The principal reasons our government fears deflation is because it will benefit responsible citizens who have been frugal, lived within their means, and have diligently accumulated a savings, while it will end the debt-based gravy train for government bureaucrats and the Federal Reserve.

The government and the Keynesian economists whom they have in their pockets will never admit that deflationary adjustments can be good for society. This is because what would be good for us will be bad for them. Deflation discourages borrowing (while encouraging saving) and is therefore bad for bankers and politicians. It's also bad for those with onerous debt, for those debts must be repaid with money that is more valuable than that which had earlier been borrowed and subsequently spent. If you have no debt, deflation will present you with a windfall.

America's Debt Addiction

When deflation increases the purchasing power of the currency, it also increases the value of any debt denominated in that currency. The more in debt you are, the more you will suffer during deflation—so the more you will desire additional inflation. This provides the government and the banking aristocracy with the justification to perpetuate our inherently inflationary monetary system. It is designed to force you increasingly deeper into debt dependency until you reach the end of your life. It is not unlike a drug dealer addicting as many of his or her future customers as possible with cheap, readily available heroine, in order to establish a reliable and sustainable source of future income—in the form of debt slaves.

Our government has lived beyond its means at the expense of the citizenry for such an extended period of time that any period of deflation will subject the government to a much more deleterious debt burden, even without additional borrowing. Furthermore, the American people have been lured into personal debt expansion over the past few decades to such an extent that it has reached an unmanageable level. Data released by the Federal Reserve Bank of New York shows that as of February, 2014 overall consumer debt stood at $11.52 trillion. More unsettling is that this individual debt —including mortgages, auto loans, student loans and credit card debt—increased by 2.1%, or $241 billion in only the last quarter of 2013. This constitutes the highest rate of personal debt expansion since the third quarter of 2007, shortly before the U.S. spiraled into recession. This puts many Americans in a perilous financial situation. More than 31% of Americans now have more credit card debt than they have in savings. As such, almost one third of the US population is financially insolvent.

---

[68]   Cantor, Paul A. Hyperinflation and Hyperreality: Thomas Mann in the Light of Austrian Economics." *Review of Austrian Economics* 7, no. 1. 1994.

This is why we are witnessing a major decline in the standard of living for the middle class. Like the heroine dealer mentioned earlier, the Federal Reserve has been doling out *free fixes* of new money to our debt-addicted government and citizenry for so long, that we are now incapable of maintaining even a basic standard of living without using more debt. We now have little choice but to continue inflating, while further indebting future generations to fund current consumption. Like a chemical dependency, our addiction to debt has become systemic such that any attempt to escape it will be accompanied by a period of excruciatingly painful withdrawal.

In essence, the government and their partners at the Federal Reserve have been committing an act no less immoral, and no less criminal, than a common thug dealing heroine on the street corner to helpless diseased junkies. Their drug of choice is debt, and they're working hard to expand their customer base.

In spite of their rhetoric to the contrary, our government is working tirelessly to enact policies that will lower the standard of living for all Americans, increase unemployment, discourage saving, expand illegal immigration, and force more people into dependency and inescapable debt. Since deflation would actually enrich those frugal and responsible citizens who have lived within their means and those who have a savings, or those with a fixed retirement income—a period of deflation would literally turn the tables on the corrupt banking aristocracy and their cronies in the political class.

Ending the Illusion

During periods of deflation, politicians can no longer pretend to shepherd an illusory growing economy based on artificially stimulated consumption. The US government is the world's largest debtor by far. For them the fear of deflation is real. The only means our government has to deal with the enormous national debt is to continue to inflate.

Therefore, the political class will vehemently resist the restoration of a sound currency. They will perpetuate any lie or any obfuscation to convince the American people that restoring a sound monetary system will be bad for America when in fact it is the only long-term solution to our economic ills. The government would much rather keep the American middle class and poor struggling and impoverished under a mountain of perpetual and inescapable debt than to give up their money-printing scheme. This demonstrates that the current political class and their puppet masters in the global fiat banking aristocracy are nothing more than parasites on society—parasites looking to further disarm and weaken their host in order to ensure their permanence.

These facts reveal that the cancerous partnership between our government and the Federal Reserve system is the enemy of individual liberty—the enemy of every American citizen aspiring to achieve self-reliance, real home ownership, and economic security. These facts reveal that the only way to restore real property rights for individual citizens in America is to end the Federal Reserve system and restore sound money as the US Constitution mandates.

Karl Marx and the United Socialist States of America (USSA)

In the book he coauthored with Friedrich Engels, Karl Marx describes the ten steps necessary to destroy free-market capitalism and replace it with a system of omnipotent government so as to affect a Communist socialist state. Those ten steps are known as the ten planks of Communism. Number 5 on the list states, "Centralization of a credit-debt system in the hands of the state, by means of a central bank with State capital and an exclusive monopoly on the creation of credit [fiat money]."

The Federal Reserve is exactly that—a centrally controlled credit-debt system that was authorized by the federal government via the Federal Reserve Act of 1913, an act that was signed into law by then President Woodrow Wilson. All US banks are members of the Federal Reserve system. The Federal Reserve has an exclusive monopoly on the issue of fiat paper money (bills of credit) and therefore has the ability to expand the money supply (in the form of debt) at will. It is a fundamentally Marxist institution.

The only distinction between the system that Marx described in *The Communist Manifesto* and the Federal Reserve system is that Marx intended that the central bank be controlled by the government. In the case of the United States, the US government is controlled by the central bank. This is neither hyperbole nor conspiracy theory. Former Federal Reserve Chairman Alan Greenspan admitted to this in a 2007 interview on the PBS *News Hour* with Jim Lehrer. The transcript is presented later in this chapter.

A Brief History of the Federal Reserve

The Federal Reserve Act was the first law in American history to have been written by people who were not part of the elected legislature or any other branch of the federal government. The law itself, written by the very bankers whom it was intended to benefit, began construction in 1910 at a meeting on Jekyll Island, GA, at the Jekyll Island Club, a private estate co-owned by J.P. Morgan.

A few years prior in 1907, a run on a number of major financial institutions caused financial panic across America. That panic was the consequence of a number of articles that were planted in the most widely read newspapers of the day (which were owned by J. P. Morgan). Those articles falsely claimed that certain major banks and trusts (Morgan's competitors) were facing financial problems. The articles went on to encourage depositors in those banks to quickly withdraw their money before they might become insolvent. Although the newspaper stories were false, they launched a run on the banks. This deliberately engineered financial panic ultimately benefitted J. Pierpont Morgan handsomely.

"The Morgan interests took advantage to precipitate the panic [of 1907] guiding it shrewdly as it progressed."

—Frederik Allen, Life Magazine, April 25, 1949

Several wealthy financiers, including Jekyll Island Club members George F. Baker, president of the First National Bank, and James A. Stillman,[69] chairman of National City Bank, met with J. P. Morgan and began examining the assets of the distressed institutions that had been subject to these runs. They decided to offer loans to any of the banks that were solvent (effectively acquiring control of them), while they orchestrated the liquidation of the competitors to those banks. The secretary of the treasury George B. Cortelyou, anxious to divert the political blowback from the situation, offered the bankers use of government (taxpayer) funds to "help prevent an economic disaster," a disaster that they had intentionally created in the first place. This constituted the first of countless bailouts that American taxpayers would provide to bankers over the ensuing century. President Theodore Roosevelt, while the panic of 1907 transpired, was on a hunting vacation in Louisiana.

The Banksters' Vision

One of the most important consequences was that J. P. Morgan gained control of most of his major competitors on Wall St. In addition to being a banker, Morgan was also an industrialist. He controlled industrial behemoths like U.S. Steel and General Electric. Not long after engineering the 1907 financial crisis as well as its recovery, Morgan together with John D. Rockefeller consolidated their power through the formation of the financial cartel, which later was established as the Federal Reserve system. Their reasoning behind doing this was nothing short of megalomaniacal genius.

Both men had been the most successful industrialists the world had ever seen, yet they were also ardent competitors. However, with the peak of the industrial revolution yet to be realized, they understood that under America's laissez-faire, free-market capitalist system, it was just a matter of time before new and more formidable competitors would come out of the woodwork—perhaps with new disruptive technologies, thereby challenging their industrial dominance. These powerful men realized that in order to retain, perpetuate, and even expand their supremacy over the economy, they would have to gain control not only of certain industries but of all industry though control of the basic means of production—property, labor, and resources. The basis to control all of these things is the nation's monetary system. By transforming themselves from industrialists to bankers and then forming a dominant central banking cartel with control over the nation's money supply, they could gain absolute power over the nation's economy and means of production. They would then

---

[69] "James A. Stillman, Banker, Former Head of National City Bank, Dies," *New York Times*, Jan 14, 1944.

be able to pass that power on to their descendants for generation after generation for as long as the monetary system remained under their central bank's control.

As competitors, Rockefeller and Morgan had clashed on many fronts. They were powerful on their own, but combined, they knew they were invulnerable. They agreed on this key idea regarding monetary reform, namely "the importance of an increased 'elasticity' of the money supply." They agreed they would both benefit if they worked together to bring it to fruition, and so they collaborated on this reform movement. These men are usually held up as having been the archetypal capitalists, but this is not an accurate description. These men were monopolists or megalomaniacs, and that is quite another thing. True capitalism is based on a system of fair competition where all players must abide by the same rules (rule of law as opposed to rule of men)—a level competitive playing field, to coin a phrase.

Monopolism and Megalomania

Monopolists are not interested in fair competition. They are interested in eliminating competition—permanently. In fact, they prefer to force (or coerce) any would-be competitors to instead work for them rather than in competition with them, particularly when those competitors are their betters.

> I'd rather have one percent of the effort of each of 100 people, than 100 percent of my own.
>
> —John D. Rockefeller

Monopolists are greedy megalomaniacs who are after absolute power. They will stop at nothing to protect and expand their powerful monopolies. According to Karl Marx, socialism depends upon a structure based on monopoly power controlled by the state. Corporate socialism also depends upon a structure based on monopoly power—controlled instead by central bankers.

Free-market capitalists are entrepreneurs who seek to harness nature. They apply their intellectual power to transform natural resources into material wealth, which benefits those with whom they choose to deal—by voluntary mutual consent. Socialists and monopolists, on the other hand, seek to harness other men. They apply political power and coercion to confiscate or steal the wealth created by entrepreneurs through fraud and deceit if necessary. Therefore, they try to place themselves above the law and force others to deal with them on terms they alone can dictate.

Free Market Capitalism operates in a competitive environment where all players are subject to the same rules of conduct. Monopolism operates in a political environment intended to evade competition. Monopolists skew the rules of conduct in their favor by using political pull in order to benefit themselves and those beneficiaries they alone have chosen.

Rockefeller and Morgan understood that they would make exorbitant amounts of money from the creation of a centralized system that was able to expand money and credit as much as they wished. In fact, such a system would put them in control of the nation's entire labor market, essentially turning every American worker into their indirect employee. In his book *A History of Money and Banking in the United States*, decorated economist Murray Rothbard explains that J. P. Morgan and John D. Rockefeller realized "the only way to establish a cartelized economy, an economy that would ensure their continued economic dominance and high profits, would be to use the powers of the government to establish and maintain cartels by coercion, in other words; to transform the economy from roughly laissez-faire [capitalism] to centralized and coordinated statism [corporate socialism]." This is the definition of converting from free-market capitalism to a form of centralized socialism (with the banking cartel in control of the state).

Under the phony guise of an entity to promote fairness and competition in the free-enterprise system, Morgan and Rockefeller created an organization to ensure the opposite, resulting in the dominance of their monopoly. Ultimately what they created was the Federal Reserve system.

> History records that the money changers have used every form of abuse, intrigue, deceit, and violent means possible to maintain their control over governments by controlling money and its issuance.
>
> —President James Madison

Today we see similar monopolistic cartels dominating every major industry on which we depend, effectively ending competitive enterprise in these areas. The US airline industry has consolidated into three huge behemoth companies. The oil industry has consolidated in the same way as has the entertainment and media broadcasting business. Today every critical industry, including transportation, energy, food and agriculture, pharmaceuticals and healthcare, and communications and information, has consolidated into a cabal of centrally controlled corporate leviathans. All of these are owned in part by major institutional investors—large commercial banks. These are the very same financial institutions that make up the ownership of Federal Reserve system and include companies such as Goldman Sachs, JPMorgan Chase & Co., Bank of America, and a few others. The banking industry has undergone the most dramatic consolidation of all. In the 20-year span between 1994 and 2014, 37 commercial banks have merged into just 4.

The most disturbing example of this trend is the consolidation of the media, which controls everything we see and hear and works to shape public opinion on just about everything. In 1983, approximately sixty different companies shared the vast majority of the news media in the United States. Today this has consolidated into just six huge corporations. They own television networks, cable channels, movie studios, magazines, publishers, newspapers, numerous websites, and music labels. They are Time Warner Cable, Walt Disney, Viacom, Rupert Murdoch's News Corp., CBS Corporation, and NBC Universal. Known as "the big six," they dominate virtually all news and entertainment in the United States.

How the Federal Reserve Came into Being

Soon after Morgan engineered the panic of 1907, Congress formed the National Monetary Commission, whose responsibility it was to review banking policy in the United States. The committee was chaired by Senator Nelson W. Aldrich of Rhode Island. Senator Aldrich also happened to be the father-in-law of John D. Rockefeller Jr., the principal shareholder in Chase Bank. His grandson, Nelson Aldrich Rockefeller, would later become the forty-first US vice president and forty-ninth governor of New York before he succumbed to a heart attack one evening in 1979 while "working with" one of his young female *aides*.

In his capacity as chair of the National Monetary Commission, Senator Nelson Aldrich toured Europe and gathered information on the various banking methods being incorporated. He met with the most powerful European banking families of the day, in particular the Rothschilds. Using what he learned as a basis, in November of 1910 Senator Aldrich invited several bankers and economic scholars to attend a secret conference on Jekyll Island, GA. While they met under the ruse of a duck-hunting excursion, the financial experts were in reality meeting to plan the restructuring of America's banking and monetary system. Aldrich sought to remodel America's monetary system after the new European fiat-banking institutions he had visited and studied in the previous year. The 1910 duck hunt on Jekyll Island included seven of the richest and most powerful men on earth at that time. Collectively these seven men represented more than an estimated 30 percent of all of the global wealth then in existence. These men included (1) Senator Nelson Aldrich (a business associate of J. P. Morgan, he was father-in-law to John D. Rockefeller, Jr., and eventual grandfather to Nelson Rockefeller); (2) former Harvard University professor of economics Dr. Abraham Piatt Andrew (who was then assistant secretary of the Treasury); (3) Charles Norton, president of the First National Bank of New York; (4) Benjamin Strong, head of J. P. Morgan's trust company (who, after the Federal Reserve Act was passed, became the first chairman of the Federal Reserve); (5) JPMorgan Chase & Co. senior partner Henry P. Davison; (6) National City Bank of New York President Frank A. Vanderlip (who was also representing the interests of William Rockefeller); and (7) investment firm Kuhn Loeb and Co. partner Paul M. Warburg (a representative of the Rothschild banking dynasty in England and France).

From the time they left their homes to travel to Jekyll Island, they conducted themselves as if they were on a covert operation. They traveled under false names and rendezvoused quietly at Aldrich's private railway car in New Jersey. From there they traveled directly to the coast of Georgia for their secret three-week conference at the Jekyll Island Club. It was there that they drafted the first rendering of the law known today as the Federal Reserve Act, a law designed solely to further the interests of the international bankers who created it.

The Jekyll Island conference remained a closely guarded secret until many years later when a magazine article by *Forbes* was published as the only acknowledgment to it. On November 5, 2010, Fed Chairman Ben Bernanke stayed on Jekyll Island to commemorate the hundredth annual anniversary of this original meeting. The event was the first official confirmation of the revelations made initially in 1949 by Ezra Pound to Eustace Mullins in his work *Secrets of the Federal Reserve* and later reported by G. Edward Griffin in his book *The Creature from Jekyll Island*, published in 1994.

What Is the Federal Reserve Really?

This question is better answered by first stating what it is not. In spite of its name, the Federal Reserve is not a part of the federal government. It is a cartel of private financial institutions whose owners are the shareholders of the Federal Reserve system. Furthermore, it is also not truly a bank nor does it have any reserves.

On September 18, 2007, Dr. Alan Greenspan was interviewed by journalist Jim Lehrer to discuss the financial crisis and collapse in the housing market. Near the end of the interview, Dr. Greenspan was asked by Mr. Lehrer, "What should be the proper relationship between the chairman of the Fed and the president of the United States?"

Dr. Greenspan answered with the following:

> Well, first of all, the Federal Reserve is an independent agency. That means basically that there is no other agency or government [including the president, congress, or the supreme-court] which can overrule actions that we take. So long as that [the Federal Reserve Act] is in place, and there is no evidence that the administration or congress or anybody else is requesting that we do things other than what we think is the appropriate thing— then what the relationships are don't frankly matter.

"What the relationships are (between the president of the United States and the Federal Reserve chairman) … don't frankly matter." The reader must fully understand the implications of Greenspan's comment. It is basically an admission that the privately owned cartel known as the Federal Reserve does not answer to anyone, not even to our federal government. Evidence suggests that our government and the US President instead answer to the Fed.

Our government is supposed to answer to the people, not to a private financial cartel. This is an affront to what the framers intended for our nation, particularly in terms of the monetary system that they mandated in the US Constitution. It's the reason that since the Federal Reserve's founding in 1913, the US government has sought relentlessly to eradicate The US Constitution and our Bill of Rights in order to ensure the permanence and irreversibility of the Federal Reserve system—a system that enables the confiscation of all of our property, labor, and natural resources for the profit and sole benefit of a few obscenely rich, powerful, and politically dominant families.

Who Owns the Private Federal Reserve?

There has been much speculation for many years about who owns the Federal Reserve Corporation. It has been one of the best kept secrets of the past century because the Federal Reserve Act of 1913 provided that the names of the owner banks be kept secret. However, R. E. McMaster, publisher of the newsletter *The Reaper*, through confidential Swiss banking contacts provided the following answer several years ago:

- Rothschild Banks of London and Berlin

- Lazard Brothers Bank of Paris

- Israel Moses Sieff Banks of Italy

- Warburg Bank of Hamburg and Amsterdam

- Lehman Brothers Bank of New York (now part of Barclays of London)

- Kuhn Loeb Bank of New York

- Chase Manhattan Bank of New York

- Goldman Sachs Bank of New York

Risk, Fractional Reserve Lending, and the Housing Bubble

One of the main forms of investments that commercial banks make is in lending. We are all taught that banks earn money in the form of interest in return for bearing risk to loan money—risk that the borrower won't be able to repay the loan. That constitutes part of the bank's investment risk. This raises the question, "Is the investment risk borne by an individual citizen the same as the investment risk borne by a banking institution?" After all, money is money, right?

Wrong. To answer this question completely, we must consider it in the context of fiat money versus sound money.

Since sound money itself retains inherent value, any loss is real. The risk and magnitude of loss is the same regardless of who bears the loss. But with fiat the consequent risk profile depends upon where you are in the financial food chain. Under our monetary system fiat money doesn't represent anything of real value until labor has been exchanged for it. Until then, it is just worthless paper. By contrast, sound money is itself valuable from the moment it comes into being because of its intrinsic value and the natural demand for it. (Gold is valuable whether used as money or not, so it is always in demand.)

Recall that banks are allowed to practice fractional reserve lending. Under this system, banks are collectively able to lend out much more money than they actually have in deposits. Banks are able to create the money they lend out of thin air simply because the borrower promises to repay it from his or her future labor. Therefore, it is the borrower who bears most or all of the risk in this transaction. The lending bank bears practically no risk. Until you borrow the money, it doesn't even exist. The bank is authorized to create it when you promise to pay it back. If you default on your mortgage, the bank will take your house, even though the money they loaned you to purchase it never existed in the first place. This system transfers all risk onto you—the borrower. In other words, comparing the lending bank's risk versus your personal risk when you take on a mortgage looks like the following:

- Bank creates money from thin air and lends it to you (secured by assets)—no risk of loss for the bank.

- You pledge your future labor for the next thirty years to repay it along with the asset as collateral—total risk of loss for you.

This demonstrates again that it is the borrower who begets value to the borrowed fiat money by promising the fruits of their future labor in exchange for it. The bank does not create any value whatsoever within the money that you are being loaned. You do. If you don't repay the money that the bank never had in the first place, you are evicted from your house, and the bank takes possession. When your mortgage application is approved (in accordance with your ability to pay) and you add your signature to the loan agreement, at that instant the money you are borrowing comes into being. As a consequence, the overall money supply is expanded. The dollar is further devalued, and the next thirty years of your labor is conscripted for the benefit of the bank and local property tax collector. At the same time yours and every other citizen's savings has been devalued by another increment because the debt which your mortgage created just expanded the total money supply.

Privatizing Profits while Socializing Losses

Therefore, consider again the subprime mortgage lending that led to the housing bubble and subsequent financial crisis that started in 2007. When that vast number of borrowers defaulted, did those banks actually lose the money they never had to lend in the first place?

Certainly not—the losses that some of those banks incurred by trying to swap the credit risk leveraged against the underlying assets were covered when they were rewarded for their malfeasance through the TARP (Troubled Asset Relief Program) and subsequent bailouts. When debtors don't repay the loans, the banks take possession of the collateral—the properties and homes against which those loans were secured. If the repossessed properties were found to have been devalued because of an oversupply, the government makes up the difference with bailouts for the banks. And from where did the government get the new money with which to bail out those banks? They borrowed it from the Federal Reserve, which created it out of thin air, increasing the national debt all at the taxpayers' expense. When it comes time to pay the interest on that additional debt, it comes from your income taxes. This is another example of how the massive wealth transfer from the middle class to the ruling class takes place.

If a citizen loses an entire life savings on a bad stock investment, the failure of a small business, or some other bad investment, he or she loses everything. The money invested was *real* money, which he or she first had to *earn* in exchange for his or her labor, in some cases a lifetime of labor. That is very real risk, and citizens are never bailed out. When financial institutions loan you money, which they are able to create from nothing, it is *you* who bears the real risk. You must pledge your home or other asset as collateral along with your future labor to repay the debt plus interest. When commercial banks lose their investments, the money they lose is essentially risk-free capital. They were able to create it from thin air and are subsequently rewarded for their mal-investments with government bailouts, which are again funded by taxpayers. This encourages mal-investment by our government, banks, and large financial institutions.

This model transfers the total burden of financial risk for all banks' lending and investing activities entirely onto the hardworking middle class. This is what is meant by *privatizing their profits while socializing their losses.* It is this insidious aspect of our monetary and banking system that seems to escape the scrutiny of so many—the fact that the financial risk of virtually all of the economic activity in society is borne entirely by the humble working class. Even the risk of mal-investment by our government and large financial institutions is eventually paid for by the blood and sweat of the middle-class taxpayer. This is a condition that is enabled exclusively by the existence our fiat money system.

The Trillion-Dollar Coin

Possibly the most absurd financial news story of 2013 was the concept of the trillion-dollar coin. This idea originated from the Yale-educated, Nobel Prize-winning, Princeton professor, and "economist" Paul Krugman, a devout Keynesian. In his January 7, 2013, *New York Times* column "The Conscience of a Liberal," Krugman explained how it would work:

> The Treasury would mint a platinum coin with a face value of $1 trillion (or many coins with smaller values; it doesn't really matter). This coin would immediately be deposited at the Federal Reserve, which would credit the sum to the government's account. And the government could then write checks against that account, continuing normal operations without issuing new debt.

Photo—Courtesy of Talking Points Memo

His idea stems from the fact that the United States was again nearing its debt ceiling, and once again the arguments ensued between the faux left and the faux right as to whether or not to raise the limit on the debt ceiling. In truth, there is no ceiling to a potentially infinite debt. Between March of 1962 and December 2013, the US debt ceiling was raised seventy-seven times, an average of once every eight months for fifty straight years. Each time it's raised, it causes a flurry of controversial debate over the ever-increasing national debt. The now predictable recurrence of the debt ceiling "crisis" is nothing more than a reality TV drama that always has the same ending.

Nevertheless, the explanation behind the trillion-dollar platinum coin goes something like this: Sovereign governments like the United States can create new money. However, after our monetary system converted to fiat paper, there was established a statutory limit to the amount of paper currency that can be in circulation at any given time. This is one reason why we now have so much digital money, with physical paper making up only about 7 percent of the money supply. Interestingly there's no similar limit on the amount of coinage. A little-known statute gives the secretary of the Treasury the authority to issue platinum coins in any denomination. This led Krugman (a former economic advisor to the bankrupt Enron Corporation) to suggest that the Treasury create a one-trillion-dollar coin, deposit it in its account in the Federal Reserve, and write checks against that deposit. This idea sounds absurd, and it should since it reveals just how absurd a fiat money system really is.

Under a sound monetary system, this would be impossible because collateralized coins are then actually valued in terms of their weight and measure. Simply stamping the words "1 Trillion" on the front of the coin doesn't make it physically worth that much. Only under a fiat monetary system can the government arbitrarily assign such a value to a coin. Nevertheless, as crazy as it sounds, the trillion-dollar coin is allowed under our fiat model.

However, as far as this author is concerned, the suggested concept is being misused. My idea would be to use this idea to eliminate our debt altogether. Thus, we should instead do the following:

The Treasury should create eighteen one-trillion-dollar platinum coins and then use those to pay off the entire national debt to the Federal Reserve and our other creditors. With no more debt there will be no more interest and no need to have a federal income tax. We can then eliminate the federal income tax, giving each and every American worker an immediate 30 percent or more increase in real annual income. This would represent a $2.8 trillion interest-free stimulus package, all of which had previously been used solely to pay the interest on the debt. That economic stimulus would be repeated annually and is nearly four times larger than the one-time-only *stimulus* included in the 2007 TARP bill (which was actually not stimulus at all, but a bank industry bailout). We can then eliminate the IRS and save their annual budget of nearly thirteen billion dollars. We then balance the US government's budget, freeze the money supply to its current volume, restore it to the gold standard, and finally repeal the Federal Reserve Act. Perhaps then the Nobel Committee could instead create a Nobel Prize for Common Sense, although few of their laureates from recent years would be qualified.

All humor aside, to have people with such a perverse sense of reality bestowed with such enormous power and influence over the public is disturbing evidence of our culture's decline. A voice of reason however, comes from Professor Hans-Hermann Hoppe, who points out the obvious.

> If governments or central banks really can create wealth simply by creating money out of thin air; why does poverty exist anywhere on earth? Why haven't successive rounds of quantitative easing by the Fed solved our economic recession? And if Fed money creation really works, and doesn't create inflation, why haven't Americans gotten richer as the money supply has grown?

All of the events of the past decade point to a complete disintegration in the value of paper money whether it is dollars, pounds, yen, or euros. In the past ten years alone the dollar has declined by over 70 percent against gold. Most currencies have declined by similar percentages. It is an illusion to believe that gold has been rising in value when it is actually the value of paper money that is disintegrating. Since precious metals like gold cannot be printed out of thin air, they are the only honest currency that exists. This is why most governments abhor gold increasing in value against their paper money. It always exposes their deliberate actions to impoverish their citizens.

In 1913, a thousand dollars could purchase fifty ounces of gold. Today it can purchase 0.67 ounces. This means that in the last hundred years the dollar has declined by 99.3 percent against gold. So in real money terms the dollar is now only worth 0.7 percent of what it was worth a century ago. An ounce of gold, on the other hand, buys just about the same assets or goods today as it did a hundred years ago or for that matter a thousand years ago. The US government (as well as most other governments) has completely destroyed the value of the dollar by issuing unlimited amounts of currency. In the next few years they will kill off the remaining 0.7 percent to make the US dollar reach its intrinsic value of zero. Once this happens they will call for a new currency, perhaps one that merges the currencies of North America, such as has been done in Europe. A single global fiat currency and a total elimination of individual property rights are two of the fundamental aims of globalization—a euphemism for global socialism.

All Federal Reserve Money Is Debt

It is counterintuitive to consider that if public and private debt (the national debt and all personal debt) were actually paid off in full, there would be no money, but this is a fact. When we hear political bickering about raising the debt ceiling on our already enormous $18 trillion debt, it is a feigned argument. The debt ceiling is actually irrelevant. Every Federal Reserve note that has been put into circulation since the founding of the Fed has been created as a debt instrument, and every Fed note is owed back to the Fed. The debt ceiling will always be raised, and there is no intention to ever reduce or eventually pay off the national debt. If all private and public debt were paid off, there would not be one single dollar in circulation.

The text on a Federal Reserve note includes, "This Note is Legal Tender." This means that we are legally obligated to accept these IOUs as payment for any good or service in the course of conducting any type of transaction. As such, you are by law required to accept your salary or wages in Federal Reserve notes in lieu of sound money as payment for your labor.

Since we are all obligated to accept this by law, we then have little choice but to transact with these IOUs amongst ourselves. Therefore, when we go to the grocery store and plunk down a ten-dollar bill to receive a pack of cigarettes in exchange, the illusion that this piece of paper has value is reinforced. As we transact with one another around the country, we are simply transferring these IOU's back and forth amongst ourselves in exchange for the products of one another's labor. This is how the ruling class forces us to cannibalize the fruits of one another's labor in return for continually devaluing paper, while they relentlessly skim whatever they want off the top. Every one of those IOUs is owed back to the Fed with interest. That interest will be paid for by your future labor—as taxes.

It is not a coincidence that the sixteenth amendment, which established the graduated federal income tax, was instituted in the exact same year as the passing of the Federal

Reserve Act. These two laws were created by the same Congress in the same year and signed by the same president—for the same purpose. Remember from chapter 3 the findings of the 1982 Grace Commission Report. Almost every dollar that is collected from the American people in income taxes is used solely to pay the interest on the national debt. The Federal Reserve system and our federal income tax were designed specifically to work in tandem to confiscate the fruits of American labor and transfer that wealth directly to the owners of the private Federal Reserve banking cartel.

If some parts of the previous sections seem redundant or even repetitious, it is by intent. I mentioned earlier in this book that the government's propagandists are relentless in repeating their lies over and over again in order to persuade the public that their lies are true. If I am guilty of repeating truth over and over again as a counter to this fraud, then I stand convicted.

The Fed's Official Mandate

The Federal Reserve Act declares that the statutory objectives for monetary policy are maximum employment, stable prices (low inflation), and moderate long-term interest rates.[70] That sounds pretty good in theory. What has the Fed been doing in practice?

The rate of unemployment is officially reported by the Bureau of Labor Statistics (BLS) using a calculated figure designated as U-3. Using this value, the government claimed unemployment had dropped from 8.9 percent down to 7.8 percent between 2009 and 2012. However, there is another BLS figure designated as U-6, which goes unreported. This figure is named "broad unemployment." During that same period, U-6 is shown on the Bureau of Labor Statistics website as varying between more than 17 percent and a low of 14.7 percent. The difference is that the U-3 calculation does not count people who have exhausted their unemployment benefits or people who have given up looking for work while the U-6 does.

The U-6 unemployment rate is the Bureau of Labor Statistics' (BLS) broadest unemployment measure. It includes short-term discouraged workers as well as those forced to work part-time because they cannot find full-time employment. However, John Williams of Shadowstats.com correctly states that even this figure does not account for the full picture.

Until 1994 "discouraged workers" were defined as those who had given up looking for a job because there were no jobs to be had. The Clinton administration then redefined discouraged workers to be counted only if they had been discouraged for less than one year. This time qualification removed the long-term discouraged workers from the U-6 calculation. Only the remaining short-term discouraged workers (less than

---

[70] Federal Reserve Regulations (2005); Federal Register—Vol. 70, No. 147. (GPO). 2005.

one year) are included in U-6.[71] So, according to the federal government, if you have been out of work for longer than one year, you don't exist at all—that's discouraging indeed.

The Real Rate of Unemployment

The seasonally-adjusted SGS Alternate Unemployment Rate reflects the current unemployment reporting methodology adjusted for the estimated number of long-term discouraged workers who were defined out of official existence in 1994. The real rate of unemployment is derived when that estimate is added to the BLS estimate of U-6 unemployment. Based upon this actual data, the real rate of US unemployment as of January, 2015 was 23.2 percent.

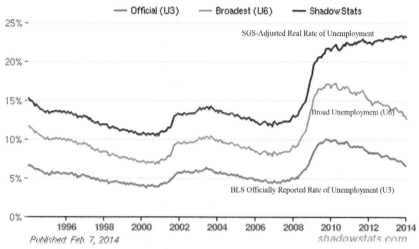

During the same time period between 2009 and 2012, the prices for food, transportation, energy, education, and other necessities have skyrocketed by between 30 to 75 percent, while the Fed has falsely claimed there is almost no inflation. Their inflation calculation is based on the Consumer Price Index (CPI), which excludes things like food, energy, heating oil, transportation, and other necessities. The price of gasoline has gone from $2.60 a gallon in 2009 to $3.68 in 2013. That's a 41 percent increase in four years. Federal, state, and local income taxes have risen 35 percent over the same four year period. During 2013 alone the cost of eggs soared 44.1 percent. As such, the real rate of inflation when one is accounting for these and other necessities is at least four times what the government reports.

---

[71]   Williams, John. Unemployment Rate, Official (U-3 & U-6) vs SGS-Alternate. *Global Economic and Investment Analytics.* Oct 22, 2012.

These economic conditions are the definition of stagflation (high inflation, low growth, high unemployment). The Federal Reserve's mouthpieces continually claim that the economy is recovering and that inflation is not an issue, yet food, energy, transportation, other basic human necessities, and the rate of labor participation are completely ignored in their calculations. By using creative accounting, the real rates of inflation and unemployment are deliberately understated by the government by a huge margin. Therefore, in violation of their congressional mandate, the Federal Reserve has acted to maximize both unemployment and inflation. They use phony government statistics to justify it while lying to the American public about their true intentions. The government and the Federal Reserve evade any accountability for this. When their bad policies lead to bad consequences for the people, the government simply manipulates and distorts the data that it reports.

The Real Rate of Inflation

The Keynesian economists who are in the pockets of the political class cherry pick data to support their flawed ideologies.

—Harry S. Dent

Officially the US Bureau of Labor Statistics (BLS) reported that the inflation rate (based upon the Consumer Price Index or CPI) for 2012 was 1.7 percent. Another report issued by the nonprofit group American Institute for Economic Research (AIER) says the US inflation rate for 2012 was far higher at nearly 8 percent. AIER used criteria based only on common daily expenditures to more accurately depict how inflation affects consumers. Their index excluded less frequently purchased items like automobiles. It's interesting to note that the Bureau of Labor Statistics (BLS) calculates the *Consumer* Price Index (CPI) excluding items that are *consumed* (food, gasoline, etc.), while including items that are not consumed (like automobiles). This is completely devoid of logic.

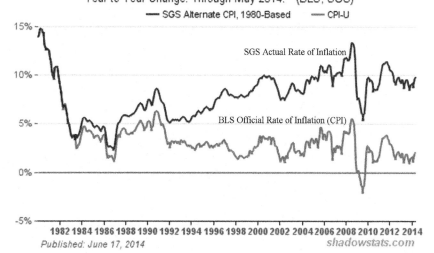

Consumer Inflation - Official vs ShadowStats (1980-Based) Alternate
Year to Year Change. Through May 2014. (BLS, SGS)

Published: June 17, 2014 — shadowstats.com

According to economist John Williams, an outspoken critic of the government's economic statistics, things are far worse. Using the government's old calculation methodology from 1980 (before politicians started to pervert the formula), he calculates the real inflation rate for 2013 as being north of 8 percent, more than five times the government's 2013 CPI figure of just 1.5 percent.

Over the years the government has made numerous adjustments to how it calculates the CPI. The claim is that this was to make it more accurate, while actual evidence suggests that the inflation rate formula has been changed in order to serve a political agenda.

Why the Government Lies about the Rate of Inflation

The government has strong motives for masking the real inflation rate. Here are at least three:

- **Political Gain**: The self-serving attitude that pervades Washington should make this obvious. Elected officials know that positive economic news, such as "inflation is under control," sound good in campaign speeches and can make the difference in a close election. Distorting numbers like the CPI helps them to avoid public pressure to do something to fix it. Government statistics that show inflation is not a problem keeps the public unaware of the issue and its consequences.

- **Big Savings**: Government entitlement programs like social security payments are linked to the CPI. Lower official numbers translates directly to lower payouts. The ruse has saved the debt-ridden US government billions of dollars that have been withheld from American citizens, hurting the retired who are on a fixed income the most. If the CPI formula had never been changed, social security payments would be twice what they are today. It's no wonder so many seniors struggle to make ends meet. In the Fall of 2012, the US Congress' debt super committee suggested basing social security increases on a variant of the CPI that would lower payments even more.

- **Justify Artificially Low Interest Rates**: The Federal Reserve uses the understated inflation figures in order to deliberately obscure its own inflationary policies. Federal Reserve policies like quantitative easing and holding interest rates near zero have driven inflation much higher, but the government's phony calculation method of the Consumer Price Index (CPI) made sure that it wasn't reported that way. If the CPI were reported accurately, the Fed would be forced to raise interest rates, which in turn would slow the consumption-based economy and hurt the stock market. That's not a headache the Fed or the elected officials in Washington want. Their long-term agenda is to allow inflation to devalue the dollar in order to help mitigate the nation's $18 trillion debt burden.

Referring again to the graph in chapter 1, it becomes clearer how policy decisions have worked to deliberately inflate the cost of living while ensuring that personal income stagnates or even declines. Inflation has deliberately been targeted at markets like food, energy, and housing, while stagflation has been the norm for the labor market between 1975 and 2008. Since 2008, the labor market actually entered a period of decline as evidenced by the reduction in household income since the beginning of the Obama administration.

Large corporations also benefit from the underreported inflation rate. Most US companies base annual cost-of-living salary increases for their employees in accordance with these figures. Therefore, they justify substandard annual salary increases to their workers based upon the government's understated inflation figures. Consequently, the average annual per-capita income does not keep pace with the real rate of inflation. The US government's Bureau of Labor Statistics website devotes an entire page to defending its methodology for calculating the inflation rate. But reality rears its ugly head every time Americans go shopping, pay bills, or try to purchase homes with their ever dwindling incomes.

The resultant divergence between the increasing cost of living and decreasing household income acts to impoverish the middle class. In effect, citizens whose intention it is to save and own property are converted into citizens who consume and own only debts.

The Agenda

There are only two possibilities. Those running the Federal Reserve are either too incompetent to carry out their mandate, or they are deliberately violating their mandate in order to destroy the middle class. Most people in America would like to believe it is the former. A great deal of evidence, however, points to the latter. Nevertheless, whether they are simply incompetent, villainous, or both, it is the American public that should hold themselves responsible for repeatedly reelecting an entire collection of incompetent, self-serving criminals to government office.

With the stroke of a pen, Congress could repeal the Federal Reserve Act and restore our constitutionally mandated sound currency. Instead, Congress has repeatedly derailed efforts by Congressman Ron Paul to call for an audit of the Fed. Everything Congress does acts to protect and preserve the Fed system, while they are instead supposed to protect and preserve our constitution per their oath of office. Our Congress has been in dereliction of their duty to the people for more than a hundred years.

There are countless examples of government malfeasance that point to the wanton and deliberate destruction of the US dollar. This unconstitutional system of perpetual debt servitude amounts to an unlawful act perpetrated by our own government and their cohorts at the Federal Reserve against the entire citizenry of the United States. It also reveals the collusion between both of the major political parties, all branches of government, and the Federal Reserve. They are complicit in their intent to perpetuate this destructive system regardless of which party controls Congress or the executive branch. In essence, whoever sits in the White House, any Senate or House seat, or any seat on the Supreme Court bench is virtually irrelevant. The separation of powers doctrine has become meaningless, and the government does not answer to the voters. They answer to the owners of the Federal Reserve. They are acting to systematically eradicate property rights for individuals so that they can take this nation's wealth all for themselves and their benefactors.

The Fed's Unofficial Mandate — Maximum Unemployment and High Inflation

Our government and the news media that brings the political process into our homes regards voting and elections as little more than a means to entertain and shape the public opinion. During the 2012 presidential elections the candidates knew beforehand that the issue on which they would most easily endear themselves to the voters was *jobs*. In response to months of opinion polling they simply regurgitated back to the American public exactly what the people had told the politicians they wanted to hear, "What are you going to do about unemployment?"

Jobs is an emotionally charged issue for most Americans. For this reason the same rhetoric on job creation has been recycled for every presidential and midterm election for at least the past two decades. During the State of the Union Address that was broadcast on January 29, 2014, Barack Obama repeated the same script yet again with the following:

"The best measure of opportunity is access to a good job."

Really? Is just having a job the key determinant of an individual's long-term economic prosperity? The jobs issue is actually used by incumbents and candidates as a clever distraction from the more crucial matter with which all should primarily be concerned—property rights. Interestingly property rights is an issue that almost no politician or media pundit will even mention (the only exception to this being Dr. Ron Paul).

Therefore, you must ask yourself, "Does simply having a job in and of itself truly provide economic prosperity for an individual in America?"

It did at one time, but not anymore.

The former Soviet Union had 100 percent employment but no economic prosperity for individual citizens. This was due to two main reasons. First under Communism, citizens have no right to property ownership, and second, the labor market is centrally and directly controlled. In the United States we also have a controlled labor market, although here it is controlled indirectly.

Neither model allows sustained economic prosperity for individuals. When the government controls the labor market, you can be sure that you will never be paid what you're truly worth. Only a free market functioning under the natural laws of supply and demand can do that. Working at a job that allows you to live paycheck to paycheck while you are never able to save for a retirement, pay off your debts, or own your home does not constitute prosperity.

A more accurate version of Mr. Obama's State of the Union comment would be the following:

"The best measure of opportunity *to become a slave* is access to a job *for which you will be underpaid, overworked, and unable to ever leave for a better paying job* ... *since there will be no other alternative under our controlled system.*"

Furthermore, when you live under a system of taxation that confiscates half or more of everything you earn, having a job becomes futile. Coupled with the skyrocketing cost of gas, food, transportation, health insurance, a college education, and all of the things we must purchase just to be able to gain employment, it eventually costs more just to be employed than the job itself pays in after-tax income. As the cost of living rises faster, it may become counterproductive just to drive back and forth to work. This is often the condition for those earning the minimum wage. Unfortunately the same career politicians who helped to create this mess often bring up the issue of raising the minimum wage as another emotional hot button they can push to garner votes from the very citizens they are deliberately acting to impoverish.

The best way to reduce and even end poverty altogether is simple. **Restore property rights**. Restore our constitutionally mandated system of sound money. Allow people to keep what they earn so they can invest it as they see fit.

Why a Minimum Wage Hurts Those It Is Purported to Help

Raising the minimum wage always has the opposite effect to the one that is promised. It is always a zero-sum game for those it is claimed to help. Employers who are forced to bear increased costs of the wage increases must then reduce nonwage-related costs, thus eliminating benefits for employees. In some cases, they have to eliminate jobs altogether, leading to a higher rate of unemployment. High unemployment causes all labor rates to go down.

When the free market determines what the cost of labor should be, the supply of workers is better matched to demand. Minimum wage legislation, on the other hand, prohibits wages to fall low enough to equate to the number of people seeking the unskilled jobs being offered. As such, the supply of unskilled labor always exceeds the demand at the government-mandated minimum wage. This amounts to creating a buyer's market for labor, giving employers a bargaining advantage over laborers. In a true free market laborers can find themselves in a stronger position than employers and demand higher wages. In other words, setting wages at an arbitrary minimum becomes a self-fulfilling prophecy, precluding unskilled but diligent workers from maximizing the wage they could otherwise demand.

Pay raises hit the bottom line (profitability), not the top line (revenue). The types of businesses affected most by minimum wage increases operate on razor thin margins, often in single or low double digits. Therefore, it makes the cost to employ someone prohibitive, eliminating jobs altogether. Those who typically employ minimum wage workers in spite of the increased cost—businesses such as gas stations, grocery stores, fast food restaurants, etc.—have no choice but to raise their prices to cover the increased payroll costs. The resultant increase in the basic cost of living is almost immediate and is borne by everyone, including those earning the newly increased minimum wage. Their cost of living goes up in direct proportion to their slightly higher wage. This renders their incremental wage increase irrelevant—and it is these lower-wage workers who are hurt the most by the consequent rising prices.

They never catch up economically. The promise of a better life through a higher minimum wage is just another fake rabbit for the poor to chase but never catch.

Furthermore, as labor costs go up, business owners must find ways to reduce headcount. We have already seen the introduction of automated checkout counters at grocery stores across the country. Restaurants are now jumping on this bandwagon with several major chains introducing tabletop tablet-ordering systems. Chili's has installed these in over 45,000 restaurants across the country, and customers can make payment through these tablets as well, so even waiters and waitresses are being eliminated.

Raising the minimum wage will not result in a rise in the standard of living for unskilled low-wage workers, but it will result in a rise of the machines. Machines don't unionize. Machines don't demand higher pay (or any pay for that matter), and they don't require their employer to provide them with a government-mandated health insurance policy. Machines don't obligate the employer to match their social security and Medicare withholdings, nor do they require the employer to spend his own resources in acting as the government's conscripted tax-collection agent since machines don't pay taxes. Machines don't call in sick, and when technology improves—as it always does—you can fire your old machine and buy a new one, improving your profitability further.

Raising the minimum wage, however, does benefit government and politicians. It dupes unenlightened voters into believing that politicians are acting in their interest so that they vote for them, donate to their campaigns, and throw them their support. A higher minimum wage means higher payroll, Medicare, Medicaid, and income tax revenues for federal and state governments collected from workers and their employers.

When the minimum wage is increased, employers and minimum-wage workers lose, while governments, politicians, and financial institutions win. Once again, the issue at hand is not income inequality, but wealth inequality. The only way to fix that is to restore property rights.

If you continue to believe that the principal economic issue facing Americans is jobs and if you further believe that our elected government employees really intend to reduce unemployment for your sake, ask yourself this basic question, "What do government and large corporations stand to gain from reducing unemployment?"

The obvious answer is *nothing*. In fact, they have a lot to lose. When unemployment is kept high, they have a large, debt-ridden, desperate, and readily available labor pool willing to work for peanuts.

In other words, if politicians truly acted to reduce unemployment, the cost of skilled labor would go up quickly. This would have an immediate negative impact on the profits of their most important corporate donors. Contrary to their rhetoric, politicians benefit from sustained high unemployment because it gives them indirect control over the labor market. Large corporations want the same thing so that they can hire and retain highly educated, highly skilled, hardworking people who are desperate and up to their eyeballs in debt. They will therefore gratefully accept any thankless job for mediocre pay and remain obedient employees until they drop dead. Don't believe for one second that either Democrats or Republicans or almost any government official for that matter is interested in creating private sector jobs. In fact, they are far more interested in eliminating them and replacing them with government jobs that will justify a larger budget and higher taxes.

As of early-2014, the average annual salary for a federal government employee was $78,500, while the average annual wage for a private sector employee was nearly half of that at $40,800.

Alan Greenspan's "Wealth Effect"

As further proof, you only need to survey recent history for your example. The decade of the 1990s is remembered as a period of unprecedented economic growth in America. The "'90s boom" as it has come to be known saw GDP increase almost continuously for nearly ten years. Although President Clinton is often credited with this boom, it was largely due to several conditions that took place in spite of the government's and the Fed's Keynesian monetary policies.

- Reagan had previously deregulated the telephone and telecommunications industry. This paved the way for the massive growth in the mobile phone industry, the fiber-optic telecom industry, computer networking, and Internet communication. This gave rise to corporate powerhouses like Cisco, Verizon, T-Mobil, Motorola, Apple, and others. This alone created new private-sector jobs for millions of Americans.

- The economy reaped gains in productivity because of the integration of technology in the workplace—computers, networking, and telecom.

- Oil prices plummeted to fifteen dollars per barrel.

- The Baby Boom generation was at its peak earnings cycle in their age demographic.

By the late 1990s, when unemployment dipped below 4 percent, employers were practically begging for talent and had to pay top dollar for it. Remember that the Fed's official mandate is to achieve maximum employment. Therefore, it should have been a reason to celebrate for having successfully met the objectives of their congressional mandate.

Instead, what was the Federal Reserve's response? Chairman Alan Greenspan spoke repeatedly on the alleged problems associated with what he called "the wealth effect," as though Americans becoming wealthier was a problem. For a ruling class bent on subjugating everyone, a wealthy and self-reliant citizenry is indeed a huge problem.

Dr. Greenspan declared that with unemployment at historical lows and the average US citizen suddenly earning more and feeling wealthier, people would spend more, thus increasing demand. Notwithstanding the fact that this is how the natural forces of supply and demand are supposed to work in a healthy growing economy, he then went on to claim that this additional economic activity would constrain supply and "lead to inflation." Any undergraduate economics textbook will tell you that inflation comes from an expansion of the money supply, not from a natural increase in economic activity.

Alan Greenspan was the chairman of the Federal Reserve for eighteen years under four different presidents of both political parties. His comments on the government's fear of a wealthy citizenry should be taken at face value. What the government and the Federal Reserve truly fear is a wealthy, prosperous, and self-reliant citizenry that has little or no need of a huge omnipotent government. The US government and the Federal Reserve have demonstrated by their actions that their real interest is in expanding and perpetuating dependency. They accomplish this by keeping the majority of Americans in debt and impoverished or at least nearly so for most of their natural lives.

So what was the government's solution to Dr. Greenspan's wealth effect?—Make Americans poorer again.

Dr. Greenspan's next course of action was to raise interest rates, which he justified by claiming that it would "stave off runaway inflation," inflation he claimed would result from this so-called wealth effect.[72] Interestingly the decade had seen prices for food, gasoline, energy, and other consumable items remain stable or even decline in some cases, so there were absolutely no signs of inflation. Nevertheless, Greenspan's action to raise interest rates immediately increased the cost of capital to large companies, leading to higher financing costs as well as compromising their access to additional operating capital. Within a year the dot-com industry imploded followed shortly by

---

[72] Tracking the Wealth Effect. New York Times. Feb 24, 2000. http://www.nytimes. com/2000/02/24/business/tracking-wealth-effect-imbalance-supply-demand-causes-greenspan-fret.html

numerous telecom industry bankruptcies. As a result, from the end of 1999 during the subsequent two years, the rate of unemployment skyrocketed by an unprecedented 37.5 percent, and by 2003 unemployment had nearly doubled. It marked the end of the greatest economic boom since the industrial revolution. The dot-com boom was stopped dead in its tracks—intentionally—simply by raising interest rates.

One could argue that the hidden agenda was to increase unemployment in order to reduce skilled labor costs for their corrupt friends on Wall St., as this was the immediate and lasting effect. Whether or not this is conspiracy theory or conspiracy fact is left to the reader to decide. In any case, this example illustrates that the only condition that made this cessation of prosperous growth possible was the dependence of every aspect of our economy on our fiat monetary system. A system that is created, controlled, manipulated, and owned by the private Federal Reserve. Beginning in 1999, the deliberate actions of just one institution put millions of American citizens out of work, and the country has not recovered since.

Today, fifteen years later, workers, white and blue collar alike, are the ones who are begging for a job, and average wages have declined by more than 11 percent over just the past five years. This is exactly as our political class intended it. Political campaign rhetoric focusing on job creation is a tapestry of lies.

When questioned by Congress about the wisdom of raising interest rates at the height of America's greatest economic boom in more than fifty years, Dr. Greenspan proclaimed that he and the Fed are just hapless innocent bystanders trying their best to react to the market's dynamics. He then continued with an almost unintelligible and convoluted dialogue, so that practically no one could decipher the actual meaning of his answer. Dr. Greenspan refers to this method of communication as "Greenspeak."

During a September 2007 interview on CNBC with Maria Bartiromo, Dr. Greenspan explains Greenspeak as "the process of using convoluted and disintegrating logic intended to subvert the general public from gaining an understanding of our private monetary system."[73] The actual interview went something like this:[74]

MB: "You are overseeing the most important institution, and leading things, and then not only are you dealing with these [financial] crises, but then you've got to convey, what's going on to people, that means Congress, The President, The Media, The Public … … so you come up with Greenspeak"

Greenspan: "Otherwise known as Fedspeak"

MB: "What is it?"

Greenspan: "It's a language of purposeful obfuscation, to avoid certain questions, coming up which you know you can't answer,

73 Blinder, Alan S. "Studies," "How Do Central Banks Talk?" International Center for Monetary and Banking, Center for Economic Policy Research. p. 66.
74 Dauble, Jennifer, CNBC – Former Fed Chairman Speaks Extensively to Maria Bartiromo, Sept. 17, 2007.

and saying 'I will not answer' or basically 'no comment' is in fact an answer, so you end up with, when say a Congressman asks you a question, and you don't want to say 'no comment' or 'I don't want to answer', so I proceed with four or five sentences which get increasingly obscure, the Congressman thinks I answered the question, and he goes on to the next one."[75]

The Merriam-Webster Dictionary defines obfuscation as "to deliberately conceal, to bewilder, to confuse, to perplex or to obscure perception." Purposeful obfuscation is a convoluted way to describe intentional lying. It's a language of deception used to avoid certain questions you can't or won't answer—questions posed by Congress, the president, the media, or the public.

Greenspeak has been institutionalized by the Federal Reserve as a legitimate media communications tool. It is even officially defined in the Federal Reserve's own documents as "a turgid dialect of English used by Federal Reserve Board chairmen in making intentionally wordy, vague, and ambiguous statements."

In a sinister irony Chairman Greenspan claims to have coined the terms Fedspeak and Greenspeak as an analogy to *Newspeak* of *Nineteen Eighty-Four*, the novel by George Orwell about a post-apocalyptic dystopian society under totalitarian rule.[76]

Used with permission – Virgin Films – UK copyright 1984.

---

[75] Bartiromo, Maria. CNBC Interview with Alan Greenspan.
[76] Jasper, William F., "Taking Delight in Deception"—*The New American*, Oct 29, 2007.

Who Dr. Greenspan sees as Big Brother is anyone's guess. The deliberately confusing and carefully rehearsed cryptic language is further described in the Fed's policy documents as "an indecipherable, Delphic dialect, that is intended to give people a sense that it is impossible for the general public to understand economics and finance, and thus to allow the Federal Reserve and government to *manage the economy without interference from the general public.*"[77]

Newsflash—the general public *is* the economy!

The reader is advised to view a video of the Greenspan interview and draw his or her own conclusions. He was once quoted as saying, "I guess I should warn you, if I turn out to be particularly clear, you've probably misunderstood what I've said." Some may view his verbal gymnastics as humorous and entertaining or even demonstrable of a powerful intellect, but when it is used to intentionally mislead the public, it is also destructive.

Remarkably, much earlier in his career, Dr. Greenspan was a confidante of author Ayn Rand and he subscribed to her objectivist and laissez-faire philosophies. In her objectivist newsletter he wrote a detailed essay on the value of the gold standard and its crucial role in limiting government's inflationary money printing. The following is an excerpt of Dr. Greenspan's essay published in the early 1960s:

> An almost hysterical antagonism toward the gold standard is one issue which unites statists of all persuasions. They seem to sense — perhaps more clearly and subtly than many consistent defenders of laissez-faire — that gold and economic freedom are inseparable, that the gold standard is an instrument of laissez-faire and that each implies and requires the other.
>
> In order to understand the source of their antagonism, it is necessary first to understand the specific role of gold in a free society. Money is the common denominator of all economic transactions. It is that commodity which serves as a medium of exchange, is universally acceptable to all participants in an exchange economy as payment for their goods or services, and can, therefore, be used as a standard of market value and as a store of value, i.e., as a means of saving.
>
> The existence of such a commodity is a precondition of a division of labor economy. If men did not have some commodity of objective value which was generally acceptable as money, they would have

---

77   Martin, Preston, "The Complete Idiot's Guide to the Federal Reserve," Alpha Books, p. 120.

to resort to primitive barter or be forced to live on self-sufficient farms and forgo the inestimable advantages of specialization. If men had no means to store value, i.e., to save, neither long-range planning nor exchange would be possible ...

The opposition to the gold standard in any form—from a growing number of welfare-state advocates—was prompted by a much subtler insight: the realization that the gold standard is incompatible with chronic deficit spending (the hallmark of the welfare state). Stripped of its academic jargon, the welfare state is nothing more than a mechanism by which governments confiscate the wealth of the productive members of a society to support a wide variety of welfare schemes. A substantial part of the confiscation is effected [accomplished] by taxation.

But the welfare statists were quick to recognize that if they wished to retain political power, the amount of taxation had to be limited and they had to resort to programs of massive deficit spending, i.e., they had to borrow money, by issuing government bonds, to finance welfare expenditures on a large scale.

Under a gold standard, the amount of credit that an economy can support is determined by the economy's tangible assets, since every credit instrument is ultimately a claim on some tangible asset. But government bonds are not backed by tangible wealth, only by the government's promise to pay out of future tax revenues, and cannot easily be absorbed by the financial markets. A large volume of new government bonds can be sold to the public only at progressively higher interest rates. Thus, government deficit spending under a gold standard is severely limited. The abandonment of the gold standard made it possible for the welfare statists to use the banking system as a means to an unlimited expansion of credit ...

In the absence of the gold standard, there is no way to protect savings from confiscation through inflation. There is no safe store of value. If there were, the government would have to make its holding illegal, as was done in the case of gold [by FDR in 1933]. If everyone decided, for example, to convert all his bank deposits to silver or copper or any other good, and thereafter declined to accept checks as payment for goods, bank deposits would lose their purchasing power and government-created bank credit would be worthless as a claim on goods. The financial policy of the welfare state therefore requires that there be no way for the owners of wealth to protect themselves.

This is the shabby secret of the welfare statists' tirades against gold. Deficit spending is simply a scheme for the confiscation of wealth. Gold stands in the way of this insidious process. It stands as a protector of property rights. If one grasps this, one has no difficulty in understanding the statists' antagonism toward the gold standard.[78]

After he rose to political prominence, Dr. Greenspan remained silent on this earlier commentary about the gold standard. Once he became the Federal Reserve board chairman, he denied his own sound-money principles.

Free Market Capitalism is only possible under a sound monetary system. It is incompatible with a fiat money system. Even according to former Fed Chairman Dr. Alan Greenspan, you cannot claim to have a system that respects property rights when its basis is fiat money. Thus, to restore individual freedom and liberty in America, we must eliminate the Federal Reserve system and restore sound money, as mandated by The Constitution. The exact steps by which to accomplish this are detailed in Chapter 26 of the latest edition of his book *The Creature from Jekyll Island*, by G. Edward Griffin.[79]

Article 1, Section 8, of the United States Constitution guaranteed the United States a system of sound money. It meant that money would be created only as coin—a precious metal commodity—as opposed to fiat, and that its unit of value should be fixed in terms of a standard of weight of that precious metal. The actual measure was not determined until later when Congress passed the Coinage Act of 1792, in which the US dollar was defined as 371.25 grains of pure silver. This definition was originally based upon the most widely used silver coin then in existence, the Spanish Reale.

Since the United States also minted gold coins as the constitution instructed, their value was regulated in terms of the weight of gold they contained and in accordance with the silver standard coin. Therefore, the United States' monetary system was originally founded upon a silver standard and not a gold standard as is commonly believed. In any case, the purpose was to establish sound money based on a specific measure of silver or gold in order to fix the value of the unit of account, the US dollar. The framers insisted on this because they understood that for a free-enterprise system to function, it depends on having a system of sound money based upon a precious metal commodity.

---

[78] Rand, Ayn. Capitalism, The Unknown Ideal. Signet. Page 101. July 15, 1986.
[79] Griffin, G. Edward. The Creature From Jekyll Island. American Media. Sept. 11, 2010.

Capitalism—Fair Competition on a Level Playing Field

Under a fiat money system, the rules of the game are vastly different for the average middle-class American than for banks and huge corporations. When you or I invest our money, it is real money because we exchanged our labor for it, so we bear real risk. When government, banks, and financial institutions invest, they create that money from nothing, and they pass 100 percent of their investment risk onto you, the citizen. When their investments fail, they reward themselves by printing more money—at our expense. We bear all risk while they bear none—privatizing profits while socializing losses. If you or I tried to do that, we would be sent to prison for fraud and counterfeiting. That hardly constitutes a level playing field in a free market.

The unaccountability of the financial elites on Wall St., the Fed, and their partners in government is what leads to financial debacles like Solyndra, Global Crossing, Lehman Brothers, Enron, and the like. These events have a great deal in common. They vastly enriched the banks that financed those companies as well as their founders, top managers, and political cronies, while at the same time they destroyed the savings and assets of common stockholders and employees. These are examples of yet another mechanism used by this nation's rulers to transfer the wealth created by the middle class to the obscenely rich.

The banks, large financial institutions, and the large corporations they control are able to conduct business based on a completely different set of rules than the rest of us—rules that are created and enforced by the government. While they bear little to no real risk and are rewarded handsomely whether they succeed or fail, the citizenry bears total risk. When a citizen is successful with a risk investment, his proceeds are confiscated through taxes. When that citizen is unsuccessful, he loses his life's savings, his home, and his children's future, and he must start again from scratch, chasing the rabbit.

When government's and banks' mal-investments are rewarded by taxpayer-funded bailouts, the overall money supply is expanded, devaluing our savings, our retirements, our 401(k)s, and our social security, further impoverishing the citizenry. While our government and huge financial institutions invest the money that they confiscate from taxpayers into speculative investments and then "purposefully obfuscate" about why these investments fail, most citizens struggle in futility just to be able to pay off the mortgages on modest homes for themselves and their families—homes they will never truly be able to own in the strictest sense of the word. Homes on which their very lives depend.

The Home Owner's Death Pledge

It's interesting to note that only the specific type of loan made for the purchase of a residential home has a unique name—mortgage. No other loan, whether for the purchase of a business, a car, or a piece of production machinery, is called a mortgage. A mortgage is a loan secured by real property as collateral. The word *mortgage* originates from the Old French language, the word *mort* meaning death and the word *gage* meaning pledge. The literal translation of this is death pledge. Upon signing a mortgage, one is literally signing away one's life in the sense that our lives depend upon having safe and secure homes. If you don't repay the mortgage (money the lenders didn't have in the first place), they figuratively take your life by confiscating the collateral, the home.

It is a basic truth that the fruits of one's labor and one's property—the security of one's home—represent more than just superficial possessions. They are a matter of life and death for every hardworking individual. Our very survival depends upon our ability to create and accumulate wealth, to earn an honest living, and to use that wealth to acquire a safe and secure home for ourselves and our children. Declared in America's founding documents is the fact that we each have a basic human right to our liberty, our property, and our own labor, in order to acquire those things upon which our very lives depend. Therefore, the best and only ethical means by which to create and distribute wealth is by the free enterprise system that respects individual property ownership.

Socialism is defined as the centralized control of the means of production—state control of land, labor, and natural resources. This is the antithesis of free-market capitalism. It bears repeating over and over again that our current monetary system is absolutely incompatible with free-market capitalism and the right to private property ownership. As such, the United States has been a fundamentally socialist country since the passage of the Federal Reserve Act in 1913. It will remain so until that corrupt institution is abolished.

Addendum to Chapter 4

The following is a collection of quotations about our monetary system that have been made by some of America's most eminent historical figures:

The few who can understand the system (check money[80] and credits) will either be so interested in its profits, or so dependent on its favors, that there will be no opposition from that class, while on the other hand, the great body of the people mentally incapable of comprehending the tremendous advantage to us, that capital [fiat] derives from the system, will bear its burdens without complaint., **and perhaps without even suspecting that the system is inimical to their interests**.

—From a letter written by Rothschild Bros. of London England to a New York firm of Bankers and dated June 25, 1863

"Unemployment as it exists today is not an economic but a monetary phenomenon, a stabilized price level with neither inflation nor deflation is the only workable solution.

—F. W. Pethick-Lawrence, financial secretary to the British Treasury (1929–1931)

Since I entered politics, I have chiefly had men's views confided to me privately. Some of the biggest men in the United States, in the field of commerce and manufacture, are afraid of somebody, are afraid of something. They know that there is a power somewhere so organized, so subtle, so watchful, so interlocked, so complete, so pervasive, that they had better not speak above their breath when they speak in condemnation of it.

—President Woodrow Wilson in 1913

Whoever controls the volume of money in any country is absolute master of all industry and commerce.

—President James Garfield

Under the Federal Reserve Act, panics are scientifically created; the present panic is the first scientifically created one, worked out much as we figure a mathematical problem.

—Charles A. Lindbergh, Sr., from his book *The Economic Pinch*, writing about the panic of 1920

---

[80] Check money was at that time, another name for Fiat money.

While boasting of our noble deeds, we are careful to conceal the ugly fact that by our iniquitous money system we have nationalized a system of oppression which, though more refined, is not less cruel than the old system of ¢hattel slavery.

> —Horace Greely in 1872, writing on his opinion of the National Banking Act, which was presented to Congress in 1872 as an earlier attempt to establish a central bank

My agency (Dept. of Treasury) in promoting the passage of the National Bank Act was the greatest financial mistake of my life. It has built up a monopoly which affects every interest in the country. It should be repealed; but before that can be accomplished, **the people will be arrayed on one side and the banks on the other, in a contest such as we have never seen before in this country.**

> —Salmon P. Chase, secretary of the Treasury (1861–1864) and Supreme Court justice (1864–1873)

Money measures things and things measure money. Each measures the other by and according to its own abundance, by comparison. **If you double the volume of money in circulation, you double the price of everything.** By doubling the price you divide the debt because it takes only half as much labor or the products of labor to pay the same debt. If you divide the amount of money in circulation, you divide the price of everything. By dividing the price of everything, you double your debts, for it will take twice as much labor or the products of labor to pay the same debt.

> —Adam Smith, the father of political economy

We have already tried borrowing and spending our way to recovery. We have made numberless hopeful and well-meant experiments, aimed to bring us out of the depression. Thus far we have not emerged, nor will we-until the fatal defects of our money system have been corrected. To those defects, more than to any other cause, I attribute the depression. What is it we want of our currency? We want money in which we will have unshaken confidence; confidence that it will be stable in its value. We want a dollar that will, in the language of the President (William McKinley), "not change its purchasing and debt-paying power during the succeeding generation.

> —Frank A. Vanderlip, former assistant secretary of the Treasury (1935)*

*Ironically Frank Vanderlip was an original member of the Jekyll Island Group, who in 1910 were the architects of the Federal Reserve Act, while he was president of the National City Bank of New York. He was instrumental in precipitating the financial conditions that caused the Great Depression.

CHAPTER 5

Environmentalism versus Conservationism

As I neared completion of this manuscript, I was engaged in a conversation with a man I've known for forty years—my dear friend, former high-school science teacher, and mentor, Mike K. Toward the end of our call, he proposed a thought provoking question that I'd immediately recognized. He had asked me this exact same question nearly two years before when I first started to write this book. As we then discussed my ideas for this manuscript, I was unclear as to how to answer his question. Fragments of the answer had been in my head for years—even decades—but the ability to connect those fragments and formulate the answer eluded me. Interestingly, on this particular night just days before submitting this manuscript to the publisher, the answer crystallized in my psyche … the conversation went something like this:

Mike K.:

I'm an environmentalist—a nature lover. I want to protect The Earth and her environment for posterity, not just for human kind, but for all living things. Given that, please tell me, what is the basis for humankind to live in an environmentally sustainable manner on this finite planet? If you could boil it down to only one thing—to a single factor or basis for humanity to be able to live sustainably and be able to preserve the natural world—what would that be?"

F.A. Grieger:

Mike, to answer this question, we must first agree upon a few principles:

• Humanity must live in accordance with the laws of nature, and therefore in accordance with the nature of man as a species.

- We must accept that humans will always deal with one another – transacting and trading their skills and the products of their skills – qua – engage in economic activity. This is the basis of social interaction—part of the inescapable nature of humankind.

- There are only two ways humans can transact with one another – either voluntarily or coercively (qua—by force). Furthermore, we can choose to act ethically, or unethically. *Coercion by force includes acting against one's will at the point of gun, as well as other forms of coercion that include: fraud, deceit, seduction, and trickery.*

- To live in accordance with the laws of nature while at the same time acting ethically, we must base all of our actions on the ethical and moral imperatives of humanity. The most important of these is that the use of force or coercion by one human against another—except in the justifiable defense of one's life, liberty, and/or property—is fundamentally immoral.

- Living unsustainably means to live beyond one's means. It is consuming more than one can produce, without permanently destroying resources while generating more waste than nature can recycle within a reasonable time-frame (reasonable in terms of human life-span). Therefore, every individual member of human society (meaning, not just individual people, but also the institutions that groups of individuals create) must live within his, her, or its own means.

Economic activity among humanity involves consumption of resources. It is the overconsumption of resources, and the overproduction of waste that leads to environmental destruction. Therefore, humans must of their own volition live, act, and transact, within their means. They must not be *coerced* into overconsumption. However, we are a complex society of specialization. For example, we have farmers specialized in dairy production and mechanical experts specialized in manufacturing agricultural machinery. The two need each other. Neither can do the work of the other and both produce far more of their respective products than each needs as an individual for himself and his family. They are therefore able to trade the excess they produce in return for that which they need. Therefore, a balance of trade is required among all of humanity in order to provide sustainability within a complex society of specialization. Otherwise, we would be relegated to return to a hunter-gatherer status as a means to attain *sustainability*.

Furthermore, in order to deal with one another on a basis of ethics, morality and fairness (without the use of force or coercion) humans must be able to trade economically through a medium of exchange that represents *a fair and equivalent value in all respective transactions.*

The use of barter for voluntary exchange is moral and fair. Barter may be used at any time by mutual agreement of the parties involved, but it is not practical as a means of transacting among the larger society for numerous obvious reasons. As I pointed out in the example of the dairy farmer and tractor manufacturer, the use of money as a medium of exchange in any fair and just economic transaction requires it to be *sound money*. It is a basic fact of economics, that when the money itself can *spoil* (just as milk or any perishable commodity can), it must be spent more quickly in order to exchange it for other economic value—before it loses it purchasing power. This leads directly to overconsumption.

It follows then that the basis of environmental sustainability is the use of sound money, while the basis for unsustainability and overconsumption is the opposite—the use of unsound or fiat money.

It has been shown that the main purpose of sound or honest money is to provide all three properties required of money: 1) medium of exchange; 2) unit of account; and 3) a sustainable store of value. Fiat, on the other hand, cannot serve as a reliable store of value, and only serves as a medium of exchange.

Fiat has features however, which enable it to be used for other purposes – purposes for which sound money cannot be used. One of these is fiat's ability to be used to distort economic demand among the members of society. The ability to create an infinite amount of money leads to the illusion of infinite resources and therefore generates infinite demand. This enables a continual expansion of consumption—an unsustainable condition in nature. It also enables the creator of that money (when issued as debt with interest) to target specific markets for increases in consumption, while ignoring other market sectors (in order to pervert the natural forces of supply and demand among the larger society). This allows them to create market-specific bubbles (inflations) at their political whim. Politicians use this as a ruse to lay claim that they are *shepherding a growing economy,* which is a fallacy—growth in consumption is not real economic growth because it is unsustainable. When something has been consumed ... it is gone. To grow this kind of economy requires consuming more, and more, and more ... forever.

Fiat can be used to coerce (or more accurately to delude) the population into believing that through debt expansion they have the ability to consume more than they would otherwise. This drives people across all of society to make economic transactions they would not otherwise have made with sound money – which cannot be created out of thin air. Fiat money expansion encourages people to over-consume, while sound money's stability encourages people to be frugal, to save, and to only spend their money judiciously. Fiat money is the fundamental basis for an unsustainable economic model. Sound money is the opposite.

Overconsumption is the basis for environmental unsustainability. When people over-consume, they also over-pollute.

Mike, these facts lead to the answer to your question. For a free, fair, and just society to live sustainably within Earth's finite environment, we must base our economic model on a system of exchange that inherently demands self-discipline—one that requires all members of society, especially those with political power – to live within their means. To have one part of humanity empowered with the ability to impose their will on another part of humanity opens the door to corruption and abuse of power.

Sound money is self-regulating. It precludes the abuse of political power by an arbitrary body authorized to create money from nothing. Sound money cannot be inflated to artificially expand demand and therefore overconsumption. It cannot be used by one part of humanity to manipulate the purchasing decisions of another part of humanity. By its very nature, sound money imparts fiscal discipline across the entire economy and it precludes over-consumptive behavior by every individual, group, institution, and unaccountable government.

Fiat on the other hand provides exactly the opposite – a medium of exchange that can be manipulated and used by one part of humanity to profit from the unbridled consumption carried out by another part of humanity. It leads to incalculable cost in terms of unsustainable depletion of our natural resources, and generation of waste and pollution in excess of nature's ability to process it.

The basis of natural law which demands the exclusive use of sound money among our society—as a means to protect the integrity of all transactions and the sustainability of our resources—was given by the original United States Constitution. Article 1, Section 8 guaranteed our nation a system of sound money based on the gold and silver standard. The US Constitution, in terms of its original meaning and intent, was the first (and remains the only) governing document ever drafted which provides this *economic recipe* for humanity to coexist peacefully, sustainably, fairly, ethically, and in accordance with the laws of nature. Indeed, the framers wrote voluminously about their intent to base The Constitution upon *Natural Law*. This was discussed extensively by their intellectual and philosophical mentors such as Adam Smith and John Locke, and goes all the way back to the Magna Carte. It was the Federal Reserve Act of 1913 and the sixteenth amendment that acted to subvert this basic principle. Their sole purpose was to create an economic model whose moral basis is diametrically opposed to the Constitution's original intent. Their intent was to enable our currently unsustainable system of consumption-based illusory growth through fiat money—solely for the benefit of the money printers. It is they who are destroying this planet as any parasite that slowly consumes its host.

So Mike, to answer your question fully, you must challenge your own accepted view of things. You called yourself an *environmentalist*, but are you really? Environmentalism is a political movement. Politics is the use of force and coercion by one group of men over another. I know you to be one who vehemently rejects this notion.

Conservationism on the other hand, is the basis for acting to **preserve** our environment and natural world **for posterity, and for future generations**—not the basis for political power, prestige, or personal gain. We have seen how this country's politicians almost universally declare themselves as *environmentalists*, while at the same time they consistently act to preserve our corrupt fiat monetary system whose purpose is to enable overconsumption.

Political environmentalists are therefore the worst kind of hypocrites.

Our fiat monetary model is based on Marxism and on the Keynesian notion of digging holes in the ground in order to fill them in again, as a means to *create jobs and economic growth*. It enables endless foreign interventionism, wars, debt expansion, mal-investment, all of which lead directly to the over-use and destruction of our natural resources. This does not enable the creation of sustainable economic value and it is absolutely incompatible with a policy of conservationism.

Fiat money can simply be re-printed if it is lost, mal-invested, or misspent. Money that you can print out of thin air can be spent frivolously, without a judicious discipline in its employment as capital. It is therefore the basis of a society bent on over-consuming until we are left with an over-polluted, unsustainable, unlivable planet covered with trash dumps, bomb craters, and other useless holes in the ground—courtesy of John Maynard Keynes and Karl Marx. Fiat money is the system we are currently living under.

Economic activity is not the same as economic growth. Real growth—sustainable value creation—comes from investment, savings, and creating real lasting value for all of humanity. The basis for this is a system of money that has shelf-life, and for which the risk of loss is real. That kind of money demands that it is employed judiciously in terms of investment in production because if it is mal-invested … it is wasted, along with the resources it was used to acquire. That kind of money is sound money—the system we abandoned in 1913.

Mike, you are NOT an environmentalist. Environmentalists are after political power. They are hypocrites. You are a Conservationist. True conservationists can achieve their ends far more effectively and far sooner by pushing for a restoration of sound money—the gold standard—as our monetary system. This therefore requires a restoration of The United States Constitution in terms of its original meaning and intent. These are the true bases for a sustainable and prosperous standard of living for all of mankind, while preserving and protecting our natural environment.

In fact, restoring the Constitution, and our system of sound money are the only chance humanity has to save this planet from environmental annihilation.

145

CHAPTER 6

A Well-Informed Public

Life is tough, but it's tougher when you're stupid.

—John Wayne

Public Education

The most important feature of childhood is the development of the child's mental powers. This consists in developing the ability to reason and perceive the world in terms of reality and in acquiring knowledge. All of these things encompass education. The capacity to reason is inherent in the human species. It is what distinguishes humans from animals. Humans are unique in that we are born with the potential to develop the ability to reason, to think critically and in abstract terms. But knowledge and skills needed for survival must be learned. Before a child reaches school age, the volumes of information, knowledge, skills, and even emotional intelligence that the child has acquired is staggering. Children acquire this knowledge largely on their own and with a great deal of help from their loving parents long before they even start attending school.

Learning is a profoundly individual process, and far more of it takes place outside of a formal school setting than within. Teaching only provides the opportunity for learning, but it is the individual who becomes educated by his or her own volition. This is exactly as nature intended since knowledge with the intelligence to act on that knowledge is the basis from which we develop survival skills and the ability to become self-reliant. Our survival depends upon our ability to acquire knowledge and skills on our own. However, in terms of survival just acquiring knowledge is not enough. One must be able to determine what knowledge is true and what knowledge is false. Acting on falsehoods can be deadly.

Most discourse today about institutionalized public education touts its importance in terms of the alleged benefits to society rather than to the student as an individual. For example, education does the following:

- prepares a person to enter the workforce and be a productive part of society,

- exposes children to their peers in order to socialize them,

- helps children develop social and organizational skills,

- helps children develop an understanding of community and world events,

- teaches right from wrong and good from evil (as defined by society),

- teaches obedience and deference to authority, and

- teaches children how to play by the rules and to wait their turn.

Many believe that it is society's foremost responsibility to educate its citizens. Society is regarded by many as an entity that holds some sort of superior status to individuals, or has overriding rights of its own. Some even hold that society can possess an evil that can be blamed for the ills of the world. But it is a basic law of nature that only an individual can exist, think, feel, know, and act on one's knowledge by one's own volition. Society is not a living entity. It is nothing more than the name we give to a group of individuals interacting with one another, each of their own accord. The notion that society is a thing that chooses and acts of its own volition or can bear a collective responsibility for individuals' problems is a fallacy. An action is a feature of a knowing and thinking mind—an attribute of the individual—and there is no such thing as a collective brain. Every individual must think and act for himself or herself, and every individual must bear the consequences of his or her actions.

Nevertheless, over the past few decades America's public schools have devolved into an institution designed to socialize children, to shape their opinions, and to instill group thinking rather than to purvey the knowledge and skills required to become self-reliant individuals who are capable of abstract and critical thinking.

Education v. Indoctrination

Education allows individuals to develop their own belief systems based upon learned facts, observations, experience, and rational analysis. Indoctrination consists in influencing an individual to accept a belief system based upon the opinion of others. Education provides students with the ability to gather knowledge in terms of truth. Indoctrination imbues opinion as being truth regardless of its veracity.

When children are trained in the notion that society, as a whole, takes precedence over their need to learn how to survive and thrive as individuals, children adopt the philosophy that their individual rights matter less than the collective will of their group (or their team). It enables children to be indoctrinated with the idea that it is not only acceptable but even super moral to subordinate an individual's unalienable right to self-determination for the sake of society and the illusive common good. In reality, there is no greater good than a society made up of healthy, self-reliant, productive, ethical individuals who respect one another's rights to life, liberty, property, and pursuit of individual happiness. This would describe a people devoted to truth and cooperating voluntarily on a basis of fairness and mutual benefit without the use of force or coercion.

Instruments of Coercion—How the Mafia Works

A school is an institution into which we entrust the care of our most valued treasure—our children. Most caring and loving parents want what is best for their children and will make any personal sacrifice for them. Because of this—more than any other type of institution—public schools wield enormous influence over our lives and over the development of our children's values and morals. These are the very foundations of our culture. Therefore, the public school system is one of the most effective instruments of control used by the political class to exert its power over the citizenry. There is a saying in the mafia that when you want to gain leverage or control over your adversaries (or your victims), you go after what they love—their family.

Schools are funded by property taxes, the nonpayment for which is a criminal offense. When state and local bureaucrats can threaten every family in this country with the prospect of seizing the family home (for nonpayment of the tax), they by default own and control your home. More disturbing is that by holding our homes and our children hostage, governments are then able to control the content, the values, and the moral basis of our children's education. It has always been the aim of central planners, tyrants, oligarchs, and dictators to steal a society's children away from the influence of their parents.

In order to indoctrinate and control children, governments establish the rules and regulations of education. Parents aren't allowed to send their children to schools that do not meet these "qualifications." This increases the power of the public school system, and the power of the bureaucrats who run it. It's time for parents to take education back into their own hands, to run the curriculum.

—Dr. Ron Paul

Education Reform

Politicians have been promising much-needed reform to public education practically since the system was first established. Perhaps the root of the problem is staring us all right in the face. Perhaps the problem is that schools simply are what they are—public.

American taxpayers have spent hundreds of billions of dollars, enormous resources of time and manpower, and immense political capital trying to find ways to improve our underperforming public schools. This usually results in measures that are based on throwing more money at the system, money that comes from bureaucrats who first confiscate it from home owners as property tax. But history has proven that monopolistic government bureaucracies such as public schools are the most economically inefficient institutions on earth. The result has been a continual decline in the quality of public education along with a systematic degeneration of the moral values instilled within our children.

Quality Comes from Economic Efficiency

When an organization consumes resources in order to deliver a product, the product quality is partly a consequence of how efficiently those resources are utilized. If it is inefficient in the allocation of resources and capital, the waste that results adds no value to the final product but produces an economic drag on the entire institution. Corners must be cut just to get the product made and delivered, and so the quality of the product is compromised. In the case of a public school organization, the product is your child's education and development.

Public schools are government bureaucracies. They are run by public employees who are members of politically influential unions. Since they are funded by local governments through taxes, they are unaccountable to the families of the children they are supposed to be educating and are instead accountable to those who provide them with money—other government bureaucracies.

Most public schoolteachers are obligated to be union members as a condition of employment (unless they are employed in a right-to-work state). Teachers' unions like the NEA and other state unions are first and foremost concerned with collecting union dues and secondarily with expanding their power as political organizations. They do not increase their revenue from union dues because student performance improves. In fact, when students do poorly, schools and unions are rewarded since they are then able to demand more money from taxpayers by claiming that the underperformance is due to being underfunded. Schools are therefore unaccountable to the parents of the children in their care and are thus inherently inefficient. In fact, government bureaucracies reward them for being as inefficient as possible. In other words, the more inefficient their capital allocation and the poorer the educational outcomes, the more tax money they will receive. Public schools are encouraged rather than discouraged to operate inefficiently mainly because of their financing model.

The Powerless Consumer

Although he or she may claim otherwise, the quality of a child's education is near the bottom of a bureaucrat's list of priorities. Therefore, we are forced against our will to pay for and accept a substandard product in the form of public education. Parents have no influence over this situation since they are unable to withdraw their financial support from schools that provide an inferior education to their children. If they try that, their home will be seized by the local sheriff. Therein lays the fundamentally corrupt nature of our model of property tax-funded public schools. In a true free market if your service provider sells you worthless, substandard junk, you may justifiably refuse to pay for it, and the provider rightfully suffers a loss. By comparison, if your public school turns your child into an imbecile and you justifiably refuse to pay them (stop paying your property taxes), they seize and auction off your house, make your child homeless, and throw you in prison for tax evasion. It is a system modeled exactly after a mafia protection racket.

There have been a great many outstanding well-intentioned teachers, school officials, administrators, and even a few government appointees who have tried in futility to fix our public education system. Most failed and left the profession in frustration. In his 2006 book *The War against Hope*, former secretary of education Rod Paige makes the comment, "To fix our public education system, we have to significantly change the way schools and school systems currently operate."[81] During his career Mr. Paige demonstrated devotion for children and educational improvement, and his book is full of many brilliant and insightful points. But this is not one of them.

Operational efficiency and therefore quality in any complex organization is to a large extent a consequence of how its resources are allocated. The basic resource on which any operation depends is money. Schools are no exception. The operational inefficiencies that result in the decline in quality of public education are an effect, not a cause. The cause of our public school dysfunctions is in how they are funded and how their financial resources are misallocated as a consequence.

To truly fix our public education system, we have to significantly change the way school systems are currently *funded*. This doesn't mean to throw more money at the problem. It means to ensure that financial resources are allocated throughout the school's operations in the most efficient manner solely to maximize the product quality (your child's education). The only way to accomplish this is to make schools accountable directly to the families of the children they are educating. This cannot happen as long as they are funded by government bureaucrats. School funding

---

[81]   Paige, Rod. The War Against Hope, How Teacher's Unions Hurt Children, Hinder Teachers, and Endanger Public Education. Thomas Nelson Publishing. 2009.

from property taxes is by nature misallocated to its most inefficient use since the consequences for doing so results in the school system being rewarded with even more money. Families have no choice but to deliver the funds. If they don't, their homes are seized, and their children are made homeless. Corrupt politicians and tax collectors benefit because the more money they can extort from hardworking Americans under the threat of taking their property, the more power they obtain. A politician's sole interest is in expanding his power. There is no better tool to achieve this than an extortion scheme that holds your home, your property, and your children hostage.

Diminishing the standards of education in America has been the goal of our political class for generations because it results in the expansion of the dependency society. A government bureaucrat like any parasite is dependent upon those he or she forces into dependency. Career politicians are bent on controlling everyone, so they enact policies that create dependency on a societal scale.

The Deliberate Dumbing Down of America's Children

From the time of America's founding to the early part of the twentieth century, the true purpose of education was to provide children with the knowledge and skills necessary to become self-reliant as a means to achieve life, liberty, and the pursuit of happiness. Today the current aim of public education is to socialize our children and indoctrinate them into a system of social dependency, a purpose diametrically opposed to the former.

Our public school system has made a science out of deliberately mis-educating our impressionable youth. They have indoctrinated generations of American children with revisionist history, absolute falsehoods, celebrity worship, and ideas and thought processes that subject them to social conformity at many levels. Their inexperience precludes them from realizing when they are being manipulated, so most children are unable to discern when opinions are being laid upon them disguised as facts. They are trained to believe that whatever someone in authority tells them is true. Therefore, after they reach adulthood, they rarely question authority.

Our kids leave childhood perfectly conditioned to enter the adult world of the working class as obedient, dependent employees who don't question authority and are incapable of critical thinking.

From Prussia with Love—Starting Them Young

To a ruler, no single target of indoctrination takes a higher priority than children. Therefore, the most effective path to indoctrination is through the school system. This principle was learned from Germany's public education system. During the 1940s many German public schoolteachers became members of the National Socialist Teacher's Union. They were obligated to join this union as a condition of employment. The term national socialism translates into German as *nazional sozialismus*. This is more commonly shortened to the better-known moniker, Nazi. Germany's public education system at that time was a legacy of its earlier Prussian mandatory public school system

The modern structure of American public school education is also modeled on the original Prussian system, which was first imported to the United States from Germany in the 1840s. The Prussian system was specifically designed to educate young children in such a way as to strip out independent thinking and replace it with obedience and conformity. The purpose was to provide the Prussian state with reliable, expendable soldiers willing to give themselves up as cannon fodder for the sake of the fatherland.[82]

The notion of socializing children is presented to parents as something positive, asserting that its purpose is to bring children together to play, interact, and have fun (i.e., teaching them to play nice). Anyone with children of their own knows that a school is unnecessary for this. Children actively seek out other children to play with on their own. What public schools actually do is use subtle training techniques to strip these children of their natural gifts, their natural curiosity, and their creativity, and most importantly their individuality and self-esteem. These individual traits are replaced with a blind allegiance to higher authority and to the state. Public schools teach children that as individuals they are insignificant, and they are indoctrinated with the concept that their value and importance is derived from their place in the larger society.[83] They are further infected with the idea that their culture (or collective) is superior to all other cultures. School children are taught that their identity is wrapped up in their school collective more so than in their family or their own person. They are conditioned to root for their team, their school colors, and their mascot and taught that success and happiness are found in defeating the other teams and in ridiculing the other mascots. This is the mentality required of mindless, unthinking soldiers or workers loyally doing their part to support the construction of a huge international empire without consideration to the cost or the consequences to themselves or to those being conquered.

Blind allegiance to the state, is always accompanied by a willing rejection of one's own individual liberty along with a passionate disrespect for the liberty of others. Public schools across America as part of their common federally approved curricula are now teaching children to report their parents' behavior to the authorities. Public school curriculum is designed to subtly encourage children to snub parental authority and to instead embrace the authority of the state. Indeed, Marxism holds that for socialism to succeed, the family unit must be destroyed.

---

[82]   From Prussia to America, How Public Schools Destroy Lives. http://www.youtube.com/ watch?v=TGg-mFBX0Kc.

[83]   Turtel, Joel. Public Schools, Public Menace: How Public Schools Lie to Parents and Betray Our Children. Liberty Books. 2005.

[Public] Education should aim at destroying Free Will, so that pupils thus schooled, will be incapable throughout the rest of their lives of thinking or acting otherwise than as their schoolmasters wish. Influences of the home are obstructive. In order to condition students, verses set to music and repeatedly intoned are very effective. It is for a future scientist to make these maxims precise and discover exactly how much it costs per head to make children believe that snow is black. When the technique has been perfected, every government that has been in charge of education for more than one generation will be able to control its subjects securely without the need of armies or police.

—Bertrand Russell, *The Impact of Science on Society*

Children and adolescents are naturally insecure and are therefore impressionable and vulnerable. Their immaturity allows those in authority to manipulate them through their natural desire to be accepted by their peers. Adolescent children are struggling to develop their identities and their sense of self-esteem. They crave the admiration of other children and the acknowledgment of adults because it makes them feel valuable. This enables some public schoolteachers to indoctrinate children with their own opinions without being challenged. There are very few who teach children the ability to think critically, to seek truth, and to always question authority.

Children are by definition—dependents. They have a natural expectation to be taken care of so they cannot yet know the sense of freedom that one derives from having achieved self-reliance. Therefore, they have a natural tendency toward embracing socialism. Socialist governments therefore seek to expand their power by targeting children for their indoctrination campaigns in order to coerce the young into rejecting individual freedom before they have the chance to grow up and taste it. The Hitler Youth was not formed by recruiting children voluntarily from their families. In March, 1939, it became a legal obligation for all German children to join the Hitler Youth—even if their parents objected. This was enforced through the public school system. Once you have perverted the minds of children, you can convince them of almost anything after they become adults.

On July 1, 1971, teenagers in America were given the right to vote under the terms of the twenty-sixth amendment to the US Constitution. It was adopted in response to student activism against the Vietnam War under the premise that "if eighteen-year-olds can be conscripted into the armed forces to die in a foreign country, then they should have the right to vote." The argument was certainly just and moral in that context, but it was based on the wrong root cause and therefore resulted in the wrong solution. The answer was not to give inexperienced, poorly educated teenagers the right to vote. The answer was to stop drafting them into the army to go to a foreign country in order to kill or be killed by other foreign teenagers. But government sociopaths always attribute the wrong root cause to every problem and therefore apply the wrong solution. Nevertheless, this wasn't some innocent mistake made by our hapless yet well-intentioned Congress. Recruiting teenagers with zero life experience to the voting booth serves the political class's interests just as well as sending them into a mosquito-infested jungle to die.

More than 64 percent of eighteen to twenty-four-year-olds identify themselves as liberal Democrats.[84] Of course they do. They haven't yet spent more than half of their lives working hard for a wage only to see most of it confiscated against their will. They haven't yet learned from experience what it is to have been robbed of your property through an act of fraud by your own government. Nevertheless, whether the ones in power are liberal Democrats or neocon Republicans really doesn't matter. Every few years our country swings from an administration of corporate socialists (Republicans) bent on expanding government justified by

---

[84]   Schaffner, Brian. Politics, Parties, and Elections in America. P188. Jan 1, 2011. Cengage Learning – 7[th]ed.

their foreign interventionism—to an administration of Marxist socialists bent on expanding dependency and the welfare state. Neither model can or will bring about individual prosperity or the ability for individuals to achieve self-reliance. Both models advance their respective agendas by confiscating the property and wealth of American citizens against their will and then transferring that wealth to various members of the political and corporate ruling classes. The statists achieve this in part by perverting the minds of our children so that upon reaching adulthood they are easily duped into embracing their own servitude.

The most recent incarnation of this is the new Common Core standard. Common Core is an attempt to standardize various K–12 curricula across the country based upon a federal standard. Examples of the sheer idiocy found within this new system are legion. For example, Common Core requires students to take standardized tests that are developed by large education corporations, such as Pearson Assessments, Inc. (a British company). In the New York state public school system students must be given a Common Core standardized test for enrollment into each level (elementary, junior high, and high school). This test may be administered to each student only once. Many children as young as four or five are being forced to take a standardized entrance test in order to be admitted at the kindergarten level of some of New York's public elementary schools. Many children at this age have not yet learned their alphabet, let alone understand how to fill in the small bubble answers with a number-two pencil. Most don't know how to hold a number-two pencil in the first place. They are given a multiple-choice test with possible A, B, C, or D answers, and when asked to color in the little bubble, they either fill in all the bubbles, reach for a crayon, or start crying. Most of these preschool children cannot read, yet they are told they are required to perform on a written test. For most children this will be the first of many experiences of being belittled and humiliated by an adult in a position of authority.

Other examples include the new history books that are compliant with Common Core standards and are being distributed to high schools across America. One of these books intended for eleventh-grade high school students misquotes the second amendment to the US Constitution as follows: "The people have the right to keep and bear arms in a state militia." Another such book presents the second amendment to the US Constitution in terms of the following convoluted statement: "The Second and Third Amendments—grant citizens the right to bear arms as members of a militia of citizen-soldiers and prevent the government from housing troops in private homes in peacetime."[85] This odd treatment not only lumps the second and third amendments together but misstates the third amendment as dealing only with peacetime. The third amendment deals with wartime conditions as well. Nevertheless, the purpose of such obfuscation is clear—to distort the meaning and intent of the Bill of Rights and subvert the possibility of any objective class discussion on the subject. If children

---

[85] *The Americans, Student Edition*, McDougal Little / Harcourt Publishing, 2011.

are to be taught civics in our public schools, they must be taught the US Constitution as it was written as well as the actual meaning and purpose for each and every constitutional right. Otherwise, the next generation will have no knowledge of what their constitutional rights actually are. Perhaps that's the intent.

The second amendment as ratified by the states is actually written as follows: "A well-regulated militia being necessary to the security of a free state, the right of the people to keep and bear arms shall not be infringed."

"To keep" means to own, and "to bear" means to carry on your person. And the words "shall not be infringed" are incontrovertible in terms of meaning. There is only one clear connotation to these words, and it is not open to interpretation. Evidently our public school system does not want the next generation to understand the irrefutable meaning of this or any of our other unalienable rights.

When criticized for the obvious problems with the aforementioned history book, a spokesman for the publisher defended it by claiming that the twenty-seven words in the original constitution's second amendment made it "too wordy," so they replaced it with their fourteen-word version simply for "verbal economy." The absurdity of this argument should elicit roaring laughter, were it not for such a glaring assassination of our Bill of Rights. I for one am not inclined to give them the benefit of the doubt. I believe their perversion of the constitution and in particular the second amendment has a clear political purpose—to program children with a distorted interpretation of our constitutional rights in order to render them irrelevant.

Some Common Core lessons advise students to reference specific web pages. Under the subject heading of mathematics, one link directs students to a passage that reads, "Some of the Constitution's authors did not trust the ability of the common voter to make the 'right' decision, so they devised the Electoral College as one way of lessening the power of the popular vote."

Another link directs math students to the following link about President Ronald Reagan: "Over strenuous congressional opposition, Reagan pushed through his 'supply side' economic program to stimulate production and control inflation through tax cuts and sharp reductions in government spending. However, in 1982, as the economy declined into the worst recession in 40 years, the president's popularity slipped and support for supply-side economics faded."

Not only are these passages blatantly false, but what could they possibly have to do with math class? Any professional teacher with any integrity should be appalled not only by the revisionist history and absolute falsehoods but by such an obscene demonstration of political indoctrination.

Common Core Indoctrination—Every Child Left Behind

Not only are the teaching materials and textbooks in question, but even more disturbing are the testing and evaluation standards imposed upon students—on which their grades and their academic futures depend. Here another example of public education's true purpose was revealed by a Texas parent whose fifth-grade child brought home a Pearson Education standardized English grammar and writing test. The actual test was purported to demonstrate knowledge about possessive nouns, and the instructions were to rewrite the underlined part of a given test phrase using a possessive noun. The first six test questions are shown below:

1. The job of a president is not easy.

2. The people of a nation do not always agree.

**Hitler Youth Poster—
"Jugend Zu Uns"**

"Youth —Join us"

3. The choices of the president affect everyone.

4. He makes sure the laws of the country are fair.

5. The commands of government officials must be obeyed by all.

6. The wants of an individual are less important than the well-being of the nation.

An English grammar test? Not hardly. Are parents supposed to believe that the purpose of these kinds of questions is to test a student's knowledge of English grammar? If this does not constitute overt socialist political indoctrination, nothing does.

The producer of this standardized test is Pearson Education, a global corporation that provides education publishing and assessment services to schools in the United States and other countries. Pearson International is headquartered in London and owns leading education media brands, including Addison-Wesley, Prentice-Hall Publishing, Penguin Books, the Financial Times Press, and others. Pearson generates more than 60 percent of its revenue in the United States. Clearly youth indoctrination is as an even bigger business in the US today than it was in 1930's Germany.

New York Times writer Gail Collins commented, "We have turned school testing into a huge corporate profit center, led by Pearson, ... Pearson has a five-year testing contract with Texas that's costing the state taxpayers nearly half-a-billion dollars."

Collins reveals that Pearson was first contracted under the No Child Left Behind Program, which was originally set up by the Bush administration in 2001.

> This is the part of education reform nobody told you about. You heard about accountability, and choice, and innovation. But when No Child Left Behind was passed 11 years ago, do you recall anybody mentioning that it would provide monster profits for the private business sector [a British Corporation no less]? [Pearson's] lobbyists include the guy who served as the top White House liaison with Congress on drafting the No Child law. It has its own nonprofit foundation that sends state education commissioners on free trips overseas to "contemplate" school reform.

If state education commissioners are open to being bribed with foreign junkets in order to contemplate *school reform* in the form of huge contracts with foreign publishers, it is clearly their kind of reform that should be in question.

The federal government's education initiatives like Bush's No Child Left Behind and now Obama's Common Core result in having foreign-contracted educational materials telling American children that they must "obey the commands of the government" and that their president decides whether or not the laws of the country are fair. The ideas surreptitiously expressed to children by such test questions are absolutely false, and the intent of such programming is obvious. Furthermore, this indoctrination process is sending billions in profits to a publisher that is headquartered in a socialist foreign country, every dime of which was confiscated from US home owners through property tax extortion.

The mass media is the other key component of the indoctrination machine. Early in 2013, MSNBC ran a segment pushing the notion that "kids belong to the collective" and that "the idea that kids belong to their parents or kids belong to their families should be eliminated."[86] This is an affront to the traditional family values and founding principles of this nation.

---

[86]   Harris-Perry, Melissa, MSNBC, "Your kids belong to us," from "Lean Forward," April 4, 2013. http://newsbusters.org/blogs/ken-shepherd/2013/04/04/msnbcs-harris-perry-americas-kids-belong-their-communities

Robbing Our Children of Their Childhood

"The stealing of a child's innocence—it's the most heinous crime, and certainly a capital crime if there ever was one."

—Clint Eastwood

Several Common Core first-grade textbooks celebrate families headed by same-sex couples. In *Who's in a Family* by Robert Skutch, the description states, "This equal opportunity, open-minded picture book has no preconceptions about what makes a family. This book catalogues multicultural contemporary family units, including those with single parents, lesbian and gay parents, mixed-race couples, grandparents and divorced parents." The Common Core curriculum's preference for political correctness over education is now promoting homosexual parenting to six-year-olds! First-graders don't yet know where babies come from. Nor should they, but our public schools are instructing children on the homosexual lifestyle before they even know what sex is. Inspiring in such young children a curiosity about sex and homosexuality is tantamount to institutionalized sexual abuse.

Furthermore, every year we see more and more news reports about public schoolteachers engaging in sex with their underage students. This kind of abuse perpetrated against our children by some public school teachers is beyond reprehensible. Many school districts do not even allow parents to move children to a different school in order to protect them from further abuse. Parents are virtually powerless to exact justice when sexual assault crimes are perpetrated against their own children. And things are getting much worse. In early 2013, a bill put before California Governor Jerry Brown specifically protects public schools (but not private schools) and other government institutions from lawsuits pertaining to sexual abuse of employees or students. It also exempts the actual perpetrators of the abuse from civil action. In other words, if you live in California and your child is seduced into having sex with a teacher or is even raped, you are not allowed to sue the school or the abuser for evading their responsibility to protect your child. This yields a system that creates teaching job opportunities that are highly attractive to pedophiles since they will have access to hundreds or thousands of children—yet be protected from the harshest possible punishment for acting on their perverse impulses. A single act of sexual abuse perpetrated against a child changes the trajectory of that child's life forever. It destroys his or her childhood and adult life. It is an act of spiritual murder and should carry the harshest punishment. Instead, local governments, school districts, and their unions are taking steps to protect these criminal pedophiles, while home owners are forced against their will to continue funding them.

National Review's Kevin D. Williamson writes,

> Exempting public schools from potential lawsuits and financially debilitating settlements is due to the political strength of

California's public sector labor unions. The unions and their political surrogates know that without that exemption, some California school districts could lose many, many millions to families of children who suffered sexual abuse at a government-run public school. Expensive settlements would bleed school budgets dry and would likely lead to staff cuts, which would deprive California's teacher unions of a small fortune.

It's difficult to calculate how much California's public schools would have to pay in sex abuse cases, but rough estimates suggest it would be in the hundreds of millions. Williamson writes,

> In the Los Angeles Unified School District alone, over 600 teachers over a four-year period were fired, have resigned, or were facing sanctions because of "inappropriate conduct" relating to students. About 60 teachers faced punishment for outright sexual relations with students or other minors, while others were punished for offenses such as: showing pornography to students, forcing students to act out "master and slave" sexual role-play scenarios, taking a student on a field trip to a sex shop, lining girls up in the classroom to judge their relative breast size before having them do jumping jacks, and old fashioned sexual harassment. Some of these teachers had complaints in their files dating back years that had not been acted upon, while another teacher had been in hot water at six successive schools for sexual misconduct.

If the system were truly about the children's best interests, such teachers would—after single offenses—be permanently stripped of their certifications and then prohibited from ever working in any childhood education role again anywhere in the country. Instead, these pedophiles and criminals are protected, while our children continue to suffer abuse. All the while we the people are forced against our will to continue funding these institutions through a system of property tax extortion that has deliberately been used to eliminate our property rights, subverting any influence we might otherwise have over the public school system.

As citizens, as home owners, but especially as parents, we must act to protect our children from this fundamentally corrupt model of public school funding and its sometimes horrifying consequences. We are being robbed of our money and our homes, while our children are being robbed of their innocence and their childhoods by a bunch of corrupt, criminal degenerates. We must regain control of our homes, our schools, and our families right now.[87]

Unfortunately the youth in this country are not offered the best alternative—a traditional education based on a devotion to truth and respect for their parents with a sense of moral obligation to their own families. Education should help children acquire the knowledge to become mentally strong and confident and to achieve self-reliance by developing their character. Our children require an objective, useful education focused on English, math, science, economics, and American history rather than the current emphasis on political correctness, cheerleading, social indoctrination, mindless obedience to the state, and various forms of celebrity worship. They need to understand that the only means by which we can realize a future of prosperity as a nation is for each of us to achieve a future of prosperity as individuals, reliant on ourselves and devoted first to our own families. This can only be achieved if our children learn self-reliance and the discipline of living within one's means. Our future lies in the hands of the next generation, but they are unfortunately being brainwashed with Marxist—Socialist dogma by our public educational institutions.

It is not one event, one president, or one political party that is responsible for forcing an entire society to reject individual liberty and instead accept totalitarianism. It is a process that is a century in the making. Part of that process involves the deliberate mis-education of our children, the destruction of their self-esteem, and the replacement of moral values with degenerate behavior.

The Bottom Line

Our current system of public school funding is unethical. It enables the ruling class to control our property, our children, our children's futures, and our very culture. To restore our free republic, our children must be educated with the knowledge and confidence to become self-reliant individuals. To achieve this, schools must be accountable to the families of the children they are educating, and not to a bunch of corrupt, self-serving career politicians. As long as public schools are funded through property tax extortion, their accountability will be misdirected.

> Whenever the people are well informed, they can be trusted with their own government; that whenever things get so far wrong as to attract their notice, they may be relied on to set them to rights.

—Thomas Jefferson to Richard Price on January 8, 1789

---

[87] Velderman, Ben, "California public schools spared from law that punishes sex abusers." EAGNews.org

CHAPTER 7

Restoring Property Rights

Home Ownership, Families, Children, and Education

As was demonstrated in the previous chapter, public school funding and property taxes are inextricably linked in the United States. Property tax revenues are used by most local municipalities to fund schools as well as local police and local fire departments, but the lion's share of it is for school districts. Policy makers have made the claim that "property tax is a critical ingredient in effective local government." Only a government bureaucrat could make such an absurd claim that the effectiveness of their governance depends upon their ability to extort money from home owners. If your dentist's effectiveness depended upon how much money he could force out of you and in terms of how much pain he can inflict otherwise, would you allow him to drill into your teeth?

The irony is that this statement coming from a politician was inadvertently honest. Stated another way, this says, "Unless we can extort as much money from you as we wish by threatening to take your home if you don't pay up, we can't effectively control every other aspect of your and your children's lives (i.e. – govern)." Indeed, it is exactly this model that provides them with the power to control the misinformation and degenerate values that are instilled in your children by public schools without your consent.

Today, public schools are operated at the state level through departments of education, and locally by school districts and publicly elected or appointed school boards. Two members of my own local school board do not even have children of their own, but sought to be on the board simply as an entry into politics. Such school board members clearly have no vested interest in the quality of childhood education. Approximately 15,000 different school districts operate in the United States, and most are run by counties. All school district employees are public employees. Most of these public employees are union-members and are therefore granted substantial entitlement benefits, such as generous pensions and health care after retirement.

This leads to the massive unfunded liabilities which are bankrupting so many local communities. Almost all of the money required to sustain this system comes from your property taxes.

Application of All Rents of All Land to Public Purpose

In Karl Marx's *Communist Manifesto*, "Application of all rents of all land to public purpose" is the first of the ten planks of Communism. "Rents of all land to public purpose" is property taxes. Literally hundreds of thousands of American families each year lose their homes and family farms to sheriff's sales because they cannot afford to pay their property taxes (rents). In Wayne County Michigan alone, more than 23,000 homes were seized during the last quarter of 2014, for nonpayment of property tax. Every child in those families is forced into homelessness by their local government employees who claim to care about childhood education. I firmly believe that a child's well-being depends far more on having a safe and stable home that his or her parents may have worked hard all of their lives to pay for than it does on gaining access to a public indoctrination camp.

Just as insidious, senior citizens who worked all of their lives and paid into our bankrupt social security system are relegated to living on the pathetic fixed income it provides in retirement. This is woefully inadequate to cover all of their living expenses on top of the relentlessly increasing property tax liability that is forced upon them in spite of their having no children in the public school system.

Across America, multigenerational family farms are being parceled and sold off piece by piece just to pay their ever-increasing property tax bills. At the same time many other large private family farms are sold into the hands of huge agricultural corporations—corporations that are owned or controlled by financial institutions that have access to cheap financing through their money-creation power. This is just another example of how America's small businesses and family farms are being wiped out through the corporatization of America.

The Property Tax Revolution

Some citizens are finally waking up and realizing that the restoration of their unalienable right to property ownership can only be effectively championed at the state and local level. In early 2012, Pennsylvania introduced H.R. 76, their version of a property tax elimination bill. In June of that same year in Bismark, ND, state lawmakers voted on a plan to abolish the property tax in their state. The Bismark newspaper quoted Mrs. Susan Beehler as saying, "When did we come to believe that the government should get rich and we should get poor? I would like to be able to know that my home, no matter what happens to my income or my life, is not going to be taken away from me because I can't pay a tax."

Catching the Rabbit

To reset the United States on a path toward sustainable prosperity for all, we must make self-reliance and prosperity achievable in the first place. We can only do this by restoring individual property rights, sound money, and the rule of law. The current federal government as well as state and local governments will resist this with every fiber of their being because their goal is to expand and consolidate their power at the expense of individual sovereignty. They will further resist it because they are charged with the responsibility to enforce and perpetuate our corrupt monetary system and our system of unfair taxation by the elitists who so amply benefit from these institutions.

For this reason the probability of successfully transforming our federal government into a group of liberty-minded, constitution-defending, freedom-fighting, property-rights advocates—is almost zero. This fight must be fought all across the country at the local community level, and in particular, at the school district level. We must take back our homes, our schools, our communities, and most importantly our children. *We the people*, parents and home owners, must lead by example, and the country will follow. If we don't each act to restore our property rights, there is no one else who will do it for us.

Restoring Property Rights

Restoring property rights must start with a respect for real home ownership for individuals. This means eliminating property taxes, and the power of the government to seize your home. Even the verbally talented Mr. Greenspeak cannot "purposefully obfuscate" around the fact that if the government can levy a tax against your home and then seize it for nonpayment, you don't really own it, and you never will. The government does. Given this basic fact, the question now becomes this: How do we eliminate property taxes?

Once again it is not the concept of taxes itself that is repugnant to constitutionalists and Libertarians. It is the form of taxes that is important. To threaten citizens with homelessness if they don't pay a tax on the homes that they might have exchanged thirty years of their labor to *own* is unethical and unconstitutional. Every American that has worked hard for most of his or her adult life in order to purchase a home should own it. Your home should be left alone as your sovereign, uncontested property because your very life depends on it. This will leave your children safe from the threat of homelessness. So then "Where will the money for education come from if we eliminate property taxes?"

The answer is simple. It will come from the same place it has always come—the families of the children being educated. Only instead of paying property taxes to an inefficient government bureaucracy and having to depend upon their integrity to honestly redistribute it, parents would be far better off simply paying tuition directly to the school.

This means to privatize—or to be more correct—to semi-privatize public schools. To semi-privatize means that some level of tax-based funding will be provided only for children of families with lesser means, to subsidize special needs children who are vulnerable and at-risk, and to cover any other public services that were formerly funded by property taxes. But those funds should not be generated by taxing the homes upon which families depend for their survival.

There is a great deal more misinformation about what school privatization means along with propaganda arguing against it than factual discourse that supports it. For one thing the meaning of privatization has been twisted into dozens of variants, none of which truly mean privatization in terms of the funding model. Privatization means schools are paid directly by those who are receiving the school's services (tuition, endowments, and voluntary charitable contributions) as opposed to public funding through property taxes levied against all home owners collectively through a government enforcement scheme.

For instance, a June 1, 2012, *Reuters* article titled "Louisiana's Bold Bid to *Privatize* Schools" stated,

> "Louisiana is embarking on the nation's boldest experiment in *privatizing* public education, with the state preparing to shift tens of millions in tax dollars out of the public schools to pay private industry, businesses owners and church pastors to educate children.
>
> Starting this fall, thousands of poor and middle-class kids will get *vouchers* covering the full cost of tuition at more than 120 private schools across Louisiana…".

The voucher system is not privatization. It is nothing more than a ruse. It is a shift of tax-based funds partially from public to some private schools. The bureaucratic collection scheme through property taxation remains the same. The dysfunctional public schools remain as they were only with some of the students leaving for better private schools using their vouchers (which may only partially cover the cost of their new private school). The schools they leave behind will then not only be underperforming but also underfunded. Since they are public, they will not be closed but will instead cry foul to their political henchmen who will then demand even more taxes to make up the difference.

The voucher system is simply a continuation of taking property tax revenue from all home owners and then redistributing some of it in the form of vouchers. People with no children continue to subsidize the education of other people's children. Property tax will continue to be extorted from all home owners forever. The public schools remain intact as they were before as does the existing model of property taxation used to fund them. This does not defuse the property tax extortion scheme, which remains in existence. In fact, it opens the door for local governments to increase property taxes even more when the public schools do indeed lose a chunk of their funding and decline in quality even further.

For the first 140 years of this country's existence, there were no public schools funded through property taxes. During the first half-century after the American Revolution, most learning happened at home. Parents taught their children with homeschooling. Massachusetts passed the first compulsory school laws in 1852 and modeled their school system after the Prussian model described earlier. It wasn't until 1920 that all American children were first required to attend at least elementary school through the sixth grade. The funding was provided directly by their parents in the form of tuition or by a tax called school tax. But this was not levied as a property tax by threatening to seize your home if you didn't pay it. Throughout that time most school systems were locally managed by county jurisdictions. The federal Department of Education did not exist until 1980, when it was created by President Jimmy Carter during the last month of his administration. The current model of public school funding through property taxation did not become pervasive across America until after the 1940s and many districts across America then still treated the tax as a school tax, which was not levied against individual property.

Real privatization consists in eliminating this model of public school funding altogether in order to eliminate property tax extortion. When schools are paid directly by the families they serve in the form of tuition, not only are they then directly accountable to the people paying them, but it also provides for accountability on the part of the families for the real cost of their children's education. If you send three children to school, why shouldn't it cost you three times as much as someone sending only one child? Fair is fair.

With privatization, property taxes could be phased out and eliminated. Families who can afford it will pay tuition directly to the school of their choice. Families who cannot afford the full tuition will pay only what they can afford (based on income) and will then be subsidized for the balance from the local and state government. That subsidy will be funded by other taxes such as a sales or some form of consumption tax but not by threatening home owners with the confiscation of their property if they don't pay whatever arbitrary amount some bureaucrat demands.

Furthermore, property taxes can continue to be levied on business property, and those residences that constitute corporate-owned rental homes. For instance, the multibillion-dollar private equity funds that are buying up swaths of foreclosed homes in order to run them as residential rentals should continue to be subject to taxes on their corporate-owned properties. Individual home owners should not.

If the revenues collected from the remaining corporate property taxes are not adequate to provide for the needy in terms of educational costs, a secondary consumption tax (sales tax) can be implemented in that county or across the state to cover the difference. In any case, these details would have to be worked out by each community in accordance with the privatization method most appropriate for it. There are numerous fair, morally acceptable, and honest ways for governments to raise revenue without threatening you, your family, and your children with the seizure of your home and the prospect of losing everything you've worked for.

The Fair Tax

When the fair tax concept was introduced in 2005 through the book by the same name, it received enormous undeserved criticism (mainly from media and the political class). That is because it is fair and would function to reduce the power of government to extort money from you. Because of the propaganda levied against it, many people scoff at the idea of a consumption or sales tax as the better alternative to any kind of asset or income tax. But consider for a moment one of the less obvious benefits that a community derives from sales taxes. When you tax sales activity, a substantial proportion of those transactions are made by visitors from outside of that community—people visiting to conduct business or just passing through. All sales tax revenue collected from outsiders adds to the public coffers of that community, enriching it with outside revenue. However, when taxes are collected solely from within a community from its own citizens in the form of income or property taxes, the government is merely cannibalizing the productive wealth of its own citizens and impoverishing them while consuming and wasting a substantial proportion of those funds through its inefficient bureaucracy. This can only provide a net reduction in wealth for that community as a whole. Consumption or sales taxes function to enrich the communities that levy them, while income and asset taxes function to cannibalize and impoverish them. And finally consumption taxes are moral and fair since the one doing the consuming can choose how much to spend, how frugal or wasteful he or she wishes to be, or whether to spend at all. It is about the inherent fairness that comes from having a choice.

There are numerous benefits to a model of privatization that eliminates property taxes, and there are few if any downsides for the working middle class.

The best reasons to eliminate property taxes altogether include the following:

- **Restore property rights and real home ownership**. You never truly own your home as long as the government can take it from you. Many people refer to property taxes as "rent paid to the government," but this is a kindness. Property tax is extortion perpetrated by the government at the point of a gun if necessary. It is nothing less than a property crime. Property tax satisfies the first plank of the *Communist Manifesto* and is a fundamentally Marxist idea.

- **Stabilize school funding.** School districts frequently struggle with steep variations in property tax revenues from one year to the next, resulting from assessment appeals by home and business owners. Funding schools with tuition based upon the real costs to deliver the education and supplemented by state funding garnered through sales taxes provides for a stable, predictable, and equitable source of revenue for schools, which is in direct proportion to the number of students they serve at any given time. Most public schools, when they incur a decline in student population find other ways to spend their annual budgets rather than simply spending less. They do this to ensure they can secure the same or even larger budget the following year regardless of the number of students. This encourages wasteful and unnecessary spending. Since direct funding by tuition is scalable to the student population, it is more efficient and less wasteful. Funding based on property taxes on the other hand encourages wastefulness and fiscal inefficiency.

- **Prevent foreclosures.** In some states monthly property tax escrow can be as high as 40 percent of a mortgage payment, exacerbating home buyers' monthly payments. Eliminating property taxes will slash the number of foreclosures across the United States.

- **Stabilize home prices more in terms of real supply and demand.** When the vastly disparate levels of property taxes are removed from the buying decision, the prices of homes will align more closely to their real demand-based value. Furthermore, inflationary shifts in home value will no longer add insult to injury to home owners by inflating their tax liabilities along with it.

- **Deliver *real* economic stimulus directly into the hands of the middle class.** In 2009, the TARP (Troubled Asset Relief Program) authorized by the US government under George W. Bush provided a $700 billion gift to failing banks and financial institutions in order to bail them out from their prior decade of malfeasance. The idea was that this would allow the rescued banks to begin lending again and thus stimulate the economy with those funds that would trickle into circulation. In that same year—in fact in every year—American home owners paid over $720 billion in property taxes, more than the one-time TARP bailout made to the banks. Returning that money to home owners to spend as they please (and on tuition to their local schools) would create a far more massive stimulus to the US economy—a stimulus that would be repeated annually—than gifting that same amount to a cabal of inefficient banks and government institutions.

- **Grow the economy through investment in personal wealth.** A home purchase is the largest and most important investment a family or individual will make in a lifetime. With the real increased asset value and no future property tax levied, home owners will finally see their personal wealth and assets (net worth) increase in real terms. This will provide a much greater ability to invest in a future for their families and their children and for their retirement. With the individual sovereignty that comes from true home ownership, the foundation is then set for sustainable economic growth through investment and savings rather than unsustainable consumption-based bubbles created by inflationary money printing.

- **Restore the prospect of a dignified retirement for our senior citizens within their own homes.** This should require no explanation either for its benefits to society or for the moral implications to our nation's elders. Our country's early values included a deep respect for our parents, grandparents, and the elderly. That cherished idea has unfortunately waned. This issue is deeply important and meaningful to those Americans who were raised with the traditional family value of "we take care of our own." This starts with a respect for our parents and our ancestors. We must restore real home ownership for those who have earned it and deserve to keep it for their golden years.

- **End wasteful, costly, unproductive activities.** With no property tax, property assessments come to an end. In Pennsylvania for example, the average cost to conduct a county reassessment is ten million dollars per county. Eliminating the need to conduct these reassessments will save states hundreds of millions annually in government spending, helping those states to better balance their budgets.

- And finally: **It will vastly improve the quality of education for our children.** The model of school funding through property taxation simply acts to absolve schools of their accountability to the families of the children they are supposed to educate. Funding schools directly is the simplest, most cost-effective, and most immediate way to make schools directly accountable to the families of the children who have been placed in their care. Our current model of funding puts tax collectors, the NEA, other teachers unions, and corrupt government bureaucrats ahead of children in the line of influence. It is time to put children *first* in the line of influence. As a parent myself, I want the school that my child attends to be accountable to me—not to a teacher's union, not to a tax assessor, and certainly not to a self-serving government bureaucrat whose primary skills are in finding new and innovative ways to rob me and my neighbors of our property.

When Your Child Finishes School and Graduates, You Should Be Finished Paying

When parents pay the school directly for their child's education, they will then have a voice that's actually heard loudest by teachers and school administrators who previously paid attention only to the bureaucrats that threw money at them in return for political support. Once your child is finished with school, you should be finished paying for it. When you pass on and leave your house to your children, they will be able to inherit and truly own a real asset rather than a perpetual tax liability that is controlled by the state.

There are a great many opponents to this idea, most of which are the unions and government bureaucrats that benefit financially from the current extortion scheme. But every hardworking American aspires to own their home. If you worked for it, you deserve to own it. It is counterintuitive that these ideas would be rejected by anyone. Unfortunately the resistance to truth and common sense is enormous. That resistance results mainly from the propaganda and misinformation that is disseminated by unions, politicians, school administrators, school boards, and a few teachers who entered the profession for the prospect of tenure and an annual three-month paid vacation.

Private Schools—Lower Cost with Higher Quality

Ironically the average cost per public school is twice that of most private schools. This fact runs counter to popular opinion, which suggests that private schools are for the rich, while public schools are for the poor and middle class. I have several good friends who are some of the most talented, knowledgeable, caring, and dedicated teachers in the profession. Almost every one of them eventually left the public school system in frustration in order to take lower-paying jobs with fewer benefits at private schools simply because they are better aligned with their values and are more dedicated to the children.

Consider further the inherent unfairness in a system that enables an unaccountable government-funded monopoly to compete directly with private schools that are fully accountable to their students' families. In spite of the huge disadvantage placed on private schools by this model, most parents who can afford it still opt to send their children to private schools even though they are forced to pay for both.

In other words, public schools function entirely in the absence of market forces. Consequently public schools have priced themselves out of what a solely private-sector education system would cost. As mentioned earlier, this is mainly due to their inherent inefficiencies and misallocation of operating resources. Property taxes have skyrocketed because of this. Plus there's the fact that only a fraction of the money collected from home owners goes toward the intended recipient. Before any government bureaucrat approves a public school budget, he first takes from the public coffer whatever he feels is required for other expenditures (including his own in many cases). In our current model, which uses taxes to provide funding for something as important as education, there is no question that there is massive fiscal inefficiency and opportunity for waste, fraud, and abuse by government employees.

Public School Dysfunction: Political Correctness Trumps Education

In New York Public School Number 139, Principal Mary McDonald ordered that the gifted program for incoming kindergartners be eliminated because "it lacks diversity." In other words, the gifted program had disproportionately more white children than children of color, and this offended Principal McDonald's sense for social justice. In her letter to the parents she wrote that the program "did not reflect the diversity of our student body and the community we live in." She further stated that "the change will allow the school to move forward as a community."

Moving forward as a community evidently means holding back the most gifted and intelligent children and relegating them to lives of boredom and mediocrity so that the parents of not-so-advanced children can feel good about themselves.

When parents questioned what the school intended to do with the higher-level students, Ms. McDonald followed up with another letter assuring them that "if they liked the gifted program, they could keep it for students already in it." It would affect "incoming kindergartners only." This is reminiscent of Obama's promise regarding our health insurance, "If you like it, you can keep it." That hasn't worked out so well for most Americans since its implementation either. However, dumbing down advanced students to socialize them in accordance with the not-so-advanced ones should certainly sit well with the liberal political agenda to attain "equality and social justice."

Some of those supporting McDonald's move tried to trivialize it by commenting that "this is for kindergarten-age children who are really just there for daycare, not for real learning anyway." That logic fits right in with the goal to dull the intellect of the brightest children from the very beginning of their academic experience. Train them right from the start that what is most important is to subjugate themselves to the desires of the collective. Train them to wait in line, to keep their heads down, to avoid shining too brightly so they don't offend anyone. Teach them to wait their turn and subordinate their abilities so those who are slower and less intelligent don't have to be challenged to try and improve themselves. Is this the principled education you wish for your child?

Waste, Fraud, and Abuse in Public Schools

A quick Internet search of public school audits reveals countless cases of waste, fraud, and abuse all across the country, amounting to millions needlessly wasted by individual districts. Added up across America, this waste of taxpayer resources is astounding. A St. Louis school district for example came under the scrutiny of a local watchdog group that began pushing for an audit. After two years of constant effort an audit was finally conducted and revealed millions in waste in a single year. In one instance a school board member had authority for approving contracts with a construction company that was also his employer and of which he was a shareholder. He approved of several construction and renovation contracts for which the company overcharged the school district by more than one million dollars in a single year. None of that money is recoverable, and the school board member has been insulated from prosecution for any crime. He was allowed to resign his board membership but basically got away with stealing millions of taxpayer dollars. This is just a single example in a single year. That school district had not been audited prior to that in more than twelve years.

In 2011, Portland public schools spent $526,901 to train teachers about the racial insensitivity of peanut butter and jelly sandwiches. After a teacher used a seemingly innocent example of a peanut butter and jelly sandwich in a lesson, Principal Verenice Gutierrez objected by saying, "What about Somali or Hispanic students who might not eat sandwiches?" As a consequence, the new school year started with "intensive staff trainings, frequent staff meetings, classroom observations and other initiatives."[88] The costs associated with political correctness are staggering.

In another example, Buffalo, NY area public schools have included in their teachers' union contract, a provision to provide free cosmetic surgery for school employees. In the 2012–2013 academic year the school district paid more than $2.9 million for nose jobs, face-lifts, boob jobs, tummy tucks, and various other cosmetic procedures. This is a district supposedly struggling with a fifty-million-dollar budget deficit that is used to justify continual increases in local property taxes. In the same school year the district's employees also spent more than $141,000 in hotels all across the United States, $48,000 in miscellaneous entertainment expenses, more than $384,000 in legal fees, and $485,902 in drug and rehabilitation services for school employees. It would be instructive to learn which of those employees who underwent drug rehab are teaching social studies or ethics to Buffalo's impressionable children. Their union contracts prevent illegal drug-using teachers from being fired. Instead, they force home owners to fund the drug rehab programs the teachers are required to attend after they are caught illegally using said drugs so that the union can protect their jobs. Who, however, is protecting our children?

---

[88] "Schools Beat the Drum for Equity," *Portland Tribune*, Pamplin Media Group, Portland, OR., Sept. 6, 2012.

Camden, NJ, city schools spent more than $306 million taxpayer dollars during the 2011–2012 school year. That works out to slightly more than $24,000 per K–12 student. For this they achieved a student graduation rate of an embarrassing 49 percent. Only one in five Camden public school students rates as proficient in math and English scores. By comparison, Rutgers University's annual tuition was approximately half that at under $13,000 annually. In other words, you could send your child to one of America's top universities for half the cost of their public school—a school which has demonstrated that it's incapable of teaching a bunch of twelve-year-olds basic math and English.

Also, during the 2011–2012 school year Camden public schools spent $987,000 on legal fees, $709,000 on consultants, $389,000 on professional conferences and workshops, and $161,000 on drug and alcohol treatment for its employees. With New Jersey having the highest property tax rates in the country, residents can rest well knowing that their property taxes are being spent to support some of the finest attorneys and consultants in the Northeast.

All across the United States the number of cases like these are legion and the amount of money being absconded from home owners by corrupt public school officials and contractors is staggering. There is only one way to end this criminal enterprise. That is to end property taxes, privatize schools, and make them accountable to the parents in their respective communities. There is no better solution.

Dozens of studies and audits have been conducted across the United States. These show that public school system costs per student are comparable to the most elite private schools and most often exceed the costs of the more efficiently run charter schools. The most insidious aspect of the current model is that parents who send their children to private schools are forced to pay for the cost of their children's education twice—in the tuition that the private schools charge plus the property taxes they are forced to pay to support the public school system.

Public education constitutes a government monopoly (a purely socialist construct). Privatizing education would open the door to a vast range of competitors fostered by the free market. This would compel each of those competitors to offer the best quality education they can rather than only the minimalist level of education in compliance with government standards. In terms of quality the current model discourages excellence since striving for this adds cost and doesn't justify their later demands for more public money. Requiring public schools to meet only a minimum set of educational standards is like saying that American schools should strive for mediocrity.

If you strive for mediocrity, you are guaranteed to achieve it, and our long-term decline in academic performance proves we're doing exactly that.

Real privatization—eliminating property taxes and delinking schools from government funding—is a model that could easily be tested on a small scale in one or more communities. This could be implemented by an appropriate state government policy change to allow one or several willing communities within a state to fully privatize.

Imagine what would happen to the value of your home if your community decided to eliminate property taxes. Instead of paying the annual tribute in return for the privilege of staying in the house you have worked so hard to pay for, you could instead pay that money directly to the school responsible for your child's education. After your child graduates, you're finished paying. The economic, social, educational, and cultural benefits enjoyed by that community would be the envy of the nation. Property values in that community would skyrocket as families would line up to purchase a home there. Residents within that community however would never want to leave. They would invest in the quality of their own homes, lives, and local culture, further enriching their local community. Inspired by the economic and social benefits derived, it wouldn't take long before neighboring communities would follow suit.

Leading by example is always better than ruling by force.

Implementing this idea carries little if any risk. Localizing this model of privatization to one or a few places in a state for a few years could allow a fair test before any statewide changes were made in the overall public education system. Once this model's vast benefits to those communities have been proven, privatization could be expanded across the country. Eventually this would render obsolete the costly and inefficient Department of Education. Eliminating that superfluous bureaucracy would save taxpayers another eighty billion dollars annually.

I am often harshly criticized for these ideas by people claiming that I'm "against education, against children, or against communities." Far from it. What I am fundamentally against is the prospect of children losing their family homes by having them seized by self-serving government parasites. I'm against children being prematurely sexualized or even raped by their teachers or other students with no legal recourse for their parents. I'm against children being indoctrinated with Marxist philosophy and revisionist history about America's founding principles. I'm against corrupt banking institutions and unconstitutional tax authorities conspiring to destroy individual property rights and with it the moral tradition of the American family.

What I am for is a prosperous future for this nation's children with the individual liberty and right to self-determination that is their birthright as handed down from the founders of this nation and as espoused in our founding declaration and the US Constitution.

Restoring Power to the People

Imagine for a moment eliminating your property taxes, increasing the value of your home, improving the quality of your child's education, removing forever the fear of losing your home by government seizure—all achieved through a single structural change in how we fund public schools.

This concept could successfully begin to unwind the oppressive and corrupt big-government vise in which the middle class is trapped and being squeezed. As I mentioned earlier in this book, Americans are being squeezed in a vice with one jaw represented by the federal government and the other represented by state and local governments. But just as with the bench tool found in your garage, it is only one of the jaws that can be unwound, yet upon doing so, both jaws must loosen their grip.

It is primarily at the community grassroots level where the American people have the chance to begin regaining their individual freedom, sovereignty, and prospects for economic security. If you as an American truly want your freedom—to be able to truly own your home and to know that the money you save for your children's future will be there for them when they need it and will retain its value over time—then it is absolutely vital that we take this country back from those who have usurped it. Most people are discouraged by the feeling that the mounting problems of this country are too vast, and that the federal government is so huge, powerful, and corrupt that there is nothing that any one person can do about it. That's what the ruling class, the government, and the media want you think.

That notion is absolutely false.

The place to start is with your own home, with your own property, within your own community, and in your local school district. To take back your home and assert your right to property ownership, you must bring your neighbors and your local community together to openly and respectfully discuss this idea and create the means with which to take your public school system out of the hands of government bureaucrats. Government must be forbidden from extorting your hard-earned wealth by threatening to take away your home—the home that you and your children depend upon for your very survival. Home ownership is not a trivial matter. It is literally a matter of life and death for every single American citizen.

The First Step to Eliminating Property Taxes

The first step is to demand a comprehensive and independent financial audit of your community's school district and tax authority in order to root out any waste, fraud, and abuse. This must be done to identify, pursue, and then prosecute those in local government who may have committed fraud against their constituency as well as to analytically determine the real costs of operating your local schools. In conducting such an audit, the school administration will have no choice but to deal directly with the grassroots of their community. Once the real costs are known the tuition-pricing model can be established based upon the next school year's enrollment. Families with children in school will henceforth no longer be billed by the government for property taxes, but instead by the school for tuition. Families whose incomes are below an appropriately calculated level will have their tuition fees adjusted down proportionally, and the mechanism for making up the difference for those families will be determined by that community based upon their local economy. The next step will be for the schools to properly manage costs and budgets rather than depend upon government largess to cover for their pattern of fiscal inefficiency.

The practical effects of ending property taxes and semi-privatizing schools are many. The money you save will be used to pay tuition for your children's education. When they graduate, you're finished paying. If you have no children, you'll have more money to spend on other things within your community, providing localized economic stimulus and further enriching the community in the process. If you choose to homeschool your children as millions of Americans do already, the money you save can be put toward paying off your mortgage and other debts and becoming a real home owner much sooner. Schools could be incentivized to work with and help parents in their homeschooling models as part of their service package. Parents would not only have choice about the process of education for their children but will also have direct influence over the school about the academic content and what moral values are being taught.

Other creative alternatives to traditional public schools would be in a better position to thrive, even in rural areas. This would create opportunities for gifted or uniquely talented children. Private schools that train musicians, dancers, and a variety of other young people with unique natural talents would ensure that those children receive a first-class education in the arts as well as in the fundamentals of math, English, and history.

The success of a community that implements the privatization alternative will lead other states to implement their own privatization models. Every community will be in a position to design its system on its own terms. Some private schools could operate on shorter school days or not conduct classes every day of the week. Bright students are often bored by the slow pace of public school instruction, and a partly online education could actually excite more advanced students for whom public education is tedious and boring. The best performing schools will become models of excellence from which other schools will learn to improve their own methods in order to remain competitive. Instead of a system that rewards minimalist mediocrity, it will be a system based on continuous improvement that always strives to raise the bar rather than lower it.

The Power of Homeschooling

Many of the greatest minds from American history did not have any public school education whatsoever. There is no evidence that Benjamin Franklin, who was at once among the greatest scientists, greatest writers, greatest diplomats, and greatest inventors in history and was fluent in at least three languages, had ever attended any formal school. Abraham Lincoln had a formal education that consisted of no more than one year's worth of classes from several itinerant teachers. Aside from this, he was an insatiable reader and was mostly self-educated. Lincoln taught himself the law by reading Blackstone's *Commentaries on the Laws of England* and other law books. Of his learning method Lincoln stated, "I studied with nobody." He was admitted to the Illinois State Bar Association with little more than one year of formal education, and had never attended any university or law school. Thomas Edison and Andrew Carnegie, whose genius transformed not just America but the world, had little if any formal education.

If eliminating public in favor of private education funding were tried just as an experiment for a few school districts in America, no great harm could result. It would most likely do a great deal of good.

CHAPTER 8

Restoring the American Dream

Prosperity, Income, Savings, and Retirement

Courage is being scared to death, and saddling up anyway.

—John Wayne

It takes courage and true grit to secure your own freedom. America's founders did it in 1776 against all odds and at enormous personal risk. We can do it again. We're Americans.

Returning to Sound Money

The American dream is not complicated. It's really a matter of choosing between two alternatives: Do you want to be a free, self-reliant, prosperous home owner who is able to earn and save an enduring legacy of prosperity for your children—or do you instead prefer to be a dependent, minimalist, debt slave who lives paycheck to paycheck and pays rent to your government until the day you die, leaving nothing but a life of debt and tax servitude to your children? The former respects property rights. The latter has no property rights.

You must choose one or the other. It cannot be both.

Our current fiat monetary system is the direct cause of the latter, and it absolutely prohibits achieving the former. As such, there is only one clear choice.

Restoring a system of sound money in accordance with the US Constitution will require the political will to do so. However, we cannot sugarcoat the reality of this fact—our current government is not only devoid of the will to do this but will vehemently reject a return to sound money. The political class depends upon the irresponsible largess and unaccountability that our fiat monetary system enables. They will resist a restoration of sound money with every fiber of their being and will go to any lengths to prevent it. Therefore, it will require that the entire Congress be replaced with a supermajority of representatives who understand this issue, who understand economics, and who have the courage and integrity to dismantle the Federal Reserve system. It is not something that can be done piecemeal. Ending the Federal Reserve system will require a repeal of the Federal Reserve Act and a restoration of the gold standard to US currency.

It is naive to presume that such challenges will be met simply because a new group of people are installed into positions of power. This is the fallacy that persists at nearly every election cycle. Voters cheer that the new guy is going to fix everything. He then winds up continuing with the policies of his predecessor—policies he denounced in order to gain votes. Excitement for *hope and change* almost always turns to disappointment and the status quo. Elections may change the players but they don't change the game. It is the game that is fundamentally flawed. The real solutions are not with politicians, but within us. Therefore, in order to have meaningful change in our federal government, virtually everyone in our federal government must be changed—in other words—replaced.

We must replace most of the members of Congress (along with their appointees) with representatives and officials that understand this and are willing to do what is necessary. We must also remove from the Supreme Court the activist judges who pervert the meaning and intent of The Constitution rather than to uphold and defend it as their oath of office demands. In other words, we the people must fire our government employees, because they are not doing their jobs, and they are stealing from their employer.

Many people mistakenly believe that this is impossible. With the current class of career politicians who have entrenched themselves permanently in our federal government, they are right. This is why the voters must rout Congress and remove every sitting career politician who objects to putting an end to the Federal Reserve system. In other words, we the people must stop allowing the entertainment media to dictate to us what the major issues are. We the people must evaluate political candidates based upon their character, as well as their understanding of these economic issues. We must make it clear that we will only support those candidates who have the courage to act to restore the US Constitution and end the Federal Reserve System. We the people will no longer tolerate corrupt career politicians dictating to us how we must live. It is we, who shall dictate to them the extent to which they will be permitted to govern—as defined in the US Constitution.

The Misguided Notion of Quantity

Many of the uninformed object to a return to sound money with comments such as, "the population is too big now and there isn't enough physical gold." This may sound logical on the surface and mainstream *economists* residing in the pocket of the ruling class do nothing to dispel such nonsense. Yet upon closer analysis, this idea is proven to be absurd. Most objections are a consequence of misunderstanding what a gold standard actually is.

First of all, approximately half of all the gold mined and produced since the discovery of the American continent, is currently stored in bank vaults and government hoards. There exists at least an additional 30% in jewelry, and private holdings. Any commodity which is stored unused, and exists to the extent of over 80 % of its total historical production since Europeans first settled America clearly does not constitute a supply constraint.

Moreover, the fact is that the supply is actually irrelevant.

Of the three purposes of money, its role as a unit of account—a tool to measure the value of items for which it is exchanged—is its most important function. In this context, money serves simply as a yardstick of value. As such, the unit of measurement has absolutely no impact on the inherent value of the item being measured.

Let's say that you measure a room in your house to be five meters in length. Expressing its dimension as five hundred centimeters, or five thousand millimeters does not make the room longer. Just as the number of measuring units has no impact on the length of a room, so the quantity of money in existence has no impact on the inherent value of all goods and services in an economy. Regardless of what measurement we use, the physical reality of what we are measuring remains unchanged.

The amount of gold that exists has absolutely no effect on its ability to serve as money. It only affects the quantity that will be used to measure the value of any given transaction.

> "We come to the startling truth that it doesn't matter what the supply of money is. Any supply will do as well as any other supply. The free market will simply adjust by changing the purchasing power or effectiveness of its gold unit. There is no need whatever for any planned increase in the money supply, or for the supply to rise to offset any condition, or to follow any artificial criteria. More money does not supply more capital, is not more productive, it does not permit economic growth."

> —Dr. Murray Rothbard

In 1913, when the Federal Reserve system was established, the average annual income for an individual was $633. In that same year, the price of Gold was $20.67 per ounce. As such, the average American worker earned 30.6 ounces of gold per year. By the beginning of 2014, more than one hundred years later, the average annual income for an individual was $40,110, and the price of gold was $1,315 per ounce. So in 2014, the average American worker earned 30.6 ounces of gold. This is exactly the same amount that the average worker earned in 1913 in terms of gold coin. A paycheck of $40,110 has the appearance of being vastly larger than one of $633, but in terms of comparing real purchasing power in 2014 and 1913 respectively, they are equivalent. The bigger paycheck is meaningless. There is one major difference however. In 1913, workers were not taxed on their wages. Therefore, the average worker in 1913 who was paid $633 actually earned about twice as much as current workers who are paid over $40 thousand, in terms of real purchasing power.[89]

Restoring a gold standard will not mean an end to the financial system as we know it. In the post-Fed America there will still be dollars, banks, ATMs, web-based systems for currency transfers, and even paper currency. A gold standard simply consists in legally defining what a dollar is in terms of a standard of weights and measures as the US Constitution demands, and then prohibiting the counterfeiting of new fiat money out of nothing. If you ask the Fed chairman today what the definition of a dollar is, his answer will be "a dollar is whatever a dollar will buy." That's a cute answer unless

---

[89] Griffin, G. Edward. The Creature from Jekyll Island. American Media. September 11, 2010.

you are trying to save for a home you intend to purchase ten years from now. What $1.00 bought in 2004 cost $1.48 in 2014.

Once the Fed's tentacles have been severed, the volume of currency will be frozen, and whatever definition of the dollar in terms of gold weight needs to be will be determined at that time. Nevertheless, the point will be to stop the irresponsible and unrestrained expansion of our money supply, which is intended to create perpetual inflation. This will prohibit government from continuing to live beyond its means. Fiscal discipline will be the consequence. Government bureaucrats do not want to see this happen because their gravy train of unlimited, irresponsible spending will be stopped.

The banking industry will remain but will undergo an adjustment. Sound banks will continue to thrive, while unsound banks will disappear, as they should. There will no longer be a process of creating money out of thin air in order to create artificially high demand intended to distort certain targeted market segments (such as the housing bubble). The obscenely rich will have to play by the same rules of the game and with the same risks of loss as the rest of us. All monetary powers would be transferred to the US Treasury Department, who answers to Congress. The Federal Reserve would be dissolved, and those who own and control it will have to either retire or find real jobs.

More importantly investment risk will be balanced across society. Sound money will immediately put an end to the possibility for government and their corporate cronies to privatize profits and socialize losses. Small business entrepreneurs will—for the first time in generations—be able to compete with large corporations on a level playing field, at least in terms of financial risk. Home prices will stabilize rather than inflate and/or deflate as we've seen over the past fifty years, and it will once again become possible for the poor to save their way out of poverty. Destructive financial speculation like home flipping will no longer be possible without substantial risks to the financial institutions that formerly enabled this sort of thing through their money-creation powers and consequent irresponsible lending practices.

The prices for goods and services will adjust according to the money supply that exists and will remain stable. Contrary to the Fed's usual propaganda, injecting new money into the supply does not confer any social benefits. If supply of goods increase (in other words, production rises) while the money supply remains stable, the price of those goods should go down. This is what we expect from efficient and competitive manufacturing concerns. Higher volume manufacturing is how unit costs are brought down. If an item costs less to make, it should cost less for the consumer to purchase. This is not deflation at work. This is supply and demand at work.

Credit markets would still function. Banks would still loan money. It would just be money that has been saved and deposited, not money that has been created out of thin air. There will still be economic growth, but it will be a healthy form of growth. It will be based on savings and real investment and not primarily unsustainable overconsumption *disguised as growth*. To use the language of business, it will be the kind of economic growth that increases enterprise value (net worth) rather than just increasing turnover (consumption).

The discipline that a gold standard imposes upon government is one of the most beneficial aspects. The wasteful largess that has been standard operating procedure within our federal government would have to come to an immediate halt. Just as this standard would impose financial investment risk evenly across society, so too would an equivalent financial risk be borne by government instead of solely by the poor and working class. The reckless and wasteful spending on digging and then refilling useless holes in the ground would be reined in with a renewed transparency regarding the cost of our foreign interventionism, unnecessary wars, and frivolous government programs.

There are two ways to end the Federal Reserve system. It can either be done in a single bold legislative act, or it could be dismantled incrementally by transitioning the system toward that goal. Either way has certain pros and cons. As far as this author is concerned, I believe that this system must be dismantled as soon and as quickly as possible so that the corrupt, self-serving members of the Federal Reserve system will not be in a position to sabotage the process of restoring sound money—for they have every reason to do so.

Restoring the Gold Standard

Some authors have suggested that the Federal Reserve system could be reformed in order to restore some stability while allowing the fiat system to continue. Those making these proposals are well intentioned, and they believe that taking such steps will set the stage for an incremental dismantling of the Fed. I disagree with these approaches and will explain why under each of their proposed tactics below:

Change the Mandate of the Federal Reserve

According the Federal Reserve's website, "The Congress established the statutory objectives for monetary policy in the Federal Reserve Act as being: maximum employment, stable prices, and moderate long-term interest rates." The Federal Reserve's actions during the past hundred years reveal that they are far more interested in achieving the opposite. They willfully create targeted inflations (economic bubbles) and enact policy that maximizes unemployment in order to ensure that the corporations owned by their banking cartel have a desperate and underemployed workforce ready and willing to work for peanuts. If they haven't fulfilled their existing mandate at any time in the past hundred years, what difference would it make to change their mandate now?

Adopting a Formal Rule to Guide Federal Reserve Decision-Making

The Fed has had formal rules intended to guide their decision-making process since it was founded. They have not followed those rules, and as Mr. Greenspan and Mr. Bernanke have told Congress on numerous occasions, they are not obligated to disclose the details of their actions and are not accountable to anyone. In fact, they have deliberately prohibited Congress any scrutiny of their adherence to those rules.[90] It is for this reason that for the past thirty years former congressman Dr. Ron Paul has worked tirelessly to bring transparency and accountability to the secretive Fed. In 2009 and 2010 he introduced: HR 1207, the bill to audit the Federal Reserve. The bill passed as an amendment in the House's Financial Services Committee and in the House itself. But eventually the most significant portions of the bill were derailed.[91]

Dr. Paul reintroduced Audit the Fed on January 26, 2011 as HR 459 along with a companion bill introduced by his son, Dr. Rand Paul, in the Senate as S202. Exactly eighteen months later on July 25, 2012, the House of Representatives overwhelmingly approved the Texas Republican's bill with bipartisan support, and it passed 327–98. The Senate version of the bill, S202, however, has remained stuck in the US Senate Committee on Banking, Housing, and Urban Affairs, as Chairman Tim Johnson (D-SD) is under direct orders from Senate majority leader Harry Reid (D-NV) "not to let it out of committee." As of this writing, this bill has remained stuck in the Senate committee on Senator Reid's orders for more than more than two and a half years. For a US Senator to deliberately quash a legitimate bill from being voted upon by the Senate—a bill that has passed the House of Representatives twice—is a blatant violation of his oath of office and his obligation to his constituency. If the other US Senators were true to their own oaths of office, they would immediately act to remove Senator Reid from his position for his repeated and egregious violations of the public trust.

Clearly the corruption has extended from the Federal Reserve banking cartel and into the halls of Congress. What good is a set of rules for decisions for either the Federal Reserve or the US Senate when the top-ranking members of both institutions willfully violate them? Clearly, Senator Reid's relationship with the Fed should be investigated for possible conflicts of interest. If such conflicts are proven, it would

---

[90] Greenspan, Alan. Testimony to Congress. October 23, 2008. http://www.c-spanvideo. org/program/281958-1

[91] 111th Congress. "Text of H.R. 1207: Federal Reserve Transparency Act of 2009.

render him as incapable of continuing in his duties as a US Senator, and he should in that case be removed from office immediately.

Adopting a Full Gold Standard by Establishing an Official Gold Convertibility Rate for the Dollar

This is essentially restoring the system back to the pre-FDR structure. This is probably the best suggestion by those trying to keep the Federal Reserve system in some form, but as FDR proved, as long as the Fed system exists in any form whatsoever, the means to corrupt our monetary system will continue to exist as well. As long as a private banking cartel controls the nation's money supply, whether on a gold standard or not, we will forever be fighting the thieves who are bent on robbing us of our property rights. We must remove the wolves from the hen house once and for all.

Allow Competitive Currencies, Including Private Currencies Backed by Gold or Silver, to Circulate against Federal Reserve Notes

Friedrich Hayek, the Austrian economist who won the 1974 Nobel Prize in economics had written extensively on his mistrust of any government to maintain even an honest gold standard. In November 1977, Hayek asserted, "I am more convinced than ever, that if we ever again are going to have sound money, it will not come from government; it will be issued by private enterprise." This form of monetary system is the model that is truest to the principles of a free-market economy. It represents the most honest monetary standard and should be held up as the ultimate goal for our monetary system. The most likely to be achievable step in this direction will be to end the Federal Reserve System and restore the gold standard with our Congress-controlled Treasury in control of our money, allowing competitive currencies to come into being based upon market demand.

What about Bitcoin?

Bitcoin is one of the most widely discussed topics on the Internet today, but it is one of the least understood. Bitcoin is a software-based open-source payment technology used for transferring value across the Internet. Therefore, it is a virtual currency. You can own units of Bitcoins via your computer or any other Internet-connected device and can even store them on a USB stick. It is possible to exchange Bitcoin units with anyone else around the world who also has a Bitcoin account. Its greatest strength is in providing a global electronic payment network that enables transactions to be low cost, to stay virtually frictionless, and to flow easily across international borders. It allows monetary value to be exchanged online without intermediaries so that users can avoid banks who skim fees with every transaction.

Many of Silicon Valley's most successful entrepreneurs have invested in Bitcoin, including some of the early backers of PayPal, Facebook, Skype, Instagram, and others. However, Bitcoin is subject to the same dynamics that occur from currency speculation. These multimillionaire investors have money they can afford to lose. Investing in Bitcoin is not investing. It is speculation. It is gambling, and its volatility at this point in time should be considered high risk. Bitcoin is not backed by anything of intrinsic value so it is not defined as sound money. It can't really be considered a fiat currency either because its value has not been declared by any government. Nor has it been declared as legal tender.

Bitcoin's price has fluctuated wildly since its inception. In 2011, the value of one Bitcoin went from $0.32 up to $32 and back down to $2. By November of 2013, Bitcoin had risen to more than a thousand dollars per Bitcoin. The value then dropped by more than 40 percent in a single day in December 2013. This occurred when China's central bank ordered payment processing companies to halt transactions involving digital currencies. Therefore, there is huge exchange-rate risk as well as political risk associated with Bitcoin.

Where Do Bitcoins Come from, and How Does Bitcoin Work?

Our current fiat paper-money system depends on a central bank like the Federal Reserve to decide how much money to print, when to loan it out, and at what interest rates. Bitcoin is not issued by any bank. Nor is it controlled by any government, and it is not *loaned* into circulation at interest. It is known as a peer-to-peer transaction medium. In that regard, it appears to be far more compatible with the free-enterprise system than our current monetary system. However, there are substantial risks and potential downsides that may have not yet become evident. For one thing it is likely just a matter of time before governments step in to regulate it. It is also just a matter of time before clever methods of committing Bitcoin fraud are concocted.

Bitcoins can be purchased using any legal tender at any given time, and there is an exchange rate for doing so. For Bitcoins to come into being in the first place, however, *miners* use software and a network of computers to solve special math problems for which the algorithm produces and issues them a certain number of Bitcoins in exchange. This is the process of Bitcoin mining. In theory, anyone can become a Bitcoin miner. The idea behind mining for these coins comes from the analogy of mining for gold to be used as physical money. The actual demand is what justifies its creation and motivates the miners to create it.

Bitcoin's inventor (or inventors) and first miner has remained anonymous but released the original software under the pseudonym Satoshi Nakomoto. The original algorithm that created Bitcoin was set up to strictly limit the total number of Bitcoins that could come into existence to twenty-one million. Each coin is divided into a hundred million pieces, which makes it scalable as a payment technology. Since there can never be any more than twenty-one million Bitcoins created, this money cannot be subject to the same kind of inflationary monetary expansion as perpetrated by our Federal Reserve System. The only thing it has in common with physical gold is that it comes into being when Bitcoin miners invest in the hardware and the software and then spend time and effort in solving the problems required to obtain the coins. If there were no demand for it, no supply would be created.

In principle, this type of money is therefore compatible with free-market principles, while Federal Reserve notes are not. In fact, Bitcoin is what is called a deflationary currency. This is because its supply is strictly limited to a maximum number of coins, and once Bitcoins start to be lost or destroyed they can never be replaced. The remaining supply of Bitcoins will see their purchasing power increase over time (deflation) as long as people continue to use it as currency.

What Happens If the Lights Go Out?

Using Bitcoin as money depends entirely on the Internet and electric grid. Turn off the switch, and no transactions can take place. Such an outage from a power failure or an EMP (electromagnetic pulse) could even cause some Bitcoins to evaporate from existence. Once lost, a Bitcoin can never be recreated. Since it is a deflationary currency, as the supply of Bitcoins evaporates, the Bitcoin economy will experience sustained irreversible deflation after the maximum supply has been reached.

Physical gold and silver can still be traded when the lights go out. Furthermore, losing a gold coin doesn't mean it simply evaporates forever into cyberspace. On July 20, 1985, treasure hunter Mel Fisher discovered off Key West, FL, the Spanish Galleon *Nuestra Señora de la Atocha* with a cache of more than forty tons of gold and silver coins. This actually represented only half of the Atocha's treasure, which remains lost—lost but not gone. The Atocha sank in 1622. After nearly four hundred years under the devastating effects of salt water and the storm-laced reefs of the Florida Keys, Mr. Fisher was able to recover thousands of gold coins that were as shiny and lustrous as the day the Atocha sank. Even the silver he recovered remained intact during that time. Thanks to his perseverance and the intrinsic value held in gold and silver coin, his children are now filthy rich and deservedly so.

The point to be made here is that precious metals like gold have been and will continue to be the most reliable form of sound money. This has been the case for thousands of years. Gold has a virtually infinite shelf life. As for me, when I trade my labor in exchange for money and I am given the choice between paper, virtual currency, or gold—in my opinion there is only one choice—the gold standard.

The Moral Contract

Money is a moral contract between the government and those who hold its currency. The point is to ensure that each unit of value that the owner has worked hard to earn, whether a peso, a pound, a euro, a dollar, or an ounce of gold, will be worth as much tomorrow as it is today. If the government allows that value to deviate, it is breeching its moral contract with the people. The proper role of government in the economy is to guarantee the integrity of market transactions. This can only be achieved with money that has integrity. Therefore, a government that forces unsound inflationary currency onto its people clearly does so for an immoral purpose—to destroy the property rights of the citizenry. Here in the US, this has been done in direct violation of the US Constitution.

Traditional American values are founded in the pursuit of the American dream. It is the goal of achieving self-reliance through hard work, delayed gratification, and saving for the future. There is no point in delaying gratification if gratification is ultimately unachievable. In the first century after America's founding, the poor in this country had a chance to escape poverty. By living frugally and putting a little bit away over time to accumulate a savings, a poor sharecropper could eventually buy a small farm. Eventually he'd become a self-reliant property owner, and his children would inherit the means to create more wealth for themselves. Today under our fiat currency model, saving your way to prosperity in this way is a mathematical impossibility. The poor are kept poor, and the middle class is systematically impoverished as inflation, debt service, and taxes devour their savings and their income.

It is only through the free-enterprise's sound monetary system that individual citizens can achieve their highest economic aspirations, and thus help the whole of society realize its maximum prosperity. It is the reason that I have asserted time and time again throughout this book that until we restore sound money as the basic monetary model, we as Americans cannot consider ourselves to be sovereign individuals functioning in a free-market capitalist system. Instead, we are adherents to a fundamentally Marxist-socialist system that forbids individual property ownership.

"Fiat money and liberty are incompatible ... therefore one must unavoidably destroy the other."

We the people who have the right to our lives, our liberty, our property, our pursuit of happiness—we who wish to bequeath these values to our children—must see to it that liberty will be the one to destroy fiat money and not the other way around.

We must therefore end the Federal Reserve system and restore sound money now.

In the beginning of a change, the Patriot is a scarce man, brave, hated, and scorned. When his cause succeeds, the timid join him, for then it costs nothing to be a Patriot.

—Mark Twain

PART 2

Who Stole My Country? Who Stole My Children's Future?

CHAPTER 9

The Assassination of Small Business and the Corporatization of America

Fascism should more appropriately be called corporatism, because it is the merger of state and corporate power.

—Benito Mussolini

Small businesses in America are dying and are being replaced by huge monopolistic corporations. Even a small independent coffee shop in your neighborhood is becoming increasingly difficult to find. They are being driven out of business by corporate chains like Starbucks and Dunkin' Donuts. The days of the small family-owned, roadside motel are gone. Even so-called economy hotels are owned by the major hotel chain corporations, and privately held franchisees remain beholden to their corporate flag. Today it is nearly impossible to find a neighborhood hardware store or drugstore that isn't owned or controlled by a large corporation. If you need a box of nails, chances are your only choices are Home Depot or Lowes.

If you are an independent entrepreneur aspiring to own a small business, you face an increasingly onerous battle to manage the risks. The financial commitment is yours alone to bear. If you finance your business using bank debt, you must pledge your future earnings to repay it along with the business itself as collateral. Large corporations have no such obligation. Their principal owners (banks, and financial institutions) use their fractional-reserve money-creation powers to make risky investments using capital that they can create out of thin air at the most favorable interest rates. If a huge corporation's venture falters, their investment bank owners can issue additional debt to cover their losses, or they get bailed out by the taxpayers. By comparison, if your small business fails, you are ruined and your family is left penniless. In that event, you may have no other option but to become an underpaid, overworked employee of one of your former corporate competitors.

This constitutes an inherently unfair competitive environment. It is another example of corporate monopolism acting to drive out small business entrepreneurship and replace it with employment servitude. This condition is exacerbated by the incessant expansion of government regulatory intrusion into small business. The latest example is the Patient Protection and Affordable Care Act (Obamacare). Between the corporate banking aristocracy and their partners in government, in time their efforts will ensure that there will be few if any privately owned small businesses in existence. Eventually almost every American will have no alternative other than to be an employee of some huge centralized monopolistic corporation. In fact, as of July 2013, small and medium businesses were surpassed as being the largest job creator in the United States. As of July 2014, the two largest employers in the Unites States were Wal-Mart and a Temp Agency.[92]

Government is the Obstacle, Not the Enabler

Home Depot, one of the largest and most successful retailer's in America, was founded in 1978 with one retail store. By July of 2013, the company had grown to more than 2,250 stores and a market capitalization of $ 113.2 billion USD. It is one of America's greatest business success stories. The company was founded during the Carter administration and was taken public in 1981 while the United States was suffering from the worst recession and highest unemployment in the previous forty years. The company thrived, creating hundreds of thousands of jobs, and it redefined home improvement retailing.

In July of 2011, Bernie Marcus, one of the original founders and the company's first CEO was interviewed by *Investor's Business Daily*. During the interview Marcus stated that Home Depot "would never succeed" if it launched today because of onerous government regulation.

When asked by *Investor's Business Daily*, "What's the single biggest impediment to job growth today?"

Marcus answered, "The US government."

---

[92]   Schow, Asche. Recovery Woes: America's 2nd Largest Employer is a Temp Agency. *The Washington Examiner.* July 8, 2013.

He then continued,

> Having built a small business into a big one, I can tell you that today the impediments that the government imposes are impossible to deal with. Home Depot would never have succeeded if we'd tried to start it today. Every day you see rules and regulations from a group of Washington bureaucrats who know nothing about running a business. And I mean every day. It's become stifling. If you're a small businessman, the only way to deal with it is to work harder, put in more hours, and let people go. When you consider that something like 70 percent of the American people work for small businesses, you are talking about a big economic impact.

IBD: "President Obama has promised to streamline and eliminate regulations. What's your take?"

Marcus:

> His speeches are wonderful. His output is absolutely, incredibly bad. As he speaks about cutting out regulations, they are now producing thousands of pages of new ones. With just Obamacare by itself, you have a 2,000 page bill that's probably going to end up being 150,000 pages of regulations.

IBD: "Washington has been consumed with debt talks. Is this the right focus now?"

Marcus:

> "They are all tied together. If we don't lower spending and if we don't deal with paying down the debt, we are going to have to raise taxes. Even brain-dead economists understand that when you raise taxes, you cost jobs."

IBD: "If you could sit down with Obama and talk to him about job creation, what would you say?"

Marcus:

> I'm not sure Obama would understand anything that I'd say, because he's never really worked a day outside the political or legal area. He doesn't know how to make a payroll, he doesn't understand the problems businesses face. I would try to explain that the plight of the businessman is very reactive to Washington. As Washington piles on regulations and mandates, the

impact is tremendous. I don't think he's a bad guy. I just think he has no knowledge of this.

IBD: "Why don't more businesses speak out?"

Marcus:

"They are frightened to death—frightened that they will have the IRS or SEC on them. In my 50 years in business, I have never seen executives of major companies who were more intimidated by an administration."

IBD: "What's your message to the business community?"

Marcus:

It's time to stand up and fight. These people in Washington are out there making your life difficult, and many of you won't survive. Why aren't you doing something about it? The free enterprise system made this country what it is today, and we've got to keep it alive. We are on the edge of the abyss. At the Job Creators Alliance, we're trying to recruit people who are willing to step up and say, "I've had it. There's no one representing me. I want to be out there and fight."

Mr. Marcus's comments are completely accurate, but this is because of a much broader premise than in terms of what the Obama administration has been doing to destroy the economy. That effort was launched long before President Obama was born. What we see happening to small business in America is a consequence of what could be referred to as *corporatization*. This consists in placing a substantially greater burden of financial risk upon small independent businesses, family businesses, family farms, and start-ups than on large corporations and the investment banks who own them. This yields a playing field of unfair competition that is engineered into the system. Its main beneficiaries are the financiers of those huge corporations and the politicians who enable their financial monopolies. Such a model is made possible under our fiat currency system. When all money is fiat debt, all investment risk is passed on to those who are obligated to trade their labor and real property in exchange for that money. This is another example of privatizing profits and socializing losses. Are you beginning to recognize the pattern?

Under a sound monetary system, the risk of loss is the same whether you are a hardworking entrepreneur willing to risk your life savings to realize your vision—or a huge bank with a legal fiduciary responsibility to wisely invest your depositors' capital. Only a sound monetary model provides for what is repeatedly referred to as the level playing field of competition in a free-market capitalist system. This is why free-market capitalism is compatible only with a sound monetary system.

It is also the reason that Karl Marx specified our current type of monetary system—fiat—as being a cornerstone of Communism and one of the principal tools used to destroy free-market capitalism. Communism is the quintessential model for privatizing profit and socializing loss (or socializing risk) while protecting the ruling class from any risks whatsoever. The system is designed to drive business activity toward a model of centralized corporate monopolies while it eliminates privately held small businesses. Marx's idea for a dictatorship of the proletariat is great so long as you are one of the dictators and not one of the proletariat.

Most Americans believe that large public corporations are owned by individual citizens like themselves through their common-stock holdings or through their 401(k) plans. However, what many don't realize is that common shareholders are subordinate to every other stakeholder in a public company. It is the preferred shareholders, bondholders (usually the original founders and their investment bankers), and major secured creditors whose ownership in these corporations is held supreme in the eyes of the law. This is true even if its principal funding came from common shareholders. However, common shareholders have absolutely no influence over management's decisions. If management decides to leverage 100 percent of the company's assets and put the company in debt up to its shareholders' eyeballs, driving it into bankruptcy, they can do so without the shareholders' consent—yet doing so will destroy the shareholders' assets.

One of the best examples of how common shareholders were fleeced out of their entire investments is the story of Global Crossing, which later came to be known as "Global Double-Crossing."

The company's founder and chairman of the board, Mr. Gary Winnick was a former partner of Michael Milken, better known as the "junk bond king" (Milken was indicted for securities fraud and racketeering in 1989). Throughout the bankruptcy, restructuring, and the reissue of new Global Crossing shares, Winnick remained as the company's chairman of the board and major preferred shareholder. In the weeks just before the company's chapter-eleven bankruptcy, Global Crossing's CEO John Legere was rewarded with a $10 Million bonus in the form of a corporate personal loan that was later forgiven and not repaid.

If you lose your own small business to bankruptcy, you lose everything you've ever worked for. When Global Crossing's management drove their public company into bankruptcy, they all paid themselves huge bonuses and took stock-option windfalls, while their common shareholders were completely wiped out. This has been the pattern in virtually every major corporate bankruptcy of the past few decades.

How Was This Shareholder Fleecing Possible?

At the height of the dot-com bust, Global Crossing had invested heavily into setting up a global fiber-optic telecommunications network with transoceanic cables that would circumnavigate the planet. Within three years of its founding the company had a market capitalization of $47.6 billion (as of February 2000). Just two years later its value stood at only $273 million (one half of 1 percent of its former enterprise value). It was the fourth largest bankruptcy case in US history.[93]

Global Crossing went from a privately funded start-up to having raised tens of billions of dollars by issuing common shares for sale on the stock market. Once capitalized with common-shareholder equity, the company borrowed multiple more tens of billions leveraged against that equity and then began to build a worldwide network of fiber-optic cables. Within months of completing the network, the company promptly went bust—all in less than four years.

However, going bust does not mean going out of business. In fact, Global Crossing continued to exist (with the same chairman and CEO) for several years after the bankruptcy. It continued to operate and earn revenue from its brand-new fiber-optic network, which was mainly paid for by the ruined shareholders. The company was eventually sold to L3 Communications. The beneficiaries were the founders, top managers, and their investment bankers. The losers were the several hundred thousand common shareholders who lost billions and the more than nine thousand employees who lost their jobs.

In a 2002 article in *The Economist* (a magazine owned by the Rothschild family) the story characterizes the events as follows:

> In that short history lies [sic] a rich parable of modern America, its excitable capital markets and its wide-eyed faith in new technology. But one lesson stands out. Global Crossing was a start-up: bankers and investors bet billions that it would dethrone the industry's ageing giants. That bet bombed.

In this passage the writer carefully chooses his words to suggest that it was a failure that the bankers could not have foreseen or avoided. It also implies that the investors (common shareholders) and bankers where in it together in terms of risk and that they both lost in the deal. But this is a misrepresentation. In truth, what the common shareholders lost, the founders and their banker friends ultimately gained.

After their bust in 2002, the company was restructured and emerged from chapter-eleven bankruptcy, issuing new common shares for sale to an entirely new group of suckers. The company continued to operate, yielding earnings for the original founders and their investment banks, and a few years hence the company was sold.

---

[93]   Survival of The Slowest, Global Crossings' Bankruptcy. *The Economist*. Jan 31., 2002.

Throughout much of this period, Mr. Winnick remained as chairman, amassing an enormous fortune in the process.

Just prior to Global's filing for bankruptcy, Mr. Winnick had made approximately $734 million by selling his original shares in the company. Afterward, he "donated" twenty-five million dollars (about 3 percent of his windfall) to Global Crossing employees who lost money in the company's 401(k) retirement plan. That amounted to a little more than two thousand dollars per employee. In March 2004, Winnick and other former company executives agreed as a group to pay a combined $325 million to settle a class-action lawsuit brought by shareholders that alleged fraud on the part of the founders and management. As part of the terms of the settlement, Winnick and former executives did not have to admit any wrongdoing in return for agreeing to pay. Winnick himself paid $55 million under the deal (less than 7 percent of what he made when he dumped his shares). His personal windfall of literally hundreds of millions of dollars came at the expense of the original common stockholders who were wiped out and wound up with absolutely nothing. His take consisted of a vast fortune. According to Forbes magazine, Winnick set the historical record for achieving a net worth of $1 billion in the shortest time after founding his company—a company he drove into bankruptcy just months after this "achievement."

Today Mr. Winnick lives in a Bel-Air mansion that is valued at more than $225 million USD. (That's a single home worth nearly a quarter of a billion dollars). He had acquired this Bel-Air estate several months prior to his company filing for chapter-eleven bankruptcy protection, wiping out twenty billion dollars' worth of common-shareholder equity.

> I love money more than the things it can buy ... but what I love more than money is other people's money.
>
> —Danny DeVito in the 1991 film
> "Other People's Money"

F. A. Grieger

Gary Winnick's Sprawling Bel-Air Estate—Valued at more than $225 Million (2013)

Several prominent politicians also gained handsomely, including Republican George H. W. Bush, Virginia Governor Terry McAuliffe (then chairman of the Democratic National Committee), and President Bill Clinton. In early 1997, McAuliffe was set up in a downtown DC office owned by Winnick's Pacific Capital Group. According to McAuliffe, he was hired by Winnick as a consultant to "work some deals with the federal government."[94] Later that year Winnick offered McAuliffe the opportunity to privately purchase a hundred thousand dollars' worth of Global Crossing stock. Not long after, McAuliffe introduced Winnick to President Clinton, who then lavished on Winnick his personal endorsement. This led to a four-hundred-million-dollar contract from the Pentagon. Shortly after this (and a round of Golf with Clinton), Winnick donated one million dollars to the Clinton Presidential Library.

Winnick was equally generous to former President George H. W. Bush, who was paid in Global Crossing stock for giving a one-hour speech to company executives in Tokyo. A few months later Bush's shares hit a value of more than $14 million after the company went public, though it is not known at what value Bush sold them. McAuliffe sold his shares at the peak of their value just a few months before the company collapsed, pocketing more than $18 million. No allegations of insider trading were ever raised. DC politicians and their donors are evidently indemnified for actions that would land any normal citizen in federal prison.

---

[94] St. Clair, Jeffrey, The Political Business of Terry McAuliffe. Counter Punch. Oct. 19, 2004. http://www.counterpunch.org/2004/10/19/the-political-business-of-terry-mcauliffe/

Global Crossing's common shareholders lost every penny of their investments. Many had invested and lost money that came from a lifetime of hard work, more than half of which was first confiscated from them by the government in the form of income taxes. Winnick, Legere, and their bankers walked away with literally hundreds of millions of dollars. At the time, Global Crossing was incorporated in Bermuda, which was exempt from US corporate taxes.

The inherent problem illustrated by this example is the fact that the rules of the game are skewed vastly in favor of those with the power and connections to the banking industry and their political cronies. Banks can use their money creation powers to make commercial loans to companies at no real risk and then bankrupt those companies at the expense of their common shareholders, all using money that they created from nothing. We the peasants, however, must trade the best years of our natural lives, laboring for these corporations for the few peanuts they throw at us as compensation, hoping to live long enough to eventually pay off the mortgage on a modest family home.

When public companies go bankrupt, the misery is shared by their employees who see their 401(k)s wiped out along with their jobs—the common shareholders whose shares are wiped out through our unjust one-sided bankruptcy laws—and retirees whose pensions and benefits evaporate. CEOs and board executives, on the other hand, receive generous compensation in the form of salary, stock grants in the newly restructured business, loans that are later forgiven, and huge multimillion-dollar bonuses. An investigation by the *Wall Street Journal* found that the median salary for CEOs at more than twenty companies, all of which filed for chapter-eleven bankruptcy, was $8.7 million. That's a median salary of nearly $40 thousand per working day in return for driving their companies into bankruptcy and destroying the life savings of their shareholders. Our system has become so perverse that we handsomely reward incompetence and failure and harshly punish diligence and success.

Bankruptcies like Global Crossing and others have revealed the same recurring pattern. This suggests that this system could conceivably be used to fleece shareholders deliberately. One merely has to capitalize a large public corporation using common shareholder equity and then intentionally drive it into bankruptcy so that the founders, preferred shareholders, the management team, and their lenders can wipe out the common shareholder equity. They can then divide up the company's assets between themselves. In other words, hypothetically it is possible to found a public company under false pretenses. Founders can then raise hundreds of millions or perhaps billions of dollars from common shareholders in equity capital all based on future projected earnings in order to establish an inflated asset value to the company. They then partner with their banker friends to intentionally take on an unserviceable debt burden by borrowing against that equity (using the bank's money-creation powers). They then promptly declare chapter-eleven bankruptcy, *restructure* the company's assets (while they use our legal system to wipe out all of the common shareholders) and then *emerge* from bankruptcy, leaving only the founders, top managers, and their investment bankers as the owners. This is hypothetical only in the sense that such intent would be difficult to prove in criminal court. But it is indeed possible, and it demonstrates yet another example of how wealth can be transferred from the middle class to the obscenely rich ruling class.

It is virtually impossible for a small business entrepreneur to compete against corporations whose investment bank owners have access to an unlimited supply of risk-free capital via their money-creation powers. The disparity in risk borne by independent business people versus that borne by huge corporations is an inescapable feature of our fiat monetary model. It enables the slow and incremental process of replacing all of our country's independent businesses with huge corporate entities. The result is that eventually almost everyone will be an underpaid and overworked employee of some huge corporation with no means to escape the dog race and compete as an independent business owner. This model does not constitute fair competition on a level playing field, and it has nothing in common with the principles of free-market capitalism. It is monopolism—central control of wealth and the means of production, the very definition of corporate socialism. America has brought Benito Mussolini's vision to fruition.

CHAPTER 10

The Inmates Are Running the Asylum—A Government of Sociopaths

I spent the last two years of high school in a daze ... attended classes sparingly, drank beer heavily, and tried drugs enthusiastically.[95]

—Barack Hussein Obama II

Lord Acton has been credited as having made the famous quotation in the late 1800s, "Power corrupts, and absolute power corrupts absolutely." But it is not power in and of itself that begets evil. It is power in the hands of a certain class of individual that does. There are those among our society that seek power over their fellow citizens solely so they can abuse it.

As such—power attracts the corruptible.

Powerful institutions are a magnet for corruptible, narcissistic, sociopathic megalomaniacs. Because of their enthusiasm for power and government, they rise to positions of influence. Once they gain enough power, they remake the organizations they run in their own image and create a culture that is unpalatable for nonsociopaths. Given enough time, the entire institution is found to be full of malevolent ne'er-do-wells. It's for this reason that a large and powerful central government will always descend into a corrupt tyranny populated by a majority of degenerate sociopaths bent on dominating the people. It's only a matter of time, and this has been the pattern throughout the history of civilization.

---

[95]   Obama, Barack. Dreams From My Father. (Times Books, 1995).

Institutionalized Unaccountability

Imagine you hire a security company to install an alarm system intended to protect your home from armed thieves or home invaders. The security company installs an elaborate system of technical accoutrements designed to monitor the comings and goings in and around your house. Your house is fitted with cameras, motion detectors, and silent alarms. After you sign the contract, the head of the security company, Mr. Alan Brownbridge, a modest, soft spoken older gentleman with large framed glasses, tells you that in order to effectively manage your security, you must also turn over the keys to your house, the contents of your safe, and your firearms, which they will hold for you for your own safety. You find him to be witty and charming. He seems very well intentioned, and you have the sense that he truly cares for you and your family's well-being. He has gained your trust, and so you believe it's in your best interest to comply. After you agree to those terms, he then tells you that the security company also needs to have unrestricted access to your financial accounts—for your own protection. You sign a document that provides them with the authority to freeze or disable all of your finances and even your personal mobility as they deem might be required to protect you in the event of any major emergency. You are left with the warm feeling of being secure in your home and the knowledge that the caring and benevolent Mr. Brownbridge and Big Brother Security, Inc., are looking out for you and yours.

Two weeks after you signed on the dotted line, you read in the newspaper that Big Brother Security, Inc., has filed for bankruptcy. Mr. Brownbridge takes an *early retirement* and is awarded a fifty-million-dollar bonus from Big Brother. The company's unrestricted access to all of your financial accounts, to which you agreed, characterizes you under the law as their unsecured creditor. Under that status all of your financial accounts are seized by the security company's secured creditors along with the contents of your safe and your guns which are sold off in order to cover the company's debts.

Purely by coincidence that evening your house is robbed by home invaders. Since Big Brother, Inc., took your firearms (for your own protection), you are left unable to defend yourself. One of the armed thieves ties you and your family up as prisoners in your own home and then casually tells you jokes while he cleans out your wallet, your family jewelry, and whatever else you didn't turn over to the security company. Angered at finding your safe empty (since the corporate thieves got their first), he decides to punish you on his way out. The thief smiles and laughs as he sets your house on fire.

Big Brother Security has no liability or obligation to you since they're bankrupt. Not only have you been robbed and victimized by a violent criminal, but you've also been defrauded by the company that you paid to protect you from such a crime.

This fiction is a fairly accurate metaphor for the current relationship that exists between *we the people* and the US government. There is only a subtle difference between the kind of covert deception described by the fictional Alan Brownbridge and the overt violence committed by the armed thief. Either perpetrator knows that what he is doing is wrong, and the fact that he is getting away with it at the expense of his victims is exhilarating to him. This kind of person engages in theft not only for economic gain at another's expense but also for the sheer enjoyment he derives from hurting, defrauding, and cheating others. Doing so gives him a feeling of superiority. The only difference between the two is that the thief is a violent aggressor while Mr. Brownbridge is deceptive and coercive. It's becoming ever more apparent that most of the members of our federal government and those running the corporatocracy are made up primarily of the latter sort.

Violence and coercion are merely tools of power. Those tools are particularly effective in the hands of those who have no morals. Most people practice self-restraint and feel empathy. They therefore do not harm others by intent. Most live by the golden rule, but there has always been and will always be that element of society that has no ethics—no sense of any moral obligation to others. They also understand something that most of the rest of us do not. This fundamental difference between us and them puts them at a tremendous advantage when they are using their coercive tools to imbalance us, weaken us, take whatever we have—in effect, to parasitize off of humanity. In fact, they consider another person's empathy or generosity a weakness to be exploited. They are ruthless, shameless, and unrepentant, and they consider themselves as being superior because of it.

According to the *Diagnostic and Statistical Manual of Mental Disorders* (DSM-IV), which is published by the American Psychiatric Association, a person who conducts him or herself in this way with a habitual pattern of behavior suggests that he or she may harbor a mental condition known as covert-aggressive character disorder. If such a person actually enjoys engaging in this kind of conduct, he or she would be considered a sadistic covert aggressive personality. The covert-aggressive personality type is the archetypal wolf in sheep's clothing.[96]

Institutionalizing Moral Decay

All around us we are witnessing a global socioeconomic and political environment in rapid decline. We can also observe a highly troubling pattern that is evident within all of the nations of the industrialized world, including the United States. It consists in the systematic consolidation of power centers along with an expansion of that power. These power centers include governments, intergovernmental organizations (such as the UN, World Bank, International Monetary Fund, etc.), financial institutions, and multinational corporations. In parallel with this process, a basis of social dependency rather than a quest for individual self-reliance has become the pervasive model of all

---

[96]   Simon, Dr. George, Jr. In Sheep's Clothing. Parkhurst Bros. Publishing. 2009.

of Western society. Trading individual liberty for a false sense of security—provided by the government—has become the order of the day.

In terms of the problems that face the current as well as future generations this situation is truly frightening. The United States has been confronted with perpetual economic recession, looming financial chaos, unrestrained monetary expansion that will inevitably lead to hyperinflation, onerous taxation, crippling regulation, a growing and overreaching police state, an expanding entitlement culture, and increasing foreign interventionism and wars.

How did the United States wind up in this condition in spite of our supposed free-enterprise system? There are those that try to blame these dysfunctions on free-market capitalism, but these same problems have happened to other countries before. From 1920s Germany and their hyperinflation to the disintegration of the former Soviet Union, these economic catastrophes have happened time and time again to countries that were anything but capitalist. So why is this happening here in America? The most logical conclusion is that America may not be truly capitalist after all. Nevertheless, it is capitalism that is usually blamed as the scapegoat for our country's economic and sociopolitical dysfunctions.

In addition to demonizing capitalism, it's usually suggested that, misfortune, carelessness, some error in judgment, or negligence are why things are disintegrating. Some claim incompetence or stupidity on the part of our government's leadership. Although many of the aforementioned elements may have a role (particularly the latter), it is minor. Potential widespread catastrophe is not the result of happenstance. When a culture disintegrates on such a massive scale as we are witnessing today, it's not just because of bad luck, carelessness, or even incompetence. It is by design.

> Sometimes I wonder whether the world is being run by smart people who are putting us on, or imbeciles who really mean it.
>
> —Mark Twain

Most of our elected government employees no longer seek office in order to represent the citizenry but instead to further their own personal interests—a lifelong high-paying government career with first-class perks, benefits, a full retirement pension, and potential media fame. The same is true for their appointees. This is why they refer to themselves as government "officials," when in fact they are our employees. Nevertheless, as of April 2013, the average federal employee salary was $78,500, nearly twice the average income for an individual working in the private sector ($40,800). Current members of Congress are paid more than $174,000 annually (not counting perks and benefits) and receive a guaranteed pension for the rest of their natural lives even after having served just a single term in office. Most of these representatives—once they're in office—never leave. Most career politicians do not seek office in order to serve, but to be served.

It was recently reported that the Department of Homeland Security (DHS) has spent over $450 thousand on fitness club memberships for the administrative personnel in their procurement office in Washington, D.C. On July 7, 2014, the agency purchased 236 memberships to the upscale Vida Fitness, which describes itself as "more than just a gym," offering an "Aura Spa, Bang Salon, Fuel Bar, Gear Shop, Endless Pools, luxurious locker rooms, and the rooftop Penthouse Pool and Lounge." Each of these DHS employees has been provided a club membership costing over $1,900 as an *employee benefit*.

For every one like this, countless other examples of egregious government waste, fraud, and abuse go unreported and remain hidden. Dozens of government watchdogs are sounding the alarm that the Obama administration is stonewalling them, in what is being described as an unprecedented challenge to the agencies they're supposed to oversee.

In August, 2014, forty-seven of the government's seventy-three independent watchdogs known as inspectors general drafted letters of complaint to congressional leaders. They accused several major agencies—the Justice Department, the DHS, the Peace Corps and the chemical safety board, among others—of imposing "serious limitations on access to records." The letter states, "agency actions that limit, condition, or delay access thus have profoundly negative consequences for our work: they make us less effective, encourage other agencies to take similar actions [of waste, fraud, and abuse] in the future, and erode the morale of the dedicated professionals that make up our staffs."

The letter to the chairmen and ranking members of relevant oversight committees in the House and Senate claimed that Obama administration agencies are withholding information by calling it "privileged." As such, the inspectors general have appealed to Congress to help them do their jobs uncovering waste, fraud, and mismanagement—the very same Congress that has demonstrated acts of incalculable waste, fraud, and mismanagement of their own.

"This is the Most Transparent Administration in History."

—Barack Hussein Obama II, February 13, 2013

Government "service" —Parasitism

Government employees, both elected and appointed, exploit the system via the *revolving door* concept. This consists in government employees hiring industry

207

professionals as consultants or advisors for their private sector experience. They then gain influence within corporations that the government is attempting to regulate or do business with and also gain political support (donations and endorsements) from those private firms.[97]

In turn, industry hires those same representatives and government employees once they are out of their government positions. This gives them access to other government employees who can provide favorable legislation, regulation, and government contracts as well as provide inside information on what is going on in government. In exchange, exiting government officials receive high-paying employment offers. Sometimes those opportunities are worth millions or tens of millions at the president or CEO level in large corporations. Lobbying is the main activity affected by the revolving door. The most important assets for a lobbyist are his or her contacts with and influence on government employees. This industrial climate is highly lucrative for ex-government employees. It means substantial monetary rewards for the lobbying firms, while those government projects and contracts can be worth hundreds of millions. This has effectively put an end to representative government and free-market capitalism.

Between 1998 and 2013, revenue earned by lobbying firms doubled, reaching more than $1 Billion. 285 former members of Congress are registered as federal lobbyists, while another 85 former members are "consultants providing strategic advice" to corporate clients—code for unofficial lobbying.[98]

Big corporate money has co-opted the government. They have pocketed the self-serving politicians (the useful idiots) to employ their legislative powers in an effort to destroy the free-enterprise system. This has enabled monopolies and duopolies to centralize control over America's most critical industries. Airlines and transportation, energy and oil, media communications, food and agriculture, pharmaceuticals, water, chemicals, all have seen hundreds of companies merge and consolidate into just three or four corporate behemoths within each industry sector. Government agencies and their officials along with the top executives of these corporations have become entangled into a malevolent symbiotic relationship intended to fleece the working class of all of their property, their wealth, and their labor. These big banks, giant oil companies, and their partners in government have coalesced into an exclusive club—a vast criminal enterprise.

---

[97] Cilliza, Chris. "The Revolving Door between Congress and K Street, Moving Faster than Ever." *The Washington Post.* Jan 22, 2014.

[98] Edsall, Thomas B. "The Trouble with That Revolving Door." *The New York Times.* Dec. 18, 2011.

The Revolving Door

Lobbyists will not run my White House ... First we will close the revolving door that has allowed people to use their administration job as a stepping stone to further their lobbying careers ... We're going to have to change the culture in Washington so that lobbyists and special interests aren't driving the process.

—Senator Barack Hussein Obama II, Campaigning for the US Presidency, October, 2008

On January 21, 2009, newly elected President Obama signed executive order 13490 which came to be known as the *no lobbyist rule*. The order prohibited anyone from being appointed to a federal post if they worked as a lobbyist for any corporation during the previous two years. On January 23, just two days after signing this order, Obama appointed Raytheon Corporation's lobbyist Mr. William Lynn as US Deputy Secretary of Defense. Mark Patterson, chief lobbyist for Goldman Sachs became chief of staff in Obama's treasury department. Chris Jennings, former lobbyist for a number of pharmaceutical and other health-care related firms, was appointed to be the Obama administration's "health policy coordinator and strategist," and assigned to *fix Obamacare*. What is the purpose of the executive order privilege, when presidents themselves do not comply with their own orders?

Government Sachs

Goldman Sachs could be considered an incubator for future Treasury Secretaries. Both Paul Rubin and Henry "Hank" Paulson went from the top position at Goldman, to the top job at Treasury. Gary Gensler, Sr. Partner and head of finance at Goldman Sachs was head of the government's Commodities and Futures Trading Commission. Steve Friedman, Chairman of Goldman Sachs was also Chief Economic Advisor to George W. Bush and Chairman of the New York Federal Reserve Bank. William Dudley, Chief Economist and Partner at Goldman Sachs also served as President and CEO of the New York Federal Reserve.

Another former New York Federal Reserve President, Timothy Geithner, went back and forth between lobbying firms like Kissinger Associates and various posts in Treasury. He eventually became president of the Federal Reserve Bank of New York just prior to being appointed as Treasury Secretary. Once in their posts as Treasury Secretary, both Paulson and Geithner were instrumental in facilitating the Fed's policies to continue money printing, bailouts for banks (their former employers) and failing auto-makers, and even providing bailouts to foreign banks (their former employers' partners).

Interestingly, in the early 1980s, Timothy Geithner became acquainted with Barack
Obama's mother, Stanley Ann Dunham (Soetoro) in Indonesia, where she worked
together with his father Peter Geithner who then oversaw a division of The Ford
Foundation. Those who believe that Barack Obama was an unknown political
outsider before his rapid rise to the US Senate leading to the presidency are hopelessly
naïve. His connections to Wall Street and the government go all the way back to his
days as an adolescent.

Hank Paulson

In the fall of 2008 Merrill Lynch was on the precipice of bankruptcy. Bank of
America, which had just received a $25 billion TARP bailout, offered to use the
taxpayers' funds to buy Merrill Lynch for $50 billion. However, after the financial
results for 2008 were posted, Merrill's staggering losses obliged Bank of America to
back out of the deal. Enter Hank Paulson—Treasury Secretary.

At the direct request of Federal Reserve chairman Ben Bernanke, Paulson ordered
Bank of America to complete the acquisition of Merrill Lynch by threatening to
remove the bank's management and board of directors if they didn't complete the
deal. In case the ramifications of this aren't clear to the reader—here we have an
unelected government employee ordering the merger of two of America's largest
financial institutions, both *publicly held* corporations. Bank of America's CEO,
Ken Lewis, gave testimony that Secretary Paulson offered to cover the bank for its
expected losses, but was unwilling to put the guarantee in writing. According to
Lewis, Paulson referred to a written commitment as a "disclosable event," which
Paulson wouldn't allow to be on record.[99]

After the agreement was made, the US Treasury provided Bank of America $20
billion in additional TARP funds along with a $118 billion guarantee to cover
further losses on Merrell's assets. Therefore, it was the struggling US taxpayers that
unwittingly financed Bank of America's acquisition of Merrell Lynch, on direct orders
from Treasury Secretary Henry Paulson (acting on the request of Fed Chairman Ben
Bernanke). One week prior to Merrell's final absorption and dissolution by the Bank,
Merrell's executives were paid $3.6 billion in bonuses—with approval from Bank of
America. That's billion—with a B.

Power brokers in positions like this are the embodiment of conflict of interest—
parasitic organisms that result from conjoining the banking cartel and government.
While he was CEO of Goldman Sachs, Paulson's competitors included: Lehman
Brothers, Bear Stearns, and Merrell Lynch. While Treasury Secretary, he organized
the liquidation of all three of his former rivals, while providing a most generous
bailout for his former employer—Goldman Sachs. The aftermath left a duopoly

---

[99]   Griffin, G. Edward. The Creature from Jekyll Island – Audio CD Book. Unabridged
Edition. (Audiobooks.com Aug 1, 2013).

of Morgan, and Goldman as the only two major investment banks left standing. This pattern of using government to consolidate these banks while destroying his competitors has an uncanny similarity to the events perpetrated by J.P. Morgan in 1907.

Let's Make a Deal – Revolving Door No. 1, Revolving Door No. 2, or Revolving Door No. 3

On the Republican side, two excellent examples of the revolving door principle are Donald Rumsfeld and Dick Cheney (former congressman, later CEO of Haliburton Corporation, and then vice president under Bush). Both men *served* in the Bush administration and were instrumental in pushing through the Patriot Act. Both started in government, left, and entered the private sector at the senior executive level and then later returned to government. All of these men have a *reported* net worth of tens and possibly hundreds of millions of dollars—that we know of. Obscenely rich career politicians have the audacity to refer to themselves as *public servants*.

Donald Rumsfeld graduated from Princeton University with an undergraduate degree in political *science*. He was first elected to Congress in 1962 at the age of thirty after a short stint in the US Navy. He later became an appointee under the Nixon administration for various posts, including head of the Office of *Economic Opportunity*, and he also became the US ambassador to NATO. In 1976, after Gerald Ford lost to Jimmy Carter and the administration changed from Republican to Democrat, Mr. Rumsfeld entered the private sector and was named president of G. D. Searle and Co., a large pharmaceutical corporation and subsidiary of Monsanto.[100] It has been alleged that he was appointed to this post largely to ensure the FDA's legalization of aspartame through his political connections.

From the time Mr. Rumsfeld graduated from Princeton until he was named president of one of America's largest pharmaceutical companies, he had never held a senior management job working for a private sector company. He had little if any experience in commercial industry including something as specialized as pharmaceuticals. His principal qualification for heading up an organization of this kind was his access to political power. He later became CEO of General Instrument, a major government contractor, and afterward he became chairman of Gilead Sciences, a biotech firm. In January 2001, he passed through the revolving door yet again and returned to government when he was appointed Department of Defense secretary by George W. Bush.

There are countless other examples that don't have Rumsfeld's celebrity status but demonstrate no less egregious conflicts of interest. Only a month before he left

---

[100] "Agricultural Biotech will find a supporter in the White House, regardless of which candidate wins the election." *Monsanto In-House Newsletter.* 2000. http://www.redicecreations.com/specialreports/monsanto.html

the Pentagon to join the board of Lockheed-Martin, Edward C. (Pete) Aldridge, Jr. approved a $3 billion contract to build 20 Lockheed planes. Before his board appointment, however, he had long criticized that same program as "overpriced" and even threatened to cancel it.[101]

There are a great many forms of bribery that don't require the direct exchange of cash and which can be structured to provide deniability by the perpetrators. It is clear that the trend is for government to be increasingly symbiotic with huge corporate interests where individual power brokers have tens of millions or even hundreds of millions of dollars at stake. For government employees, whether elected or appointed, their self-interest clearly supersedes their duty to the people, to their oath of office, or to the constitution. Their positions in government give them unique access to opportunities with enormous financial rewards. More often than not, those opportunities in the corporate sector present a clear conflict of interest with their responsibility to the American people.

Given these conditions, one can conclude that under the current or any future regime there is not going to be any meaningful change in the direction in which the United States is headed until a genuine crisis causes the existing order to collapse. In fact, this trend will accelerate.

The main reason is that the world's most powerful institutions and the US government in particular have been infiltrated by a certain type of person—persons having one or more basic character disorder. In other words, a type of moral decay has become so pervasive that it is now institutional in our government as well as in the leadership of our largest corporations and financial institutions.

This class of people, who now control many major institutions, suffer from one of three basic types of character disorder. Some have a combination of several of these mental illnesses: covert-aggressive personalities, narcissists, and sociopaths. Their public rhetoric starkly contradicts their common hidden agenda, while their actual beliefs and ambitions are revealed by their actions. The consequences are evident throughout the economic, political, and cultural framework of the United States. If the American people want to understand what the true intentions of our political class are, it is important to stop listening to what they say and instead pay strict attention to what they actually do.

Every branch of our federal government has been populated with covertly aggressive personalities, narcissists, and fundamentally dishonest career politicians. What this means to us in terms of our nation's governance is not a trivial matter. Throughout history this has been a matter of life and death. The evidence for this is the tens of millions of victims who suffered under Stalin, Hitler, Mao, Pol Pot, and countless

---

[101]   Wayne, Leslie. "Pentagon Brass and Military Contractors' Gold." *New York Times.* June 29, 2004. http://www.nytimes.com/2004/06/29/business/29door.html

other socialist dictators. The founders of this country and their ancestors also faced this issue while they suffered under the tyranny of the British monarchy. They took responsibility for their own lives and decided to settle in the New World which had better prospects and more freedom. After the British monarch extended his oppression onto the colonists, they again took charge of their own destiny. They pledged their lives, their fortunes, and their sacred honor in order to fight for the cause of individual liberty. The founders of this country were devoted to truth, honor, and moral justice, not political power as a means to abuse their fellow citizens.

Most Americans believe that what happened in places like Nazi Germany, the Soviet Union, Mao's China, and dozens of other countries in recent history could not happen in the United States. In fact, there is no reason that it won't. All of the institutions that made America exceptional—A belief in free-market (laissez-faire) capitalism, devotion to family and to God, respect for individual property rights, an aspiration toward achieving self-reliance, and the restraints of the constitution—are now historical relics.

What Does This Mean to Each of Us as Individual Citizens?

The population distribution of those with mental disorders, such as narcissism or sociopathology, is completely uniform across space and time. On a per-capita basis there was no greater proportion of evil people in Stalin's Russia, Mao's China, or Hitler's Germany than there is today in the United States.[102] The only thing required is to have favorable conditions for them to flourish much as mushrooms do on manure. Conditions for them in the United States have become extremely favorable during the past two decades. This is why tens of thousands of people enthusiastically sought employment by the TSA—so they could grope, fondle, degrade, and humiliate law-abiding citizens. What motivates a person to seek out a career that consists in digging through other peoples' luggage and inspecting their underwear while subjecting them to all sorts of other indignities? Most would find this sort of work repugnant, yet these people were attracted to—not repulsed by—an occupation where they wear a government provided costume and are granted the authority to abuse their fellow citizens day after day. The tens of thousands of government workers now employed by the TSA and various other Department of Homeland Security divisions are the same sort of people who joined the Gestapo—enthusiastically participating in the mission to control their countrymen. Not a single person was drafted into the Gestapo. It was purely a voluntary organization.[103]

Today, every law-abiding middle class citizen has been made subservient to the authority of a vast and expanding government bureaucracy, made up primarily of this sort.

---

[102] Casey, Doug. "The Ascendance of Sociopaths in US Governance." *Casey Research*. March 21, 2012

[103] Casey, Doug. "The Ascendance of Sociopaths in US Governance." *Casey Research*. March 21, 2012.

Being Truthful –vs– Being Right

Typical career politicians have such inflated egos and exaggerated sense of self-importance that they believe they are never wrong about anything. They believe that their intentions are the only good intentions so they must win every debate irrespective of truth. By their actions however, they demonstrate repeatedly that they are devoid of ethics and integrity. These are the types of people in whom we have vested authority over our lives, our families, our property, and our children's futures.

Having integrity and a devotion to absolute truth requires a degree of humility and courage. If you are devoted to truth, you must accept that you may be wrong in your knowledge or interpretation of an issue. Being devoted to truth requires a willingness to see all sides of an issue, admit error, and change one's thinking when proven wrong. Conversely individuals with a character disorder such as covert-aggression or narcissistic personality are not interested in truth but in winning at any cost. Such people are willing to pervert the truth in order to prove their point and retain or, whenever possible, expand their power. Politicians rarely if ever admit when they are wrong. They are expert in using purposeful obfuscation and other techniques like *Fedspeak* in order to evade truth. In essence, most of the people whom we have empowered to run our lives are mentally ill to varying degrees.

Narcissism is a character disorder or mental illness. It manifests itself in individuals who are described as being extremely preoccupied with matters of personal adequacy, power, prestige, and vanity. It is a condition that affects about 1 percent of the population. The classification of narcissistic personality disorder was first described in 1968 and was historically called megalomania. It is characterized as severe egocentrism. Narcissism is most often accompanied by covert-aggressive behavior.[104]

According to the *Diagnostic and Statistical Manual of Mental Disorders* (DSM-IV-TR), the characteristics of those with narcissistic personality disorder include the following:

- grandiose sense of self and entitlement, pursuing selfish goals

- very manipulative personality covered by superficial charm

- inability to take criticism, reacting with anger, retaliation, humiliation

- taking advantage of others to reach one's own goals

- exaggerating own talents, importance, or achievements no matter how insignificant

---

[104]   Millon, Theodore. Disorders of Personality: DSM-IV-TM and Beyond. New York: John Wiley and Sons. 1996.

- surrounding him or herself only with people who agree with everything he or she says

- imagining unrealistic fantasies of success, beauty, power, intelligence, or romance

- requiring constant attention, admiration, and positive reinforcement from others

- a desire to always be in the spotlight, adored, and recognized

- prone to being envious, jealous, and contemptuous of his betters or those perceived as a threat

- an instinct to attack the person (opponent) and not the message when losing an argument

- display of arrogance with a condescending demeanor

- seeking power and displaying a sense of superiority

- becoming easily hurt and rejected yet appearing unemotional

If you do not admire, revere, and adore this person, they will denigrate, belittle, and discard you without any regret. Spend any amount of time with a typical career politician, and you will observe a demonstration of many of the aforementioned characteristics.

Because narcissists have no conscience, they are quite often successful in business and other areas where ruthless behavior can help you to get ahead. Narcissists possess an inflated sense of self-worth in that they value themselves as being fundamentally better than others. Their inflated sense of self-esteem is delicate, so they are unable to take criticism. They often compensate for this inner fragility by belittling, marginalizing, or disparaging others in an attempt to validate their own self-worth.

> If you've got a business, you didn't build that. Somebody else made that happen.
>
> —Barack Hussein Obama II, July, 2012

Think of this when you listen to the vitriol spewed by Democrats against their Republican rivals and vice versa, or by both against whom they crudely refer to as

Tea Baggers. To the extent that people are pathologically narcissistic, they can be controlling, blaming, self-absorbed, and intolerant of others' views. They are not concerned with others' needs or of the effects their behavior has on others. They insist that others see them as they wish to be seen, not as they truly are. In personal relationships, they can destroy their friendships, their families, and the lives of their spouses and children. In positions of political power, they can destroy their countries and the lives of their countrymen.

Extreme character disorder is what is called sociopathology. Indeed, many sociopaths are also narcissistic, and this combination of personality traits should be considered dangerous. Narcissists and sociopaths have no consciences or at least severely underdeveloped ones. They have a diminished capacity for experiencing genuine shame or guilt, and they rarely if ever show remorse for wrongdoing. They generally view others as objects and as a means to an end. What may appear to some as a defense mechanism on their part is in fact a power tactic used to manipulate others so that they can resist making concessions to societal demands.

Narcissists see others as a means to validate their superiority, so they seek the admiration of the public. Sociopaths may or may not need to be validated, and they see others mainly as tools to be used to achieve their own ends. As such, they simply seek authority over people in order to use them as a resource. A narcissistic sociopath seeks validation and adoration from the public as well as self-advancement, so that person uses other people to attain both ends. In any case, either type of disordered person has an innate need to dominate and control others. In layman's terms, they are control freaks. Both seek to exploit people, and neither has any remorse or conscience in doing so. Institutions offering political power are magnets for these types of people. The common denominator is that they are mentally ill to a greater or lesser degree.

What Happens when Sociopaths Gain Powerful Political Positions?

They tend to evade responsibility for having engaged in bad behavior and justify wrongdoing by making excuses, feigning innocence or haplessness. They pervert facts and distort logic in order to claim that an immoral act is actually moral … simply because it was they who perpetrated it.[105]

They truly believe that they are above the law and that they are ordained with a privileged place in society. Therefore, they feel they are exempt from the same rules of conduct as the rest of us. The most recent example of this behavior was when the members of Congress collectively exempted themselves from having to comply

---

[105] Lobaczewsky, Andrew M. and Laura Knight-Jadczyk. *Political Ponerology (A Science on the Nature of Evil Adjusted for Political Purposes)*. Red Hill Press. 2007.

with the Obamacare law that they so zealously forced upon the rest of the American population.

Most important is that character-disordered people do not think the way most others do. How we think, what we believe, and the attitudes we have developed largely determine how we will act. Psychological researchers have identified the common thought patterns of character-disordered people as being self-centered, possessive, extreme (all or nothing), egomaniacal, shameless, guiltless, dishonest, and ruthless. In character-disordered individuals these are not defense mechanisms but fundamental aggressive traits of their personalities. As such, these are individuals who will never change their behavior unless they are forced to do so against their will. When these people obtain positions of power, they will abuse that power continually for as long as they are able to hold on to it.

> After we win this election, it's our turn. Payback time. Everyone not with us is against us, and they better be ready because we don't forget. The ones who helped us will be rewarded. The ones who opposed us will get what they deserve. There's going to be hell to pay. No election to worry about after this is over, and we have two [Supreme Court] judges ready to go.[106]
>
> —Valerie Jarrett, Senior Advisor to
> Barack Hussein Obama II

The two judges mentioned by Valerie Jarrett in the above quote, were liberal activist judges Sonja Sotomayor and Elena Kagan, both appointed by Obama soon after he first took office.

What Does All of This Have to Do with Our Government?

It has *everything* to do with our government. I mentioned earlier that power attracts the corruptible. Those who have these types of personality disorders make up the corruptible element of humanity. Therefore, powerfully structured institutions will always attract these types of people—those who are seeking access to power. Therefore, it is just a matter of time before institutions endowed with great power become fundamentally corrupt as a whole.

In a free society where market forces determine who fails and who succeeds, such dysfunctional institutions ultimately self-destruct on their own. But under a system of central planning, those in power get to pick and choose who fails and who doesn't based upon which provides them with the most political capital. It is here that certain

---

[106] Wolf, Dr. Milton R. Tyranny in Our Time. *The Washington Times*. May 24, 2013.

privileged organizations are considered as "too big to fail" while others are deemed unworthy because they are of no political value to those in power. As a consequence, dysfunctional institutions are left to continue with their destructive actions usually at the expense of the people they harm—the taxpayers. Therefore, corrupt leaders always seek to circumvent the forces of the free and fair market. They attempt to control outcomes in order to perpetuate their flawed model of central planning and control.

The framers understood this and partly for this reason avoided establishing the US as a democracy (majority rule). Instead they constructed the original US government as a constitutional republic (rule of law) with *limited* and *separated* powers. It was the check and balance of this separation between the different branches of government that sought to avert a degeneration of our government into a centralized structure of omnipotent power, which would attract the sort of people who would transform it into a fundamentally corrupt institution. Unfortunately it has become clear that the framers failed in preventing this. It is therefore only *we the people* who can fix it.

Investor and economist Doug Casey explains how this degeneration has taken place in practice:

We have to understand Pareto's law. That's the eighty-twenty rule, which tells us that 80 percent of your revenue comes from 20 percent of your customers or that 20 percent of the population are responsible for 80 percent of the crime.

In general, 80 percent of people are basically decent. Their fundamental values are to live ethically by the golden rule with a wish to do no harm. Twenty percent of people, however, are what one might call potential troublemakers. These are people who given an opportunity would be inclined toward doing the wrong thing if they believed they could get away with it. They don't overtly misbehave, mainly because they fear getting caught. These are people on the more benign end of the character-disordered spectrum. They might now be retail sales clerks, postal workers, waitresses, or white-collar professionals. They seem perfectly inert, living during normal times in a kind of holding pattern. They play baseball on weekends and pet the family dog. However, given the opportunity, they will sign up for the Gestapo, the KGB, the Stasi, the TSA, or the Department of Homeland Security. Many are well intentioned but are more likely to favor force or coercion as the solution to any problem [particularly if they are the one charged with the authority to wield it]. [107]

---

[107] Casey, Doug. "The Ascendance of Sociopaths in US Governance," Casey Research, March 21, 2012.

Casey goes on to explain that this is only part of the story. Twenty percent of that 20 percent are truly fundamentally evil. They are attracted to government and other positions of power where they can impose their will upon others. Since they're enthusiastic about government, they are relentless in their drive to climb the ladder and gain positions of authority. These people may be on the more extreme end of the character disorder spectrum. They usually fall into the category of narcissism, and they may even be sociopaths. In order to preserve their status, they remake the culture of the organizations they run in their own image. Gradually nonsociopaths can no longer tolerate being there. The best people leave, and soon through attrition the whole barrel is full of bad apples. This is exactly what has happened to the US government and to some of our most powerful institutions.

Most people generally assume that another person is telling the truth. Therefore, most don't recognize soon enough that the person who is habitually lying to them is in fact a sociopath. Sociopaths take great pains to cultivate a charming and socially attractive veneer, and they rarely telegraph their malevolent intentions. You can rely on them to be politically correct in public. They're expert at using facades to disguise reality, and they are remorseless about doing so.

A sociopath's lack of regard for the welfare of others and typical lack of conscience can make him or her dangerous. In positions of political power, they will always seek to expand their power with the goal to achieve absolute power. They have no qualms about destroying even their own country in the process. Examples include the most notorious and powerful socialist dictators of the twentieth century.

Political elites today primarily consist of sociopaths and narcissists. They are indeed unlike the rest of us not because of any superior intellectual qualities—as they would like to believe—but because they are differentiated by their dysfunctional psychological characteristics.

Franklin D. Roosevelt—Eliminating of the Separation of Powers Doctrine

Career politicians who have entrenched themselves in our government during the past century have been successful in consolidating and expanding their power. One of the best examples of this was Franklin D. Roosevelt, who died during his fourth presidential term. Most Americans are unaware of the repeated attempts by Roosevelt to fundamentally transform the Supreme Court in order to further his socialist agenda, unhindered by the constitution. During his first term six of his New Deal projects and one proposed new government agency failed because they were deemed unconstitutional by the Supreme Court. What Roosevelt did next was to draft a bill that came to be known by him and his inner circle as "the Supreme Court Packing Plan." It was officially titled with the more palatable moniker, the Judiciary Reorganization Bill of 1937. The goal of the plan was to increase the number of Supreme Court justices from nine to fifteen, enabling Roosevelt to pack the Supreme Court with a majority of liberal judges only he had the power to appoint. The obvious goal was to add enough left-leaning judges who supported his New Deal initiatives in order to dilute the votes of the constitutionally conservative majority. This would tip the judiciary's voting in his favor and thus allow his socialist programs to go unchallenged for their constitutionality. FDR treated the separation of powers doctrine and The Constitution as obstacles to his personal agenda, his sworn oath to uphold and defend them notwithstanding. The Senate voted seventy to twenty against his bill, and so we continue to have only nine justices to this day.

Nevertheless, Roosevelt was relentless in his quest to expand his political power, successfully seeking reelection to four terms as president. During his subsequent terms and his more than twelve years in office, he managed to appoint eight of the nine sitting Supreme Court justices as their predecessors left the bench through attrition. Except for George Washington, who nominated all of the members of the nation's first Supreme Court, FDR is the only president in US history to have accomplished this. This *plan B* court-packing initiative was ultimately successful and ensured that subsequently every socialist program he signed into law would remain unchallenged for its constitutionality. Roosevelt established the precedent for placing activist judges on the Supreme Court. He thus forever transformed the United States by having completely subverted the separation of powers doctrine. Every subsequent president has made one end-run after another around the Constitution. This is the reason that today we continue to labor under numerous bankrupt social programs such as social security and now the misnamed Patient Protection and Affordable Care Act (Obamacare). Roosevelt ensured America's complete transformation from a free-market capitalist system into the current corporate socialist model that was first initiated by Woodrow Wilson.

The *modus operandi* demonstrated by John D. Rockefeller in business, was that if you can't effectively destroy a competitor (obstacle), you find a way to conscript him and make him work for you. American politics has worked in much the same way. Roosevelt employed the same tactic, by conscripting the Supreme Court to be his servant, thus eliminating that body as a check on his executive power. To gain the power of a tyrant one must subvert the separation of powers doctrine. The tactics Roosevelt employed to achieve that proved to be very effective.

Roosevelt's successors have continued his tradition. They have driven America incrementally deeper into a system of interdependent corporate socialism that is so complex and difficult to decipher, that it is now nearly irreversible. Furthermore, his contemporaries have convinced the American people that socialist systems like FDR's "New Deal" and Lyndon Johnson's "Great Society" are features of American capitalism. Today we are witnessing the last stage of this transformation with the construction of the American Police State.

Evildoers

In the years following the World Trade Center attack on September 11, 2001, the American people faced a continual onslaught of media commentary by the Bush administration which referred to the perpetrators as evildoers. As a result, the people became desensitized to the existence of evil within our own government. Americans began to believe that evil only existed in distant places like North Korea, Iraq, and Iran, countries that were and continue to be irrelevant backwaters.[108] More likely, the oil producing countries in the middle-east are strategically chosen as manufactured enemies not because of disparate ideals but because they have something we want. Their oil export transactions to all foreign nations have been denominated exclusively in US Dollars since 1972. This was due to an agreement made that same year between Secretary of State Henry Kissinger and the Saudi royal family. That agreement inaugurated the *petrodollar concept* as the means to have the US Dollar continue as the world's reserve currency, in spite of the cancellation of its gold-backing that same year (see Nixon and The Bretton Woods Agreement).

While the Bush administration was purveying the concept of evil and unsubstantiated *weapons of mass destruction* to justify a long-standing agenda to invade Iraq, real evil continued to grow in strength and intensity all around and within our own government. Unfortunately for the American people this has been nourished by turning the United States into a national security police state. The unconstitutional Patriot Act has moved the United States a substantial leap closer to the national socialist model that was practiced in Nazi Germany. It is the Patriot Act that authorized the NSA's illegal spying on US citizens, which was revealed in mid-2013 by NSA contractor Edward Snowden. Continuing President Bush's policies, Barack Obama signed into law the National Defense Authorization Act. This now authorizes US law enforcement agencies to arrest and detain US citizens indefinitely without charge—a direct violation of the US Constitution. Our activist Supreme Court has refused to challenge the constitutionality of either law.

More than a decade after the Patriot Act was passed things are clearly getting out of control. The United States is in a protracted and lingering economic depression, and we are on the brink of a currency meltdown. The labor participation rate is the lowest it has been in nearly fifty years, yielding a real rate of unemployment that is more than four times the official rate reported by the Bureau of Labor Statistics. As of December 2014, more than ninety-three million Americans or almost one third of the US population have given up looking for work and are no longer considered part of the labor force. The talking heads continue to spew nonsense about the jobless recovery when in fact there can be no recovery when more than a third of the working population does not even try to participate in the productive side of the economy. While huge corporations enjoy an economic windfall (provided mainly by cheap, desperate, overworked employees living in fear of losing their jobs),

---

[108]   Casey, Doug. The Ascendance of Sociopaths in US Governance. *Casey Research*, 2012.

individual Americans continue their debt-fueled consumption while becoming even more impoverished in terms of real savings and net worth.

The sociopaths in government will react by accelerating the pace toward a national police state domestically, while starting another major war abroad, probably against Iran, Syria, Iraq, North Korea, or some combination thereof. In order to fund this consumption based illusion of economic growth, the government will continue with the only thing they know—deficit spending, money printing, and bailouts for their corrupt Wall Street friends. Eventually this will lead to hyperinflation and a complete collapse of the US dollar. This is mathematically inevitable. It is completely predictable. It is what sociopaths do.

Police states are borne out of regimes that are bent on centrally controlling the economy and the people. Once their oppressive tactics reach such a level that the citizenry begins to express intolerance for it, such regimes feel the need to crack down. They become paranoid about their ability to hold on to power. They begin implementing draconian measures to suppress dissent and to ensure the people will be too fearful to express any objections.

The laws passed by Adolf Hitler's government just prior to embarking on his final solution consisted in controls over the press, radio and film media, free speech, restrictions on international travel, emigration, capital controls, and gun ownership. His next step was to militarize the police force, and from this the Gestapo was born. Social problems become exacerbated once a highly politicized central government expands its control over the citizenry. This has always been the case in Europe, and we have seen this phenomenon take root in the United States as our federal government has consolidated and grown its power. A government full of power-mongering sociopaths will always seek to take advantage of and enflame social unrest in order to justify its expansion. This is why our federal government continues to meddle in the lives of the citizenry with regard to issues that are completely outside of the scope of the proper role of the federal government.

In a healthy society a typical sociopath usually stays under the radar. Perhaps he'll commit a petty crime when he thinks he can get away with it, but social customs keep him restrained to a large extent. However, once the government becomes powerful enough to change its emphasis away from protecting its citizens from illegal force being used against them (the only proper role of government) to initiating force against its own citizens with onerous laws, taxes, and confiscation of their property, the restraints of those customs are abandoned. Regard for social conduct and morality—the forces that keep a healthy society orderly—are replaced by regulations enforced by militarized police and funded by confiscatory taxes.[109] When government no longer functions to secure individuals' rights but instead begins violating them, sociopaths start coming out of the woodwork, drawn to the

[109] Casey, Doug. The Ascendance of Sociopaths in US Governance. *Casey Research.* 2012

state bureaucracies and their regulatory agencies where they can be authorized and paid to do what they've always wanted to do—gain power over their fellow citizens and then abuse it.

There are only two ways people can relate to one another—voluntarily or coercively. A government is an instrument of pure coercion, and sociopaths are drawn to its power and authority to use force. Once they gain control of a government, their only desire is to make that government omnipotent. It is through this principle that the US government, which once had limited and separated powers has been perverted into what it is today—a leviathan of centralized power that considers itself totally unaccountable to the people of the United States.

Only free, self-reliant, and moral individuals subscribe to societal interaction on a voluntary, mutually respectful basis. Parasites, on the other hand, must compel others to interact with them by force. They are incapable of dealing with others on a basis of fair exchange because they have nothing of real value to offer. The United States today has fallen under the governance of sociopathic, narcissistic parasites who are intent on enslaving the entire population under a mountain of inescapable debt.

Free and self-reliant people do not willingly subjugate themselves. They must be tricked into it.

We have to pass the bill so you can find out what's in it.[110]

—Nancy Pelosi, US Representative and
former Speaker of the House

Why the Majority of Americans Will Continue to Accept the Status Quo

As evidenced in the 2012 presidential election, socialists in America now outnumber those who are devoted to a constitutional form of governance. The majority will accept the status quo because it's what they want. Those in power will continue to subvert the rule of law that limits government's power and will instead expand the federal government by virtue of the will of the majority. This demonstrates precisely why pure unrestrained democracy is an inherently flawed system. It is what Ben Franklin meant by "three wolves and a lamb voting on what to eat for lunch." Democracy is fine unless you're a lamb, and it's the middle class that is being devoured. Fifty-one percent of the population denying the rights of the other

---

[110] Pelosi, Nancy. In a Speech to the Legislative Conference for the National Association of Counties - March 9, 2010.

forty-nine percent is not a basis of fairness. It is a basis of tyranny. Karl Marx called it "the dictatorship of the proletariat."

Secondly even those with a strong work ethic who lean toward a desire for self-reliance have no philosophical anchor on which to base a framework for self-governance. Too many successive generations have been educated with public-school propaganda about American democracy and revisionist history. Most Americans no longer have any real core beliefs, and most of their opinions, such as "national health care is a human right" or "our brave troops should fight evil over there so we don't have to fight it over here" or "the rich should pay their fair share," are reactive and comforting. Such babble emanates from the daily bombardment of media propaganda. "The purpose of media-spin-doctors is to produce comforting sound bites that appeal to people purely at the emotional level, while eluding the ability to be tested against reality."[111]

Thirdly Americans look to the television news and entertainment media to tell them how to think, what to think, and why they should think it. They have been inculcated to believe everything they hear from celebrities as being true on its face simply because those celebrities are popular. Most absorb virtually all of their information from the news and entertainment media and then wait for those same outlets to tell them what their conclusions should be. People rarely try to look beyond what they are being told by asking, "Why is the media reporting these things in this way by this person?" Such is the nature of propaganda. The purpose is not to inform people but to shape their opinions and thus surreptitiously dictate how they will vote in order to validate political candidates that have already been preselected by the ruling class.

And finally Americans have become too pampered and comfortable. We have for too long been living under the misconception that the safe, comfortable, and convenient lifestyle we all enjoy is not only normal but that we are entitled to it. In fact, the quality of life we currently have is for the most part an illusion, and it is unsustainable. The real world is a harsh and difficult environment and requires real survival skills in order to thrive. It requires that individuals be able to cooperate and exchange their skills and the fruits of their labor by peaceful, voluntary, mutual consent. Using force and coercion to drive individuals to deal with one another in ways they would not otherwise freely deal—in order to artificially expand consumption disguised as growth—yields unintended consequences. Doing so destroys economic value and creates disincentives for individuals to produce and save, once they come to understand that the fruits of their labors, their assets, and their savings will be confiscated by taxes and rendered worthless by inflation.

The concept of perpetual, infinite, economic growth (based upon consumption) is a scientific and physical impossibility. There are countless aspects of our current quality of life that are unsustainable, but in spite of that we continue to live as a nation of

---

[111]   Casey, Doug. "The Ascendance of Sociopaths in US Governance," Casey Research, March 21, 2012.

freeloaders without wondering or caring how long it can last. We routinely lie to ourselves that all of this is the way it's supposed to be. "I don't need to be self-reliant because my government will force someone else to take care of me."

We the People Are Ultimately Responsible for Our Decline

The idea of public opinion polling for presidential election campaigns started with FDR in 1936. Today the candidates spend tens of millions of dollars taking the pulse of the public in bogus opinion surveys and then simply regurgitating the poll results back to the people from a teleprompter. The population is told exactly what they all want to hear virtually word for word. Therefore, the majority of Americans is where the decay stems from.

> Once a country buys into the idea that an above-average privileged lifestyle is everyone's minimum entitlement, whether they earned it or not; when the fortunate few can lobby for special deals to scrape whatever they want off the table, as they squeeze wealth out of others by force; that country is on the decline. Lobbying and onerous taxes, as the alternative to production, innovation, and self-reliance, have never been able to achieve and sustain prosperity. The wealth being squeezed out of the American middle class today took at least two centuries to produce, but it has its limits and is reaching the end.
>
> —Doug Casey

Class Envy as a Tool of Political Power

It is politically incorrect but true that people generally fall into several different economic classes.

Today there are actually four economic classes in America. The three that we are most familiar with are the poor, the middle class, and the rich. The rich are what the media has been referring to as *the 1 percent*. To be part of the 1 percent, you must earn more than $350,000 annually in gross income, according to data published in 2013 by the Bureau of Labor Statistics.

These rich, however, are nowadays really part of the middle class, albeit the upper middle class. Those highly educated professionals and small business entrepreneurs earning $350,000 or more annually are in reality up to their eyeballs in debt like the rest of us. They are in more or less the same boat as the average middle-class chump who is just a few paychecks from bankruptcy or homelessness at any given time. They just have a lot more to lose. This is the category that politicians actually refer to when they talk about the rich in the context of who pays their *fair share* in taxes. Their purpose is to provide a straw man for the poor and lower middle class to envy for being able to earn more.

The Fourth Class—The Obscenely Rich

The wealth gap that we hear so much about is generally mentioned as being between the poor and this illusory 1 percent. But this gap is economically meaningless compared to the real wealth gap undermining overall economic prosperity. This is the gap between the middle class (including the upper middle class) and the obscenely rich and ruling class. These are people whose net worth is in the high tens of millions to several hundreds of millions or more. It's really this one tenth of 1 percent of the population that is raking the lion's share of wealth off the economic table, in return for nothing of real value. According to a new study by Thomas Piketty of the Paris School of Economics and Gabriel Zucman of the University of California, Berkeley—at the very top, wealth is distributed as unevenly as it was in the early 20th century. The wealthiest 0.1 percent and especially the 0.01 percent have left the rest of the 1 percent far behind. This is because the net worth of the obscenely rich is measured by real wealth or hard assets, such as land, ownership in private companies, and foreign properties and investments. The wealth of the middle class, on the other hand, is measured in worthless paper—US dollar savings, stocks, bonds, 401(k)s, all of which are denominated in Federal Reserve Notes, all of which is more or less vapor and based upon debt.

We hear a great deal from the entertainment news media about *income* inequality but rarely if ever do they mention *wealth* inequality. The distinction is vast. Income is what you earn. Wealth is what you can keep, invest, and save for the future. Someone earning $250 thousand annually and living paycheck to paycheck may appear to be better off than someone earning $50 thousand annually and also living paycheck to paycheck. However, both are just a few weeks from bankruptcy upon losing their respective jobs. In this context, income inequality is far less relevant than wealth inequality. It is the growing wealth inequality that is decimating the middle class. The obscenely rich can keep and grow their wealth, while the property of the middle class is confiscated and squandered by inept and corrupt government wealth redistribution programs.

Within this fourth obscenely rich economic class is a subcategory—the anonymous ruling class, who are economically so far beyond even the obscenely rich that they are interested primarily in power. Here I'm talking about people with several billions or more in terms of net worth. The concept of net worth has to do with assets—property rights. The people in this class of wealth have access to investment products in legal jurisdictions that are not available to the rest of us. That allows the obscenely rich and ruling class to retain, expand, and protect their property and assets in ways that are impossible for the middle class. These are the owners and managers respectively of the dog track on which the poor and middle class (and even most of the so-called 1 percent) are all chasing rabbits. For the middle class our property and our assets are there for the taking by those in power. For the obscenely rich and ruling class their assets are protected and off limits.

The main distinction between all social classes is that the obscenely rich and the ruling classes enjoy real property rights. The rest of us do not.

It is the ruling class who owns and controls our central banks, the media, and our political system. They use the media to foster class envy between the poor, the middle class, and the illusory 1 percent while they insulate themselves from the ensuing conflict—Divide and Conquer.

Over the centuries oligarchs and tyrants have learned that when they directly rule a people, overtly fleecing their wealth and fruits of their labor in order to satisfy their own greed and personal gain, it is just a matter of time before the people rise up and overthrow those rulers. Some have even lost their heads to violent revolution. Thus was developed the covert means of rule that is prevalent today. As such, most of the obscenely rich and all of the political class are the puppets of the ruling class. They are the useful idiots used to manage and control the population. Their other purpose is to insulate the ruling class from those they exploit. The political class should be considered a subcategory of the obscenely rich since most career politicians who are not obscenely rich when they enter politics, are very likely to be when they get out.

> "[We] came out of the White House not only dead broke but in debt ... [we] had no money and *struggled* to piece together the resources for mortgages and [her daughter] Chelsea's college education ... You know, it was not easy."
>
> —Hillary Clinton, in a June 9, 2014
> interview with Diane Sawyer

The Clinton's left the White House in January, 2001. Just prior to that in 1999 and 2000 they purchased 2 homes for $4.5 Million, one of them in New York, the other in Washington DC. This was necessary to establish New York state residency since Mrs. Clinton had been *selected* to be New York's next US Senator.

Dead Broke? Since leaving the White House in 2001, former President Clinton's taxpayer funded perks have included most of his basic expenses including all of his phone bills and a more than $579,000 annual rent bill for his nearly 18,000 square-foot *office* in Manhattan—according to a 2008 ABC news report. In 2011, the former president moved his offices to an even larger site in lower Manhattan's financial district sprawling over more than 25,700 square feet. This is more than 21 times larger, than an average single family American home.

Bill Clinton has received more of almost every benefit available to former presidents— from his pension to his staff's salaries and benefits. Between 2001 and 2011, the taxpayers have paid more than $720,000 in phone bills and more than $5.5 million in rent for his Manhattan offices. These expenses have far surpassed the totals rung up for those purposes by Bush (both of them), Carter and the late former presidents Gerald Ford and Ronald Reagan combined.

These figures come from congressional reports and from summaries of annual budget requests by the U.S. General Services Administration, which administers the program. Clinton family tax documents show that the Clintons pulled in $111 million in total income between 2000, their last year in the White House, through the end of 2007. Most middle class Americans would not consider that as *dead broke*.

From Left to Right: Hillary Clinton, Sir Evelyn de Rothschild, Bill Clinton, Lady Lynn de Rothschild – at the Rothschild Estate attending a party given by The Rothschilds for Mrs. Clinton in 2003.

According to the Obama administration, a hardworking neurosurgeon who spent more than a decade studying for his profession, who likely invested hundreds of thousands in his education and then earns $350,000 annually is *rich* or in the so-called 1 percent. Or an entrepreneur that risks his entire life savings to start and run a small business that might be earning $350,000 annually is *rich* by Obama's standards. Neither of these people could even afford Bill Clinton's phone bill.

Nevertheless, people earning that kind of money are indeed wealthy as compared with the very poor in this country. Never mind the fact that they take risks and work hard to *earn* their wealth. Begrudging them success is the basis for the culture of envy fostered by the ruling class in order to foment the infighting between the citizenry. This is partly what keeps the dog race going.

The real wealth gap is the one between the middle class and the obscenely rich, and it is diverging at an exponential rate.[112] In fact, the wealth gap between the poor and the upper middle class is actually narrowing. It is the middle class and the upper middle class that are disappearing. For them, under our current monetary and tax system, there is nowhere to go but down. It is mainly the middle class that is relentlessly taxed into poverty and whose property, assets, and net worth are constantly being confiscated. It has become evident to many that the American middle class is evaporating permanently. This is not hyperbole. It is a mathematical fact.

Hope and Change for America—Becoming A Third World Economy

The data provided in the following table (The Global Wealth Data Table) reveals that although the United States is near the top of the developed world in average or mean wealth, this is due mainly to the many multibillionaires in the United States. The median wealth per US adult, however, is substantially lower (column 4 in the table). For those unfamiliar with statistics, it is another way of saying that the enormous wealth held by America's multimillionaires and billionaires is a statistical anomaly. The average wealth therefore is not a representative measure of the vast cross-section of Americans. The *median* wealth however is far more indicative. It is that value where 50% of the population owns more, and 50% of the population owns less in terms of real assets. In fact, a direct measure of the magnitude of this wealth gap is given by the ratio of median to mean wealth (column 5 in the table). This is lower in the United States than in every other country except Russia. The startling impact of this huge wealth gap is best illustrated in column 6 of the table. This data shows that adults in the United States with a median level of wealth (as assets) hold a substantially smaller percentage of the nation's overall wealth than any other country except China and India. Again this is a reflection of America's lack of respect for individual property rights.

In other words, referring to column 6 of the data table itself, the reader can see that a middle-class citizen of Finland owns $122.50 for every one billion dollars of Finland's wealth. A Canadian owns $13.40 for every one billion dollars of Canada's wealth. A citizen of Czech Republic owns $49.40 for every one billion of his country's wealth. In Thailand it is $5.40. By comparison, in the United States, a middle-class citizen owns just sixty cents for every one billion dollars of total wealth in the country. Only the citizens of China at forty cents and India at thirty cents hold less than Americans in terms of assets in proportion to their national wealth. Therefore, the only two countries in the industrialized world whose citizens have fewer property rights than in the United States are China and India. This is clear evidence that America's middle

---

[112] Lowery, Annie. The Wealth Gap In America is Growing. *New York Times*. April 2, 2014.

class has already descended to the standard of a Third World country in terms of real wealth. Even the former Communist nations of Czech Republic and Russia enjoy substantially more property rights than Americans.

Wealth Gap – The Global Wealth Data Table

	1	2	3	4	5	6	7	8
	Adults	Tot. Wealth	Mean	Median	% Med / Mean	*% Total*	Number	Number
	Millions	Trillions	Wealth	Wealth		*Wealth per Billion*	Millionaires	Billionaires
Australia	16412	5.8	$354,586	$193,653	54.6	33.4	905	18
Brazil	133355	3.3	$24,600	$5,852	23.8	1.8	227	37
Canada	26822	6.1	$227,660	$81,610	35.8	13.4	842	29
Chile	12255	0.5	$44,198	$13,073	29.6	26.1	42	5
China	987184	20.2	$20,452	$7,536	36.8	0.4	964	122
Czech	8413	0.3	$40,259	$14,820	36.8	49.4	24	4
Denmark	4171	0.9	$214,396	$87,121	40.6	96.8	117	6
Finland	4173	0.6	$145,693	$73,487	50.4	122.5	57	1
France	47896	12.7	$265,463	$81,274	30.6	6.4	2284	24
Germany	67031	11.7	$174,526	$42,222	24.2	3.6	1463	58
India	751287	3.2	$4,250	$938	22.1	0.3	158	55
Indonesia	155294	1.7	$10,842	$2,293	21.1	1.3	104	25
Ireland	3447	0.5	$152,563	$60,953	40.0	121.9	59	5
Israel	4865	0.6	$129,526	$37,019	28.6	61.7	69	17
Italy	48998	10.4	$212,910	$123,710	58.1	11.9	1170	23
Japan	104303	28.1	$269,708	$141,410	52.4	5.0	3581	22
South Korea	37955	2.6	$69,646	$27,080	38.9	10.4	208	24
Netherlands	12844	2.2	$173,910	$61,880	35.6	28.1	323	6
New Zealand	3194	0.5	$156,428	$63,000	40.3	126.0	57	3
Norway	3695	1.2	$325,989	$79,376	24.3	66.1	229	6
Russian Fed	110813	1.3	$12,161	$1,267	10.4	1.0	97	110
Singapore	3885	1	$258,117	$95,542	37.0	95.5	156	10
South Africa	30800	0.7	$21,458	$3,822	17.8	5.5	44	4
Spain	36936	3.9	$104,773	$53,292	50.9	13.7	313	20
Sweden	7245	1.7	$237,297	$41,367	17.4	24.3	343	14
Switzerland	6062	2.8	$468,186	$87,137	18.6	31.1	562	13
Thailand	49163	0.4	$7,415	$2,166	29.2	5.4	20	10
U.K.	47883	12	$250,005	$115,245	46.1	9.6	1582	37
U.S.	236502	62	$262,351	$38,786	14.8	0.6	11023	442

The one characteristic common to all Third World countries is that there is no middle class, or if there is one, it is disproportionately small as compared to the ruling class. Virtually all Third World countries are dominated by a small, obscenely rich ruling elite who own and control virtually all land, resources, and means of production along with a large population of poor and destitute who have no property and no means of ever escaping poverty. This is exactly the direction that America has been headed for the past several decades.

The Food Stamp Nation

In November, 2008, 39.8 million Americans lived in poverty. Four years later in November 2012, the US Census Bureau reported that 53 million people lived in poverty, including almost 20 percent of America's children, the highest level ever (These figures do not include illegal immigrants). This means that the number of Americans who have joined the ranks of those living in poverty increased by more than 33 percent in just the first term of Obama's presidency. Every one of those people was formerly part of the middle class. And thanks to our inflationary fiat money system, it is far easier to fall into poverty than it is to escape it once you are there.

Washington politicians and their media mouthpieces never refer to their friends in Hollywood, professional athletes, or talk show hosts—basically the entire entertainment industry—who are earning tens of millions or in some cases even hundreds of millions annually when they mention the rich. They also aren't referring to their Wall Street friends who might have a net worth of a hundred million dollars or more and who sit as board chairmen or CEOs of the world's largest multinational corporations like GE, GM, Exxon-Mobil, Monsanto, McDonald's, or others. This is because the political class aspires to join the ranks of the obscenely rich—that is, if they aren't already among them when they take office. These could be categorized as the "one tenth of 1 percent," but no one talks about them.

It should also be understood that the people in this obscenely rich category of wealth do pay a share. It's just not a fair share (compared to the middle class), and they don't pay it in the United States. Most of their wealth is earned through investments in legalized, international, money-laundering programs called offshore private equity funds. These are incorporated in low-tax jurisdictions like Bermuda, the Cayman Islands, Luxembourg, Dubai, and numerous other offshore tax havens. Ultra-high-net-worth families around the world invest their assets in such funds primarily for the purpose of avoiding US taxes. That type of investment, however, is exclusive and unavailable—even to most of the so-called 1 percent. For example, Luxembourg levies only a 3 percent corporate tax rate on the earnings of some private equity funds incorporated in that country. However, the minimum subscription required to invest in a single share of such funds is at least five million dollars. Even those Obama considers rich don't have that kind of money lying around for a single share of a fund in a tax-haven country. However, billionaire golfers or talk show hosts worth hundreds of millions consider that kind of money to be disposable income. This is where the ever-widening wealth gap is occurring. It is not the gap between the poor and the so-called 1 percent. It is the gap between the middle class, which pays virtually all of this country's taxes, and the 0.1 percent—the obscenely rich and ruling class, which pay almost none of it.

F. A. Grieger

The Carrot and Stick Principle—Ruled by Fear and Confusion

The news, sports, and entertainment media establishment is one of the most important tools of the ruling class with which to control and manipulate the poor and middle class. It is through this body that they use the carrot and stick principle to instill in us false hope for a prosperous future and then bombard us with fear-mongering news stories about unemployment, the debt ceiling, racism, terrorism, and war. By combining false hope and fear, they keep the masses confused, hungry, and in fear of losing their job, their credit rating, or their home. At the same time they dangle the carrot providing false hope that as long as we keep running on the hamster wheel we might get lucky. We might just win the lottery, get a promotion at our thankless job, or be discovered and strike it rich. It is this psychological basis that keeps every hardworking American chasing rabbits that they can never catch for the entirety of their natural lives, while cheerleading for their favorite NFL star, billionaire golfer, hip-hop artist, or political party. The American people have willfully enslaved themselves and even express reverence and gratitude to their oppressors for the privilege.

The Classes Defined

The poor are characterized by apathy. They have nothing. They are downtrodden, devoid of hope, and so they don't really care. They believe they have neither anything to lose nor anything to gain. They're resigned to their fate of accepting whatever scraps are thrown to them by the political class—scraps that have first been confiscated from the middle class, whom the poor have been convinced are actually rich. Any politician that promises them something more like a raise to the minimum wage or expanded welfare benefits (at the expense of the middle class) will get their vote. They will even forego working in order to volunteer their time to support a politician who promises to punish those in the so-called 1 percent by forcing them to pay more of their *fair share*. This kind of political activity is what is meant by community organizing and redistributing wealth. This is the politics of envy.

The middle class is ruled by fear and false hope—fear from the knowledge that they're only a few paychecks away from falling into the poor class. Indeed, at least fifteen million of them have fallen into poverty between 2008 and 2014. They fear that they can't pay their debts or might be unable to borrow more. They fear that they don't have a realistic prospect of improving their quality of life. At the same time the media bombards us with images of what we must buy in order to be successful—the newest fashion, the latest model of BMW, the newest hit albums from this year's Grammy winners. We are relentlessly indoctrinated with false hope that our lot will improve and our future will eventually be secured, both of which are lies. Many believe that they might actually have the chance to rise to the obscenely rich class if they just work harder or risk a bit more of their life's savings in the fraud-laden stock market. Some

232

even religiously pay into *the idiot tax*—the Powerball and Mega-Millions lotteries, which are voluntary hidden tax-schemes set up by politicians to further fleece the citizenry by enticing them with more false hope. What most don't realize is that the obscenely rich class is a club, and outsiders are not invited.

False hope is sold to members of the middle class also by our university system and by our system of corporate employment. Many white-collar workers believe that if they can just invest fifty, sixty, or even a hundred thousand more of their hard-earned (after tax) dollars in another university degree or an online executive MBA, it will propel them to a higher rung on the corporate ladder, possibly getting them a little bit closer to economic freedom and self-reliance. However the closer they get to the rabbit, the faster it will be speeded up in order to make sure they never quite reach it. University education in the US is part of the racket involved in luring America's young people into inescapable debt-servitude by selling false hope. Today, anyone with a credit card and internet access can acquire an MBA or Ph.D. without ever attending a class or leaving their sofa. While this has rendered advanced university education as essentially worthless, the student loan debt crisis has reached epic proportions. As of April 2014, student loan debt defaults have reached $145 billion with total outstanding student debt estimated to be $1 trillion. This is the politics of fear and false hope.

The obscenely rich are characterized by greed and arrogance. They have everything, and they think they deserve it—whether they actually earned it or not. Those in media and the entertainment industry enjoy extraordinary financial rewards mainly because they are the useful idiots used by government and the ruling class to distract the people with entertainment and propaganda. Celebrities provide the public with an unrealistic vision of what they call *the American dream.* They spend their lives polishing their image for appearances on television, film, and in print, telling the American people which sneakers to buy, what laundry detergent to use, what to think, and which politicians to vote for. Television programs targeted at children start their celebrity worship indoctrination at toddler age. Celebrity worship is one of the most effective weapons of mass distraction. It dupes the public into wasting their mental and emotional energy on irrelevant issues rather than reading a book and learning something useful. American politics has also become a mainstay of the entertainment industry, with objective news reporting having been replaced by opinion-entertainment programs. Their purpose is to entertain, indoctrinate, and distract, while at the same time polarizing the citizenry by fostering envy and rivalry.

And finally *the ruling class* is all about absolute power and control. They have so much real wealth and power that you won't easily find their names or images anywhere. The notion that people like Carlos Slim, Bill Gates and Warren Buffet really are the richest men in the world is preposterous. They don't have the authority to print money and force us to borrow it from them for use as the sole medium of exchange, but there are those in the world who do have that power. The truly richest on earth will never let the peasantry know who they really are. Would you if you were one of them? These are the people who control the world's central banks and the issuance of fiat currencies—the dollar, the euro, the yen, the pound, etc. They are the people who truly own and control all of the property, labor, and means of production in this and the other industrialized countries. Their goal is to centralize the means of production on a global basis under their control via their power to issue the various fiat currencies around the world. This centralization of their economic dominance has been the real purpose of globalization.

What's Next?

If *We the American people* do not act to restore our individual property rights, sound money, and a respect for the founding principles of the US Constitution at the federal, state, and local levels of governance, things will continue to decline further until we live under a global socialist totalitarian dictatorship. There will be no place to go where individual property rights will be respected. In that case, the run up to it will look something like this:

The wealth gap will continue to widen. More of the middle class will evaporate, and the obscenely rich and ruling class will become even more powerful and entrenched. They will remain protected. Eventually the middle class will disappear, and we will consist of a mass of working poor with no real assets and no savings, all living paycheck to paycheck, working for companies that are owned either directly or indirectly by the central banking aristocracy. Since they also control the military-industrial complex, every Western country will devolve into a surveillance-based police state. People will begin to spy on one another out of self-preservation.

Martial Law and the Militarization of Local Law Enforcement

In a June 2012 report put out by the Department of Homeland Security, the DHS lists hundreds of types of domestic terrorist threats. This was part of the NDAA or National Defense Authorization Act, which authorizes law enforcement to arrest and detain indefinitely and without charge anyone who might be a potential terrorist. The DHS considers anyone an "extreme right wing potential terrorist" if they fit any of the profiles on this list. A small sample of these types of domestic terrorists follows. You might be a terrorist if you are one who:

- believes that one's personal and/or national way of life is under attack,

- is against abortion (pro-life),

- homeschools your children,

- talks about or has reverence for individual liberty,

- talks about the first amendment,

- talks about the second amendment,

- talks about the tenth amendment (states' rights),

- talks about defeating communism,

- is a member of the family research council,

- is against illegal immigration,

- is suspicious of centralized federal authority,

- is concerned about grave threats to national sovereignty,

- is part of "the patriot movement,"

- is a "tea partier,"

- complains about media bias,

- has bumper stickers that are patriotic or anti-UN,

- talks about their constitutional rights,

- believes in conspiracy theories,

- is a gun owner,

- is a Ron Paul supporter,

- is a survivalist,

- is a returning war veteran,

- is an Evangelical Christian.

More than two thirds of the US population can be described by at least one of the aforementioned. Perhaps this is why police departments across the United States are being militarized with training and equipment. Recently the Department of Homeland Security has purchased 2700 MRAP (mine-resistant ambush-protected) sixteen-ton armored vehicles in order to deploy them to local US law enforcement agencies.

These vehicles were designed specifically for urban warfare in the Iraqi and Afghani theater of desert war. They are so heavy that some bridges across the United States are unable to support their weight. The unit cost for a single MRAP vehicle is more than $650,000. The total maintenance cost with spare parts and periodic overhauls per vehicle can be as high as $115,000 annually, and they only get four miles per gallon. All of these operating costs will be imposed upon taxpayers who have had absolutely no influence over the introduction of these vehicles to local law enforcement agencies across the country, even though it is being done at taxpayer's expense. If your local police department is funded through your property taxes and they receive one of these, the resultant increase to the extortion tax on your home will be used to pay for its maintenance and operation. That property tax increase will be imposed without your consent and if you refuse to pay it, your home will be seized and auctioned off—perhaps to an illegal immigrant that has been granted amnesty by the federal government and then given favorable zero-interest loan offers—also guaranteed by the federal government.

For what purpose these vehicles are being deployed on US soil is a question the reader must answer for him or herself. What is clear is that American taxpayers are again being forced without their consent or foregone knowledge to feed the beast that is bent on controlling and subjugating all of us.

Government Power Run Amok

As Bush said, "If you're not with us, you're against us," and with the passing of his Patriot Act, he may as well have said, Constitution? What's a Constitution?" But that document has been viewed by the current and prior administrations as nothing more than an obstacle to expanding federal government power. The Obama administration's contempt for The Constitution along with the Supreme Court's demonstration of compliance with his personal agenda have rendered this country's founding documents as practically irrelevant.

You may find it difficult to remain quiet when you see these things going on. However, you'd better keep your mouth shut, or you may be indefinitely detained. And in today's world just keeping quiet won't be enough. As the Edward Snowden-NSA spying story unfolded, it revealed that the national security state has an extensive and growing file on almost every citizen as well as the means to monitor all of your communications.

Given the level of sophistication of analytical marketing software today, your e-mails, purchases, vacation trips, websites you've visited, programs you've watched, etc., have all been used to determine your purchasing habits, beliefs, desires, fears, and even with whom you associate. What we face today is far more dangerous than tyrannies of the past. Personal security and privacy will be difficult if not impossible to find anywhere in the world in the years to come.

What's Next?

If the past is any indicator, things don't look good for the next generation. The 20th century was human history's most barbaric period. Approximately 50 million to 60 million people died in international and civil wars. However, that figure pales in comparison with the number of people who were killed at the hands of their own government. The late Rudolph J. Rummel, former professor of political science at the University of Hawaii and author of *Death by Government*, estimated that since the beginning of the 20th century, governments killed 170 million of their own citizens. Topping the list of well-organized government mass-murderers were the Soviet Union, which killed 62 million of its own citizens, and the People's Republic of China, which was responsible for the deaths of 35 million to 40 million of its citizens. In a very distant third place were the Nazis, who exterminated almost 16 million Jews, Slavs, Serbs, Czechs, Poles, Ukrainians, noncompliant Germans, and others deemed misfits, such as homosexuals and the mentally ill. Every one of these countries was a Socialist Dictatorship of one form or another.

Why was the 20th century so vicious? We created a vast military industrial complex, owned and controlled by bankers—and war became their greatest profit center. A system which profits from war and waste is the quintessential Keynesian economic growth model. Peace and efficiency are the enemies of such an absurd system. Since any normal and rational person would object to such a system, it must operate under a cloud of secrecy, requiring central control of the economy. This led to the emergence of concentrated power centers that arose during the period. Had Josef Stalin, Mao Zedong or Adolf Hitler been around in earlier times, they could not have engineered the slaughter of tens of millions of people. They would have had neither the authority nor the financial resources to do so. It was the fiat monetary system that took root in Europe during the first decade and in the US during the second decade of the 20th century, that enabled this.

> Power kills … absolute power kills absolutely
>
> —Rudolph J. Rummel, *Death by Government*

"The more power a government has, the more it can act arbitrarily according to the whims and desires of the [moneyed] elite, and the more it will make war on others and murder its foreign and domestic subjects." That's the long, tragic, ugly story of government: the elite's use of government to dupe and forcibly impose its will on the masses.[113]

Government achieves that power by forcing its population into dependency and servitude by whatever means possible. The most effective means is to eliminate property rights.

Today, the most important aspect to this is our astounding and ever-expanding national debt crisis—a direct consequence of our unconstitutional fiat monetary system. It is the key element that has allowed the federal government to morph into the unwieldy and corrupt behemoth it is—entirely at the expense of the middle class and poor.

This debt, along with the debts held by all of our state and local governments can never be paid off. When governments default it is the citizens who pay. As time marches on, income taxes will increase, other new taxes will be added, and more homes and farms will be confiscated for nonpayment of increasingly unaffordable property taxes. Such confiscatory taxes will eventually be extended to any other real assets that individuals might hold, such as gold and silver—just as FDR did in 1933. More controls over the labor market will be instituted through increasing minimum wages that will ensure high unemployment. Interest rates will eventually be driven up. The inevitable hyperinflation that is to come will *not* increase the value of your home because there will be fewer qualified borrowers. The hyperinflation will *not* be accompanied by a proportional increase in your earnings since the controlled labor

---

[113]   Williams, Walter. Evil Leaders Don't Reach Positions of Power Without Help. *Politics Today.* April 7, 2014.

market lags inflation by several years. More people will be forced to use debt just to finance the cost of a subsistence standard of living. This is in fact the ruling class's goal, since it is they who issue that debt and profit from the interest.

Just as today everyone will continue to find that they are working harder and harder for less and less, continually playing catch up but with the continued false hope that "better days are ahead." By the time you reach retirement age, any savings you might have accumulated will have been rendered worthless in terms of buying power, and you will have little or nothing to leave to your children. What little you might save for your kids, estate taxes will eat up in probate upon your death.

President Obama has demonstrated that he does not have the will to change the self-destructive trajectory that this country has been on for decades. Neither did President Bush before him, nor will Obama's eventual successor. On the contrary, both the Democrat and Republican leadership today are working in collusion for a different agenda, and it's not on behalf of the electorate. The two-party system is a fraud intended to give *we the people* the illusion that we actually participate in our own governance. We do not. Both political parties have been charged by the nation's clandestine ruling class of sociopaths with the same responsibility—to destroy the dollar, eradicate individual property rights, further enslave the middle class to an inescapable system of perpetual debt servitude, and bring the US another step closer to being a subservient lackey to the United Nations and their vision for socialist global governance.

Is this the country you wish to leave to your children?

CHAPTER 11

Fear and Loathing—Why the Government Is Like the Mafia

It is to be regretted that the rich and powerful too often bend the acts of government to their selfish purposes. Distinctions in society will always exist under every just government. Equality of talents, of education, or of wealth cannot be produced by human institutions. In the full enjoyment of the gifts of Heaven and the fruits of superior industry, economy, and virtue, every man is equally entitled to protection by law; but when the laws undertake to add to these natural and just advantages artificial distinctions, to grant titles, gratuities, and exclusive privileges, to make the rich richer and the potent more powerful, the humble members of society—the farmers, mechanics, and laborers—who have neither the time nor the means of securing like favors to themselves, have a right to complain of the injustice of their Government.

—Andrew Jackson

In the first James Bond film, author Ian Flemming introduces perhaps the film industry's best criminal character of all time, the evil Dr. No. He first enters the Bond film franchise as the head of the notorious SPECTRE, Special Executive for Counterintelligence, Terrorism, Revenge, and Extortion. Today this seems a more appropriate acronym for the US government.

Socialist governments generally follow the same MO (method of operations) as organized crime syndicates. They go after what you love, depend upon for your livelihood, or simply cannot live without. America's federal, state, and local governments pretend to take an interest in the well-being of this country's citizens, while they threaten us with homelessness and imprisonment if we refuse to allow their various extortion schemes to be carried out against the hardworking, the innocent, the productive, and the best among us. The US government makes the mob look like a bunch of schoolgirls in terms of scale. Any nongovernment body doing the same things would be considered as operating a criminal enterprise of biblical proportions. From their various Ponzi schemes like social security to conscripting all employers as their tax collection agents—from their foreign interventionism and overthrowing democratically elected governments through economic hit men[114] to their collusion with the Federal Reserve to commit counterfeiting—a cartel between SPECTRE, Chaos, and Dr. Evil's criminal empire would pale in comparison.

How Banks and the Government Intend to Steal Your Savings

On March 15, 2013, the small Mediterranean island nation known as the Republic of Cyprus found itself on the brink of financial collapse. Cypriot banks became overleveraged (having taken on too much debt) to their investments in local property companies and because of their involvement in the Greek debt crisis. On this day two of their major banks, the Laiki Bank and the Bank of Cyprus, abruptly closed until further notice. As a consequence of credit downgrades from both Moody's and Fitch, they were disqualified from issuing bonds as collateral for access to credit from the European Central Bank. Unable to benefit from an American-style bailout from taxpayers, they instead conducted what has been called a bail-in.

This basically consisted in confiscating their depositors' money. In other words, individuals who in good faith put their savings into these banks woke up one morning to learn that their bank was now authorized to take their money in order to cover the banks' bad debts. Depositors in those banks flooded the streets, trying to access ATM machines and bank branches in order to withdraw their money before it was seized only to find the banks had been *closed for business.*

What happened next was that depositors themselves were forced against their will to bail out Cyprus's largest bank. Their deposit accounts were raided in a so-called bail-in via the confiscation of 47.5 percent of their savings for account balances exceeding 100,000 euros.

Why Is the Cyprus Financial Crisis Important to Americans?

It was the IMF (International Monetary Fund) together with the European Central Bank and the European Commission that came up with the mechanism for this bail-in as the means to rescue Cyprus. And where did they get the idea?

Three years earlier in 2009, the G20 Financial Stability Board in Basel, Switzerland, (as part of the Bank for International Settlements) asked the IMF to suggest ways through which the financial sector might be able to contribute to its own bailouts.

---

[114] Perkins, John. *Confessions of an Economic Hit Man.* Plume Publishing. Dec 27, 2005.

In response, the IMF released a study in 2010 that proposed several types of new taxes—a levy on financial institutions to create a pool of bailout funds and a tax on financial transactions.

Most interesting is that these and the IMF's other suggestions had been implemented several months earlier in the United States via the 2010 Wall Street Reform and Consumer Protection Act, also referred to as the Dodd-Frank Act. It was Martin Gruenberg, the head of the FDIC (Federal Deposit Insurance Corporation) who coauthored the Cyprus bail-in plan.[115]

Raiding your Bank Account

On December 10, 2012, two years after this initial IMF study was released, there emerged another study called the FDIC-BOE Plan (Federal Deposit Insurance Corporation—Bank of England Plan). Therein are the policies that allow bank accounts in the United States and United Kingdom to be taken over in the same fashion as the Cypriot banks' so-called bail-in. This plan added provisions to deliver clear title to funds from unsecured creditors. What most people do not realize is that legally as soon as you deposit your money in the bank, the bank owns your funds. Your money becomes the bank's liability, and you become the bank's unsecured creditor, holding nothing more than an IOU from the bank for your money on deposit. For US bank account holders, the FDIC insures your IOUs against loss.

Under FDIC-BOE, however, your IOUs would be converted into equity shares in the bank in exchange for your deposit in the event of the bank's insolvency. In this case, the bank's equity would be virtually worthless, so your money would be exchanged for worthless shares in a bankrupt financial institution. In Cyprus as of September 2013, one of the bailed-in banks was already bankrupt, and the other was being wound down, so their newly conscripted shareholders were wiped out and lost that part of their savings, which was confiscated and exchanged for the worthless shares.

In the United States, the FDIC-BOE plan has language calling for "no exception to the seizure of deposits." This means that there is no amount of funds that would be protected by FDIC. Since your savings would be converted into equity shares of the defunct bank, those shares would no longer be covered under the FDIC deposit insurance, and they could then be wiped out. In other words, when all of your cash deposits are converted into worthless stock in bankrupt banks, none of it will be covered by the FDIC insurance system. The potential for losing every nickel in your bank's savings account is a very real possibility.

What this means is that the FDIC (Federal Deposit Insurance Corporation) has the authority to confiscate any portion of your savings anytime it deems that there is a

[115]   Advani, Ashish. Cyprus Shutdown: Did the FDIC Orchestrate it? *Money News*. April 3, 2013.

financial emergency taking place. As we learned in 2008, when a financial emergency occurs in America, *we the people* are among the last to find out. By that time your savings will have already been absconded.

The precedent for this kind of wealth confiscation in the United States has already been established when on April 5, 1933, FDR signed executive order 6102. This order criminalized possession of monetary gold and gold bullion and authorized the forced confiscation of sound money in exchange for fiat Federal Reserve notes under penalty of law. At the time FDR's gold confiscation was implemented, the price of gold was fixed and defined by the US Constitution as being $20.67 per ounce. Weeks after FDR's confiscation was completed, the treasury re-priced the dollar at thirty-five dollars per ounce. Treasury retained convertibility of Federal Reserve notes to gold at that rate only for foreign exchange banks, giving the US government a 75 percent windfall—all at the expense of American citizens who had exchanged their gold for paper money at the lower exchange rate in the preceding months.

Imposing Another Hidden Tax on Your Savings

Title II of the Dodd-Frank Act also includes language that establishes an "orderly liquidation authority." Under this provision, the FDIC is now allowed to impose additional taxes that are called assessments or fees to dozens of bank-holding and insurance companies that have fifty billion dollars or more in assets. They use these fees to build what is called an orderly liquidation fund. This is basically a bailout fund that will allow the government to take over systemically risky financial institutions, recapitalize them, and then permit them to once again conduct business as usual in the financial markets. In the end those fees and assessments are passed on to the depositors, savers, and consumers of financial products in those banks. Prior to Dodd-Frank's passage, the organization *Americans for Limited Government* warned Congress that this was "an affront to private property rights." They were ignored.

Setting Us Up for a Run on the Banks

Banks earn some of their money by taking the savings of ordinary depositors and lending it out to others in the form of mortgages or business loans through an investment banking division. We've already seen how this depositor's money is leveraged tenfold through fractional reserve lending. At any given time a typical large multinational bank might have as much as 90 percent of its capital lent out to other investments. As long as all savers don't try to withdraw their money at the same time, the system works. Once the perception that there isn't enough money to go around takes hold, depositors flock to their banks to get their money before the banks' reserves are cleared out. This becomes a runaway freight train that's impossible to stop. It is what drove actor Jimmy Stewart's character George Bailey to attempt suicide in the iconic film *It's a Wonderful Life.*

The Countdown to Confiscation

What event might trigger a Cyprus-style confiscation of savings in the United States?

A rapid rise in interest rates may be all it would take. The availability and vigorous flow of credit is essential to the functioning of our debt-based system. The higher interest rates go, the more economic activity will be constricted. As this process continues, the cost of capital rises, and it becomes more expensive for federal, state, and local governments to borrow money. It will also be more expensive for companies and businesses to borrow money to fund operations. The interest payments on the national debt will increase. Unemployment will rise. Consumer debt and mortgages will become much more expensive, and fewer people will qualify for home loans. Consequently the housing market may crash again. But even these are child's play compared to what awaits. What very few in America see coming is that there is a good chance that the $441 trillion interest-rate-derivatives bubble could implode.[116]

What Is an Interest Rate Derivative?

Imagine entering a Las Vegas Casino and placing a bet that the yield on ten-year US treasuries will reach 2.9 percent in the following month. If it reaches that level, you win, and if it doesn't, you lose. That's an interest rate derivative. There are many types of investment derivatives, including options, futures, and other investments, which are essentially bets on the changes in value of underlying assets. They are called derivatives because they derive their value from an underlying asset but have no intrinsic value of their own. Warren Buffett characterized derivatives as "financial weapons of mass destruction." The total size of the outstanding derivatives market is over $700 trillion. To put this figure in perspective, if you counted out $700 Trillion one dollar at a time, and you counted one dollar per second every second for twenty-four hours per day for 365 days per year nonstop until you got to 700 trillion, it would take you 22,181,661 years to be able to count the entire amount.

The fact that this figure is so unimaginable is why its magnitude and potential impact escapes the understanding of most people. Since global GDP is approximately seventy trillion dollars, the total derivatives investment exposure is more than ten times the GDP of the entire planet. There is not enough money or productive capacity on earth to cover the losses that would result from an implosion of this bubble. The largest part of this is the $441 trillion interest rate derivatives market.[117] It consists of a large number of entities (mainly financial institutions) speculating on whether or not interest rates will go up or go down at certain points in time.

---

[116] Snyder, Michael. "The Coming Derivatives Panic That Will Destroy Global Financial Markets." December 4, 2012. www.theeconomiccollapseblog.com.

[117] European Bank for International Settlements. Annual Report. 2013.

Rapidly rising interest rates have the potential to take down the entire global financial system from the exposure of interest rate derivatives alone. Most banks use these derivatives to hedge their lending and investment risks, but some use them to speculate as well. Normally these investments are not problematic because interest rates tend to move slowly and the system remains balanced. However, interest rates have been kept artificially low for so long (in order to fuel our unsustainable consumption-based economy), it is just a matter of time before those rates will start to skyrocket. When that happens, this massive derivatives bubble has the potential to burst catastrophically.

As of June 2013, the interest rate derivatives exposure by major banks included the following:

- Bank of New York Mellon: $1.375 trillion

- State Street Financial: $1.390 trillion

- Morgan Stanley: $1.722 trillion

- Wells Fargo: $3.332 trillion

- HSBC: $4.321 trillion

- Goldman Sachs: $44.192 trillion

- Bank of America: $50.135 trillion

- Citibank: $52.102 trillion

- JPMorgan Chase: $70,151 trillion

The total derivatives exposure of the nine largest US banks is $ 228.72 trillion. Just JPMorgan Chase's derivatives exposure alone is roughly equal to the current global GDP.

To be fair, however, it must be understood that many of these bets are actually bets on bets of yet other bets, so many of the derivatives risks cancel each other out. This is the point of hedging. Therefore, the actual cash at risk amounts to about 20 percent of the face value of the derivatives exposed or about forty-six trillion dollars. This is no consolation since this represents three times the entire US GDP (gross domestic product).[118]

---

[118]   McDonald, Robert L. Derivatives Markets, 3rd Edition; New York: Prentice Hall. 2009.

When interest rates begin a long-term climb, many financial institutions will begin losing massive amounts of money on interest rate derivative contracts. The bankruptcies that will ensue will happen virtually overnight. Among those banks it will inevitably lead to the FDIC-BOE plan's provisions being implemented. Depositors in US banks will lose their money just as happened in Cyprus in mid-2013. It is almost inevitable

The Bond Bubble

The bond bubble is far more ominous than the other bubbles we have witnessed in recent decades. The bond market is much larger than either the stock market or the housing market. The Fed's policies of incessant quantitative easing and artificially low interest rates have taken bonds to the highest levels in the past 30 years. According to investor Doug Casey, it has created *a balloon in search of a pin*. That pin may be a rise in interest rates, or any number of economic imbalances that are likely to occur in the near future.

Government bonds are issued so that the government can continue deficit spending on entitlement programs. One of the greatest yet least understood risks to this market is the looming shift in population demographics. The imminent explosion in retirement of the baby boom population provides underlying fundamentals that will help precipitate the bursting of this bubble. The retiring baby boom population is accelerating in number. As they enter the population of entitlement recipients, their social security and health care benefits will be paid for by the working population which will be younger, earn less than those who have retired, and be fewer in number. This represents a $70 trillion bubble, whose expansion is now just beginning to accelerate (as of July, 2014).

This in combination with the costs of our continued military foreign interventionism and the expansion of the domestic police state, makes it clear that our deficit spending will not stabilize, but expand also at an accelerated pace. All of this is funded by more government bond issues.

The greatest risks facing Americans today, although they appear to be economic or financial, are actually political. Therefore, the most prudent means by which to protect your family and your future is to diversify by internationalizing your assets and your ability to earn a living.

No matter what country you live in, your country sees you as a milk cow. If things get tough for them [the political class], they will treat you as a beef cow.

—Doug Casey

Who Does the Federal Reserve's Zero-Interest-Rate Policy Benefit?

At the Federal Open Market Committee meeting in October 2013, the Federal Reserve board of governors suggested imposing a negative interest rate on deposits held with the Fed. In other words, a depositor will have to pay the bank a fee, to hold its money. This clearly reveals the intent by the Fed to continue devaluing the dollar as a means to escape the long-term consequences of our unmanageable national debt. Governments and central bankers love this strategy because it encourages higher risk investing in the stock market while it discourages saving (since the bank is paid a fee to hold deposits rather than having to pay out interest to depositors). However, in our economic model where uncertainty has become systemic, investors seek less risk and not more.

Most people think that banks make more money through higher interest rates on lending, but that is not necessarily true. Just ask yourself this question: "If you can create money out of thin air, what is the lowest interest you can charge and still earn a profit?"

The answer is any interest above zero. Even 0.00001 percent is profitable when you can lend money you create from nothing. So the real winners in this incredibly low-interest-rate environment are big banks, big corporations, and most of all, big government. People who are retired and living on a fixed income and savers who live within their means are the big losers. They cannot earn any interest on their savings, which continually devalues in purchasing power. Those who risk putting it into the stock market more often than not wind up losing their investments thanks to recurrent stock bubbles or devious public companies like Global Crossing.

For big corporations, sustained low interest rates are a windfall, and many public companies are posting record-setting profits. But instead of hiring more American workers, paying their existing workers more, or investing in the expansion of their US operations, they are instead investing in low-cost countries where they have more favorable tax policy than in the United States. While they create jobs in China and elsewhere, some others are just sitting on mountains of cash that they then disburse to their top executives with obscene compensation packages and huge bonuses.

According to the Economic Policy Institute, the typical public company CEO in America now earns 231 times what his employees are paid on average. In 2013 the mean annual paycheck for a CEO of a publicly traded company was $9.7 million. In one of the most egregious examples, the average worker at Wal-Mart earns $22,000 a year while the company's CEO is paid $23.1 Million (more than one thousand times more). To put it another way, the CEO of Wal-Mart earns in just two hours what an average Wal-Mart worker earns in an entire year. These huge payouts are a consequence primarily of the stock bubble, which in turn has been enabled by the Fed's artificially low interest rate policy and incessant money printing.

Another winner in this is the big commercial banks. They are able to borrow money at near zero percent from the Federal Reserve and then loan it out at 4 percent or more, while they further expand it through fractional-reserve lending. Since they don't need to rely solely on depositor's funds in order to meet their reserve requirements, they pay virtually nothing in terms of savings interest to their depositors.

The biggest beneficiary of all however, is the federal government, which has been able to borrow an extra $1.5 trillion annually with an interest payment of only $26.9 billion. Every year the interest is paid by your income taxes plus additional borrowing by the government. That's what makes our monetary system the mother of all Ponzi schemes. But take note that if interest rates rose to a level that reflected our real economic conditions and treasuries were closer to their average of around 6.7 percent, the interest on this annual debt would increase four fold—to more than a hundred billion dollars annually. In other words, if interest rates rise, the government will not be able to cover the nation's debt service even if your individual federal income taxes are more than tripled.

Who Determines Interest Rates?

Under a sound monetary system (in other words—in a free market), where all money has intrinsic value and therefore bears the same risk exposure, interest rates are determined by the market itself. In the free market, interest rates are determined by the supply and demand for money loaned out by competing banks, every dollar of which is backed by a tangible asset. Under such a system, lenders actually compete for clients on the basis of the interest rates they can offer which are based on the risk they're able and willing to bear, and in terms of the borrows actual ability to pay back the debt. As such it is the lenders themselves who assess the risk of loss when they are lending money that is backed by something of tangible value. The natural risk-based interest rate comes out of this.

Under our fiat money system, however, it is twelve men and women who are voting members of the Federal Open Market Committee (FOMC) who have the power to arbitrarily set interest rates for interbank lending that are then the baseline for all subsequent commercial lending rates. Interest rates under this model are not a reflection of real risk. Nor are they even related to the rate of inflation since our government grossly understates it by perverting the calculation.

All of these facts together should raise the following question: Has the Fed been keeping interest rates artificially low for so long solely to keep the economy stimulated and our bubble economy inflated, or have they been doing so to delay an inevitable implosion of the derivatives market?

It is most likely a combination of both. But what is most disturbing is that with the Federal Reserve being in direct control of interest rates, it suggests that the few people with their hands on the levers of our monetary system actually have the power to destroy the economy anytime they wish simply by raising interest rates at a pace that is fast enough to implode the derivatives bubble. A system where such power resides in the hands of only a dozen people—the power to impoverish more than three hundred million citizens with nothing more than a mouse click—is not compatible with free-market capitalism. As stated earlier, the main purpose of our fiat monetary model is to preclude individuals from the possibility of having real property rights, and to subvert real free-market capitalism in order to replace it with socialist central planning. Confiscating the wealth and savings of the middle class is part of that process, and the clear purpose of the Dodd-Frank Act along with the FDIC-BOE plan is to do exactly that. It's been suggested that the Cyprus confiscation was merely a test run of bigger plans to confiscate the savings of the middle class by intentionally imploding the economy.

Why Would They Do This?

The purpose is clear: in order to realize Karl Marx's dream of permanently and irreversibly destroying capitalism by using our fundamentally socialist monetary model to destroy individual prosperity and eradicate property ownership. They then falsely blame the country's failure on the free-enterprise system we no longer practice, so that it will never be restored.

The United States is headed for the worst financial crisis in modern human history, one that will make 2008 look like a minor speed bump. Our debt-fueled prosperity, which we have been enjoying for so many decades, is illusory. It will evaporate as quickly as will the bank accounts of every American saver who is unfortunate enough to have placed his or her trust in our banking system and in our government—which is supposed to be protecting our property rights rather than trying to find surreptitious ways to destroy them.

What Can You Do?

There is a particular class of banks (the too-big-to-fail banks) that is classified by the BIS (Bank for International Settlements) as G-SIFI (Global systemically important financial institutions). If you have an account at one of these banks, you may want to consider moving your account to a smaller local bank. Also, ask your bank's managing director to provide you with their financial statements to determine how heavily they are leveraged and how invested they are in hedge funds using interest rate derivatives. Better yet, join a credit union. The list of G-SIFI banks is included in appendix A.

The Global Currency Bubble

In chapters 3 and 4, we examined the bubble economy, how it works, and who it benefits. In particular was the fact that here in the United States our Federal Reserve and their member commercial banks use their money creation power and fractional reserve lending to create market-specific bubbles in order to achieve certain ends to which only they are privy.

I had also mentioned that since the beginning of the twentieth century every industrialized nation on earth had adopted this fiat currency model. Consequently the bubble-economy shenanigans are going on for every other major currency as well. In every industrialized country central banks are expanding the supply of every currency in order to manipulate each of their respective markets to create bubbles in certain targeted asset classes. They are also beginning to competitively devalue their currencies to try to stimulate their own exports. Therefore, while these market-specific bubbles are created and subsequently burst as a means to fleece the working classes around the world, a larger bubble is being relentlessly expanded on a global scale—the global fiat currency bubble.

Socialist governments all over the world have been using their central banks' money-creation power to hide the scope of their respective fiscal problems, their unfunded liabilities, the cost of their entitlement programs, and the wasteful spending perpetrated by each of their political classes. All of them have used fiat debt to artificially stimulate consumption-based *growth* to greater or lesser degrees. Nevertheless, every country that uses the fiat currency model is now beginning to buckle under their respective debt burden. The top eighteen economies in the world together have a government debt to GDP ratio of more than 85 percent, while the private sector debt in all of these countries is three times that. There is not enough labor productivity on earth to cover this debt service.

Eventually the entire fiat currency bubble will burst as well, and paper currencies around the globe will no longer be able to function as money. This implosion will involve all of the world's major currencies, and not just in a single country or in a specific asset class like housing, but everywhere. Unless the United States acts to restore a sound money system before this occurs, the global implosion will take the United States down with it in a worldwide economic catastrophe of a scale that no one alive today has ever seen or can possibly imagine.

The Cashless Society—The Final Blow to Property Rights

The technical foundation for a completely cashless society already exists. When the cash-based fiat currency system finally implodes, governments around the world will begin imposing the cashless utopia upon the hapless citizenry—as this is the ultimate goal of the fiat banking aristocracy. They will use government authority to implement it. It will of course be sold to the public as being "for your own convenience and security." This would mean that all currency and coin would be replaced with purely electronic *funds*.

What will be the consequences? Consider the fact that banks today are forced to have at least some modicum discipline in their lending policy due to the requirement they hold 10% of their depositors' cash in reserve as physical money. We have already learned that a "run on the banks" occurs when all depositors try to withdraw their money at the same time, and the bank lacks enough physical cash to satisfy its liabilities.

When physical money no longer exists, the reserve requirement becomes irrelevant since there will no longer be any risk of a bank run. Banks will merely create as much electronic money as required to satisfy the demands of their depositors as well as borrowers. With no reserve requirement, banks will be absolved of any fiscal discipline whatsoever. They will then also be absolved of paying any interest to depositors at all. Negative interest rates on deposits will become the norm. In other words, you will pay the bank for the privilege of managing your electronic deposits rather than the bank paying you interest for holding and re-lending your money. They can then write loans to all comers and expand the money supply to infinity. All it will take is a few keystrokes on a computer keyboard.

The outcome will be unrestrained hyperinflation and a rapid expansion of poverty. No person will be able to conduct any transaction without paying a commission to a financial institution which will be required to process the electronic transfer. Never again will you even be able to sell your used television to your neighbor without government interference. Just conducting a garage sale will require you to first obtain permission from the government as well as access to a bank's electronic transfer services—for a fee of course. If you exercise your first amendment right to free speech by saying something the government (or the bank) doesn't like—you might find yourself deprived of the ability to conduct any transaction at all.

The end result—Slavery.

CHAPTER 12

The False Left-Right Paradigm—The American Form of Government

Democracy is three wolves and a lamb voting on what to have for lunch. Liberty is a well-armed lamb contesting the vote."

—Benjamin Franklin

Totalitarianism is defined as a political system where the state, usually under the control of a single political party, recognizes no limits to its authority and strives to regulate every aspect of public and private life wherever feasible. Totalitarianism is generally characterized by the combination of authoritarianism (where ordinary citizens have no significant share in state decision-making) and ideology (a pervasive scheme of values promulgated by institutionalized media as a means to direct the most significant aspects of private life through propaganda and shaping opinion).[119]

According to Karl Loewenstein, "The governmental techniques of a totalitarian regime are necessarily authoritarian. But a totalitarian regime does much more. It attempts to mold the private life, soul, and morals of citizens to a dominant ideology. The officially proclaimed ideology penetrates into every nook and cranny of society; its ambition is total."[120] As such, the ambition of totalitarian regimes is to control every aspect of your life—your values, your children's values, their education, the kind of home you occupy and your standard of living, the value of your labor—everything—Central Economic Planning.

Thus to establish a totalitarian regime requires that individual property rights be eradicated.

---

[119]   Mises, Ludwig Von. "Omnipotent Government, The Rise of the Total State and Total War." 1985. ISBN 0-910884-15-3.

[120]   Loewenstein, Karl. "Political Power and the Governmental Process," June 1965.

On September 17, 1787, after four months of debate and deliberation, Pennsylvania delegate Benjamin Franklin exited the Constitutional Convention in Philadelphia to walk to his favorite pub, the City Tavern. Just after he left Independence Hall, he was stopped in the street by a woman who asked him, "What have the delegates given us?"

Franklin's answer was, "A republic, madam, if you can keep it."

Since at least the 1950s, most Americans have been taught in public school that America is a democracy. Much of this belief is reinforced with the repeated misuse of the term by our media and educational institutions. In fact, children in American schools have been taught absolute falsehoods about the form of the US government for decades, so most American's have been persuaded that the United States is a democracy. We even refer to our foreign policy of interventionism and empire building as "spreading democracy throughout the world."

The United States was founded as a constitutional republic. The framers intended that it remain so.

There are vast differences between a constitutional republic and a democracy. In fact, these two forms of government have very little in common. Democracy is rule by a majority. Constitutional republicanism is rule by law (natural law as espoused in The Constitution). The only aspect of democracy that was included in the founding of the United States is purely procedural. The framers structured the US government to utilize the democratic process (voting) in selecting its legislative and executive representatives. By extension, that same democratic process would be used by the legislative branch of government to either enact or reject legislation proposed by its members. However, the voting process for such legislation required compliance with certain rules for passage in order to comply with the *spirit and intent* of the constitution. For example, a simple majority was not sufficient to sign a measure into law. A supermajority would be required. This was so that 51 percent of the legislature could not authorize any laws that would encroach on the liberties of those represented by the other 49 percent. Furthermore, any law proposed that was outside of the scope of what was authorized for the federal government by The Constitution was deemed unconstitutional and therefore not enforceable as federal law. This would ensure that individual and states' rights would take precedence over federal authority. This is the central purpose of the Tenth Amendment.

The code of federal laws was intended to be small and manageable, but it has instead become a collection of unintelligible, confusing, and sometimes ridiculous nonsense. The number of egregiously stupid federal laws on the books is legion. Consider the following examples:

- With the Equine Equality Rule, as of March 15, 2011, hotels, restaurants, airlines, and other service providers became legally obligated to modify policies, practices, or procedures to accommodate miniature horses as service animals. According to the Department of Justice, which administers the rule, miniature horses are a "viable alternative" to dogs for individuals who are observant Muslims and others whose religious beliefs preclude canine accompaniment.

- There is a statute that states it is a felony to wear a bulletproof vest while you are committing a murder.

- No pilot in command of an aircraft shall permit a person to enter or leave the aircraft during flight without a parachute.

- According to the Internal Revenue Code, no person may appear as a contestant in more than one game show in a calendar year.

- In the United States it is illegal to operate a train that does not have an F painted on the front. Evidently without the F most Americans would be unable to discern where the front of the train is.

- In the United States it is illegal to milk your cow and sell the milk to your neighbor. Armed federal agents have actually raided many US private family farms for having done this.

- In the United States it is illegal to sell natural cures for cancer—even if they work.

- If you register with a false name on MySpace or Facebook, you could potentially spend five years in federal prison.

An Alaskan inventor who'd never had a traffic violation was arrested and prosecuted by the federal government because he failed to put a certain type of sticker on a UPS package. He had no idea the sticker was required. No one at UPS informed him of it, and everything else about his shipment was perfectly legal. Nevertheless, after he was arrested and handcuffed, he was forced face down on the pavement by a half-dozen SWAT-team officers pointing assault rifles at his head and upper body. He was sentenced to almost two years in federal prison.

There are at least 4,450 offenses in federal criminal law, and at least 454 federal crimes were added from 2000 to 2007. That's an average of more than one new federal crime per week.

When the will of a majority (democracy) overpowers the rule of law (republicanism), this is what you get. US taxpayers pay members of Congress each a salary of more than $174,000 annually to sit around and think up nonsense like the aforementioned. These are more examples of why the framers intended the federal government to have limited and separated powers.

In order to form a more comprehensive understanding of the differences between a constitutional republic and a democracy, one must understand governance across its many forms.

The False Left-Right Paradigm

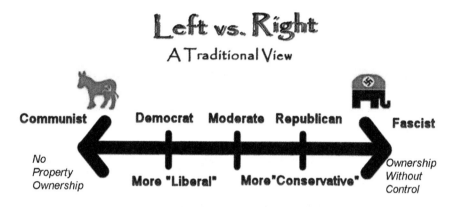

Most Americans have been led to believe that the overall political spectrum consists in a left-right paradigm with groups like Communists and socialists on the far left and fascists or dictators on the far right, moderates or centrists being somewhere in the middle. But this is a mischaracterization.

The True Left-Right Paradigm

A more accurate depiction of governance would show the political spectrum in terms of government power. A government having zero power (no government) on the far right to a government having 100 percent power (total government) on the far left as in the figure below.

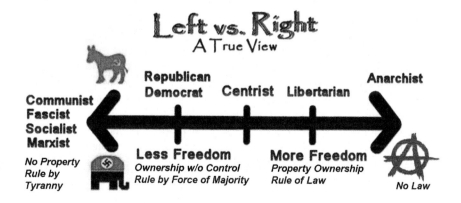

F. A. Grieger

At the extreme right is no government whatsoever—anarchy. At the extreme left there is total omnipotent government under such forms as Communism, socialism, Nazism, fascism, monarchy, and other forms of tyranny. By this depiction, on the left there can be no property rights. On the far right we can have whatever property rights we are able to protect for ourselves. Those who claim that fascists and Nazis are right wing never properly define the context. This creates confusion about the characteristics of these various forms of government. In other words it is false to refer to Communism as far left and National Socialism (Nazism) as far right. Both are variants of socialism and are founded in the notion of centralized control of the means of production with little or no individual control over property. Both subordinate the individual to the state. The most important distinction between the two lies in the means by which they limit or prohibit property rights.

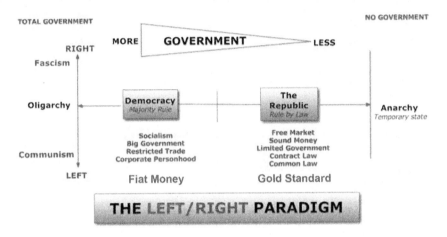

The type of government that has limited powers can be found near the middle of the political spectrum. Democracy, which is depicted in the figure above to the left of center of the political spectrum, has its powers defined by the will of the majority. Here the majority determines just how limited the government's powers shall be at any given time. Under a democracy a corrupt majority will always seek to expand government power rather than limit it, and rule by majority will permit this. On the other hand, under a constitutional republic (rule of law) the government's powers are defined and limited, and those powers are intended to remain limited over time in accordance with the law. Under such a system, minority rights are protected equally since no majority can subvert the rule of law. The most important distinction lays in which type of monetary system is compatible with which system of governance. This is what ultimately determines the nature of property rights under its respective system. As can be seen in the diagram above, fiat money is incompatible with the free enterprise system under the rule of law. Only the gold standard provides a system where individual property rights are respected.

Germany in the 1930s was a parliamentary democracy that evolved into a dictatorship when the national socialists under Adolf Hitler gained the majority of the seats in parliament. Democracy has always had the weakness of being malleable to the whim of the majority, which is able to expand and redefine the role of government over time if left unrestrained. This ultimately leads to a tyranny of the majority, or as Karl Marx called it, a "dictatorship of the proletariat." To protect the rights of minorities requires a body of law that restrains government power and ensures that those restraints are sustained over time. Limiting government to its proper role requires that the government itself abide by laws that restrict expansion of central government power. Such law cannot be perverted in terms of its meaning or application by the will of any majority. This is found only in the rule of law within a constitutional republic. This is the form of government depicted just to the right of center (to the right of pure Democracy) in the figure above.

So What Is the Proper Role of Government in a Free Society?

Government is an institution that holds the exclusive power to enforce certain rules of social conduct in a given geographical area. If a society's government should become fundamentally corrupt, having that exclusive power can lead to bad consequences for the people. This is when the lambs get eaten by the wolves in spite of their objections.

The only proper purpose of a government is to protect man's rights, which means: to protect him from physical violence. A proper government is only a policeman, acting as an agent of man's self-defense, and, as such, may resort to force only against those who start the use of force. The only proper functions of a government are: the police, to protect you from criminals; the army, to protect you from foreign invaders; and the courts, to protect your property and contracts from breach or fraud by others, to settle disputes by rational rules, according to objective law. But a government that initiates the employment of force against men who had forced no one, the employment of armed compulsion against disarmed victims, is a nightmare infernal machine designed to annihilate morality: such a government reverses its only moral purpose and switches from the role of protector to the role of man's deadliest enemy, from the role of policeman to the role of a criminal vested with the right to the wielding of violence against victims deprived of the right of self-defense. Such a government [democracy] substitutes for morality the following rule of social conduct: you may do whatever you please to your neighbor, provided your gang is bigger than his.[121]

—Ayn Rand

---

[121] Rand, Ayn. Atlas Shrugged. Signet. Page 1062. Sept. 1, 1996.

The source of the government's authority is the consent of the governed. This means that the government is not the ruler but the servant or agent of the citizens. It means that the government has no rights or powers except those delegated to it by the citizens for a specific purpose. This means *all* citizens and not solely those in a majority. It also means that the government cannot of its own accord expand those powers that have been delegated to it.

A republican form of government based on a rule of law, and not a rule by a majority of men is the only form of government that brings about liberty for individuals and minorities. In this case, all people, including the majority and the government itself, must all abide by the law of the land. That law first and foremost must respect the property rights of all individuals.

The purpose of the rule of law is to protect the rights of all of the people, not just those in the majority. This is where the Constitution of the United States resides. Those who advocate this form of government are called constitutionalists or constitutional moderates. Those who repeatedly refer to the United States as a democracy do so either out of ignorance or in order to intentionally fool the public into believing that our rule of law can be manipulated, changed, or otherwise perverted by the whim of an unenlightened majority. These are the people who espouse the concept of a *living constitution*. Our constitution is based on ethics, and moral truths which are absolute and do not change over time. As such the spirit and intent of the US Constitution was meant to endure and to transcend the generations in order that the moral values it espouses would be upheld for every succeeding generation. The fallacy of a living constitution is discussed more fully in chapter 15.

The fundamental difference between private action and governmental action—a difference thoroughly ignored and evaded today—lies in the fact that a government holds a monopoly on the legal use of physical force. It has to hold such a monopoly, since it is the agent of restraining and combating the use of force [by the people against one another or by foreign invaders against its people]. For that very same reason, its actions have to be rigidly defined, delimited and circumscribed; no touch of whim or caprice should be permitted in its performance; it should be an impersonal robot, with the laws as its only motive power. If a society is to be free, its government has to be controlled. Under a proper social system, a private individual is legally free to take any action he pleases so long as he does not violate the rights of others, while a government official is bound by law in his every official act. A private individual may do anything except that which is legally forbidden; a government official may do nothing except that which is legally permitted. This is the means of subordinating "might" to "right." This is the American concept of "a government of laws and not of men."[122]

—Ayn Rand

The various other forms of government are described as follows in accordance with the true left-right paradigm:

Monarchy as a dictatorship no longer exists in practice in the world today. The current form of dictatorship is generally a group that elevates one of its members to the role of figurehead. Monarchs have counsels and lower-ranking royals such as princes, dukes, earls, while dictators have their czars, commissars, or bloated bureaucracies under them. It isn't truly rule by one, even though there may be a single visible leader that rules.

At the far right is anarchy—no government. History reveals that the most hideous crimes against humanity were committed by powerful governments. Therefore, some citizens adopt the concept that having no government at all—anarchy—would be a good idea. However, this is a fallacy. As the ancient Greeks said, "Without law there can be no freedom." Anarchy always ends in oppression and tyranny. This is because in a state of anarchy every individual must guard against life, liberty, property, and harm to one's family. Property rights may exist under anarchy but only for those who are strong enough and able to defend their property from anyone who would take it. And many will try. Therefore, everyone must be heavily armed, and movement and travel must be severely restricted. This is because every individual must protect his or her own property at all times. If you leave property unattended, it is likely to be stolen or destroyed. Under anarchy most individuals would be afraid to leave their homes unattended, or it could be found empty (or worse, occupied by killers and rapists) when they return to them.

The early American frontier of the 1800s saw pockets of anarchy from which came the moniker of the Wild West. But once communities hired private law enforcement, a town sheriff, or a local police force to protect and to serve, the people had more freedom, not less. They could leave their properties unattended in order to work in the fields and attend to their business. It is the application of rules of conduct, the law, and the proper amount of limited government to enforce it that makes everyone freer.[123]

[122] Rand, Ayn. Capitalism, The Unknown Ideal. Signet. July 15, 1986.
[123] The American Form of Government. *The John Birch Society, Overview of America.* 2007.

There are those, however well-intentioned, who seek to use anarchy as the means to incite revolutionary change when they are not satisfied with their current government. This always backfires. The aforementioned problems with anarchy always leave a vacuum in society, and what rushes in to fill it is usually undesirable. This occurs when the violence and chaos that accompanies anarchy becomes so overwhelming for the citizenry that they appeal to those among them who are best able to put an end to the violence. This is usually the same people who started it. Once in power the anarchists create a government run by them and for their own benefit. Ultimately, they create an oligarchy where they have absolute power.

Remember that power attracts the corruptible. It is why revolutionary anarchists virtually always become violent dictators. It is exactly what led to the regimes of Vladimir Lenin, Joseph Stalin, and Mao Zedong. Anarchy is always an unstable transition between what exists and what is desired by the corrupt and power-hungry.

Oligarchy, or rule by a select group, is the most common form of governance in history. Most nations of the world are ruled by powerful elite, so oligarchy remains as the most pervasive form of governance worldwide. Earlier in this book I made the case that the purpose behind establishing a central bank with a monopoly on the issuance of fiat money is to enable those with the money-creation power to subjugate both the government and its people to its authority. Money is not "the root of all evil." It is the root of all production. Whoever controls the issue of a society's money controls the means of production—the economy and therefore controls the government. Therefore, every country today whose economy is based on a central bank's fiat-money system is in reality an oligarchy under the rule of whoever controls the central bank. When this model is combined with a vast entertainment media establishment whose main purpose is to shape the ideas, opinions, and morals of the populace, you have what is defined as a totalitarian state. This is what America has devolved into. America today differs from other totalitarian regimes only by matters of degree.

Some people believe that the only just alternative to having either no government or total government is democracy. This might sound like it has some fairness, but suppose the majority votes to take away your home or business or to break up your family and take your children? Democracy is fundamentally flawed because a majority with power is not restrained. Every example of pure unrestrained democracy in history has over time become fundamentally corrupt, evolving into anarchy and then into some form of tyranny or oligarchy. It is just a matter of time. The rise and fall of the Roman Empire is the quintessential example.

In a constitutional republic it is the constitutional law that provides the only restraints on power. The US Constitution was based in natural law and not only provides the basis for that law but also defines the form and extent to which government power can take. From this came the separation of powers doctrine along with the limits to federal government authority. Limited and separated powers are the keys to sustaining the integrity of America's founding form of governance. Our current regime willfully ignores both the constitution and the separation of powers doctrine. They do so in order to protect and perpetuate their unconstitutional monetary system. They use the false claim that as a democracy, the will of the majority can allow them to pervert and change the meaning and intent of the constitution in order to expand and consolidate their power.

The American Revolution officially ended in 1781, with the actual peace treaty with England being finalized in 1783. However, it would be another four years before the United States had adopted the US Constitution and thereafter in 1791 the first ten amendments to the constitution known as the Bill of [Unalienable] Rights.

In the years between the cessation of hostilities and the drafting of the constitution, the founders had the unique opportunity to start clean. They could have established any form of government they wished at that time. There were some members of the first Congress who actually called for George Washington to be proclaimed king. However, the founders were not only highly educated products of the enlightenment but were also pragmatic idealists devoted to natural law and individual liberty. They instead chose to give us the rule of law in a republic and not the rule of a majority under a pure democracy.

It is clear why they chose Republican governance instead of Democratic governance. Consider this passage from the film *The American form of Government*:

> Consider the period of the old West during the early years of the US. Imagine a "lynch mob" under a democracy. Forty riders in a posse chase and eventually catch a lone gunman, and then vote forty to one to hang him until dead. Democracy triumphs and a man is left hanging by the neck from the nearest oak tree without trial, without any defense, without any due-process of law. Under a Republic, the riders vote forty to one to hang the gunman, but the Sheriff arrives and stops the mob telling them, "You cannot kill this man, he has a right to a fair trial." The man is taken back to town and is then put on trial before a jury selected from among those in town considered his peers. He is able to state his case, and to defend himself, and it is the jury that decides whether or not he should hang. In a Republic under a rule of law, even the Jury cannot decide such a case by majority rule. In order to convict a citizen of murder; the jury must find against the citizen unanimously, or he cannot be hanged. The rights of the governed are not subject to majority rule under democracy, but are subject to the law under a Republic. This is the essence of the Republican form of governance. It is the only form that can prevent the innocent, from being unjustly lynched.

The word democracy does not appear in a single instance in the nation's founding documents—not in the Declaration of Independence, the US Constitution, or any single constitution of any of the fifty states respectively, as the framers did everything possible to preclude the United States from having a democracy.

In essay number ten of *The Federalist*, James Madison wrote, "Democracies have ever been spectacles of turbulence and contention; have ever been found incompatible with personal security or the rights of property, and have in general been as short in their lives as they have been violent in their deaths."

Alexander Hamilton also is quoted as saying, "We are a Republican government. Real liberty is never found in despotism or in the extremes of democracy." And Samuel Adams said, "Democracy never lasts long, it soon wastes, exhausts, and murders itself."

The entirety of the historical record demonstrates that the founders had great contempt for democracy. The framers of the constitution were highly educated in classical literature and history, and they knew that the democracies of the ancient Greek city-states had all collapsed after they produced some of the wildest examples of government largess imaginable. In every historical example the pattern was the same. Democracy led to mob rule and turned to anarchy, which eventually evolved into oligarchy. This happened every single time in history without exception.

It was the ancient Greek Solon who urged Greek society to establish a fixed body of law that would not be subject to the whims of an unenlightened majority. The Greeks rejected Solon's ideas, but the Romans eventually embraced those principles. From this they built "the twelve tables of Roman law," and with it they built the Roman republic, which limited government and left the people alone. Since the power of government was restricted, the citizenry were free to produce and transact as they wished and by their own volition. They were able to retain the fruits of their labor. In a short time Romans became wealthy, living in a thriving economy that was the envy of the world. Their monetary unit was the gold *Solidus*, a system of sound money that lasted for 700 years without inflation.

After centuries of riding the wave of success that liberty had enabled, the Romans eventually forgot that the essence of freedom is the proper limitation of government. Once the Roman people became too comfortable in their prosperity, they forgot that the freedom they were enjoying was not free and that it, too, had a price. That price was vigilance, discipline, and the responsibility of self-reliance. Eventually the Roman people put down their guard in favor of a blind trust in government endowments. Subsidies and entitlements of all kinds were introduced in addition to housing and welfare programs. Inevitably taxes were imposed on the public, which perpetually rose over time, and productivity declined rapidly. Eventually fewer and fewer people produced, which led to shortages, while more and more began to exploit entitlement systems. Eventually mobs and gangs roamed the streets, demanding government handouts while the rest of Roman society began to trade away their liberty in exchange for security. Eventually the Roman Empire collapsed. They had started as a republic, transformed into a democracy, and finally degenerated into an oligarchy ruled by a progression of Caesars.[124]

History has demonstrated repeatedly that democracy is not a stable form of government. It represents a gradual transition between a republic and an anarchy that ultimately leads to an oligarchy. As such, it is the transition from the rule of law of a republic to the omnipotent power of a tyranny. This is the process we are witnessing in the United States today.

The Democratic party is the bastion of progressivism (e.g. socialism). They are believers in the idea of pure majority rule. They reject the restrictions placed on government power by the rule of law. The Republican party has also lost its way. It was at one time in America's history the party that respected the meaning and intent of the constitution, property rights, limited government, and individual sovereignty. Today the Republican party has betrayed its own core values. They simply promote a different variant of socialism. The establishment GOP espouses corporate socialism as the only alternative to statist socialism, while they falsely claim that they represent free-market capitalism. Nothing could be further from the truth. The actions and decisions of our government over the past several decades and through several administrations from both political parties demonstrate a pattern of collusion between them. The country vacillates every eight to twelve years between a Republican and a Democrat administration or between a Republican- and a Democrat-controlled Congress, yet nothing substantial changes in terms of government largess, overreach, and expansion of power. When a Republican administration dominates, they institute laws like the Patriot Act that expand the police state and further empower government to erode our constitutional rights to free speech and privacy. When a Democrat administration dominates, they institute laws like the Community Reinvestment Act, the Patient Protection and Affordable Care Act (Obamacare), or the National Defense Authorization Act, all of which expand the nanny state as enforced by the police state. They subordinate America's interests to those of the United Nations and even act to subvert our Bill of Rights. They sign international treaties whose terms are incompatible with our constitution and actually violate US law. Both political parties act to incrementally eradicate our rights to private property ownership and to self-determination. They enact laws that benefit the obscenely rich international banking aristocracy and their puppets in the political class. This pattern has remained unchanged since before JFK was assassinated in 1963.

---

[124] Gibbon, Edward. The History of the Decline and Fall of the Roman Empire: Volumes 1–6. 1776–1781.

F. A. Grieger

Monopolism Is Socialism

We are presented with a distorted view of American history by our media and our public schools. We have been taught that historical figures like J. P. Morgan, John D. Rockefeller, and the Rothschilds—the actual creators of our Federal Reserve System—are the icons of capitalism. But this is intentionally misleading. These men were monopolists, not capitalists. Capitalism consists in fair competition on a level playing field where all must abide by the same rules. Monopolists abhor competition. Monopolism consists in obtaining enough power in order to be able to make the rules, skew them in your own favor, eliminate your competition, and then expand your power.

John D. Rockefeller himself was quoted as having said on many occasions, "Competition is a sin."

Central Planning

The claimed justification for socialism or Communism is based on the promise for equal distribution of wealth. The premise of Marxist communism was "from each according to his ability, to each according to his need." Everyone in society receives an equal share of the benefits derived from labor (e.g., food and money). Therefore, in order to ensure that everyone receives an equal amount, all means of production must be controlled by the state. There can be no private property under any form of socialism. It is by definition rule by force. The idealists who espouse socialism and Communism intentionally ignore the fact that corruption and fraud run rampant when power is consolidated. In practice, the notion that wealth can be equitably and fairly distributed among society as enforced by a powerful centralized government made up of corrupt sociopathic bureaucrats is ridiculous. The free-enterprise system has and shall always remain the only fair and moral means by which to distribute wealth and the fruits of individual labor on a basis of free, voluntary exchange.

Fascism claims to allow for private enterprise, but its economic system is focused entirely on strengthening and glorifying the state. Fascist Italy and Nazi Germany both strived for self-sufficiency so that each country could survive entirely without trade with other nations. In order to achieve this, the disposition of property in its use for production still had to be controlled by the state in order to subordinate the goals of private individuals and enterprises to the goals of the state. Therefore, although fascist leaders claim to allow property ownership, property rights remain under the control of the government.

Socialism can take on many forms, such as Communism, fascism, National Socialism (Nazism), corporate socialism, etc. The subtle distinctions between these have mainly to do with how property rights are restricted and controlled by the state collective. In a free-enterprise system property rights are not granted to anyone by anyone, as it is the unalienable right for every individual citizen who has earned his or her wealth in the form of that property to own and control it as he or she sees fit, provided that person's usage does not infringe upon the property rights of others. Under the free-enterprise system only you are the sovereign over your own property, and the rule of law is intended to protect your property from infringement by others including the government.

The Anti-Free-Market Agenda

Opponents of the free-enterprise system relentlessly spew absolute falsehoods about it.[125] Some examples include the following:

Lie: "The free market creates scarcity and increasing prices."

Truth: A free-market system fosters productivity in an environment that functions solely on the natural forces of supply and demand, where value and price are synonymous. As the demand for a good or service increases, its price will increase for as long as its supply is constrained. However, suppliers will always increase production to meet increasing demand once they determine that demand to be sustainable, which in turn will result in price stabilization. If new entrants create a glut of supply in response to short-term demand increases, prices go down. Where supply of certain items cannot be increased because of limited natural resources, entrepreneurs are encouraged to develop and offer alternatives (e.g., alternatives to fossil fuel energy sources). This fosters innovation driven by real demand. It is only through a centrally controlled economy where demand is artificially stimulated through debt-based money creation that prices are made to continually increase through inflation.

Consider this in terms of the cost of the money itself. This is known in financial circles as the cost of capital or the price of borrowing money. In a sound money system where all money is asset-based, the interest rate applied to borrowing is a reflection of the very real risk of loss in terms of the available supply versus demand for the money itself. In such a system there can never be a zero interest rate. Under America's current fiat monetary model, we have seen several years with zero interest rates on interbank lending. This would suggest there is zero risk of loss, which of course is preposterous.

In a system that allows certain entitled members of society (central bankers) to print money from thin air, what emerges is a system with no real risk of loss for them (since they can simply print more), but with total risk of loss for the working class—privatizing profits and socializing losses. We have seen how this model leads to rampant mal-investment, ultimately leading to various bubbles, busts, and bankruptcies in an engineered business cycle that has little or no relationship to the natural forces of

---

[125] Mises, Ludwig Von. The Anti-Capitalistic Mentality. Libertarian Press. 1970.

supply and demand. Therefore, it is the centrally controlled or mixed economies like ours that deliberately create scarcity and continually rising prices.

Lie: "In the free market, businesses get special privileges from the government."

Truth: The free market is free precisely because it denies special privileges to any single person, corporation, group, or entity. In a free market no one is granted any unfair advantage over anyone else since in a true free market, government has no power to grant such advantages. This does not mean that individuals or groups cannot attain advantages. They can when such advantages are earned on the basis of fair competition and are not gained through fraud, government pull, or physical force or coercion against the person or property of others. Indeed, the motivation for continuous improvement in manufacturing is the goal of gaining sustained competitive advantages over one's industrial peers. When your competitors catch up, you must innovate again in order to survive in business. This leads to real progress. Having certain businesses or sectors gain special privileges through political pull isn't about continuous improvement. It is about bribery and buying favors. Referring to this corruption as crony capitalism is a misnomer. Capitalism is fundamentally incompatible with this concept, so it is socialism's centrally controlled economy that begets political cronyism.

Lie: "The pre-Obamacare health-care industry was based on free-market principles."

Truth: The health-care industry has been highly interventionist for decades. Through prior anticompetition regulations individuals were not permitted to purchase health insurance from providers across state lines. This created miniature monopolies within each respective state, which hardly constitutes a free market for health care or health insurance (which are two different things). It was the failure of the prior interventionist system that the statists used to justify the even more interventionist model of Obamacare, which will prove to be even less efficient and more costly than the previous system. Obamacare was not the answer to the rising cost of health care. The answer was to restore a true free-market model to the health-care system that was abandoned generations ago. America has gone in exactly the wrong direction.

There are those who try to claim that universal health care is a human right. But health care can only be obtained from a health-care provider. To claim that every person has a right to a professional service provided by another for free is preposterous. This is no less ridiculous than claiming that every American then also has a human right to free plumbing and electrical services, free refrigeration, free air conditioning, free entertainment, free pharmaceuticals, free food, and free haircuts. Where do we draw the line?

Jobs, food, clothing, recreation, homes, medical care, education, etc., do not grow in nature. These are man-made values – goods and services produced by men. Who then is to provide them? If some men are entitled by right to the products of the work of others, it means that those others are deprived of rights, and are condemned to slave labor. Any alleged "right" of one man, which necessitates the violation of the rights of another, is not and cannot be a [human] right. No man can have a right to impose an un-chosen obligation, an unrewarded duty, or an involuntary servitude on another man. There can be no such thing as the right to enslave. Observe, in this context, the intellectual precision of the Founding Fathers: they spoke of the right to pursuit of happiness – not the right to happiness. It means that a man has the right to take the actions he deems necessary to achieve his happiness; it does not mean that others must make him happy.[126]

—Ayn Rand

Lie: "The free market is pro-war."

Truth: The free market is anti-war, because it is unprofitable under a sound monetary system. Wars provide economic benefits primarily to those who can finance them by printing money, while they provide horrific pain, suffering, and enormous cost to those who fight them. Under a sound monetary model, the real cost of waging war makes most wars unaffordable and economically counterproductive. It is not a coincidence that the largest wars in terms of scale and cost that have been fought in the history of the world were all financed by fiat monetary systems. This is true even for the American Civil War, which was financed by the union with the introduction of the greenback. The principal beneficiaries of the two world wars, the Korean conflict, the Vietnam War, and the more recent wars in the Middle East have been the central banks that financed them. Under a fiat currency system where the ruling class can print as much money as it wishes out of thin air and which will eventually be repaid by the future labor of the citizenry, waging war is highly profitable and yields no financial risk to the money printers. In contrast, under a sound money system where all money is real money, both the direct costs as well as the opportunity costs of waging war are real—the potential for financial loss being a true measure of the associated risks. Therefore, a true free-market system is pro-peace, not pro-war. The fact that the United States abandoned true free-market principles in 1913 and has been in a continual state of war ever since is a testament to that fact.

---

[126]   Rand, Ayn. Capitalism, The Unknown Ideal. Signet. July 15, 1986.

Institutionalizing the False Left-Right Paradigm

Stealth and deception has enabled the corporatocracy to manipulate the American people, keeping us ignorant, uninformed, and confused since the beginning of the twentieth century. In *Tragedy and Hope*, Dr. Carroll Quigley described the manipulative tactics over our American political process via the false left-right paradigm.

> The chief problem of American political life for a long time has been how to make the two Congressional parties more national and international ... (therefore) the argument that the two parties should represent opposed ideals and policies, one, perhaps, of the Right and the other of the Left, is a foolish idea acceptable only to doctrinaire and academic thinkers. Instead the two parties should be almost identical, so that the American people can 'throw the rascals out' at any election without leading to any profound or extensive shifts in policy.

What Dr. Quigley describes here is exactly what we have witnessed in the governance of our country since almost the beginning of the twentieth century. It is the reason that the issues argued by presidential candidates today are the exact same issues that were argued by H. Ross Perot, George H. W. Bush, and William J. Clinton in 1992; the same issues argued by Ronald Reagan and Jimmy Carter in 1980; and others for decades before them. It has been clear for some time that nothing substantial will change in American governance at the federal level no matter whom we vote for, no matter what we do. Therefore, it is entirely up to us. We the people must take our country back community by community, town by town, city by city, and state by state. We must peacefully engage in the form of activism that was intended by America's founders—from the bottom up.

CHAPTER 13

The Fool

You can't fool all of the people, all of the time; but you can fool
enough of the people enough of the time to rule a large country.

—Will Durant

The US Constitution went into effect on March 4, 1789, thus establishing the rule
of law with the basic framework for a free-market capitalist economic system. Just
fifty-eight years later in 1848, Karl Marx and his partner, Friederich Engels, wrote and
published the *Communist Manifesto*. Neither Marx nor Engels had ever set foot in the
United States, so neither had ever personally experienced life in a truly free-market
capitalist country. Nevertheless, both men considered themselves to be expert in the
dynamics of capitalism. One of the central themes of the Communist Manifesto is to
criticize capitalism as a system that does not provide for social justice.

Since then, proponents of social justice have continued to pervert the notion of rights, defining them as entitlements granted by government. America's founding principles, on the other hand, espoused our rights as being unalienable or God-given. Such rights derive from natural law, not man-made laws. A right to something of value created by someone else who provides that value is an entitlement granted by force rather than by voluntary exchange, and therefore, it is not a right.

The writings of Karl Marx address the idea of social justice extensively. What he does not address is ethics or moral justice. Nor does he reconcile the fact that socialism can only be enacted by means of force. There is not a single phrase or statement within any of the writings of Karl Marx that explores the moral implications of using force to redistribute wealth.

Few socialists will admit to the fact that one of the fundamentally immoral features of socialism is that it cannot be enacted without the use of force. The free-market system is based on the idea that all economic transactions between parties should be voluntary and under mutually agreed terms. In other words, it is immoral to use force or coercion during the conduct of any economic activity between people, and it is free will that should determine how people interact and whether or not they decide to interact at all. There is a Christian values basis for this in the sense that man is endowed with free will. It is up to each man to decide how to act and then to bear the consequences and cost of his actions. Acting morally will lead to a righteous, clean, successful, and happy life.

The opposite of free will is enforcement. The use of force by one individual or group against another is fundamentally immoral. The notion that free will should not enter into the dealings among and between men is one of the reasons that socialism espouses atheism. Pure democracy is rooted in the principle of majority rule. It provides that force and coercion is justified as long as it is perpetrated by a majority against a minority. It is the reason that establishing the United States as a constitutional republic rather than a democracy was as much a moral decision as it was a political one—in fact more so. The founders rightly considered that the use of force (unless in the act of self-defense or exacting justice for a crime) is considered to be unethical and fundamentally immoral.

Inherent in The Constitution are the Judeo-Christian notion of free will and the principle of personal responsibility. Socialism espouses the antithesis of this, seeking to govern people by force without any basis of ethics or fundamental morality—a purely secular model. Under socialism everyone must follow arbitrary rules laid down by men who happen to be in a powerful majority instead of following a set of principles that stem from self-evident truths based on ethics and fundamental morals. Under socialism, therefore, lays the paradox that in order to achieve social justice (equal outcomes), it requires the commission of a moral injustice (the use of force).

Logic should then dictate that committing a moral injustice negates the value of the so-called social justice achieved. Therefore, socialist schemes intended to ensure equal outcomes through the use of force are not only inherently immoral but also illogical. This is why they always yield unintended consequences. Leftists have made a science out of misusing language in order to invert moral principles. They are experts in taking something that is inherently immoral and portraying it as being super moral by virtue of being well intentioned, but this is a fraud. The use of force by anyone against anyone else (except in self-defense or in exacting justice for a criminal act) is always immoral.

The urge to save humanity, is almost always a false front for the urge to rule.

—H. L. Mencken

Throughout Karl Marx's life, he never visited the United States, which at that time in history was the first and only true free-market capitalist (laissez-faire) nation on earth. In fact, neither Marx nor Engels ever set foot outside of Europe. Every idea and principle that they argued in opposition to the free-enterprise system was based solely on what they had learned from their own readings and discussions with other devout socialists in Europe and from their observations while they lived in London. Neither Marx nor Engels had a single firsthand experience of what life was truly like under a real free-enterprise system as the one that existed in the United States at that time.

Like many others, Marx was beset with confirmation bias. When one critically analyzes his own writings, such as in the *Communist Manifesto*, this is revealed repeatedly. He had a deeply rooted bias against the free-enterprise system because he believed in the use of force and the subjugation of all individuals to the collective. Marx clearly had a persistent bias toward sources of information that confirmed his already preconceived beliefs, so he sought out information and studies that only reinforced his personal value system while he rejected any information that disagreed with his convictions. He certainly never traveled to the United States to see for himself how a free-enterprise system worked in practice. His goal was not to seek out the objective truth of the matter. His goal was to prove his own point and satisfy his own ego like any power-hungry politician. His ideas and philosophies about life sprang from a markedly dysfunctional childhood that scarred him deeply and set the trajectory for his entire adult life as well as the development of his values and ideology.

His conclusions about the evils of free-market economics were as deeply flawed as his zealous endorsement of what he believed to be the superior and benevolent principles of collectivism and socialism. It is Marx's *benevolent* socialism that led to the mass killing of between 85 Million and 100 Million innocents in China, the former Soviet Union, Europe, and Southeast Asia throughout the 20th century. Marx was a fool and numerous assertions he makes in the *Communist Manifesto* demonstrate his deeply flawed logic.

For example, in the ten planks of Communism, Marx defines the preconditions that a society must implement in order to destroy a free-enterprise system and replace it with an all-powerful omnipotent government. One of those planks refers to public education. He states, "The Government must provide free education for all children in public schools."

While on the surface this sounds like a good thing, it is impossible in practice. In the real world, nothing is free. Everything has a price and someone has to pay it. Marx doesn't define his terms honestly as there is no such thing as a *free education*. With this one sentence, he garners from the reader the impression that he is a caring and benevolent man who wants only the best things for society's children. What he is really saying is that education should be free for the children receiving it, but the cost of their education should be distributed among the rest of the population through taxation and wealth redistribution as enforced by the central government. The operative word here is *enforced*.

It is instructive to look at all of Marx's ten planks of Communism and then compare them to the socioeconomic model that we have in place today right here in the United States.

The ten planks of Communism given in the *Communist Manifesto* are as follows:

1) Abolition of private property and the application of all rents of land to public purposes.

Rents of all land to public purposes are property taxes. This has been implemented in America also in other ways with actions such as the fourteenth amendment of the US Constitution (1868), giving the federal government far more eminent domain power than was originally intended. Local governments also gain control of private homes through zoning regulations, and through property taxes levied primarily to fund public schools and in most cases police and fire departments as well.

2) A heavy progressive or graduated income tax.

Americans know this as the misapplication of the sixteenth amendment of the US Constitution, which was passed in 1913. It has been further instituted through the Social Security Act of 1936, the Joint House Resolution 192 of 1933, Medicare and Medicaid taxes, and various state and local income taxes. Progressives call it *paying your fair share*. But in truth, you don't pay this voluntarily, it is confiscated from you against your will as a condition of employment. Here it needs to be understood what the definition of income is. There are two basic forms of income for individuals— income from your labor (wages and salaries) and income from corporate activity (dividends and capital gains from investments in business enterprises like stocks, bonds, etc.). This is explained in great detail in chapter 3.

The graduated taxes on income are not uniform throughout the United States as expressly required by the constitution. But our graduated income taxes are indeed modeled exactly after the Marxist prototype of taxation described in the *Communist Manifesto*. The framers never intended that individual citizens should be taxed on their income in terms of how they defined income (compensation as wages, salaries, and tips). Taxing this form of income is a tax on your property. In fact, since you have exchanged hours, days, and years of your life in return for that compensatory wage, it is a tax on your very life.

3) Abolition of all rights of inheritance.

These are currently our state and federal estate taxes (enacted in 1916) and the reformed probate laws providing for limited inheritance through arbitrary inheritance tax statutes. Once again this constitutes a violation of property rights, and its purpose is to allow the government to confiscate your children's inheritance. This ensures that economically your children will have to start adulthood from scratch, impoverished and with no significant assets or wealth with which to begin their lives. This condition will ensure that your children will have no choice but to use debt in order to finance the cost of starting their independent adult lives, especially if they aspire to obtain a university-level education. Once they have been sucked into the debt cycle, they will probably never get out, a fate that will most likely also befall their own children and so on and so forth for generation after generation. The purpose is to ensure perpetual, intergenerational debt-slavery.

4) Confiscation of the property of all emigrants and rebels.

These are what we currently refer to as government seizures and tax liens. These are found under Public Law 99-570 (enacted in 1986) or Executive Order 11490, section 1205 (enacted in 2002), which gives private land to the Department of Housing and Urban Development and authorizes the US government to imprison suspected terrorists or those who speak out or write against the government (in accordance with the 1997 Crime/Terrorist Bill). This was later expanded in the misnamed Patriot Act. Property confiscation without due process (a violation of the Fifth Amendment to the US Constitution) is routinely perpetrated by local authorities for nonpayment of property taxes as well as by the Internal Revenue Service, the DEA, the ATF, other federal law enforcement agencies.

5) Centralization of credit in the hands of the state by means of a national bank with state capital and an exclusive monopoly on the creation of fiat money.

This is the cornerstone of it all. It is embodied in the Federal Reserve system, which is a privately owned credit/debt system allowed by the Federal Reserve Act of 1913. All local banks are members of the Federal Reserve system and are regulated by the Federal Deposit Insurance Corporation (FDIC), another privately owned corporation. The Federal Reserve banks issue fiat paper money in the form of debt, and their commercial bank members practice economically destructive fractional reserve lending.

6) Centralized control of the means of communications and transportation in the hands of the state.

This has been long-established in the United States via the Federal Communications Commission (FCC); the Department of Transportation (DOT); the Interstate Commerce Commission (ICC) established in 1938; The Federal Aviation Administration (FAA); state-mandated driver's licenses and vehicle registrations; and Department of Transportation regulations.

7) Extension of factories and instruments of production owned by the state, the bringing into cultivation of wastelands, and the improvement of the soil generally in accordance with a common plan.

This was embodied in the collective farms in the former Soviet Union that proved to be miserable failures. Here in the United States we have been expanding government control over agriculture through farm and dairy subsidies, acreage allotments, and land-use control. The Desert Entry Act and the establishment of the Department of Agriculture, Department of Commerce, Department of Labor, Environmental Protection Agency, Bureau of Land Management, Bureau of Reclamation, National Park Service, Bureau of Mines, and IRS control of business through corporate regulations. Furthermore, with the ever-increasing property taxation that is driving the corporatization of family farms, agricultural production is falling further under the centralized control of both corporate (bank-owned) and government institutions.

8) Equal liability of all to labor and the establishment of industrial armies, especially for agriculture.

Perpetual inflation has obligated families to rely on two incomes, driving both parents in a family to work. One of the purposes is to wrest children away from their parents' influence and make them subjects of the state (through the public school system). The push to bring women into the workforce was disguised as "the women's liberation movement," which was funded largely by the Rockefeller foundation.[127] Its true purpose was to increase the number of working taxpayers and to increase gross household income in the short term in order to establish a new economic equilibrium for the long term. This would then require two incomes per family in order to maintain the same standard of living over the long term, further leading to the breakup of the family unit. Other examples include the nineteenth amendment

---

[127] Russo, Aaron. Film: America, From Freedom to Fascism. www.freedomtofascism.com. 2007.

of the US Constitution, the Civil Rights Act of 1964, assorted socialist unions, affirmative action, and federal public works programs.

9) Combination of agriculture with manufacturing industries and a gradual abolition of the distinction between town and country through a more equitable distribution of population over the country.

This was established in America through the Planning and Reorganization Act of 1949, zoning (Title 17 1910–1990), and super-corporate farms, as well as executive orders 11647 and 11731 (ten regions) and Public Law 89-136. These provided for forced relocations and forced sterilization programs like in China.

It is a little-known fact that the United States was the first country to undertake compulsory sterilization programs for the purpose of eugenics.[128] The principal subjects of the program were the mentally ill, but also targeted under many state laws were the deaf, blind, epileptics, and physically deformed. According to activist Angela Davis, Native Americans and African-American women were sterilized against their will, usually without their knowledge while they were in a hospital for other reasons.[129]

10) Free education for all children in public schools. Abolition of children's factory labor in its present form. Combination of education with industrial production.

In chapter 6, we discussed at length the fact that Americans are being taxed on their private property to support public schools. Even private schools are regulated by the government. The purpose is to train and indoctrinate the young to become obedient adult workers in support of our Marxist debt-based fiat monetary system. At the federal level we have the Department of Education and the National Education Association (NEA teacher's union) that have pushed outcome-based education. These are used so that all children can be indoctrinated with government propaganda like "The United States is a democracy," "In a democracy the majority rules," and "Pay your fair share." The concept of fair share is not inherent in the constitution, Bill of Rights, or even the Internal Revenue Code. The philosophical concept of fair share comes from the Communist maxim, "From each according to their ability, to each according to their need." This concept is pure socialism and demonstrates another example of the socialist's inversion of moral principles. To share constitutes a voluntary act, while the socialist concept of "share" has to do with forcible redistribution of wealth. There is nothing fair about the use of force against someone's will. Just as there is no such thing as a *free education*, there is no such thing as a *fair share* when achieved through government enforcement.

---

[128] Iredale, Rachel. "Eugenics and its relevance to Contemporary Healthcare"—*Nursing Ethics*, (Arnold, 2000).

[129] Davis, Angela. *Women, Race, and Class*, 1981. ISBN 0-394-71351-6.

I have personally known hundreds of well-intentioned Americans who espouse Marxist socialism as being superior to free-market capitalism, believing it to be better at providing for the poor. However, very few of them have actually read the *Communist Manifesto*. Most have never spent any appreciable time in or even visited a communist country. In fact, of those who have acted over the years in Marx's name—inciting bloody revolutions and wars; and in supporting repressive governments and justifying massacres—very few knew anything about the man himself. Although much of his personal life has never been revealed, it is enlightening to learn about the life of the man who is the grandfather of the progressive socialist movement that persists around the world.

A Brief Background on the Character of Karl Marx

Karl Heinrich Marx was born in Trier, Kingdom of Prussia on 5 May 1818, as an Ashkenazi Jew, to Hirschel Mordechai (a lawyer) and Henriette Pressburg. Marx's Jewish name is Chaim Hirschel Mordechai. Marx descended from Talmudic rabbis on both sides of his family. His paternal ancestors had provided the rabbis of Trier since 1723, a post that was last held by his grandfather.

He studied at the University of Bonn and the University of Berlin, where he became interested in the philosophical ideas of the Young Hegelians. In 1836, he became engaged to Jenny von Westphalen, whom he later married in 1843. He received a Doctorate in Philosophy in 1841, but was turned down for a teaching position because of his revolutionary activities. After his studies he wrote for a radical newspaper in Cologne and began to work out his socioeconomic theories. He was then expelled from Germany after which he moved to Paris in 1843 to study Economics. It was in France where he met Friedrich Engels, learned about French communism, and began writing for other radical newspapers. He and Engels then worked together on a series of books. He was later thrown out of Paris and was exiled to Brussels, where he became a leading figure of the Communist League.[130] In 1849, he was exiled again and moved to London together with his wife and children. In London, where the family was reduced to poverty, Marx continued writing and formulated his theories about the nature of society and how he believed it could be improved through socialism.[131]

In 1844, Friedrich Engels published a booklet called *The Condition of the Working Class in England*. It was Engels' philosophy that established the basis for the ideas which were later developed by Marx.

One of Marx's grandparents was Nanette Salomon Barent-Cohen, from a wealthy Amsterdam family. Her cousin Hannah had married Nathan Mayer Rothschild and gave birth to Lionel Nathan Rothschild, later a Member of Parliament for the

---

130 Mehring, Franz. Routledge, *Karl Marx—The Story of His Life*, 2003.
131 Kegan, Paul. Routledge. *Marx's Critique of Political Economy, 1844–1860*, 1984.

City of London. Aside from Marx being a cousin of the Rothschild family, during his lifetime others associated with the Barent-Cohen side of his family had married into other international financial dynasties. He was actually related to Hannah Rothschild on both her paternal and maternal side.

It should be noted that before Marx penned a single word, the socialist movement already existed in Germany, France, Britain and elsewhere, each with their own ideas about how to improve the situation of the working-class. The question has often been raised as to who supported Marx. In the book *Der preußische Regierungsagent Karl Marx* by the German author Wolfgang Waldner, it suggests that Marx worked as an agent of the Prussian government. Waldner mentions the fact that Marx married Jenny von Westphalen in 1843. She came from a wealthy family, the daughter of a Prussian baron. Her brother was Ferdinand von Westphalen, who was Prussian Minister of the Interior from 1850-1858. Perhaps the most revealing political alliance Marx made was with David Urquhart, a Scottish member of parliament. Urquhart's campaign was instrumental in ensuring British participation in the Crimean War—a war that was funded by Marx's cousin Lionel de Rothschild.

Prior to authoring *Das Kapital* in the British Museum reading room, Nathan Rothschild had given Marx two checks for several thousand pounds to finance the cause of Socialism. The checks were put on display in the British Museum. During this same time period, his famous cousin Lionel de Rothschild (Nathan Rothschild's father), was the Member of Parliament (MP) for the City of London (1847–1868 & 1869–1874). Interestingly, the name "Rothschild" is completely absent from *Das Kapital.*

History books have depicted Marx as a poor, frustrated, unemployed, academic who had been fired from numerous jobs. He had been expelled from Paris and deported from France, and had eventually immigrated to England. Most accounts of his life during this time, claim that he lived on the grants of his main benefactors (mainly Friedrich Engels, who had been born into a very wealthy family).

It is a little known fact that Marx was commissioned and paid a fee to write *The Communist Manifesto* by the Central Committee of the Communist League, a small London-based organization of German refugees. In fact, the original title of the book was *Manifesto of the Communist Party.* Marx was not credited as the author until 20 years after its publication, after several small revolutions had failed. The Manifesto was described by Marxists as "The Charter of Freedom of the Workers of the World."

Marx never felt any obligation to earn a living. Perhaps this was because he had been born into a wealthy family in the Prussian Rhineland and was a blood relative to the Rothschild banking dynasty. Neglecting his responsibility to provide for his six children, three of them literally died of malnutrition in infancy. Later two of his surviving daughters and a son-in-law committed suicide. One of them, his daughter Eleanor, had later in life woken up to the reality of her father's irresponsible and selfish lifestyle. Her most startling revelation came in 1895 when she discovered that one of her closest friends (possibly her lover, but this was never acknowledged), the forty-five-year-old Freddy Demuth, turned out to be her half-brother. Before Eleanor was born, Marx had abandoned his illegitimate son to a foster family in 1851 and had never provided him with any material support. Nevertheless, Eleanor, her siblings, and her mother had all built their lives around Marx and his ideas. Her life was centered on the notion of self-sacrifice for the sake of her father's goals.

Once in England, Marx and Engels shared a London apartment until Marx's death. When he died on March 14, 1883, only six people attended his funeral. Afterward Engels spent the next twelve years editing and publishing the rest of Marx's writings, but none found any substantial success. In the years after his death some saw an opportunity to exploit Marx's idea to establish what he called "a dictatorship of the proletariat" as a means to gain political power over society. As such, they sought to sanitize the facts of Marx's life in order that his vision of a utopian, classless society would not be discredited. His daughter Eleanor took part in this sanitization until just a few years before her suicide when she realized the truth of her father's character and then attempted (though unsuccessfully) to have his more revealing personal letters and journals published.[132]

Marx's theories about society, economics, and politics, collectively known as Marxism, hold that all societies progress through the dialectic of class struggle. He defines this as a conflict between an ownership class that controls production and a lower class that provides the labor. Heavily critical of the then current socioeconomic form of society, he called it the "dictatorship of the bourgeoisie," believing it to be run by the wealthy classes purely for their own benefit. He considered this to be capitalism and predicted that it would inevitably produce "internal tensions" that would lead to its self-destruction and replacement by a new system—socialism. He argued that under socialism society would be governed by the working class in what he called the dictatorship of the proletariat, "the workers' democracy." He believed that socialism would itself subsequently be replaced by a stateless, classless society called Communism. Along with believing in the inevitability of socialism and Communism, Marx actively fought for the former's implementation through revolution in order to topple capitalism and bring about socioeconomic change.

This raises the question, "If Marx truly believed that capitalism would self-destruct and inevitably lead to socialism on its own, why would organized revolutionary action even be necessary?" Clearly Marx himself didn't fully believe in the efficacy of his own theory.

Interestingly Marx considered that the economic system in England under which he and Engels lived from 1849 until their respective deaths was capitalism. They were

[132]   Gabriel, Mary; *Marx the Man vs. Marx the Myth*; Love and Capital Little Brown & Co. Publishers, Oct 11, 2011.

rightfully outraged at the horrible working conditions for the poor in England at that time, particularly in terms of the child labor being used. However, the UK form of government at that time was a parliamentary monarchy. Parliamentary monarchy has very little in common with a free-market capitalist economic system as was being practiced in the United States. Nevertheless, Marx's ideas about class struggle were based upon his observations under England's parliamentary monarchy, not under true free-market capitalism. He was outraged at the idea of a rich ruling class that owned all of the wealth and the means of production, and used an impoverished working class to produce the labor. In terms of his experience in the late 1800s in England, this was likely true. However, he considered this structure to be capitalism. He was mistaken.

The greatest irony is that it is Socialism and Communism that produce a citizenry of impoverished workers and an obscenely rich ruling class which exploits them. The cornerstone of Marxist Socialism is central banking with a monopoly on the creation fiat money. The idea that vesting the power to print money out of thin air, in a small elite powerful cabal would somehow lead to a fair, just, and equitable distribution of wealth, is absolutely absurd. Furthermore, history has proven it to be a system that has brought obscene and unimaginable wealth to Marx's extended family—the Rothschild banking dynasty.

Could Karl Marx Have Been a Psychopath?

In the book he co-wrote with Paul Babiak, PhD, titled *Snakes in Suits*, Professor Robert Hare offers the hare checklist as a tool for trained professional psychoanalysts to identify the character traits of a psychopath. Most people usually associate a psychopath with a criminal serial murderer who eats his victims, like Hannibal Lecter or Jeffrey Dahmer. However, as we already saw in chapter 10, what distinguishes a psychopath (a criminal sociopath) is the absence of any emotional connection—no sympathy, no empathy, no remorse, no guilt, no shame, no conscience. Whether people act on their compulsions by putting their victims through a wood chipper or defrauding them out of billions of dollars is just a matter of distinction. Both exhibit the behavior of a psychopath.

The Hare Psychopathy Check List—Revised (PCL-R)

Factor 1: Aggressive Narcissism (malignant narcissism)

1. Glibness/superficial charm

2. Grandiose sense of self-worth

3. Need for stimulation/prone to boredom

4. Pathological lying

5. Cunning/manipulative

6. Lack of remorse or guilt

7. Shallow (superficial experience and expression of emotions)

8. Callous/lack of empathy

Factor 2: Deviant Lifestyle

9. Parasitic lifestyle

10. Poor behavior control, particularly in childhood

11. Promiscuous sexual behavior

12. Lack of realistic long-term goals

13. Impulsive

14. Irresponsible

15. Failure to accept responsibility for consequences of own actions

16. Many short-term marital relationships

17. Juvenile delinquency

Karl Marx was known to have been dirty, unkempt, and reeking of offensive body odor. He had poor personal hygiene and suffered extensively from skin rashes and boils. The only known record of actual employment was a short stint as a postal clerk, a job from which he was fired after just a few weeks because of his unkempt appearance and lack of personal hygiene. He was known to have been a heavy drinker and was also a paid informant for the Austrian police, spying on revolutionaries whom he'd befriended.[133] His family on both sides was descended from a line of Jewish rabbis, but his parents had converted to Lutheranism in order to advance themselves in business and politics. Marx had rejected his family's values and all Judeo-Christian values, declaring himself an atheist. He was a juvenile delinquent and spent his year at University in Bonn drinking heavily and amassing a large debt that his father eventually paid on his behalf.

---

[133] McClellan, David. *Karl Marx—His Life and Thought*, (Harper & Row, New York, 1973).

Marx did have a grandiose sense of self-worth. He was cunning and manipulative. He was callous, and he lacked empathy. He indeed had many traits associated with psychopathy and narcissistic personality disorder. Marx's most devout followers turned out to be psychopaths themselves—Vladimir Lenin, Joseph Stalin, Mao Zedong, Pol Pot, and a long line of mass-murdering dictators.

Most of the biographies of Marx consider him to be one of the greatest economic and social thinkers in history, but these writings ignore the facts of his life as well as the fatal economic, logical, and moral flaws inherent in socialism. It is a system that is embraced by those seeking power over other men, power that they will be in a position to abuse. Every so-called classless society based on Marxism has devolved into a savage dictatorship with three classes—the small elite ruling class and intellectuals, a small middle class of worker drones, and a disproportionately large class of kulaks or useful idiots who are driven into poverty and starved to be made an example of in order to keep the citizenry fearful.

Every Marxist system of governance that has been implemented has failed, generally with great suffering and loss by the citizenry. Social democracy in Europe is failing today. The only reason it has lasted this long is because since the end of World War II, the United States has provided defense and military resources to those countries, enabling them to divert their own tax revenues toward generous but unsustainable socialist entitlement programs.

America embraced this statist-collectivist vision in 1913, when Woodrow Wilson's administration implemented the most important parts of Marx's ten planks of Communism. Marxism is clearly discredited by its flawed economic philosophy and immoral tenets. However it is also a political failure, as revealed through the incompetence and corruption inherent in large centrally controlled governments and monetary systems. Our Federal Reserve and current Congress are perfect examples. The attraction of Marxism is not that it can deliver a perfect utopian system that will provide for the poor—the propaganda usually submitted by its useful idiots. The attraction of Marxism is for psychopaths who are intoxicated with the prospect of wielding absolute power over the lives of others. Marxists seek to divide and conquer the citizenry and will destroy anyone who gets in the way.

> Socialism may be established by force, as in the Union of Soviet Socialist Republics—or by vote, as in Nazi (National Socialist) Germany. The degree of socialization may be total, as in Russia— or partial, as in England [and The United States]. Theoretically, the differences are superficial; practically, they are only a matter of time. The basic principle, in all cases, is the same.

The essential characteristic of socialism is the denial of individual property rights; under socialism, the right to property (which is the right of use and disposal) is vested in "society as a whole," i.e., in the collective, with production and distribution controlled by the state, i.e., by the government.[134]

There is no difference between communism and socialism, except in the means of achieving the same ultimate end: communism proposes to enslave men by force, socialism—by vote. It is merely the difference between murder and suicide.

—Ayn Rand

Most of the people who embrace Marxism are those who can be bought with unearned entitlements or charity for which they don't have to thank the one who provided it. Marxist politicians and their allies are fundamentally dishonest. Their true intentions are to enrich themselves at the expense of the middle class and the poor. There is no better indictment of the failure of socialism, communism, or any variant of Marxist philosophy than the lessons of history.

The Welfare State is the oldest con game in the history of the world. First you take people's money away quietly, and then you give some of it back to them flamboyantly.

—Dr. Thomas Sowell

---

[134]   Rand, Ayn. The Ayn Rand Lexicon – Harry Binswanger, Editor. Plume. Jan. 1, 1988.

CHAPTER 14

False Flag Capitalism

One of the methods used by statists to destroy Capitalism, consists in establishing controls that tie a given industry hand and foot, making it unable to solve its problems, then declaring that freedom has failed and that stronger controls are necessary.

—Ayn Rand

The concept of a *false flag operation* has its origins in naval warfare. It consists in the use of a flag other than the aggressor's true battle flag as a ruse prior to engaging an enemy so that one's political enemy is falsely blamed for the aggression. In modern principle, employing a false flag is used by a political movement to stage a catastrophic event in such a manner that casts blame on that movement's political opponents. This causes the opposition to be viewed with distrust and contempt by the general public.

One of the best examples of a false flag was America's Operation Northwoods in 1962. This was a proposed false flag that was never actually carried out. Nevertheless, the proposal went something like this: The plan called for the CIA and other paramilitary operatives to commit perceived acts of terrorism in US territory and then blame those acts on Cuba. The purpose was to gain public support for a war against Cuba, which had recently come under the control of Fidel Castro. One of the main parts of the plan was to use Cuban exiles living in the Miami area to develop a faux-Communist terror campaign in South Florida and along the East Coast of the United States. This campaign would consist of attacks that would include hijackings and bombings of public events and buildings. These would then be followed by the introduction of phony evidence that would implicate the Cuban government.[135] The plan was drafted by the US Joint Chiefs of staff and was then sent to Secretary of Defense Robert Strange McNamara (yes, that is his correct middle name, derived from his mother's maiden name). The plan was rejected by President John F. Kennedy.[136]

Another one of the most noteworthy examples of a false flag was the Reichstag fire in Berlin. (This is alleged because it was never proven to have truly been a false flag.) This event was the catalyst that led to Adolf Hitler's rise to absolute power. On February 27, 1933, at 9:25 in the evening, the Reichstag building's main chamber of deputies (the lower house of the legislature in Germany's parliament) was engulfed in flames.

The police conducted a thorough search inside of the building and found Marinus van der Lubbe, a mentally handicapped Dutch council Communist. The next day the *Preussische Pressedienst* (Prussian Press Service) reported that "this act of incendiarism is the most monstrous act of terrorism carried out by Bolshevism in Germany." The *Vossische Zeitung* newspaper warned its readers that "the government is of the opinion that a danger to the state and the nation existed and still exists."

The consensus among the then German leadership was that this marked the beginning of a Communist *putsch* (revolution). Just four weeks before this occurred on January 30, Adolf Hitler had been sworn in as the new chancellor of Germany. The fire was used as evidence by the Nazis that the Communists were beginning a plot to overthrow the German government. Van der Lubbe and four Communist leaders were subsequently arrested. Chancellor Adolf Hitler urged President Paul von Hindenburg to pass an emergency decree called the Enabling Act to counter the "ruthless confrontation of the Communist party of Germany." This allowed the Hitler government to suspend civil liberties, after which the government instituted mass arrests of Communists, including all of the Communist parliamentary delegates. With the Communists' seats empty, the Nazis gained the two-thirds supermajority they required to pass and enact any legislation they wished. Subsequent elections confirmed this position and thus allowed Hitler to consolidate his power.

Since then, it is often claimed that the Nazis themselves orchestrated the fire by coercing the Communists to perpetrate it so that they could be blamed and then ousted from parliament. In truth, it remains only a theory that the Reichstag fire could have been a false flag operation. Nevertheless, the Reichstag fire was such a pivotal event that it has come to be the archetype of a false flag operation.

---

[135] U.S. Joint Chiefs of Staff. Justification for US Military Intervention in Cuba (TS). U.S.DOD. March 13, 1962
[136] Horne, Douglas P. Inside the Assassination Records Review Board: The U.S. Government's Final Attempt to Reconcile the Conflicting Medical Evidence in the Assassination of JFK, Volumes I – V. November, 2009.

At the time it was the Weimar Constitution (Weimarer Verfassung) that governed Germany during the Weimar Republic (1919–1933). The constitution declared Germany to be a democratic parliamentary republic.

The Enabling Act, which was passed as a consequence of the Reichstag fire, was a special law that gave the chancellor, Adolf Hitler, emergency powers to pass laws by decree without the involvement of the *Reichstag* (parliament), thereby circumventing the German Constitution. These special powers would remain in effect for four years, after which they were eligible for renewal. Under article 48 of the existing Weimar Constitution, the president could rule by decree in times of emergency.

The analogous power held by US presidents is known as "the executive order privilege." In the US however, there is no four year limit on these powers. Executive orders have been used—or more accurately misused—by US presidents for generations. The excessive use of executive order by US presidents over the past century should be viewed as an egregious abuse of power.

In the case of pre-war Germany, the Enabling Act was only supposed to be passed in times of extreme emergency, and in fact, it was only used once before in 1923–24, when the government used such an act to rescue Germany from hyperinflation. To pass an enabling act, a party required a vote by a two-thirds majority in the Reichstag. In January 1933, the Nazis had only 32 percent of the seats and thus were in no position to pass an enabling act. Once the Communists were out of parliament, the Nazis had the supermajority and total control of Germany.[137] The rest is history.

America's Reichstag

The most sophisticated and far-reaching false flag in the history of the world has been the concept of American free-market capitalism in the twentieth and twenty-first centuries.

I've tried to point out in earlier chapters that the Federal Reserve system, the graduated tax on individual incomes, and the existence of taxes on homes and properties are all fundamentally Marxist constructs. Real free-market capitalism is completely incompatible with our current systems of fiat money and taxation on property and earnings. As such, the United States has been a socialist country since 1913. This assertion is further supported when one reviews the *Manifesto's* ten planks of Communism and compares those against America's current socioeconomic model.

In spite of these facts, we are told practically every hour of every day over and over again by our public schools, our media, and our politicians, that America is a capitalist country practicing the free-enterprise system. This is another example of the principle that if you repeat a lie often enough, it is eventually accepted as being true. While

---

[137]   Pritchard, John. Reichstag Fire: Ashes of Democracy, Ballantine Books.1972.

America's leaders have been deceptively flying the flag of free-market capitalism, they have surreptitiously implemented capitalism's archenemy—socialism.

The American people have been subject to a false flag operation of biblical proportions. It is a false flag operation that has been ongoing for the past hundred years and is on the verge of coming to complete fruition. The false flag operation to which I am referring is false flag capitalism.

By having convinced the American people that the socialist model under which our country has been suffering is capitalism, the ruling class can continually marginalize, discredit, and disgrace real capitalism. In blaming every socioeconomic problem of the past century on capitalism, many have come to believe that capitalism is evil and a failure. Indeed, an increasing number of American journalists routinely express contempt for "American Capitalism," while it is in fact American Socialism they are condemning. The American people never seem to see through this fraud. Some just scratch their heads, wondering why the free-enterprise system isn't working while others regurgitate the nonsense they were taught about socialism being better at providing a fair distribution of wealth. In fact, it is our current system of American socialism that is not working. It is Wilson's *progressivism*, Roosevelt's *New Deal*, Johnson's *Great Society* that are all dysfunctional and corrupt systems. Referring to these socialist systems as "capitalist" is absurd.

A Government of Traitors

Oran's *Dictionary of the Law* (1983) defines treason as "a citizen's actions to help an enemy or foreign government overthrow, make war against, or seriously injure the parent nation."

The United States has fought several bloody wars under the premise that Communism is America's enemy—North Korea, North Viet Nam, and the long cold war against the former Soviet Union being the best-known examples. Meanwhile, most members of our nation's leadership have advanced, defended, and continue to support the fundamentally Marxist models inherent in our monetary system and our tax systems. One could make the case that their protection and advancement of America's Marxist institutions have acted to *overthrow and seriously injure the United States* through their subversion of our US Constitution and our founding principles. As such, by definition, these politicians have committed treason against the United States and against the American people.

America in Wonderland—Deception and Obfuscation

If I had a world of my own, everything would be nonsense. Nothing would be what it is, because everything would be what

it isn't. And contrary wise, what is, it wouldn't be. And what it
wouldn't be, it would."

—Lewis Carroll from *Alice in Wonderland*

A Successful False Flag Depends on Propaganda

One of the most popular films of 2009 was *Capitalism: A Love Story*, a film written,
directed by, and starring Michael Moore. The film focuses on the period of the late
2000s, the financial crisis, the bank bailouts, and the TARP stimulus. The film
delivers a scathing indictment of the current economic order in the United States. In
doing so, it demonizes capitalism as the culprit. Topics covered include Wall Street's
casino mentality, for-profit prisons, Goldman Sachs's influence in Washington, DC,
the poverty-level wages of many workers, the mortgage lending frauds perpetrated
during the past twenty years, credit default swaps, home foreclosures, and the
consequences of runaway corporate greed. The film fails to admit however, that these
problems are the end result of the policies enacted by our central bank – The Federal
Reserve. It is the fiat money and fractional reserve banking systems that make all
of these dysfunctions possible. The film fails to admit that our model of fiat money
and fractional reserve banking are the cornerstone of our fundamentally Marxist
economy. Instead, the film seeks to convince the viewer that these institutions are
"capitalist."

The film also features a religious component where Moore examines whether or
not capitalism is a sin and if Jesus would be a capitalist. The film implies that
there are ideological contradictions among evangelical conservatives who support
free-market principles, and that they are therefore hypocrites. In this aspect of the
film, Moore ignores one of the main ideological bases that formed our constitution
and the true free-enterprise system—namely the biblical concepts of free will and
property rights. According to this understanding, Jesus would indeed have been
a free-market capitalist. He espoused fair and peaceful interaction and voluntary
exchange among people, value for value by mutual consent, and property rights
as espoused in the Ten Commandments. Jesus denounced the authoritarian use of
force and coercion as espoused in the *Communist Manifesto*. Jesus also denounced
usury by the moneychangers—the basis for central banking and fiat money, which
are also espoused in the *Communist Manifesto*. By that standard it is Moore's film
that is replete with hypocrisy. Michael Moore himself has a net worth of well over
$50 Million.

The film closes with Moore placing crime-scene tape around numerous banks and
around several areas of Wall Street, which is in keeping with his sensationalist
style. He is admittedly very good at injecting cynical humor into his films, and this
certainly plays well to America's entertainment culture. The crime-scene analogy is
actually correct but not for the reasons Moore implies. The criminals on Wall Street
are not capitalists. They are monopolistic corporate socialists, and their crimes against

the United States are far greater than just fraud and theft. Their crimes include high treason against the US Constitution.

In his closing remarks while he is narrating the film, Moore declares that capitalism is an evil that can only be eliminated and replaced with "the goodness of democracy—rule by the people, not by money" (corporatocracy). In fact, Democratic Socialism *is rule by money*—fiat money. He omits any discussion on the distinction between these aforementioned variants of socialist rule versus the rule of law (constitutional republicanism). It is a fraud to claim that one form of socialism is a better alternative to another form of socialism, while never submitting true free-market capitalism under a rule of law as one of the options.

Moore concludes the film by encouraging the American public to "speed it up" in terms of the process of destroying capitalism in favor of pure democracy—democratic socialism.

It is this *bait and switch* along with other false flag tactics used by the media, government, and our educational institutions that is used to delude the public into believing that America's ills are a consequence of capitalism. In fact they are a direct consequence of a century of American Socialism.

Other False Flags

Most of the American people are hopelessly confused by all of this. They're supposed to be. We have been indoctrinated with the notion that the elite robber-barons and bankers of early twentieth-century America were capitalists, and so their progeny and legacy institutions are also purported to be models of capitalism. Anyone who has ever played the Milton Bradley game of Monopoly should recognize the banker character in the card decks as having been modeled on the likeness of J. P. Morgan. Moreover, the Monopoly game's rule book states: "The bank never goes broke. If the bank runs out of money, the banker may issue as much more as needed by writing on ordinary paper." This would not be possible under the sound money system required by free-market capitalism. Even the board game Monopoly functions under rules established for a Marxist monetary model (which depends on monopolism). However, life for America's struggling poor and middle-class is not a board game. It is a matter of survival.

Monopolists abhor competition. They abhor capitalism because the free market enables the best among us to rise by virtue of our own ability and become formidable competitors to the likes of the Rockefellers, the Warburgs, and the Rothschilds. It allows the poor to escape poverty and become self-reliant, depriving the ruling class of desperate, poor, obedient employees. The monopolists' goal is not only to preclude potential competitors from rising but to enslave their betters into producing for their benefit. They achieve this pervasively across all industries and across the entire population by controlling the monetary system and the government who keeps the working class impoverished through unfair taxation. They are parasites, in motive and in form.

Whether the rulers centralize control over the means of production in the hands of the state (as in Soviet-style socialism) or in the hands of a few international bankers (as in the United States) is a minor distinction. Either model is the enemy of a free market where the means of production resides with those who actually do the producing, and where the individual right to private property ownership is truly respected.

> One also finds in the human heart a depraved taste for equality, which impels the weak to want to bring the strong down to their level, and which reduces men to preferring equality in servitude to inequality in freedom.

> —Alexis de Tocqueville (1848)

Obamacare: Attacking the Free Market

When Obamacare, Social Security, and Medicare have bankrupted, America, They will Falsely Blame the Free Market.

Health care and health insurance are two different industries. The former is a service-based industry where the providers are highly trained in specialized medical technologies. Their revenue is earned in return for providing patients with care and sometimes life-saving medical treatment. The latter is a financial industry where the providers are administrators and paper-pushers. Their revenue comes from lobbying government in an effort to force Americans to buy their insurance policies whether they want them or not. Media mouthpieces, however, continually portray Obamacare (an enforced tax disguised as an insurance scheme) as an institution that provides health care. Obamacare does nothing of the kind. In fact its deployment immediately drove costs upward and even deprived many people from maintaining their existing health insurance policies. Obamacare has made most liberty-loving Americans quite ill.

The health insurance industry was already heavily regulated before Obamacare. In recent years, if you lived in state A, you couldn't buy insurance from state B. That gave insurance companies in state A, a local monopoly on health insurance. This drives the price up and the quality down. It also means that fewer people get insurance—even though it's lower quality. The fact that this problem was created by the government in the first place was consistently ignored when people were fielding the countless objections to the Obamacare legislation.

More regulations and subsidies have been foisted upon America like never before because of the Obamacare law. What have the consequences been? The price has gone up. The quality has gone down. Formerly full-time jobs are being replaced with part-time jobs in every US industry. People have lost their health insurance and are now forced to sign up for policies only approved by the government. Companies will have a preference for hiring part-timers so people will get fewer hours to work. In short, people are getting a lot less of what they desperately need and now have to work a lot harder for it. Obamacare will be a complete and total economic failure. But in terms of the statist's principle goals, it will be a runaway success. It will provide them with the ammunition to claim what they always do—that the free market has failed again and that we need full-fledged socialized government-run health care.

> You know Obamacare is really the worst thing that has happened in this nation since slavery … It is slavery in a way, because it is making all of us subservient to the government, and it was never about health care. It was about control. That's why when this administration took office it didn't matter that the country was going off the cliff economically. All forces were directed toward getting this legislation passed. Vladimir Lenin, one of the fathers of Socialism and Communism, said that socialized medicine is the keystone to the establishment of the socialist state.[138]

> —Dr. Ben Carson, director of pediatric
> neurosurgery at Johns Hopkins

Crony Capitalism

The term *crony capitalism* is another misuse of language intended to instill the idea that capitalism is inherently evil. The concept of real capitalism is incompatible with what is meant by crony capitalism, so why use the word at all? Why not call it what it is—influence peddling, pay off, bribery, or something like that? Calling it what it is, however, doesn't benefit the political class, whose goal it is to discredit and destroy real capitalism. Once again it is about politicians trying to pervert or obfuscate meaning through the subtle misuse of language in order to advance their political agenda.

Crony capitalism has absolutely nothing in common with free-market principles. It consists in using political power and influence to gain unfair advantage by skewing the rules of business in one's own favor in order to eliminate competition. This is consistent with monopolism—not capitalism. Using the word capitalism even with

---

[138]   Carson, Dr. Ben. Remarks from his speech at the Value and Voter's Summit in Washington, DC. Oct. 11, 2013.

the descriptor crony before it falsely implies that monopolism is a form of capitalism, which it is not. It is the very basis of socialism and socialist institutions.

The American "Experiment"

Propagandists often refer to America's founding principles as "The American Experiment." But how can a social order based upon natural law, ethics, and which espouses individual liberty and respect for property rights, be characterized as an "experiment?" In fact, individual liberty and economic freedom are the natural order of things—all else is just folly.

It is the myriad forms of collectivism and centralized governance that constitute an endless stream of failed experiments. Those who refer to America's founding principles as an "experiment," are again perverting logic, and inverting the truth as a means to destroy the concept of American freedom.

Natural law as the basis for American governance comes from the writings of John Locke in the 1600s, and later Adam Smith. Prior to their time, the larger society based much of its philosophy in superstition. Remember that this was the time of Galileo, who was imprisoned and tortured for more than 6 years after announcing his scientific discovery that the Sun, and not The Earth, was the center of our Solar System.

Experimentation is done when you lack knowledge about something and endeavor to seek the truth of the matter. During man's earlier attempts at central governance, principles were derived experimentally and through superstition because of a lack of knowledge. From the Inquisition to the Salem Witch trials to the Soviet gulags, despots have tried and failed repeatedly to quash the God-given natural rights of individuals. They were experimenting to find the best means by which to destroy mankind's natural right to self-determination.

The "American Experiment" is no experiment at all. Our founding principles are a reflection of knowledge and truth that was first gained and then passed on to America's founders over centuries of experimentation culminating with the historical period of The Enlightenment. These truths, based upon ethics and science, and which are espoused in our founding Declaration and US Constitution, obviated the need to continue "experimenting" and thus governing by superstition. Thousands of years of experimentation proved that arbitrarily governing by men or by a majority of men would always lead to despotism and failure. America's founders thus chose for America to be governed by The Rule of Law—Natural Law.

Experiments can fail, and when they do, we abandon the theories that led us to conduct those experiments. Tinkering around with different monetary models and political tactics to centrally control the economy is by definition, experimentation. By contrast, the natural order of things—the free enterprise system—is the only economic model that is consistent with the laws of nature, and that is therefore based in rational truth. America's founding principles were the product of social trials and tribulations conducted over thousands of years. America's founding principles are the conclusion—not the experiment.

Over the past hundred years, those who refer to America as an "experiment," are simply planting the notion that our founding principles are arbitrary, subject to trial and failure, and therefore we should dispose of these ideals if they don't "work for us." They then surreptitiously enact socialist policies that were already proven failures. When—as predicted—those policies fail again, they point to them as *America's failings*, while the media blames Capitalism and the Free Market as the culprit. Thus the con is sealed. The False Flag Capitalists (who are actually socialists) can beat their chests and claim, "see, I told you so, the American experiment has failed."

Referring to America's founding as an experiment is yet another false flag tactic used by her enemies to destroy her founding principles, so that they will never be restored.

Those seeking to destroy the free enterprise system and the concept of individual Liberty, label everything associated with America: liberty, Capitalism, free enterprise, individualism, and morality, as that which they are not. They do this in order to try to dupe the public into believing that slavery is freedom, renting is ownership, wrong is right, immoral is moral, cronyism is capitalism, and that individual liberty is nothing more than a trivial "experiment." Absolute power is their objective, and inverting truth is their tactic.

There are many variants of collectivist oppression, but there is only one form of individual freedom. If you're free, you're free. If you're not, you might be a socialist, a Nazi, a communist, a corporate socialist, or some other type of slave. It would be more correct to call it crony socialism, crony fascism, or crony corporatism, but this would not serve the purposes of the propaganda ministry in trying to discredit and destroy real capitalism by employing subtle false flag tactics at every opportunity.

Some might label this assertion as mere semantics, but semantics are important. Words have meaning, and the political class has become expert in perverting meaning and truth through the subtle misuse of language. Truth is truth. A is A; and B is B. A is *not* B. Immoral is *not* moral. Renting is *not* ownership. And the United States of America has *not* practiced free-market capitalism in at least a century.

The true free market operates with an extremely efficient invisible hand that guides people's choices through price movements. Those price movements, in a purely supply and demand dynamic (under a sound money system), are a consequence of the billions of daily decisions and transactions made by the hundreds of millions of Americans—the whole of the people. In a free market, price guides people to make the most efficient choices that are economically possible. What happens when you violate the free market? The economy is distorted, and wealth is destroyed. It is a basic law of economics.

Karl Marx claimed that capitalism would self-destruct and be replaced by socialism on its own. History has proven the opposite to be true. Every socialist dictatorship that has been established around the world has eventually failed, usually with great loss of life and hardship. American socialism is in the process of failing as well. Socialism was instituted in America by surreptitious means, by fraud, by incrementalism, through force and coercion. It has been proved time and time again to be the unnatural condition of society. It is socialism's inherent flaws that render it to be the self-destructive system.

CHAPTER 15

The Living Constitution—A Living Death

> I hate people who say, "Can we speak frankly?" It means they're
> bullshittin' me the rest of the time.
>
> —Lawrence Garfield (Danny DeVito)
> from *Other People's Money*

On December 10, 2012, Supreme Court Justice Antonin Scalia discussed his judicial philosophy of reading the US Constitution on its textual basis and original meaning.

"The fairest reading of the text is what the law means," he said to an audience of more than seven hundred at Princeton University—the bastion of progressive indoctrination. "When we read Shakespeare, we use a glossary because we want to know what it meant when it was written. We don't give those words their current meaning. So also with a statute—our statutes don't morph. They don't change meaning from age to age to comport with whatever the zeitgeist thinks is appropriate." [139]

Scalia's talk was titled "Reading Law," which is also the title of the book he coauthored with legal language expert Bryan Garner and published in early 2013. The notion of a living constitution has risen dramatically during the past half century and has become pervasive throughout American society. Even Hollywood celebrities have gotten in on perpetuating this myth. Several years ago actor Richard Dreyfuss began a crusade to restore the study of civics to public schools, and he has conducted hundreds of public speaking engagements to promote that idea. His efforts have been

---

[139] Patel, Ushma; Princeton University Office of Communications. "Scalia favors 'enduring' not 'living' Constitution." *News at Princeton*. Dec 11, 2012.

well intentioned, and indeed, the study of the workings of our government in terms of our founding principles should be required subject matter in every school. However, in listening to one of Mr. Dreyfuss's earlier speeches he repeatedly reinforced this idea of a *living constitution*, even spewing the popular nonsense about it having been written "by a bunch of old, rich, white, slave owners." However, the fact that George Washington was one of the richest men in all of the colonies at the time of the revolution actually serves to reveal the eminent character embodied in him and the other founding fathers. A man with so much to lose and practically nothing to gain, yet having the courage to risk his wealth and his life for the principle of individual liberty for all of his countrymen is a rare breed. Old, rich man indeed—our country should be so fortunate to have another such man leading us today.

Mr. Dreyfuss doesn't mention that today's old, rich, white, slave owners who control the Federal Reserve, and his multimillionaire friends in the entertainment industry have done little to restore individual liberty and property rights for all Americans. It was the founders of this country who established those American values in the first place. They did so at great personal risk. Such a disrespectful statement about our founders from a privileged Hollywood multimillionaire is shameful. To his credit however, in some of his later remarks Mr. Dreyfuss revealed that he has abandoned the party-line stating, "I ceased being a Democrat a while ago, and thought that it would hurt this [civics] endeavor, and because I thought that there was very little difference between the two parties." Mr. Dreyfuss has at least decided to think for himself rather than marching in lock step with the rest of the Hollywood elite. For that and his efforts he deserves great respect. One can only hope that he will eventually realize his errors in subscribing to the notion of a living constitution.

The term *living constitution* was coined by Franklin D. Roosevelt in the same year he first attempted his Supreme Court packing plan. Prior to FDR's efforts to pack the Court with liberal activist judges, it was still populated largely with originalists (those who properly render legal interpretation based upon the Constitution's original intent). Today, Scalia and Justice Clarence Thomas are the only originalists on the Supreme Court. The other seven members have at one time or another espoused an adherence to the notion of a malleable constitution. This is perhaps one of the most damaging legacies of the FDR presidency—that he successfully transformed the judicial branch of government from one of independent review in accordance with the rule of law to one of subservience to the political will of the executive branch.[140] The fact that the majority of Supreme Court justices have adopted this idea is one of the main bases for the degeneration of this country's founding principles. This has led to the elimination of the separation of powers doctrine, thereby consolidating our government's ever-expanding power over the people. The fact that Supreme Court justices are appointed for life by the sitting president has proven to be a serious weakness in our governing principle, which was intended to keep the branches of government separated and independent of one another.

---

[140]   Alexander, Mark, *Essential Liberty*, (Publius Press, Inc. Chattanooga, TN, 2010), p. 17.

Scalia went on to say, "I have classes of little kids who come to the court, and they recite very proudly what they've been taught [in public school], 'The constitution is a living document.' I tell them it isn't a living document! It's dead, dead, dead, dead!" Scalia said, eliciting laughter from the audience. "No, I don't say that. I call it the enduring constitution. That's what I tell them."

The power to amend or add to the constitution does not implicitly empower our Congress to change its original meaning and intent. In fact, the framers did everything they could to prevent the constitution from becoming a malleable, living document subject to the whims of some unenlightened majority. They anticipated clearly the long-term threats to their hard-won liberties that confront us at every turn today.

The constitution and Bill of Rights is not and was never intended to be a living document. This assertion is supported by both logical inference and historical fact.

Included in the US Constitution are elements that define the core aspects of our free-market economic system (the most important of which is its guarantee of sound money). It contains the basic rules of the game in terms of commerce, trade, and business. If you are playing poker with two other opponents, would you allow them to change the rules in the middle of play for their own convenience and benefit just because there are two of them and only one of you?

The fundamental concept of unalienable rights is that we are endowed with these by nature, by God (or whatever God means to the individual). These principles never change. One of the most important reasons that the constitution is not a living document is that it is based upon natural law and therefore on ethics, and fundamental moral truths. If you hold that the constitution's fundamental premises should live or change with the times, then you must hold that fundamental morality, ethics, right and wrong, should change with the times.

That is a dangerous path to follow.

The most important of these ethical principles is that no individual, group, or institution, even if it is in the majority, shall have the right to use force (either physical or coercion) against any other individual or minority group. Doing so is a violation of their unalienable, God-given right to their own life, and their own property. These are not rights that have been granted by our government, by any majority, or by any arbitrary authority. Such rights that have been granted by men can also be removed by men, especially if there are more of them with guns than there are of you without guns.

To claim that the US Constitution is a living document is to say that any majority can remove or change an individual's constitutional rights to life, liberty, and property. This is not espoused anywhere in the US Constitution. If that were the case, those rights would not be *unalienable*. Unalienable means inseparable—inseparable from man as a species—that is any man, woman, or child. The constitution was specifically intended to protect the unalienable rights of minorities and individuals, not to violate those rights at the whim of any majority. The second amendment in particular was intended to ensure that American citizens would have the right to be at least as well armed as the very government that might, at some point in time act to deny the citizenry of all of their other unalienable rights.

> When governments fear the people there is liberty; when the people fear the government, there is tyranny.
>
> —Thomas Jefferson

It is that pesky little word *unalienable* that is hated and disavowed by liberals, which precludes the US Constitution from being treated as a living document. This is exactly as the framers intended. Unalienable means inseparable or unable to be taken away. To change the meaning of an unalienable right is no different than taking it away. The point of a constitutional republic is to establish governance based upon a body of natural law that must be abided by all, including the government itself. Its primary purpose is to protect the citizenry—*all* of the citizenry—against government overreach. Perverting the law of the land defeats the entire purpose of the constitutional republican form of government.

Our government has no power to grant rights to anyone. Therefore, it cannot take any of those rights away. Nor can it change any of them. In fact, it is the constitution, which is legally considered to be a treaty among the sovereign states that ratified it, which defines and delimits the powers delegated to the federal government and not the other way around. The framers clearly did not trust any government wielding too much power to perpetually respect the rights of individuals. Thus, the Bill of Rights was made part of the US Constitution.

> The Constitution of the United States cannot protect us, unless we protect the Constitution.
>
> —Dr. Thomas Sowell, Senior fellow on public policy at Stanford University

If you think you want to live under a living constitution so that you can bend the rules to suit you whenever you please, you must realize that this is a double-edged sword. You may not be part of a minority today, but sometime in the future each and every one of us most certainly will be, as the demographics of this country change in the coming decades. In fact, even if you are a young, educated, white man and you are lucky to live long enough, eventually you will be part of the minority of the elderly and infirm.

With a living Constitution, some day in the future you may find that a self-serving majority of which you are no longer a part of will have sole authority over your destiny, your savings, retirement, wealth, health, property, and how the fruits of your labor shall be disposed of. Do you want a majority of which you are not a part to have the power to deny you of your formerly unalienable rights—possibly even to deny you the medical care required to extend your life?

With a living constitution that is exactly what will happen to you. It is already happening to millions of Americans as they watch their property confiscated and their rights violated by our own government on a daily basis.

> The smallest minority on Earth, is the individual; One who would deny individual rights, cannot then claim to be a defender of minorities.
>
> —Ayn Rand

The constitution is about guaranteeing the unalienable rights of the individual. It is not about manipulating those rights over time by a majority who have empowered a corrupt and overreaching government that has more guns than do the citizens—and a demonstrated willingness to use them against those citizens. In a country with a living constitution, it is not a matter of if but when the government functioning under it will eventually attain enough power to become a totalitarian oligarchy. It is vitally important to understand this objectively. It is not an academic question, for someday in this country, perhaps for your children and most certainly for your grandchildren, it will become a matter of life and death.

Since power attracts the corruptible, powerfully structured institutions will eventually become fundamentally corrupt. It is just a matter of time. For this reason, the framers constructed our government to have limited and separated powers, as defined by our Constitution. Those limits on central government power were meant to be perpetual and permanent. Those who promote the idea of a living constitution in an effort to pervert its meaning and original intent, clearly do so in order to gain and expand power by subverting this basic principle. Their goal is to consolidate and then expand government's powers so they can eventually abuse that power for their own personal gain.

Whether you're a liberal or a conservative who has been indoctrinated to believe that we have a malleable living constitution, you must ask yourself objectively why the establishment wants you to believe this. Do you truly believe that an all-powerful fundamentally corrupt government will restrain itself from violating your rights and taking your property? If the constitution forbids them from doing so it won't matter because they'll just change it, and they can so long as you consent to the absurd idea that it is a living constitution.

This is not a conservative versus liberal issue, or a Republican versus Democrat issue. This issue plays directly to every hardworking American family that is struggling to own their home, save for the future, and establish long-term security for their children. These are aspirations that we all share independent of our political affiliations. As long as *we the people* allow our public schools, universities, and propaganda media to indoctrinate the population with the myth that the constitution is a living document, we will continue further along the path to full-on tyranny. Eventually your children and your grandchildren will "wake up homeless, and penniless, on the continent their forefathers conquered." Once our freedom and our unalienable rights have been lost, do you truly believe that an all-powerful government run by narcissistic sociopaths will simply give them back to a bunch of powerless peasants?

The Arguments of the Useful Idiots

Previously Justice Scalia had written, "There's the argument of 'flexibility,' and it goes something like this: The constitution is over two hundred years old, and societies change. It has to change with society like a living organism, or it will become brittle and break. But you would have to be an idiot to believe that the constitution is a living organism. It is a legal document. It says something and doesn't say other things."

Indeed, and what it says is based upon natural laws and moral truths that are as true today as they were two hundred—or two thousand years ago.

Justice Clarence Thomas has also stated,

> There are really only two ways to interpret the Constitution, try to discern as best we can what the framers intended or make it up. No matter how ingenious, imaginative, or artfully put, unless interpretive methodologies are tied to the original intent of the framers, they have no basis in the Constitution ... At least originalism has the advantage of being legitimate, and I might add, impartial.

Based on states' efforts to pass laws restricting the use of eminent domain after a Supreme Court decision upheld its constitutionality, another Princeton student asked Justice Scalia, "Do you think there's any hope for federalism?"

"I think there is hope for state activism," Scalia said. But he added,

That's not what federalism is about. What federalism is about is that there are certain things the federal government can't do even if it wants to. That [state activism] doesn't limit the federal government's powers at all. *Wringing your hands about states' rights ... forget it. They're gone. Basically the federal government can do whatever it wants now. Who's going to protect the states? My court? Ha, we're feds!*

With this, Scalia's meaning was a clear admission that the separation of powers is a thing of the past much to his chagrin and more to the detriment of the American people.

This view of the constitution as malleable, Scalia said, has two practical problems. The first, he said, is a question of legitimacy. The constitution does not say that the Supreme Court should decide the "evolving standards of decency" in society. This is a task better suited to the Congress.

"Why would you think these nine unelected lawyers living in a marble palace have their thumb on the pulse of the American people so that they know what the evolving standards of decency are? I don't know what they are. I'm afraid to ask," Scalia said.

"The second argument," Scalia said, "is that the text and its original meaning are the only objective standards to which all judges themselves can be held."

Herein lays the distinguishing characteristic of a constitutional republic as opposed to a pure democracy. Under a constitutional republic even the government authorities themselves must abide by the law of the land (the constitution). They have no authorization to change the meaning or intent of those laws over time in order to suit their personal agendas, even if they represent a majority. This is the only means by which all of the people, especially those in the minority, can be protected from a tyrannical government. A government that seeks to exert powers it does not have (in order to confiscate the people's wealth and property for example) will always seek to pervert the law in order to legalize actions the government wishes to take but which are otherwise prohibited by its constitution. The Supreme Court used to be the only thing standing in the way of a government bent on distorting the Constitution's protections of individual rights.

Given these facts, it's clear that the continual propaganda asserting that the constitution is a living document and the ongoing assault on its meaning and intent has a specific purpose—a means to an ultimate end. The ultimate goal of the statists is to render the constitution inert, and with it the Bill of Rights. This will allow them to take power over every aspect of our lives, giving them complete control of the fruits of all of our labor and all of our property. The power of the federal government has already gone through dramatic expansion along with consolidation and the virtual elimination of the separation of powers doctrine. But even this isn't enough for the power mongering sociopaths in our government. They want their expanded power and control over our lives to be irreversible. To achieve that permanence, they must change the meaning and intent of The US Constitution. To do that, they must convince the American people that the constitution is a living document.

Control equals ownership. When the government eventually owns and controls all property, we will all be serfs. When the government controls the entire labor market, we will all be slaves. This is the ultimate goal of the statists. This was also the goal of the monarchy against whom our founders led the revolutionary idea of a free people with a right to own their own homes, their own land, the fruits of their labor, and to be able to choose their own destinies. It appears that history indeed repeats itself and American patriots must fight the American Revolution all over again.

Our elected government employees and their appointees are charged with the responsibility to protect the unalienable rights of American citizens against violations of those rights. For that reason, the president, every member of Congress, the Supreme Court, their appointees, and the military must take an oath of office. Their oath binds them to uphold and defend the US Constitution and Bill of Rights, not to pervert its meaning and intent.

The Presidential Oath of Office reads,

> I do solemnly swear that I will faithfully execute the office of The President of the United States, and will to the best of my ability, PRESERVE, PROTECT, and DEFEND, the Constitution of the United States."

Members of Congress and All Commissioned Military Officers' Oath of Office reads,

> I do solemnly swear that I will support and defend the Constitution of the United States against all enemies, foreign and domestic, that I will bear true faith and allegiance to the same, that I take this obligation freely without any mental reservation or purpose of evasion; and that I will well and faithfully discharge the duties of the office on which I am about to enter: So help me God.

This latter oath, which is taken by military officers, binds them to disobey any order that violates our constitution. Therefore, these oaths mandate the preservation, support, and defense of our constitution exactly as it was written and ratified by the states and not as a so-called living constitution.

CHAPTER 16

Restoring Prosperity—Government

Which is better, to be ruled by one tyrant three thousand miles away or three thousand tyrants one mile away?

—Mather Byles to Nathaniel Emmons of Massachusetts, 1776

The Patriot
©2000 Global Entertainment Productions GmbH
& Co. Movie KG. All Rights Reserved.
Courtesy of Columbia Pictures

A variation of this quote was made famous by Mel Gibson in the film *The Patriot*. As profound as it is, the character played by Gibson, who is the better known source, was a far cry from the original. Mather Byles was a loyalist and an outspoken advocate of British colonial rule. In 1777, he was placed under house arrest and was constantly under guard by a sentry whom he referred to as his Observe-a-Tory. [141] Even supporters of tyranny can have a charming sense of humor.

However, enslaving an entire population is no laughing matter, and to answer Byles' question, *neither form of rule is better or acceptable in a free society*. Men can be a danger to themselves and to others. Corrupt men with power acting in combination with other men are particularly dangerous. Therefore, being governed by the rule of law is the only ethical and moral condition of a just society. It is without question preferable to rule by any man or combination of men regardless of their distance. And for those who haven't yet seen the film, Gibson's character finished the quote by saying, "An elected legislature can trample a man's rights as easily as any king can."

Our Congress has proved him right. This is the reason the framers established the United States as a constitutional republic with limited and separated powers under the rule of law. It only works, however, if the government follows the law. Ours has not.

Byles' quote exemplifies the concept of being coerced into choosing the lesser of two evils while inferring by omission that there is no other alternative. In doing so, you are still choosing evil. Tyrants and dictators have exploited this idea for millennia. Their aim is to convince the people to embrace their own enslavement under one form of tyranny, by claiming that the alternative form of tyranny would be worse. Tyrants never offer true individual freedom, and self-determination as one of the options, and thus the con is sealed.

In the previous fifteen chapters I described a consistent pattern of rights abuses perpetrated against the poor and middle class by our own government and the Federal Reserve. Their goal is to eradicate our property rights and our liberty and then to destroy the US Constitution, and to ensure that we can never regain those values. The perpetrators are clearly revealed by their actions and by their own words. When a Fed chairman proudly proclaims his skill at "purposeful obfuscation" as a means to dupe Congress and the American people—when they knowingly place society's entire burden of financial risk on the hapless, hardworking population—when families and children face the possibility to lose their homes or farms even if they have paid off their debts in full—then we are already living under a totalitarian regime.

For the past century the US government in collusion with the private Federal Reserve banking cartel has acted to deliberately eradicate individual property rights for all Americans. They have done this primarily through our Marxist and unconstitutional

---

[141]   Gates, Henry Louis, Jr., *The Trials of Phyllis Wheatley. America's First Black Poet and Her Encounters with the Founding Fathers*, 2003. p10.

systems of fiat money and graduated income taxes confiscated from us by our own employers. The state and local governments hold our homes, our properties, our jobs, our businesses, our local schools, and our children hostage in an elaborate property tax extortion scheme modeled after a Mafia protection racket. They don't hide it, and their agents even appear on national television to boast about their skill at willfully lying before Congress in order to mislead the American people about their real agenda. The greatest tragedy is that they have been doing it with our consent.

In the preceding chapters I demonstrated that the United States was fundamentally transformed into a socialist country with the means of production (land, labor, and natural resources) placed under the control of an unelected ruling class of financial elites. They did this with the sanction and support of our own government. I referred to this as *corporate socialism*. I've made the case that these actions reveal the government's true objective—to gain the powers of a totalitarian state and to ultimately make those powers permanent and irreversible. The tyrant achieves these things by destroying individual property rights, expanding dependency, rendering self-reliance unachievable, destroying our constitution, destroying the moral character of the people, and then using false flag tactics to wrongfully blame all of these things on his enemy—free-market capitalism. This all started in 1913 with Woodrow Wilson's passage of the sixteenth and the seventeenth amendments, and the Federal Reserve Act. The year 2013 marked the 100th anniversary of Socialism in America. This anniversary was actually celebrated by Ben Bernanke and selected members of the government and the Federal Reserve, at a ceremony conducted at Jekyll Island, Georgia—the original location where the Federal Reserve System was conceived.

In part 1 of this book I asserted that the American poor and middle class are caught in a vice that squeezes each of us out of our hard-earned assets as well as the fruits of our labor. I went on to explain that one jaw of the vise is represented by the state and local government, which robs us of our money through a sophisticated property tax extortion scheme—while the other jaw is represented by our federal government, which robs us of the fruits of our labor through income taxes and deliberately engineered inflation. These are the means by which our property rights have been eradicated.

Here in part 2, I have explained how our government has been usurped by financial interests who have corrupted our system of representative government and thereby transformed our constitutional republic into its antithesis—democratic socialism. In this final chapter, "Restoring Prosperity—Government," I will outline some ideas for peacefully restoring constitutional authority to our system of governance, accountability for the oaths of office taken by our representatives, and a restoration of the separation of powers doctrine.

We can only restore America, our constitution, our liberties, our property rights, and our founding principles if we are able to exert our power as citizens from a position of strength. As long as we live under the constant threat of homelessness, unemployment, and poverty, we will always be functioning from a position of weakness and dependency. It is our own federal government that has systematically relegated the citizenry to this weak position. It's for this reason that I believe we must first act to restore our property rights and individual sovereignty at the state and local level. Chapters 7 and 8 presented the most effective ways to accomplish that goal. Once we restore our property rights and take back our homes and control of our children's education, we will be in a far stronger position to exert pressure on the political class at the federal level in order to end the cancerous partnership between the private Federal Reserve system and our federal government. Until we end the Federal Reserve and restore sound money, we will never have a government of, by, and for the people. Unless we act to reassert our authority over the federal government, we will forever be serfs—subjects of the global banking aristocracy. We will forever live under the incessant threat of homelessness, and our children and grandchildren will suffer immeasurably more and more with every successive generation.

Restore Constitutional Authority and the Separation of Powers

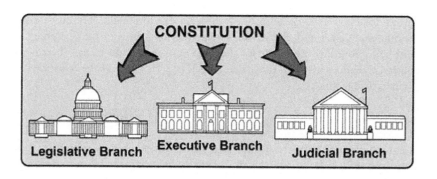

In 2009, a Harris Poll conducted by the American Bar Association revealed that more than 20 percent of Americans believed the three branches of government were Republican, Democrat, and Independent. This reveals how few Americans understand the framers' intent behind the structure of our government in trying to ensure separate and distinct powers. It was British political theorist M. J. C. Vile who wrote, "For the establishment and maintenance of political liberty, the government must be divided into three branches ... in this way each of the three branches will be a check on the others and no single group of people will be able to control the machinery of the state." In the "Federalist #51," James Madison said, "The necessary partition of power among the several departments—by so contriving the interior structure of the government, its several constituent parts may, by their mutual relations, be the means of keeping each other in their proper places. The separate and distinct exercise of the different powers of government is essential to the preservation of liberty."[142]

As Justice Roberts's unconstitutional ruling on Obamacare demonstrated, the consolidation of power vested in the executive branch has become most egregious between the White House and the Supreme Court. This is a weakness in our system that must be corrected if we are to restore constitutional authority and liberty to the people. In "Federalist #51," James Madison also wrote, "Each department should have a will of its own, and the members of each should have as little agency as possible, in the appointment of the members of the others."

Given this statement, how is it that the appointment of Supreme Court justices became vested in the authority of the president? Clearly the actions of FDR throughout his 12-year presidency—starting with his failed attempt to pack the Supreme Court with liberals and followed by his patient transformation of the court through attrition—demonstrated the flaw in this model.

Should the President Nominate Supreme Court Justices?

Restoring America to the rule of law requires that we reestablish a meaningful separation of powers to the branches of the federal government. This must start with the Supreme Court and US Senate. Presidential nominees to the Supreme Court must be approved by the Senate for their appointment to take effect. Therefore, the political dynamics between the Senate, the White House, and the Supreme Court are inextricably linked.

Supreme Court justices are not democratically elected by any majority vote because their purpose is not to represent the will of any majority. Their responsibility is to ensure that our laws are strictly compliant with what is permitted by the US Constitution in order to ensure that the unalienable rights of all people, especially minorities and individuals are protected. If they were intended to bend and manipulate the law in compliance with the will of some majority of the people or some special interest, a Supreme Court judgeship would be an elected office. It is not, precisely because the US Constitution must be enforced in terms of a strict interpretation of its original meaning and intent. This also implicitly prohibits the US Constitution from being treated as a living document.

Under article 2 of the constitution the president has the power by and with the consent of the Senate to appoint judges to the Supreme Court. Once nominated, the Senate Judiciary Committee conducts a series of hearings with the nominee prior to any Senate confirmation vote. Once vetted as a nominee, the appointment is confirmed with a majority vote in the Senate. Originally, this required a two-thirds

---

[142] Hunt, Gaillard—Editor. 1900. *The Writings of James Madison*—nine volumes. New York, G. P. Putnam & Sons.

supermajority (67 Senators). Several decades ago however, this was changed to a three-fifths majority (60 Senators). Late in 2013, even this was changed to a simple majority of just 51 Senate votes for confirmation—pure Democratic Socialism as opposed to the Rule of Law. How did this systematic degeneration take place?

Tyranny's Inauguration—Eliminating the Separation of Powers Doctrine

Senate Majority Leader Harry Reid has acted consistently and predictably in his quest to subvert the separation of powers doctrine. On July 15, 2013, Senator Reid appeared at the Center for American Progress to lay out his plan for what he called the "nuclear option."[143]

When Senator Reid began his speech, he started with the following comment: "Congress is extremely unpopular for a couple of main reasons. Any poll you look at indicates that they're unpopular for two reasons: one, gridlock, gridlock, gridlock; two, not getting things done."

Indeed, the Gallup poll he is referring to indicates gridlock and not getting things done as the top two reasons for disapproval by those polled. It would be interesting to know, however, which demographic was targeted for conducting this poll. A great many Americans are finally waking up to realize that whenever the government does anything, we suffer as a result. By definition any action the government takes is intended to limit, remove, prohibit, and destroy more of your liberty. Therefore, Americans are better off when Congress is in gridlock and precluded from doing something destructive. We should put them in gridlock and keep them there.

On November 21, 2013, Harry Reid and the Democrat controlled Senate exercised his "nuclear option" and changed the rules so that federal judicial nominees and executive-office appointments can advance to confirmation by a simple majority of senators, 51 votes rather than the 60-vote supermajority that has been standard for nearly four decades.

The rationale for the move was to allow the confirmation of three picks by President Obama to the U.S. Court of Appeals in the District of Columbia Circuit. The vast majority of Americans still have little understanding about the ramifications. The main network news programs reported this by stating something like the following: "Senate Majority Leader Harry Reid is calling for the 'nuclear option' on reform of senate rules for confirmation hearings." A statement like that means nothing to the average listener at home. It's not supposed to mean anything. The goal of such media reporting is to ensure that you don't *get it* but still have the feeling that you're informed. As such, you have no idea about what you just heard. You express no

---

[143]   DePillis, Lydia. Washingtonpost.com, "Harry Reid's speech on how he'll save the Senate from becoming 'obsolete'," July 15, 2013.

outrage, and so you do nothing other than to take another sip from your beer and flip the channel over to the playoff game. The media never explained to viewers what the nuclear option was, what its implications were, or what it will mean to your life, your future, your constitutional rights, or the future lives of your children.

In fact, its ramifications are alarming. Its purpose is to further neuter the US Constitution and bring it another step closer to becoming an irrelevant letter.

Justice Roberts's Supreme Court opinion on Obamacare has already demonstrated the extent to which the separation of powers has been diminished. However, Harry Reid's nuclear option may have pushed the sinister consolidation of the executive and other branches of government past the tipping point. It is FDR's Supreme Court-packing strategy on steroids. The reader must clearly understand the overwhelming ramifications of this and the irreversible damage this has already caused to the republic. This will allow the president, with sole authority to appoint SCOTUS nominees, to completely pack the Supreme Court, all US Federal Courts, and any other branch of government with his own team of activist lackeys that are subservient for life to their presidential benefactor—even after he leaves office. Henceforth, the people of this country will have absolutely no recourse to unconstitutional and illegal legislation passed by our Congress and signed into law by our president. Our government will be able to conduct any illegal activity against the citizenry it wishes, with no recourse by the people whatsoever. Not only the Supreme Court, but all circuit courts, courts of appeals, in fact the entire judicial system will be beholden to corrupt self-serving politicians, rather than to the law.

Any member of Congress who would even suggest such a thing clearly has one goal in mind—to castrate the constitution, make socialism permanent in America, and enable the consolidation of the US government into a centralized, monolithic, totalitarian oligarchy which already bears an unsettling similarity to the former Soviet Union.

What Senator Reid accomplished with his *nuclear option* was to fully transform the country into a pure democracy—"three wolves and a lamb voting on what to eat." It is the middle class who will be served up on the dinner plate. And Reid used a meaningless Gallup poll, citing gridlock to justify it. Reid's recent success in implementing his nuclear option has enabled any presidential nominee's appointment to be confirmed by a simple majority of 51 percent in the Senate. Therefore, the probability that any presidential nominee could be rejected is essentially zero.

The Supreme Court has already shown itself to be nothing more than an enforcement arm of the White House rather than a defender of the constitution. Thanks to Harry Reid, this condition will be even more onerous and may be irreversible. Whichever tyrant sits in the Oval Office will then be able to sign into law any unconstitutional act he wishes, and the judiciary—most appointed by and beholden to him—will then rarely if ever challenge its constitutionality. They will instead use their power to pervert the meaning of their so-called living constitution in order to uphold any unconstitutional law, as has been demonstrated with Obamacare. Their goal is to ensure that unconstitutional laws will be virtually impossible to overturn, and they have already demonstrated this in practice.

It could be argued that the SCOTUS decision on Obamacare was just a dry run to test the waters for what level of public outrage would arise. In fact, there was very little outrage to speak of. Many Americans still don't fully grasp the profound consequences behind Justice Roberts' decision and still believe that it was really only about the Obamacare law itself. It wasn't. Roberts' decision was a demonstration that our federal government's legislative, executive, and judicial branches of government have been consolidated into a monolithic, overreaching power center. It was a dry run to prove that tyranny in America is achievable. What Harry Reid has accomplished with his nuclear option was to prove that tyranny in America is not only achievable but indefinitely sustainable. We the people cannot allow them to deliberately and irreversibly destroy forever the spirit and intent of our constitution, and the rule of law that is intended to protect our individual and unalienable rights. The Senate must restore the supermajority confirmation rule, as it forms a key element of the separation of powers doctrine.

Supreme Court Judges as Political Activists

In 2009, while still acting as the US solicitor general and prior to her nomination to the Supreme Court by Barrack Hussein Obama II, Justice Elena Kagan contributed to a book titled *Change for America: A Progressive Blueprint for the 44th President*. The book, edited and compiled by Mark Green and Michele Jolin, was funded and published by the Center for American Progress Action Fund, a leftist think tank. Contributors were invited based upon their liberal progressive leanings. Its purpose was stated to "presciently and insightfully offer ideas for the renewal of progressive governance in America." Progressive is well known as the code word for socialist. The book begins by rightfully demonizing the Bush administration policies but then falsely characterizes those policies as laissez-faire.[144] Bush's policies were anything but laissez-faire. This condemnation is made either out of ignorance of basic economic theory, or it constitutes further false flag tactics intended to discredit true laissez-faire free-market capitalism. The consistent pattern of behavior by the left would suggest it is the latter, having yet again deliberately misused that label to describe Bush's corporate socialist policies in expanding the police state. Later in Kagan's book is a chapter on the economy titled "A Pro-Growth Progressive Economic Agenda." This chapter starts with the following typical liberal hyperbole: "A pro-growth progressive economic agenda must focus on policies that both raise the economic tide and lift all boats—boosting productivity and our Gross National Product, while fostering the shared prosperity that defines our nation's values."

---

[144] Green, Mark. Progressive Patriotism—*Change for America: A Progressive Blueprint for the 44th President*. 2009, P. xviii. ISBN-13: 978-0465013876.

The book then goes on to redefine the role of government by stating that the way to achieve this would be as follows: "The role of government is to make investments in areas that the private sector will under-invest in, relative to their 'social return,' such as fundamental research and a skilled workforce, and to create a policy environment that will foster competition, innovation, and entrepreneurship."[145]

The utter nonsense of these statements in terms of economic reality cannot be overstated. A sound economic return on an investment *is* a social return if it adds to economic prosperity. And something like social return in this context cannot be measured. Only a lawyer or a government bureaucrat that has never exchanged real work in return for an honest day's pay could embrace the ridiculous notion of a *social return* that comes from risking an economic investment.

Here are some actual examples of the fundamental research on which the federal government spends taxpayer money hoping to gain a *social return (and you can't make this stuff up)*:

- $3 million to study penguins to determine the magnitude of rectal pressure required to eject fecal matter over a distance of at least 50cm

- $20 million to help students from Indonesia earn Master's degrees

- $200,000 study to develop a new tattoo removal system

- $3 million to University of California to fund research on video games

- $500 Million on various studies by Department of Health and Human Services including: to solve the problem of 5-year old children that can't sit still in a kindergarten classroom.

- $30 million to research ways to help Pakistani farmers produce more mangos

- $700,000 to study methane gas emissions from dairy cows

- $615,000 to University of California at Santa Cruz to digitize photos, T-shirts, and concert tickets belonging to the Grateful Dead

- $1 million from the National Science Foundation, for Indiana University to create a database designed to detect "political smears, suspicious memes, and other *social pollution*, with a major focus on online political speech"

---

[145] Sperling, Gene, *"Change for America: A Progressive Blueprint for the 44th President."* 2009, P. 93.

- $2.6 million to train Chinese prostitutes to drink responsibly

- $216,000 on a study to determine whether politicians gain or lose support by taking ambiguous positions

- $100,000 for a San Francisco Theater Company to create a stage play on same-sex marriage

- $35 million budgeted for 2014 for salaries and expenses related to the 2008 TARP (Troubled Asset Relief Program) bailout.

- $24 million for the AeroMarti program – a US plane that flies around Cuban airspace beaming American sponsored TV programming to the island's inhabitants (the broadcast signal for which is jammed by the Cuban government so that few if any Cubans can see the broadcasts).

And the list goes on and on.

Economic reality is simple. When you are spending your own money, you are far more scrupulous about the return on its investment than when you are spending other people's money. Every nickel the government spends is other people's money, money those other people had to work for and which the government took from them by force. The ridiculous notion that government spending "in areas in which the private sector would under-invest" should "foster competition, innovation, and entrepreneurship" is absolutely absurd. If the private sector chooses not to invest in something, it is because it is an uncompetitive, un-innovative use of their hard-earned capital, so no real entrepreneur would ever touch it because the opportunity cost for doing so is too high. This is why it is only an inept, incompetent, and corrupt government that is willing to spend money digging holes and then filling them in again another area in which the private sector would never invest. There is no such thing as a social return that is distinct from an economic return. Just ask any recent college graduate with a useless degree in social studies and a $200,000 student loan debt. The only social return from that kind of financial investment is debt slavery.

It's likely that Ms. Kagan's contribution to Obama's instruction manual on expanding socialism in America added to her credibility with him and reinforced his reasons for nominating her for her lifetime appointment to the bench. This is exactly the reason neither he nor any president should wield this power. The degeneration of our Supreme Court started with four-term progressive President Franklin D. Roosevelt, and it has been downhill ever since. Progressivism is simply a kinder-sounding proxy for socialism. And what is the *progressive blueprint for America*? Eradicate your property rights, destroy the minds of your children, threaten you with homelessness, steal your money, keep you in poverty, send your sons to foreign deserts to kill or die for the benefit of an oil company, and make sure that you have no constitutional basis by which to object.

The Government Works for Us, Not the Other Way Around

Restoring the separation of powers doctrine should require that the American people have the right to impeach and remove from office any elected or appointed federal employee, including a Supreme Court justice who clearly violates the US Constitution or his or her oath of office. Most people believe we actually have this right. We don't. Only once in the history of the SCOTUS was a Supreme Court justice served with articles of impeachment. In 1804, Samuel Chase, one of the signers of the Declaration of Independence, was impeached by the House of Representatives after he was accused that his federalist leanings affected his rulings. He was acquitted of all charges by the Senate, establishing the right of the judiciary to independent opinion. Chase remained on the court until his death.

This demonstrates that the probability of successfully removing a corrupt, self-serving activist Supreme Court judge from the bench is practically zero. Therefore, we must establish term limits for SCOTUS judges and members of Congress.

A limited Constitution can be preserved in practice no other way than through the medium of courts of justice, whose duty it must be to declare all acts contrary to the manifest tenor of the Constitution void. Without this, all the reservations of particular rights or privileges would amount to nothing. To deny this would be to affirm ... that men acting by virtue of powers may do not only what their powers do not authorize, but what they forbid.

—Alexander Hamilton

The nation's founders were very clear that their central purpose was to defend the rights and liberties of individual American citizens against any encroachment by an out-of-control federal government. That requires following the constitution as the highest law of the land as it was written and in terms of its original intent. As George Mason stated, "No free government, or the blessings of liberty, can be preserved to any people *but by frequent recurrence to fundamental principles.*"

To be true to these fundamental principles, we first cannot accept the concept of a malleable living constitution, and secondly we must have a Supreme Court that is accountable solely to the law, and to the American people—not to either of the other two branches of the federal government.

The framers of the constitution intended that the Supreme Court would protect the citizenry from the imposition of unjust and unconstitutional laws. The Supreme Court's purpose was to be the second-to-last barrier that protects our freedoms from a potentially tyrannical government. The last barrier is the militias of well-armed individual citizens themselves. However, when the chief executive of that tyrannical government has the sole authority to appoint those judges to our highest court, how can its integrity, objectivity, and mandate be maintained? As has been demonstrated by many of its decisions over the past few decades, it cannot—once the court has been besieged by activist judges who willfully distort the US Constitution.

Supreme Court judges are appointed for life. This leaves a vestige of power extended from the president who appointed them until long after he is gone from office. In fact a Supreme Court judge should not be involved in the political spectrum at all. Since the constitution does not specify any qualifications to serve as a Supreme Court justice, the president may nominate anyone he wishes. History has demonstrated that presidents always nominate individuals who share their ideological worldviews and a willingness to promote their political agenda. As such, the politicization of our judiciary takes place from the very beginning of the process. Judicial activism is inherent in the system. It is the system that is flawed.

Once a nominee goes before the Senate Judiciary Committee, special interest groups come out of the woodwork and lobby the senators in order to influence them on whether to confirm or reject that nominee. Anyone familiar with lobbying in Washington, DC, understands that this is where millions of dollars or other perks are exchanged in order to buy the support of those senators. Once the hearings are completed, the judiciary committee then votes on whether or not the nomination should proceed to a full Senate vote. By the time this has happened, those senators on the committee have already built their coalitions within the Senate who will vote in accordance with them—and therefore in accordance with the special interests who lobbied them.

The final confirmation vote by the Senate formerly required a three-fifths majority (60 percent). Thanks to Harry Reid, 51 percent of the Senate now has the ability to deny the constitutional rights of the other 49 percent of the nation's voters. Reid has repeatedly demonstrated his contempt for the citizens' Constitutional rights by driving our government in exactly the wrong direction. For the good of the country, we need to strengthen the separation of powers doctrine, not weaken it. We must have the Senate restore the requirement for a two-thirds supermajority to confirm any SCOUTUS nominee. In addition, the president should be stripped of the nominating privilege altogether.

As of 2014, there have been a total of 151 nominations to the Supreme Court since the nation was founded. Not a single nominee was ever rejected as a consequence of the Senate Judiciary Committee hearings. This raises the question: What is the purpose of the Senate Judiciary Committee hearings if every single nominee that has ever gone through them is approved for the Senate vote anyway? Is it nothing more than the proverbial dog and pony show? In any case, the point is that the entire process of nominating, screening, and then confirming appointments to the Supreme Court is intensely political in spite of the government's claims to the contrary.

The Supreme Court is the final authority that determines the enforceability of laws in accordance with their compliance to the US Constitution. It was not intended to be an instrument of political will, bending, transforming, manipulating, and perverting the meaning of the constitution in order to fit it to any law or to support whatever hidden agenda is held by those with the power of the majority. It's clear that the Supreme Court has become nothing more than another wing of the White House, and its responsibility to objective scrutiny has given way to political pull and influence peddling.

An institution as important as the Supreme Court should not be subject to the whims of a single elected government bureaucrat, especially one as potentially destructive as a president who is inclined toward Marxism. This is probably the single most profound weakness in our constitution. The framers likely never envisioned the extreme politicization of the Supreme Court or the rise of political activism among the justices. Yet this is exactly the situation we face, as evidenced by Ms. Kagan's contributions to Obama's instruction manual on implementing socialism—*A Progressive Blueprint for the 44th President.*

Thomas Jefferson warned repeatedly that the greatest threat to the rule of law and to limited government was an unrestrained judiciary.

> The original error was in establishing a judiciary independent of the nation, and from which the citadel of the law, can turn its guns on those they were meant to defend, and control and fashion their proceedings to its own will. The opinion which gives to the judges the right to decide what laws are Constitutional and what are not, not only for themselves in their own sphere of action but for the Legislature and Executive also in their spheres, would make the judiciary a despotic branch.
>
> —Thomas Jefferson

Unfortunately, Mr. Jefferson's prophecy has come to pass. "Jefferson understood that should our Constitution ever become a straw man for a politicized judiciary to interpret as it pleased, Rule of Law would gradually yield to rule of men—the terminus of the latter being Tyranny."[146] The idea behind the lifetime tenure was the belief that this would place justices above partisan politics. The framers believed that being appointed for life to the highest court in the land would leave the justices free to opine and make decisions based upon their basic moral virtues and principled understanding of the constitution. As such, with lifetime tenure they should gain nothing from doing otherwise. This notion, however, has proven to be false, and it has backfired on the American people. The framers likely never counted on a Supreme Court of dishonorable activist judges devoid of ethical and moral virtues and who lack a principled understanding of the constitution. Nevertheless, this, too, can be fixed. A single term of a limited time period will come closer to accomplishing what the framers intended.

Proposals to Reform Our Supreme Court Nomination and Appointment Process through Constitutional Amendment

We must change the Supreme Court nomination process to ensure that this judicial body is accountable to The Law and to the people of the United States—not to any president who appointed them. Therefore, the nominee selection process should be conducted by the states, and not by any other branch of the federal government. The following are some of the conditions that must be applied:

- Appointment confirmation should require a two-thirds supermajority vote by the Senate.

- There should be a realistic possibility of impeachment for violating their oath of office.

- Justices should be held to a single nine-year term and a mandatory retirement age of seventy.

- The president should be stripped of the privilege of Supreme Court nominations.

Numerous ideas have been put forth as alternative means by which to nominate justices to the US Supreme Court. Several of the more interesting ideas follow:

When an opening on the court avails itself, candidates are nominated from among the fifty states. Each respective state legislature would nominate a candidate and in compliance with a defined set of minimum qualifications for those candidates. States may abstain from presenting a nominee candidate if they so choose. Those nominee candidates presented by the states are vetted by a judiciary committee in the House of

---

[146] Alexander, Mark. Essential Liberty and the US Constitution. *Publius Press—The Patriot Post*. 2010

Representatives that would select a nominee finalist from among them. Alternatively, a rotating board made up of ten state governors could select nominees. Every successive nomination would be made by governors from a different group of states. The ten governors of each respective board would represent different geographic regions of the country. The nominee would then be subject to confirmation by a supermajority (three-fifths) vote in the Senate.

Either model or one similar to it has merit since it gives the states more authority over which judges are eventually considered for the federal bench. The US Constitution is intended to protect the rights of all US citizens against federal government overreach. The federal government's powers are strictly limited to what is defined in the Constitution. The tenth amendment mandates that states' rights and individual rights supersede federal power. It is the US Supreme Court that decides on the constitutionality of laws created by the US Congress, so having a Supreme Court's authority derived from the states' participation in the selection process provides a more balanced check on federal authority and the potential for abuse thereof.

Another idea would be to have multiple nominating and confirming authorities. This is what is done in France, Germany, Italy, and Spain. In those countries no single person, office, or institution has a monopoly on appointments to the court. Typically this authority is shared between the upper and lower houses of the parliament. In Spain, four judges are appointed by the upper house, four by the lower house, two by the government, and two by a judges' council.

Many scoff at the idea that the president should be stripped of the privilege to nominate Supreme Court justices. But there is another little known reason why it should be done: It is technically possible for the president to nominate himself to the Supreme Court. All he would have to do would be to step down as president during his final months in office after he was confirmed in the Senate in order to accept his lifetime tenure on the highest legal authority in the land. There is no law or statute that prevents him from doing this. The very fact that this would be legally permissible is reason enough to strip from any US president the privilege of Supreme Court nomination and appointment.

Term and Time Limits for All Elected and Appointed Government Employees

Sitting on the Supreme Court has become a privilege of the political elite. They may try to claim otherwise, but Supreme Court justices are political players, no different in their personal motivations than any member of the House, Senate, or aspiring tyrant who sits in the White House. Like any career politician, they are seduced by the prospect of having power. Activist judges especially are after as much power as they can get because as far as they are concerned, their personal agenda trumps their oath to uphold the constitution. Any activist judge should be considered as harboring an inherent conflict of interest and should immediately be disqualified from appointment to the SCOTUS. All career politics in Washington must be put to an end, and this includes putting an end to lifetime tenure for Supreme Court judges. This is a necessary step toward restoring the separation of powers on which the integrity and enforceability of The Constitution depends.

What must also be prohibited is the revolving door within and between the branches of government. Politicians aspire to begin their careers in the House of Representatives and move after a few terms to a Senate seat. There are few if any members of Congress who don't covet the power, prestige, glamour, and access to obscene wealth that can be gained from becoming president. A career politician who might serve just three terms in the House, two terms in the Senate, and then two terms as president will have by then held elected office for a total of twenty-six years. Sitting in Washington for decades and living off of the public dole is not what the framers intended with respect to representative government. They intended for our representatives to be statesmen, not career politicians.

A term limits bill with any teeth must not only call for a limited number of terms but for limited total years of service in any elected or appointed federal office. For example, the term-limits amendment I would propose would be as follows:

No federal government employee may hold elected or appointed office in any or all of the three branches of the federal government for a cumulative total of more than 12 years. No person may be elected to the House of Representatives for more than four terms. No person shall serve as Supreme Court justice for more than nine years. Any person who has served in either the legislative or executive branch of government may not be appointed to the Supreme Court, and no former Supreme Court judge may hold any federal elected or appointed office after leaving the court. No person shall hold the office of president for more than a single term of 6 years, or a total time in office of 8 years in the case of a vice presidential accession to the presidency. All elected and appointed employees of the federal government shall be subject to the same laws and programs to which all US citizens are subject.

First term presidents spend more than half of their time campaigning to win a second term. Every second term president is always referred to as a *lame duck*. Limiting a president to a single 6-year term will put an end to this waste and abuse of taxpayers' resources. This rule would also limit Supreme Court appointments to a period of time equivalent to one and a half presidential terms and would prohibit a career senator or congressman from ever becoming president, as it should be. Under this model, if you aspired to be president, you could not have first served for more than six years in the Congress. Therefore, no two-term senator could ever be president of the United States. If you served in the House of Representatives for three two-year terms (six total years), you could then only serve one Senate term and could in that case never serve as president. Or if you aspire to be president after three terms in the House, you would not be able to serve a single Senate term. Such a clause would put an effective end to the *Potomac two-step* hopping from one branch of government to another and corrupting the entire system from within. More importantly it would also require that representatives eventually get a real job after their time in government. Once they return to work in the real world, they like the rest of us will have to live with the destructive consequences of the legislative actions they had taken while holding office.

Finally, Congress must be prohibited from passing any legislation from which any member of the executive branch, legislative branch, judicial branch, or their appointees are exempt. All employees of the federal government must be subject to the same laws and programs that they force onto the American people.

Repeal the Sixteenth Amendment and End the IRS

We discussed earlier how to end the Federal Reserve system and restore sound money. With the fiat currency system abolished, there will no longer be a need for us to pay a federal income tax that is used solely to pay the interest on the debt created by the fiat system. Eliminating the IRS budget will save the US taxpayers more than fourteen billion dollars annually and will free the entire middle class of this insidious burden. Every American business will be free from the cost of compliance, reducing their overhead, increasing their profitability and even allowing retailers to reduce prices in accordance with their lower costs. This will provide real economic stimulus that will benefit the citizenry, rather than a few politically connected banks and corporations.

In its place, we would institute *the fair tax* to raise the revenue required for the federal government to function. This model will require that government live within its means just as the whole of the American people must do. The government will no longer be able to pick winners and losers in their centrally controlled too-big-to-*jail* economy, and everyone will be treated equally in terms of economic opportunity.

The fair tax is simple. It is a national consumption tax (sales tax) that treats every individual on US soil equally, does not discriminate on the basis of economic class, allows small businesses to thrive, and can provide the federal government with all the revenue it needs to function—while it demands the discipline for government to live within its means. Under the fair tax every person transacting in the United States, whether they live here or are just visiting, pays a sales tax on purchases of new goods and services excluding necessities (for citizens). The fair tax rate after necessities will initially be 23 percent, which is equal to the lowest current income tax bracket (15 percent) combined with the employee payroll taxes (7.65 percent), both of which will be eliminated along with the IRS.

With no further obligation to continue paying interest on the national debt, federal revenue requirements will be substantially reduced. Once the budget is balanced and federal spending stabilized, the fair tax rate can be scaled back as appropriate for the reduced federal spending requirements. One of the basic advantages of the fair tax is that it is quickly and easily scalable.

Immediate benefits of the fair tax include the following:

- Americans will for the first time in generations be able to keep what they earn.

- A paycheck that is nearly twice as big as before represents an unprecedented economic stimulus package for the country.

- Employers will no longer incur the cost of administering tax collections from their employees on behalf of the government, and businesses' profits will increase.

- Americans living below the poverty line will pay no federal sales tax.

- Social security and Medicare will be put on more solid financial footing.

- People pay taxes only on what they spend. The more wasteful and irresponsible you are, the more taxes you pay.

- It encourages thrift and frugality and discourages wastefulness. This fosters environmental conservation and reduced pollution.

- The obscenely rich cannot avoid it by funneling their earnings through tax-haven countries, so more of their money will remain in US banks.

- There will be no more IRS filing.

- Those in the country illegally will not be able to avoid taxes.

- Foreign tourists and visitors will pay the same sales tax as everyone else and will add to the nation's wealth with the foreign capital they bring, enriching our economy from the outside.

- Eliminating the corporate tax rate, the highest in the world, will allow companies to operate in America free of income tax. This will bring jobs back to America and increase real economic growth from investment rather than illusory growth from unsustainable consumption.

- It will allow us to rescue social security from future bankruptcy, and once restored to sound financial footing, we can restructure it as it was promised—as a trust fund.

- It will reduce the federal budget by at least thirteen billion dollars by eliminating the IRS.

- It will eliminate the cost to incarcerate in US prisons, tens of thousands of American citizens for the noncrime of tax evasion.

Other Reasons We Should Eliminate the IRS

In 2013, Americans spent a staggering 6.4 billion hours complying with the maze of regulations in the federal tax code. That equates to over $130 Billion in labor cost. The number of hours spent by corporations is far greater, adding to their cost of doing business—costs they passed on to their customers.

The budget of the IRS has increased by more than 58 percent since 2000, and the federal tax code has more than tripled in length between 2001 and 2013.

Investigations revealed that high-ranking officials within the Obama administration used the IRS as a political weapon by targeting groups and individuals who exercised their first amendment right to free speech by disagreeing with many of the administration's unconstitutional policies.

The data collected by the IRS constitutes an intrusive violation of privacy. If you're concerned about the NSA collecting your phone calls or monitoring your e-mails, consider that every April 15 you hand over to the IRS data about how much money you make, where you make it, who you give it to, what you spend it on, and information about your children and dependents. None of these things are anyone's business outside of your own family.

Concentrating so much power in a single government agency is a design ripe for corruption. The IRS has great discretion over how tax law is enforced—discretion that has been abused under multiple administrations and by both parties. IRS agents are considered federal law enforcement and can be armed like any other law enforcement agency. The Tea Party suppression scandal is just the latest example of abuse perpetrated by the IRS against the citizenry. The IRS engages in government sponsored extortion, and they are trained to carry and use loaded guns against the citizenry to enforce it.

The current tax code is a political tool used by incumbents to entrench themselves in government and expand their power. The link between the tax code, lobbying activity, political fundraising, and incumbent protection is a clear and present danger to the nation's future. It constitutes an egregious conflict of interest within our government.

End the Revolving Door between Government and the Lobbying Industry

Disgraced Washington lobbyist Jack Abramoff once said,

> A representative who stayed in Washington for decades, and was a friend, was worth his weight in gold. But permitting people to rule for decades is a recipe for disaster. Is there really a difference between a permanent Congress and a president for life? Representatives should be allowed to serve for three terms of two years, senators for two terms of six years. Then they should get out of town.

Abramoff should know. He was one of the most successful lobbyists in history. His comments support my own term-limits proposal, which would go a long way to diminishing the influence that lobbyists have over members of Congress. The attraction of post-public service employment as a lobbyist must be eliminated. The revolving door between elected office and corporate lobbying is one of the greatest sources of corruption in government. If you choose to serve in Congress or if you accept an appointed position on a congressional staff, you should be prohibited from working for any company or organization that lobbies the federal government. Just imposing a ban on lobbying is not sufficient. Nor is it constitutional. Congressmen looking for financial gain for themselves and for their campaign coffers know full well how to circumvent any ban on lobbying anyway. They simply go to work as consultants, which is the same thing.

The framers intended that we be governed by statesmen who had professions, businesses, or careers apart from their public service. Statesmen are there to serve the people, and once they have completed their service, they go home and return to a real job. This is how it was intended, and our system must be restructured to attract that kind of public servant.

Prohibit Gifts and Donations from Lobbyists

Limiting the size of political contributions made by individual citizens, while completely ignoring the contributions made by government lobbyists, federal contractors, or others who benefit from government funded programs defeats the purpose of campaign finance restrictions. Anyone, whether an individual, a union, a company, or a nonprofit association, who receives perks or public money from an elected official should not be permitted to reciprocate with campaign contributions. If you earn money from government contracts or are paid by any entity that does, you must be prohibited from giving campaign contributions.

None of the aforementioned is intended to suggest that we somehow prohibit lobbying. This would be impossible. Furthermore, lobbying to some extent is part of the means by which elected representatives acquire knowledge and information about what is going on in industry. The US Constitution is clear about the people being allowed to petition Congress, and whether you are an individual or a group with a common interest, you should be able to do that. What should be prohibited, however, is being able to provide financial incentives and promises of lucrative private-sector careers to politicians in return for their political influence.

End Pork Barrel Spending

Pork barrel spending consists of federal government spending on localized projects that benefit a state or congressional district. Bringing home the bacon is how politicians suck up to industry as well as their constituents—including local businesses and contractors—in order to buy political support in return for access to federal money. This is how federal politicians use federal taxpayer money to buy votes in the local jurisdictions that elect them. It is a blatantly corrupt practice and must be prohibited.

Repeal the Seventeenth Amendment

The current practice of electing senators by popular vote is not a feature of our founding principles. It began on May 31, 1913 (the same year as the Federal Reserve Act and the sixteenth amendment establishing the individual income tax). Before that time, under the original provisions of the US Constitution, US Senators were elected by their state legislatures. This was intended to prevent the federal government from indirectly making off with the powers and funds of the states. Repealing the seventeenth amendment would restore to the respective state houses the election of their senators. It would ensure that some of the buffoons who are able to marshal funds and media attention will not have such easy access to such an exclusive and powerful institution as the US Senate.

One of the best examples of this principle is found with former Democratic Senator Max Baucus of Montana. Baucus is a classic career insider to Washington politics. Prior to being appointed as the US Ambassador to China in February, 2014, he had held some kind of elected office in federal government since 1975 after he served only two years in his state legislature from 1973 to 1974. Baucus had been a member of the US Congress continuously for thirty-eight years. This is longer than any Supreme Court justice in history (who is appointed for life). Before he entered politics, his only experience in the private sector was as a practicing attorney for about two years (the second year of which he spent campaigning for his first political office). More absurd is that in spite of being the U.S. Senator for Montana, he did not even own a home in that state for the eleven years between 1991 and 2002. Upon being challenged for his non-residency, he *bought* half of his mother's house in order to reestablish legal residency in the state he was supposed to be representing.

During his 2008 reelection campaign Baucus raised a record amount of money, 91 percent of which came from campaign donors living outside of Montana. According to the Center for Responsive Politics, Baucus's campaign raised $11.6 million, more than 80 percent of which came from health care and other industries overseen by the very committees on which Baucus served. The overwhelming ratio of special interest and out-of-state monies versus donations from Montana citizens is staggering, and it raises serious ethics questions.

The prior 2002 Montana primaries gained media attention when Baucus's campaign ran ads suggesting that his opponent was gay. The ad was paid for by the Democratic Senatorial Campaign Committee and alleged further that his opponent had embezzled funds from the cosmetology school he once owned. It showed suggestive film footage from the early 1980s of his opponent massaging another man's face while he was wearing a tight suit with an open shirt. His subsequently dropped out of the race, and Baucus won with 63 percent of the vote. Several months later his opponent was cleared of any embezzlement charges. Nevertheless, Baucus remains an entrenched career politician, one of the untouchables.

Statesmanship, character, and integrity have been replaced with dirty politics and corruption in a climate of unaccountability. There is no question that we must act to end career politics at every level and within every branch of our federal government.

Restore Individual Liberty and Preserve It for Our Children

When one has read the voluminous writings of all of the founding fathers, including their personal letters, the common theme is the preservation of individual liberty and the protection of our property rights. Therefore, it should be recognized that the spirit of this principle is the key thread woven into the fabric of all of our country's founding documents, most especially The US Constitution. Today the number of political candidates who are devoted to preserving this traditional American value are in the extreme minority in both our federal and state governments. *We the people* need to relearn and deeply understand those principles on which our individual liberty and our national sovereignty depend—property rights, the free-enterprise system, sound money, governance by character, integrity, and statesmanship, a limited government with the discipline to live within its means, a non-interventionist foreign policy, and a meaningful separation of powers between the branches of our federal government. These were the cornerstones of our founding principles of governance. These were the principles that ensured our individual liberty and which remain enshrined in our constitution—if only we enforced it.

> Honor, justice, and humanity forbid us tamely to surrender that freedom which we received from our gallant ancestors, and which our innocent posterity have a right to receive from us. We cannot endure the infamy and guilt of resigning succeeding generations to that wretchedness which inevitably awaits them if we basely entail hereditary bondage upon them.

—Thomas Jefferson

And finally to reiterate an earlier point: No president, senator, congressman, Supreme Court justice, or any combination thereof will restore your individual rights to property and liberty. Only you can act to restore your liberty, or it will not be restored.

AFTERWORD

Silence is acquiescence. Doing nothing and remaining silent constitutes implied consent. If you refuse to speak out against tyranny, whether out of fear or complacency, then you are already a slave and have condemned your children and your countrymen to a life of servitude and destitution. If we the people do not rise up and shout from every rooftop that we object to being robbed of our property, our earnings, our moral values, our children, our families, and our national sovereignty, then we deserve to lose everything our founders fought, bled, and died to win for us. If we do not fight to restore our constitution, our property rights, our liberty, and the rule of law, then we have earned our enslavement and the enslavement of our children. As a father I will not sit silent. I will not consent to my own servitude. I will not consent to the enslavement of my children or my neighbors. If you consider yourself a true American, I humbly ask that you too refuse to consent to the dissolution of our founding principles and begin to take action to restore your liberty and your property rights within your own community.

It is the Duty of the Patriot, to protect his country from its Government.

—Thomas Paine

List of G-SIFI (Global-Systemically Important Financial Institutions)

United States

- Bank of America

- Bank of New York Mellon

- Citigroup

- Goldman Sachs

- JPMorgan Chase

- Morgan Stanley

- State Street

- Wells Fargo

Asia-Pacific

- Bank of China

- Mitsubishi UFJ

- Mizuho

- Sumitomo Mitsui

Europe

- Barclays

- BNP Paribas

- Commerzbank

- Credit Agricole

- Credit Suisse

- Deutsche Bank

- Dexia

- Groupe BPCE

- HSBC

- ING Bank

- Lloyds Banking Group

- Nordea

- Royal Bank of Scotland

- Santander

- Societe Generale

- UBS

- UniCredit

Recommended Reading

The United States Constitution

The Creature from Jekyll Island by G. Edward Griffin

For a New Liberty by Murray N. Rothbard

Liberty Defined by Ron Paul

The Market for Liberty by Morris and Linda Tannehill

Confessions of an Economic Hit Man by John Perkins

Democracy: The God that Failed by Hans-Hermann Hoppe

Economics in One Lesson by Henry Hazlitt

The Communist Manifesto by Marx and Engels

From Bretton Woods to World Inflation by Henry Hazlitt

End the Fed by Ron Paul

Capitalism: The Unknown Ideal by Ayn Rand

Atlas Shrugged by Ayn Rand

The Road to Serfdom by F. A. Hayek

Roads to Sound Money by Alex Chafuen and Judy Shelton

Failure of The 'New Economics by Henry Hazlitt

The Federalist Papers

Aftershock by David and Robert Wiedemer, Cindy Spitzer

Man versus The Welfare State by Henry Hazlitt

America the Beautiful by Dr. Ben Carson

Hostile Takeover by Matt Kibbe

The Fountainhead by Ayn Rand

The Lorax by Dr. Seuss

Recommended Web Pages

Ludwig Von Mises Institute for Economics, http://www.mises.org/

African Americans for Libertarianism, https://www.facebook.com/AAforLiberty

Campaign for Liberty, http://www.campaignforliberty.org/

Education Action Group Foundation, http://eagnews.org/

Western Center for Journalism, http://www.westernjournalism.com/

The CATO Institute, http://www.cato.org/

Shadowstats.com, http://www.shadowstats.com/

Original Intent, http://www.originalintent.org/

The Sovereign Society, http://sovereignsociety.com/

Casey Research, http://www.caseyresearch.com/

The Adam Smith Institute, http://www.adamsmith.org/

The Hoover Institute – Stanford University, http://www.hoover.org/

National League of Taxpayers, http://leagueoftaxpayers.com/

The Fair Tax, http://www.fairtax.org/

Ron Paul, http://www.ronpaul.com/

BIBLIOGRAPHY

Buchanan, Patrick J. *Where the Right Went Wrong*. New York: Thomas Dunn Books, 2004.

Chemerinsky; Erwin. *Constitutional Law: Principles and Policies, 4th Edition*. New York: Aspen Publishers, 2011.

Chodorov, Frank. *The Income Tax—Root of All Evil*. Auburn, AL: Ludwig Von Mises Institute, 2007.

Tocqueville, Alexis de. *Democracy in America*. London: Penguin Books, 2003.

Epstein, Richard. *Takings, Private Property and the Power of Eminent Domain*. Boston: Harvard University Press, 1985.

Federal Reserve Bank of Chicago. *Modern Money Mechanics*. Chicago: Federal Reserve Bank of Chicago Press, 1992.

Flynn, John T. *The Roosevelt Myth*. Auburn, AL: Ludwig Von Mises Institute, 1955.

Foster, Ralph T. *Fiat Paper Money, The History and Evolution of Our Currency*. Berkeley, CA: Ralph Foster, 2011.

Freeland, Chrystia. *Plutocrats, The Rise of the New Global Super Rich and the Fall of Everyone Else*. New York: Penguin, 2012.

Goebbels, Joseph. *Goebbels on the Power of Propaganda*. [City]: Shamrock Eden Publishing, 2009.

Griffin, G. Edward. *The Creature from Jekyll Island*. Westlake Village, CA: American Media, 1994.

Hamilton, Madison and Jay. *The Federalist Papers*. New York: Penguin Group, 2003.

Hayek, F. A. *The Road to Serfdom—Definitive Edition*. Chicago: University of Chicago Press, 2007.

Hayek, F.A. *The Constitution of Liberty*. Chicago: University of Chicago Press, 1960.

Hazlitt, Henry. *Economics in One Lesson*. New York: Arlington House Publishing, 1979.

Hoppe, Hans-Hermann. *Democracy—The God that Failed*. New Brunswick, NJ: Transaction Publishers, 2007.

Keynes, John Maynard. *The General Theory of Employment, Interest, and Money*. Harcourt Brace & World, May 12, 1965

Kibbe, Matt. *Hostile Takeover*. New York: Harper Collins, 2012.

Lobaczewski, Andrew M. *Political Ponerology—Science on the Nature of Evil, Applied to Political Purposes*. Grande Prairie AB, Canada: Red Pill Press, 2006.

Marx, Karl, and Friedrich Engels. *The Communist Manifesto*. [City]: Swenson & Kemp, 2003.

Mencken, H. L. *Notes on Democracy*. New York: Dissident Books, 2009.

Mises, Ludwig von. *The Anti-Capitalist Mentality*. Auburn, AL: Ludwig von Mises Institute, 1970.

Mises, Ludwig von. *The Theory of Money and Credit*. Auburn, AL: Ludwig von Mises Institute, 1952.

Mises, Ludwig von. *Omnipotent Government*. Auburn, AL: Ludwig von Mises Institute, 1945.

Mises, Ludwig von. *Human Action—The Scholar's Edition*. Auburn, AL: Ludwig von Mises Institute, 1998.

Mises, Ludwig von. *Socialism—An Economic and Sociological Analysis*. Auburn, AL: Ludwig von Mises Institute, 1922.

Paige, Rod. *The War against Hope*. Nashville, TN: Thomas Nelson Publishing, 2009.

Paul, Ron. *End the Fed*. New York: Grand Central Publishing, 2009.

Paul, Ron. *Liberty Defined*. New York:Grand Central Publishing, 2011.

Peck, Dr. M. Scott. *The Road Less Traveled*. New York: Simon & Shuster, 1978.

Pohl, Rüdiger F. *A Handbook on Fallacies and Biases in Thinking, Judgment, and Memory.* New York: Psychology Press, 2004.

Quigley, Carroll. *Tragedy and Hope, A History of the World in Our Time.* [City]: GSG and Associates Publishing, 1975.

Rand, Ayn. *Capitalism: The Unknown Ideal.* New York: Penguin Books, 1966.

Rockwell, Llewellen H. *The Gold Standard: An Austrian Perspective.* Auburn, AL: Ludwig von Mises Institute, 1992.

Rockwell, Llewellen H. *The Left, the Right, and the State.* Auburn, AL: Ludwig von Mises Institute, 2008.

Rothbard, Murray N. *Man, Economy, and State.* Auburn, AL: Ludwig von Mises Institute, 2009.

Rothbard, Murray N. *For a New Liberty—A Libertarian Manifesto.* Auburn, AL; Ludwig von Mises Institute, 2006.

Rothbard, Murray N. *What Has the Government Done to Our Money?* Auburn, AL: Ludwig von Mises Institute, 1963.

Savage, Charlie. *Takeover: The Return of the Imperial Presidency.* New York: Back Bay Books, 2008.

Shelton, Judy. *Fixing the Dollar Now.* Washington, DC: Atlas Economic Research, 2011.

Sowell, Thomas. *Race and Culture.* New York: Basic Books, 1995.

Sumner, William Graham. *A History of American Currency.* Auburn, AL: Ludwig Von Mises Institute, 2008.

Tannehill, Morris and Linda. *The Market for Liberty.* Lansing, MI: Laissez Faire Books, 1993.

Turtel, Joel. *Public Schools, Public Menace: How Public Schools Lie to Parents and Betray Our Children.* Staten Island, NY: Liberty Books, 2005.

Tye, Larry. *The Father of Spin—Edward L. Bernays and the Father of Public Relations.* New York: Henry Holt & Co., 2002.

Wiedemer, Robert. *Aftershock.* Hoboken, NJ: John Wiley & Sons, 2011.

INDEX

ABOUT THE AUTHOR

F. A. Grieger is an aerospace engineer, entrepreneur, and businessman. He holds undergraduate and graduate degrees in engineering, finance, and international business economics. A first-generation American, he has started and sold several businesses, has run two privately held companies, and has lived both in Europe and the United States. He is the youngest of seven children, speaks three languages, and is entirely devoted to his family. A proponent of self-reliance, he grew up in a small family business where he started working at age twelve. As a young man, he worked as a bartender, bouncer, shoe salesman, road-paving worker, commercial diver, offshore oil-rig roughneck, SCUBA instructor, security guard, house painter, roofer, draftsman, computer programmer, and mental health technician, all in the course of working his way through college and graduate school. His mother is his greatest inspiration. It was from his parents' remarkable life-story of courage, survival, and perseverance through World War II where he learned that adversity does not build character but rather reveals it.

CPSIA information can be obtained at www.ICGtesting.com
Printed in the USA
BVOW07s0119160615

404432BV00005B/8/P

9 781490 862880